Early Modern Prophecies in Transnational, National and Regional Contexts

Volume 2

Brill's Studies in Intellectual History

General Editor

Han van Ruler (*Erasmus University, Rotterdam*)

Founded by

Arjo Vanderjagt

Editorial Board

C.S. Celenza (*Johns Hopkins University, Baltimore*)
M. Colish (*Yale University, New Haven*) – J.I. Israel (*Institute for Advanced Study, Princeton*) – A. Koba (*University of Tokyo*) – M. Mugnai (*Scuola Normale Superiore, Pisa*) – W. Otten (*University of Chicago*)

VOLUME 324

Brill's Texts and Sources in Intellectual History

General Editor

Leen Spruit (*Radboud University, Nijmegen*)

Editorial Board

J. Lagrée (*Université de Rennes 1*)
U. Renz (*Universität Klagenfurt*)
A. Uhlmann (*University of Western Sydney*)

VOLUME 23/2

The titles published in this series are listed at *brill.com/btsi*

Early Modern Prophecies in Transnational, National and Regional Contexts

Volume 2: The Mediterranean World

Edited by

Lionel Laborie
Ariel Hessayon

BRILL

LEIDEN | BOSTON

Cover illustration: William Blake, 'The Angel of Revelation' (c.1803–1805)

Library of Congress Cataloging-in-Publication Data

Names: Laborie, Lionel, editor. | Hessayon, Ariel, editor.
Title: Early modern prophecies in transnational, national and regional contexts / edited by Lionel Laborie, Ariel Hessayon.
Description: Leiden ; Boston : Brill, 2020. | Series: Brill's studies in intellectual history, 0920-8607 ; volume 324/1- | "This edited collection of primary sources originates from a major international conference on early modern prophecies, which we organised at Goldsmiths, University of London, in June 2014"–ECIP acknowledgements. | Includes bibliographical references and index. | Contents: v. 1. Continental Europe – v. 2. The Mediterranean world – v. 3. The British Isles.
Identifiers: LCCN 2020040926 (print) | LCCN 2020040927 (ebook) | ISBN 9789004442658 (v. 1 ; hardback) | ISBN 9789004442634 (v. 2 ; hardback) | ISBN 9789004442641 (v. 3 ; hardback) | ISBN 9789004342668 (hardback) | ISBN 9789004443631 (ebook)
Subjects: LCSH: Prophecy–Christianity–History–Sources.
Classification: LCC BR115.P8 E27 2020 (print) | LCC BR115.P8 (ebook) | DDC 231.7/4509015–dc23
LC record available at https://lccn.loc.gov/2020040926
LC ebook record available at https://lccn.loc.gov/2020040927

Typeface for the Latin, Greek, and Cyrillic scripts: "Brill". See and download: brill.com/brill-typeface.

ISSN 0920-8607
ISBN 978-90-04-34266-8 (hardback, set)
ISBN 978-90-04-44265-8 (hardback, vol. 1)
ISBN 978-90-04-44263-4 (hardback, vol. 2)
ISBN 978-90-04-44264-1 (hardback, vol. 3)
ISBN 978-90-04-44363-1 (e-book)

Copyright 2021 by Koninklijke Brill NV, Leiden, The Netherlands.
Koninklijke Brill NV incorporates the imprints Brill, Brill Hes & De Graaf, Brill Nijhoff, Brill Rodopi, Brill Sense, Hotei Publishing, mentis Verlag, Verlag Ferdinand Schöningh and Wilhelm Fink Verlag.
All rights reserved. No part of this publication may be reproduced, translated, stored in a retrieval system, or transmitted in any form or by any means, electronic, mechanical, photocopying, recording or otherwise, without prior written permission from the publisher. Requests for re-use and/or translations must be addressed to Koninklijke Brill NV via brill.com or copyright.com.

This book is printed on acid-free paper and produced in a sustainable manner.

Printed by Printforce, the Netherlands

Contents

Abbreviations   VII
Notes on Contributors   VIII

Mediterranean Apocalypticism: An Introduction   1
    Mayte Green-Mercado

5 Sebastianism: A Portuguese Prophecy   20
    Jacqueline Hermann

6 "Hopes of Portugal" by Antonio Vieira: 17th-Century Portuguese America, a Luso-Brazilian Fifth Empire and Prophetical Views of History   72
    Luís Filipe Silvério Lima

7 Prophecies in Early Modern Spain: Deceit, Scandals, and the Spanish Inquisition   159
    Monika Frohnapfel-Leis

8 The So-Called Italian Quietism: Siena in the 1680s   201
    Adelisa Malena

9 Saints in Revolt: The Anti-Ottoman "Vision of kyr Daniel"   246
    Marios Hatzopoulos

Bibliography   277
Index   299

Abbreviations

ACDF   Archive of the Congregation for the Doctrine of the Faith, Vatican City, Italy
AGS   Archivo General de Simancas, Valladolid, Spain
AHN   Archivo Histórico Nacional, Madrid, Spain
BNE   Biblioteca Nacional de España, Madrid, Spain
BnF   Bibliothèque nationale de France, Paris, France
BNP   Biblioteca Nacional de Portugal, Lisbon, Portugal
EBR   *Encyclopedia of the Bible and its Reception* (*EBR*) *Online*
OED   *Oxford English Dictionary*, online

Notes on Contributors

Monika Frohnapfel-Leis
is a postdoctoral researcher and assistant lecturer at the University of Erfurt, Germany. She specialises in divination and magic in early modern Europe and in spatial history. Her publications include her PhD thesis on the perception of sorcery and false saintliness in pre-modern Spain (*Jenseits der Norm. Zauberei und fingierte Heiligkeit im frühneuzeitlichen Spanien* [Bielefeld: 2019]). Recent areas of interest are mantic practices in early modern Venice and Ernestine Saxony.

Mayte Green-Mercado
is Assistant Professor of History at Rutgers University–Newark. She specialises in early modern Islamic, Iberian, and Mediterranean history. Her recent publications include the book *Visions of Deliverance. Moriscos and the Politics of Prophecy in the Early Modern Mediterranean* (Ithaca, N.Y.: 2019), and she recently edited a special issue titled "Speaking the End Times: Prophecy and Messianism in Early Modern Eurasia," *J.E.S.H.O.—Journal of the Economic and Social History of the Orient* 61 (2018), 18–90. Her main areas of interest are Moriscos, Mediterranean history, the history of Iberia and North Africa, Ottoman history, political, religious, and social history.

Marios Hatzopoulos
is a researcher at the Research Centre for Modern History (K.E.N.I.), Panteion University of Social and Political Sciences (Athens, Greece). He also teaches at the Hellenic Open University. He is a historian specialised in nationalism and national identity in south-east Europe and the Mediterranean world. He has recently contributed the chapter "Eighteenth-century Greek Prophetic Literature", in David Thomas & John Chesworth (eds), *Christian-Muslim Relations. A Bibliographical History, Volume 14 Central and Eastern Europe (1700–1800)*, Leiden: Brill 2020, 382–402. His areas of interest are modern Greek history, Ottoman history, prophecy and political radicalism in early modern Europe, nationalism and religion, and digital history.

Jacqueline Hermann
is Associate Professor at the Federal University of Rio de Janeiro. She specialises in Portuguese-Brazilian messianism and the Iberian Union. She is the author of "Política e Profecia: resistência antonista e difusão do sebastianismo na Europa (1578–1580)", in *Poderes do Sagrado*, ed. J. Hermann and W. de S. Martins (Rio

de Janeiro: 2016); "Between Prophecy and Politics: The Return to Portugal of Dom Antônio, Prior of Crato, and the Early Years of the Iberian Union", in *Visions, Prophecies and Divinations Early Modern Messianism and Millenarianism in Iberian America, Spain and Portugal*, ed. L.F. Silverio Lima and Ana Paula Megiani (Leiden: 2016); "Pelas letras dos profetas: D. João de Castro e a 'fábula mística' portuguesa (1580–1603)", in *O universo letrado da Idade Moderna* (São Leopoldo, 2019). Her areas of interest include the history of sebastianism and of Luso-Brazilian messianisms, as well as the history of the Iberian Union and its developments in Europe and America.

Luís Filipe Silvério Lima
is Associate Professor of Early Modern History at Federal University of São Paulo (Unifesp). Author of *Império dos sonhos: narrativas proféticas, sebastianismo e messianismo brigantino* (Alameda: 2010) and co-editor of *Visions, Prophecies, and Divinations. Early Modern Messianism and Millenarianism in Iberian America, Spain, and Portugal* (Leiden, 2016), he is currently working on a study of the hopes of the Fifth Monarchy and prophetical connections in the 17th-century Atlantic.

Adelisa Malena
is Associate Professor of Early Modern History at the University of Venice 'Ca' Foscari'. Her main fields of interests are: women and gender studies, cultural history, and religious history. She has been mainly working on the Roman Inquisition, the Catholic Spiritual Direction and Female Mysticism in the 17th century, and is the author of the *L'Eresia dei perfetti. Inquisizione romana ed esperienze mistiche nel Seicento italiano* (Rome: 2003). She is now working on trans-confessional relationships and networks between Italy and Germany (17th–18th centuries).

Mediterranean Apocalypticism: An Introduction

Mayte Green-Mercado

In recent decades, ideas of connectivity, exchange, and a productive and at times conflictive interface between Christians, Jews, and Muslims, have dominated the scholarship on the early modern Mediterranean. One of the phenomena that best embodies these themes is apocalyptic thought and practice. In a recent article, Ottoman historian Cornell Fleischer proposed the idea of a discrete Mediterranean apocalyptic phenomenon in the early modern period.[1] Tracing the entangled nature of Muslim and Christian apocalyptic beliefs that circulated after the Ottoman conquest of Constantinople in 1453, Fleischer argued that in the Ottoman-Habsburg rivalry for recognition as legitimate claimants to the world empire of the last age of history, prophecies became central to contemporary understandings of history and politics. Fleischer's analysis centred primarily on the mid-fifteenth to the first three decades of the sixteenth century, after which he sees the apocalyptic phenomenon wane (at least in the Ottoman context). Drawing from Fleischer's proposition, this introduction delineates the main contours of apocalyptic beliefs and practices in the different geographic, cultural, and political areas around the early modern Mediterranean basin: a shared and competing idea of universal empire to which all Mediterranean powers aspired, the conversion of infidels before the End Times, messianism as a political ideal in the figure of a Hidden King, among others, to argue for a veritable Mediterranean apocalyptic phenomenon between the fifteenth (and one could even extend it as far back as the thirteenth century) and the seventeenth and early eighteenth centuries. While it is impossible to cover all aspects of early modern apocalypticism in this essay, this introduction aims to provide a general Mediterranean context in which the apocalyptic texts presented in this volume are to be located.

---

1 Cornell H. Fleischer, "A Mediterranean Apocalypse: Prophecies of Empire in the Fifteenth and Sixteenth Centuries", in *Speaking the End Times: Prophecy and Messianism in Early Modern Eurasia*, ed. Mayte Green-Mercado, JESHO—*Journal of the Economic and Social History of the Orient* 61 (2018), 18–90.

The Early Modern Mediterranean: Apocalypticism in Context

In his famous book *Mohammed and Charlemagne,* Henri Pirenne proposed that the Islamic conquests of the seventh/eighth centuries cut Europe from the Mediterranean, casting what had previously been a unified and vibrant political and economic whole into an impoverished backwater. The collapse of the Roman Empire in the West (and the subsequent European "dark ages") had not been the result of the so-called Barbarian or Germanic invasions, but had, according to Pirenne, taken place with the Muslim conquests, which cut Europe from the eastern Roman world. Although Pirenne's thesis has been rejected by scholars, the idea that during the Middle Ages the Mediterranean served as a border between Islamdom and Christendom still holds.[2] It was certainly a space where "no power could completely triumph despite the hegemonic aspirations of the most powerful states".[3] Pirenne's theory aimed to suggest that the medieval Mediterranean was a barren place that functioned as a frontier. However, as historians have amply shown, what characterised the medieval Mediterranean was its centrality in world trade networks. It was as much a space of competition and confrontation as it was a place of contact and exchange.

During the early modern period, the Mediterranean seems to have lost this central position in world trade, at least when viewed from the perspective of Western Europe, though not from the eastern Mediterranean.[4] Its connectedness, however, remained as vibrant as in earlier times. During the early modern period, at least since the Ottoman conquest of Constantinople in 1453, an imperial mode dominated the political discourse of Christian and Muslim polities alike, and the recreation of the Roman empire, with its ideal of universal rule, was a central piece of that puzzle.[5] As we shall see, the articulation of the idea of universal empire (and therefore the competition between powers, which in the early modern period were Christian and also Islamic) was expressed in an apocalyptic language, and ideas about the End Times, and the restoration of justice and peace became an integral part of political discourse, at least among certain circles. As the evidence discussed in this introduction

---

2 See Dominique Valérian, "The Medieval Mediterranean", in *A Companion to Mediterranean History,* ed. Peregrine Horden and Sharon Kinoshita (Hoboken, N.J.: 2014), 77–90.
3 Ibid., 78.
4 Molly Greene, "The Early Modern Mediterranean", in *A Companion to Mediterranean History,* ed. Peregrine Horden and Sharon Kinoshita (Hoboken, N.J.: 2014), 91–106.
5 For the imperial idea in early modern European monarchies see the classic work by Frances A. Yates, *Astraea. The Imperial Theme in the Sixteenth Century,* 2nd ed. (London: 1993), 1–28.

will demonstrate, although it has been argued that the Mediterranean lost its centrality in world trade during the early modern period, it was still a node where the circulation of people, goods, news, and apocalyptic ideas created a fertile ground for the germination of universalist political discourses.

In this contest for the control of the Mediterranean, for example, the Ottomans saw themselves as rightful heirs to the Roman Empire after conquering its capital. This was precisely what the Greek Humanist Niccolò Sagundino expressed upon his return from the recently conquered Constantinople. Addressing the Aragonese king Alfonso the Magnanimous (r.1416–1458), Sagundino wrote that Meḥmed II (r.1444–1446; 1451–1481) had been fortified by "prophecies and prognostications that promised the sultan the Kingdom of Italy and the conquest of the city of Rome, and that the see of Constantine was granted to him by the heavens, and that this see appears to be in reality Rome, not Constantinople, and thus it is just and well corresponds, that just as the sultan had taken possession of the daughter [Constantinople] by force, the mother would be conquered [Rome]".[6] Not only had Meḥmed II been assisted by God in his conquest of Constantinople, but, more importantly, it was predicted through prophecies that he would also conquer the city of Rome; thus, by uniting the eastern and western parts of the empire, Old and New Rome, Meḥmed II was destined to revive the Roman Empire as its divinely sanctioned ruler. The idea of an Ottoman conquest of Rome was not solely the reflection of Christian fears after the conquest of Constantinople.[7] We know that at least from the ninth century Muslims had been looking at the Italian Peninsula, and in particular to Rome, as a possible target they could conquer. As a result, a large Muslim army had sacked the basilicas of Old Saint Peter's and Saint Paul's Outside-the-walls in 846, and had engaged in the naval battle of Ostia in 849. The Muslim project of conquering Rome came to be one of many Muslim apocalyptic scenarios, especially in prophetic literature, or ḥadīths—sayings, actions, and tacit approvals of Muḥammad. For example, citing al-Kindī (d.870 C.E.), the historian and polymath Ibn Khaldūn (d.1406) recounted Muslim apocalyptic narratives to the effect that after conquering the Iberian Peninsula and Rome, the Mahdī, or eschatological redeemer in Islam,

---

6 "Ad serenissimum principem et invictissumum regem Alfonsum Nicolai Sagundini opratio", in *La caduta di Constantinopoli. L'eco nel mondo*, ed. Agostino Pertusi (Verona: 1976), 129–135.

7 For a discussion of the idea of an Ottoman conquest of Rome, see Mayte Green-Mercado, *Visions of Deliverance. Moriscos and the Politics of Prophecy in the Early Modern Mediterranean* (Ithaca, N.Y.: 2019), esp. ch. 3. I am currently preparing a project that explores this idea more in depth and in a more connected way.

would conquer all of the east, and finally Constantinople, becoming Lord of all the earth, and that only then the true religion would triumph.[8] According to this prognosticative narrative then, the whole of the Mediterranean would be conquered by Muslims before the End Times. Other Ottoman texts also foretold an Ottoman conquest of Rome. For example, in his second recension of his *el-Müntehā* (Epilogue), written in 1465, Yazıcıoğlu Aḥmed Bīcān (*d. c.*1466) stated that the conqueror of Constantinople would inaugurate the End Times. According to Bīcān's prognostication, not only would he defeat the Christians, but he had the intention of conquering Rome, "because the Day of Resurrection was nigh".[9]

The image of the Ottoman sultan as messianic redeemer became apparent in the figure of Süleymān the Magnificent (1520–1560).[10] Numerous prognosticative texts circulating in the court represented the ruler as the eschatological redeemer of Islam. For example, in his *Cāmiʿüʾl-meknūnāt* (Compendium of Hidden Things), the Ottoman Sufi writer Mevlānā ʿĪsā (*b.*1474/75) specifically identified Süleymān as the Mahdī whose command would "reach from East to West".[11]

The Habsburgs, especially after the election of Charles V as Holy Roman Emperor, also strove to achieve the ideal of universal empire. This is particularly evident in the Ghibelline program of Mercurino di Gattinara, Charles V's advisor, for whom "the title of empire legitimises the acquisition of the entire globe, as was ordained by God himself, foreseen by the prophets, predicted by the apostles, and approved in word and deed by Christ our Saviour by his birth, life, and death".[12] Charles V was not only the legitimate claimant to the

---

8   Ibn Khaldūn, *Muqaddimah: An Introduction to History*, ed. and trans. Franz Rosenthal, vol. II (London: 1958), 191. Cited in Giuseppe Mandalà, "Tra mito e realtà: L'immagine di Roma nella letteratura araba e turca d'età ottomana (secoli XV–XVI)", in *Italien und das Osmanische Reich*, ed. Franziska Meier (Herne: 2010) 47.

9   Istanbul, Süleymaniye Kütüphanesi, Ms. Hacı Mahmud Efendi 1657, fols 3ª–3ᵇ, Yazıcıoğlu Aḥmed Bīcān, *el-Müntehā*.

10 See especially Cornell H. Fleischer, "The Lawgiver as Messiah: The Making of the Imperial Image in the Reign of Süleymân", in *Soliman le Magnifique et son temps*, ed. Gilles Veinstein (Paris: 1992), 159–177.

11 İstanbul, Üniversitesi Kütüphanesi, Ms. T. 3263, fol. 52ª, Mevlānā ʿĪsā, *Cāmiʿüʾl-meknūnāt*. For a discussion of this text, see Barbara Flemming, "Public Opinion under Sultan Süleymân", in *Süleymân the Second [i.e. the First] and His Time*, ed. Halil İnalcık and Cemal Kafadar (Istanbul: 1993), 49–57. See also Barbara Flemming, "The Cāmiʿül-meknūnāt: A Source of ʿĀlī from the Time of Sultan Süleymân", trans. John O'Kane, in *Essays on Turkish Literature and History* (Leiden: 2018), 169–182.

12 Rebecca Ard Boone, *Mercurino di Gattinara and the Creation of the Spanish Empire* (London: 2014), 91–92.

Holy Roman Empire, but through marriage ties and conquest he appeared as the veritable universal ruler, the Lord of All the World. Charles v's universalist aspirations were in part motivated by an ideal of holy war, of Crusade, against Islam and against one of his main challengers, Süleymān the Magnificent.[13] He would not only defeat the infidels, but he would also unite the world under one law and one rule. The defeat of Muslims and conquest of Europe and the Mediterranean, the main military achievements of the emperor of the End Times, is evident in a prognostication purportedly sent by pope Leo X to king Ferdinand of Aragon, grandfather of Charles V, in 1515. According to this prophecy Charles V would "subjugate the Anglian, Hispanics, Gauls, Lombards. [He will] destroy Rome and Florence … and then will cross the sea with a great army, and he will enter Muslim lands and will call himself king of the Greeks".[14]

These messianic and universalist aspirations were not confined to the Ottomans and the Habsburgs. We have a striking example of this in the aftermath of the battle of Wādī al-Makhāzin or Alcazarquivir in 1578. The so-called Battle of the Three Kings saw the armies of the sultan of Morocco, ʿAbd al-Malik, confront an alliance of the deposed sultan, Abū ʿAbd Allāh Muḥammad, and the king of Portugal, Sebastian I. Despite its scale, the battle had no winners, but its political consequences were nevertheless important. Sebastian I was killed—his body never to be found—and the vacant Portuguese throne fell into the hands of the Spanish monarch, Philip II. ʿAbd al-Malik died during the battle of natural causes, and Abū ʿAbd Allāh Muḥammad survived two more years, but with no real support from the nobility. It was in this way that ʿAbd al-Malik's brother, Aḥmad al-Manṣūr, became the sultan of Morocco. As remarkable as the geo-political consequences were, the widespread, cross-confessional messianic expectations that followed the disastrous battle had a lasting effect on the religio-political landscape of the Mediterranean. The new sultan of Morocco would come to be seen as the expected Mahdī, the promised messianic figure who would restore justice and order to the world. Al-Manṣūr's conquest of the Songhay Empire in the Western Sudan in 1591 was interpreted

---

13 For Charles V's idea of crusade, see Youssef El Alaoui, "Carlos V y el mito de la cruzada contra el islam", in *Autour de Charles Quint et son empire*, ed. Augustin Redondo (Paris: 2005), 113–130.

14 Cited in Geoffrey Parker, "Messianic Visions in the Spanish Monarchy, 1516–1598", *Calíope: Journal of the Society for Renaissance and Baroque Hispanic Poetry* 8/2 (2002), 7. The text was also analysed by Bethany Aram, "La reina Juana entre Trastámara y Austrias", in *Gobernar en tiempos de crisis: las quiebras dinásticas en el ámbito hispánico (1250–1808)*, ed. José Manuel Nieto Soria and María Victoria López-Cordón (Madrid: 2008), 31–44.

as proof of his God-chosen role as Universal Emperor of the Last Days.[15] The chronicler al-Ifrānī described the conquest of Timbuktu as one "of the numerous foretelling signs of the imminent coming of the Mahdī", and stated that Oran would be regained from the Spaniards "by the Mahdī or under his order".[16] In Portugal, similarly, Dom Sebastian's death, and more importantly, the accession of Philip II of Spain to the Portuguese throne, sparked a messianic myth that would last for centuries. Inspired by the prophetic verses of a shoemaker named António Annes Bandarra, and because the young king's body was never recovered from the battlefield, it was rumoured that Dom Sebastian had not died, but rather was hiding (*encoberto*, Port.; *encubierto*, Sp.), and was expected to return in order restore the Portuguese throne to the House of Braganza. Jacqueline Hermann's contribution in this volume charts the development of Sebastianism in the late sixteenth and early seventeenth centuries, and Luís Felipe Silvéiro Lima's piece discusses its exportation to the Americas through the works of António Vieira.

The myth of the hidden Dom Sebastian drew its host of impostors and impersonators. In the late sixteenth century, a baker from the town of Madrigal de las Altas Torres in Ávila named Gabriel de Espinosa claimed to be none other than the real Dom Sebastian who had emerged from hiding and, in a complicated scheme of court intrigue and connections to the religious establishment, he sought to dethrone the king, Philip II, claiming his crown.[17] The myth of Dom Sebastian elicited curiosity and interest around the Mediterranean and beyond. Its imagery of a hidden king, the geo-politics of the battle of Alcazarquivir from which the myth emerged, the crusader ideology that it embodied, and the intense circulation of the story, make this a truly Mediterranean phenomenon—one with Atlantic reach.

While there is no doubt that messianic imperialism was one of the modes that dominated political discourse in the Mediterranean, prophecies and apocalyptic prognostications also served as a medium for the articulation of the political ambitions of early modern imperial subjects. In the Iberian Peninsula, baptised Jews and Muslims, known as Conversos and Moriscos respectively,

---

15   See Stephen Corey, *Reviving the Islamic Caliphate in Early Modern Morocco* (Farnham: 2013); and Mercedes García-Arenal, *Ahmad al-Mansur: The Beginnings of Modern Morocco* (Oxford: 2009).

16   García Arenal, *Ahmad al-Mansur*, 128.

17   For an excellent analysis of this case see Ruth McKay, *The Baker who Pretended to be King of Portugal* (Chicago: 2012). The baker of Madrigal was not the only impersonator of Dom Sebastian in the sixteenth and seventeenth-century Mediterranean. For others see for example Eric Olsen, *The Calabrian Charlatan, 1598–1603: Messianic Nationalism in Early Modern Europe* (Basingstoke: 2003).

read apocalyptic prophecies that spoke to their condition as newly converted Christians. Through the circulation of these prognostications imperial subjects could insert themselves in the politics of their time. Take for example the Moriscos, for whom prognostications known as *jofores* served to bolster rebellions such as the two-year uprising in the Alpujarras mountains of Granada between 1568–1570.[18] Prophecies were also central to the insurrection plans of Greek subjects of the Ottoman empire in the Morea who, scarcely two years after the Morisco revolt, appealed to the Spanish king Philip II, requesting military assistance. They promised to deliver Greece and Trabzon to the Spanish king, who would become "emperor of Constantinople", and therefore, of Rome, as was predicted in their prophecies.[19] Not only did prophecies serve as mobilisation discourses for ethnic and religious minorities, but, as the Greek example shows, prophecies could also serve as diplomatic discourses that allowed non-state actors in the Mediterranean to communicate their political aspirations to powerful rulers.[20] The text analysed by Marios Hatzopoulos in this volume demonstrates the lasting power of prophecies, well into the eighteenth century. As Hatzopoulos shows, Greek subjects of the Ottomans continued to turn to prophecy to make sense of their present, and to project onto the future their political aspirations of an Ottoman defeat.

Around the Mediterranean basin, apocalyptic excitement also took root among mystics, spiritual groups, and lay people alike. Movements like that of the seventeenth-century kabbalist and ascetic Sabbatai Zevi (1626–1676), a Jew from Izmir, likely of Sephardic ancestry, became infused with messianic expectations. Sabbatai Zevi was trained as a rabbi, but instead devoted himself to mysticism. In 1648 he declared himself as the awaited Messiah. His messianic message received harsh criticism from the local Jewish community, and he was exiled from Izmir. He lived in Salonica, Istanbul, Aleppo, Jerusalem, and

---

18 For an analysis of the uses of apocalyptic prophecies among Moriscos see Mayte Green-Mercado, *Visions of Deliverance*; and "The Mahdi in Valencia: Messianism, Apocalypticism, and Morisco Rebellions in Late Sixteenth-Century Spain", *Medieval Encounters* 19 (2013), 193–220.

19 Valladolid, Archivo General de Simancas (Hereafter AGS), Estado, Leg. 1214, doc. 143. For more on Greek contacts with Iberia see José Manuel Floristán Imízcoz, "Felipe II y la empresa de Grecia tras Lepanto (1571–78)", *Erytheia: Revista de estudios bizantinos y neogriegos* 15 (1994), 155–190; and the indispensable work by the same author, *Fuentes para la política oriental de los Austrias: la documentación griega del Archivo de Simancas (1571–1621)* (León: 1988).

20 For more on the diplomatic uses of prophecy see Mayte Green-Mercado, "Morisco Prophecies at the French Court (1602–1607)", *Journal of the Economic and Social History of the Orient (JESHO)* 61 (2018), 91–123.

Cairo, and returned to Izmir in 1665, taking over the leadership of the local Jewish community after silencing the rabbis of the city. Soon his reputation as the awaited Messiah spread from Isfahan to London, and from Yemen to Moscow and Morocco.[21] Surrounding Sabbatai were prophets and other visionaries, like Nathan of Gaza, who prophesied the restoration of Israel, and his wife Sarah, who was considered a messianic figure in her own right. Like other messianic and prophetic movements of his time, Sabbatai attracted the attention of the authorities. While initially the Ottomans were not particularly concerned with his message, as his influence grew, and he began to gain more followers, the Grand Vizier accused him of fomenting sedition, and forced him to convert to Islam. On the one hand, Sabbatai's messianism continued to influence Jewish communities around the Mediterranean. On the other, his conversion prompted some in Salonica to follow suit, and this group came to be known as the Dönme (converts).[22] Salonica was a major centre of Dönmes until 1923, when they were forced to abandon their homes during the Greek-Turkish population exchange.

In Iberia, visionaries and prophets weighed in on proper religious observance, commented on political news, and made predictions about political matters. One of the most interesting and well-known visionary cases in the sixteenth century was Miguel de Piedrola, a Spanish soldier who had served in Granada, Flanders, North Africa, Naples, Florence, and Rome.[23] He claimed to have been taken captive in Istanbul, where he had allegedly begun to hear certain "voices" that he claimed had helped him escape. He was said to have received political information and advice from these voices, whose intended recipients were the Spanish authorities in Naples. He was allegedly captured twice more and taken to Istanbul, where he again managed to escape with the help of the "voices", and he ended up in Sicily with new divine messages for the Viceroy and the Commander of the Navy. He then went to the court in Madrid and began to offer assistance to King Philip II. During these years

---

21   The literature of Sabbatai Zevi is vast. For recent treatments of the subject see Matt Goldish, *The Sabbatean Prophets* (Cambridge: 2004); and Cengiz Şişman, *The Burden of Silence: Sabbatai Sevi and the Evolution of the Ottoman-Turkish Dönmes* (New York: 2015). For Sabbatai Zevi's wife, who was also considered a messianic figure, see Alexander van der Haven, *From Lowly Metaphor to Divine Flesh: Sarah the Ashkenazi, Sabbatai Tsevi's Messianic Queen and the Sabbatian Movement.* (Amsterdam: 2012).

22   For more on the Dönme see Marc David Baer, *The Dönme: Jewish Converts, Muslim Revolutionaries, and Secular Turks* (Stanford: 2010).

23   For an excerpt of Piedrola's inquisitorial autobiography see Abigail Dryer and Richard Kagan, *Inquisitorial Inquiries. Brief Lives of Secret Jews and Other Heretics*, 2nd ed. (Baltimore: 2011), 88–115.

Piedrola offered all manner of advice on governance, he interpreted news, and gave political messages to the king, viceroys, religious officials, and other powerful men. After eventually being banished from the court, he began to claim the title of Prophet and warned of great calamities for those who did not believe in his messages. Like many prophets and visionaries, Piedrola ended up in the hands of the Inquisition, where he described his mission to the inquisitors in the following manner:

> As you know, I am a prophet. As such, I have spoken to pontiffs, kings, and magnates and to the guardians of these kingdoms. Many of my prophecies have come true, I state this clearly because I don't want harm to come to you, as has come to all others who have dared to persecute me without my having committed a crime deserving [of punishment]. I won't tell you any more than I've told everyone else.[24]

Miguel de Piedrola was by no means singular. Numerous prophets and visionaries peppered the streets of Madrid, Ávila, Toledo, and other Mediterranean cities like Venice or Istanbul.[25] As Monika Frohnapfel-Leis's piece in this volume shows, the presence of these prophets prompted a debate on the discernment of visions and prophecies. While it was believed that women and men could receive divine revelations (an idea that Christians, Jews, and Muslims shared), during the early modern period the secular and religious authorities increasingly saw the need to control these messages, which they considered potentially subversive. Adelisa Malena's study on Sienese quietism in this volume highlights the role of the Inquisition in controlling orthodoxy. With regards to mystics, visionaries, prophets, and messiahs, the Inquisition in Iberia and Italy became the primary institution charged with investigating these claims. In fact, in most cases we know about these characters precisely because of the rich archives of the Inquisition. In Islamic lands, as the case of Sabbatai Zevi shows, while initially the control of his message was in the hands of the local rabbis, when it became a matter of public control it was the Grand Vizier who would be charged with controlling the spread of messianic activity.

---

24 Dryer and Kagan, *Inquisitorial Inquiries*, 98.
25 For visions and apparitions in early modern Spain see the classic work by William A. Christian, *Apparitions in Late Medieval and Renaissance Spain* (Princeton: 1989). For visionaries and prophets see for example Richard Kagan, *Lucrecia's Dreams Politics and Prophecy in Sixteenth-Century Spain* (Baltimore: 1990); María V. Jordán, *Soñar la Historia. Riesgo, creatividad y religión en las profecías de Lucrecia de León* (Madrid: 2007); Gillian T.W. Ahlgren, *The Inquisition of Francisca: A Sixteenth-Century Visionary on Trial* (Chicago: 2005).

While the Mediterranean was indeed the space through which apocalyptic and messianic ideas spread, the intellectual genealogies of early modern apocalypticism also show it to be a distinctively Mediterranean phenomenon. The following section will explore the characteristic features and most salient topoi found in the apocalyptic literature produced in the Mediterranean basin.

Intellectual Genealogies and Apocalyptic Imagery

In his influential article on the connected nature of the early modern world, Sanjay Subrahmanyam focused on the apocalyptic theme to weave the threads that linked Europe to Asia, while shedding important light on the shared nature of Christian, Jewish, and also Muslim ideas of the End Times. Subrahmanyam's macro perspective served to contest comparative studies that downplayed the global and connected nature of the early modern period, while privileging national histories, and therefore making western European history the standard for historical analysis. Although the focus of the present introduction is regional, and in this sense narrower than his intended global scope, Subrahmanyam's connected approach is useful in analysing the shared nature of apocalyptic imagery of the early modern Mediterranean.

While this introduction has made it a point to explore the theme of apocalypticism in a particular historical moment—the early modern age—no discussion of ideas about the End Times in this period can ignore its deep late medieval roots. In fact, when it comes to the matter of apocalypticism, such distinctions become muddled, especially when considering the preoccupations of people living around the Mediterranean basin, and the intellectual genealogies from which they drew to give meaning to their past, interpret their present, and project their aspirations for the future.

There is no doubt that one of the figures that left the most indelible mark on the political theology of the Christian Mediterranean was the Calabrian abbot known as Joachim of Fiore (*d*.1202). Without delving into the vast and complex literature on the subject, one can suggest with confidence that one of the most enduring of Joachim of Fiore's ideas was his division of history. Interpreting scriptures, Joachim of Fiore developed a tripartite theory of time according to which three ages succeeded one another: the Age of the Father, or of the law (the Old Testament), the Age of the Son (the period of the New Testament), and the Age of the Holy Spirit, culminating in the inauguration of a new dispensation of peace and love. The Age of the Holy Spirit, which would begin with a great cataclysm, would be followed by the restoration of the Christian faith with the spiritual unity of Latins and Greeks, the conversion of the Jews, and the "renovation of the world" (*renovatio mundi*).²⁶ One of the most appealing aspects of this conception of time was the promise of the renovation of the Church. Late medieval authors viewed the Great Schism of 1378–1417 with anxiety and interpreted it as one of the birth pangs of the End Times. Thus, the apocalyptic scenario of the destruction and renovation of a corrupt Church is present in most Christian Western European apocalyptic writings from the fourteenth century onwards.

Combining the dreams of universal empire with the desire for the reformation of the Church, the French monk Jean de Roquetaillade's (John of Rupescissa, *d*.1362) work titled *Vade Mecum in Tribulatione*, that circulated from the fourteenth to the sixteenth centuries, emphasised the reformation of the Church after its destruction by Muslims, and announced the Joachimite vision of the perfected rule by an angelic pope and a messianic emperor.²⁷ Similarly, the French theologian and astrologer Pierre D'Ailly (*d*.1420) viewed the history of the Church as a series of persecutions that culminated with the arrival of Antichrist.²⁸ It was to D'Ailly, among others, that Christopher Columbus would turn when composing his *Book of Prophecies*, in which he viewed his own evangelising mission—and Ferdinand and Isabella's role as Emperor of the End Times through their conquering of Jerusalem—as key events that signalled the Latter Days.²⁹

At times the Joachimite visions of reformation and renewal could coalesce with other apocalyptic narratives in a single text, as is the case of a sixteenth century rendition of a prophecy attributed to the Crusader king of Jerusalem Guy de Lusignan (*d*.1194), that circulated in the Italian Peninsula for more than

---

26   For a classic work, see Marjorie Reeves, *Joachim of Fiore and the Prophetic Future* (New York: 1977). See also Bernard McGinn, *The Calabrian Abbot: Joachim of Fiore in the History of Western Thought* (New York: 1985); Gian Luca Potestà, *Il tempo dell'Apocalisse: vita di Gioacchino da Fiore* (Roma: 2004); Brett Edward Whalen, *Dominion of God: Christendom and Apocalypse in the Middle Ages* (Cambridge, MA: 2009).

27   For a study of the works and thought of Jean de Roquetaillade, see Leah DeVun, *Prophecy, alchemy, and the end of time: John of Rupescissa in the late Middle Ages* (New York: 2009).

28   Louis Pascoe, *Church and Reform. Bishops, Theologians, and Canon Lawyers in the Thought of Pierre D'Ailly (1351–1420)* (Leiden: 2005), 12–13. For an in-depth study of the apocalyptic thought of Pierre D'Ailly, see Laura Ackermann Smoller, *History, Prophecy, and the Stars: The Christian Astrology of Pierre D'Ailly, 1350–1420* (Princeton: 1994).

29   For more on Columbus' apocalyptic thought, see Alain Milhou, *Colón y su mentalidad mesiánica en el ambiente franciscanista español* (Valladolid: 1983); and Djelal Kadir, *Columbus and the Ends of the Earth. Europe's Prophetic Rhetoric as Conquering Ideology* (Berkley: 1992). For an edition and translation of Columbus' Book of Prophecies see Delno C. West (trans. and ed.), *The Libro de las profecías of Christopher Columbus* (Gainesville: 1991).

a century, and that also ended up among the papers of the Spanish ambassador to Venice in 1575.[30] In this oracle, the unlikely prophet Lusignan predicted the events that would take place in the 1450s. The prophecy reads as a providential history, the framework of which is Mediterranean in scope, with roles played by the major powers of the time. It begins with the destruction of the Church at the hands of the Ottomans, who would conquer Constantinople and charge against Hungary. The Ottoman sultan would proceed to Rome, but the pope of the time would call upon the Holy Roman Emperor, who would not defend Christendom. Instead, Venice was to emerge in the Adriatic in order to resist the Ottoman forces. The Holy Roman emperor would demand from the pope the restitution of his imperial dignities from him, but the Pope would decide to confer the imperial title to the Venetians. As revenge, the Holy Roman Emperor would assist the Ottomans in conquering Rome, after which the Ottomans would conquer all the Venetian lands. Jesus would then send a holy man to Rome to cleanse the church from its corrupt priests and cardinals. Echoing the sentiment of pope Pious II's famous 1461 letter to Sulṭān Meḥmed II, in which he offered his support and legitimacy in exchange for the Ottoman ruler's conversion to Christianity, Guy de Lusignan's oracle makes the Ottoman ruler convert after seeing the miracles of the "holy man" in Rome.[31] The Ottomans would then rule over all of Christendom, Muslims were to convert, and all laws would be annulled. The idea that at the End of Times the Ottoman sultan would conquer Rome and would convert to Christianity is repeated in other early modern texts. For example, in his 1466 letter to Sulṭān Meḥmed II, the Greek Humanist writer George of Trebizond adulated the Ottoman ruler with the following words: "In your victory, God transferred the kingdom to you in order to gather through you all the races into one faith and one church, and to exalt you as the autocrat of the whole world and king not merely of things perishable, but also of the very heavens." According to George, it was prophesied that Meḥmed II would conquer Rome, and that Islam would be eradicated. He encouraged the conversion of the Ottoman sultan in the following terms:

> If the conqueror strives for the unity of the faith and of the church, and if he demonstrates his zeal by deeds and not merely by words, then through

---

30   AGS, Estado, Leg. 1498, doc. 256. For an in-depth analysis of this prophecy see, Mayte Green-Mercado, *Visions of Deliverance*, ch. 3.
31   For an analysis of Pious II's letter see, for example, Margaret Meserve, *Empires of Islam in Renaissance historical thought* (Cambridge MA: 2008); and Nancy Bisaha, "Pius II's *letter to Mehmed II*. A reexamination'", *Crusades* 1 (2002), 183–200.

him God will destroy Muhammad's creed and make the conqueror and his descendants lords of the whole world. And they will be hailed as the kings of heavens.[32]

In the mid-fifteenth century the image of the Ottoman sultan as the model of a universal ruler, or the Emperor of the End Times, possessed wide currency. Meḥmed II had just conquered Constantinople, and the ever-expanding Muslim empire seemed unstoppable. But the appeal of Lusignan's oracle in the sixteenth century, as attested most remarkably by its appearance in the Spanish court as late as 1575 (after the Ottoman defeat at Lepanto), demonstrates on the one hand the enduring power of prophecies, while on the other it reflects the continued apocalyptic anxieties that accompanied the Ottoman-Habsburg confrontation in the Mediterranean.

Returning to Lusignan's apocalyptic narrative, the French prognosticator announced that the Ottomans would bequeath control of Jerusalem to Venice. As a final dramatic scene, in a Joachimite vision of dual sovereignty, the Ottoman sultan would rule as universal emperor alongside the holy man, and the whole world would live in perfection. The scenario presented in this prophetic text brought together different intellectual and theo-political threads that wove together the net of apocalyptic thought and practice across the Mediterranean. From the visions of the conquest of Jerusalem, to the conquest of the city of Rome by Muslims, the eradication of all laws, and the gathering of humanity under a perfected religion, the apocalyptic prophecies that circulated in the Christian as well as the Muslim shores of the Mediterranean weaved a common horizon of coexistence, exchange and also—simultaneously—confrontation of the three Abrahamic religions.

In the eastern Mediterranean, the ideas expressed in a vast corpus of literature produced by Ibn ʿArabī (d.1240), an Iberian-born philosopher and mystic, shaped apocalyptic narratives in the Islamic world. This is not a place to assess the impact of Ibn ʿArabī's unitarian mystical theology on Muslim intellectual traditions in the early modern period, but what is pertinent for our purposes is the presence of prophecies attributed to Ibn ʿArabī that concerned a future Ottoman conquest of Constantinople and Rome. According to one such text titled *al-Shajarat al-nuʿmaniyya fī dawlat al-ʿUthmāniyya* (The Crimson Tree on the Ottoman State), which appears to have circulated widely in the early modern period, the dynasty founded by the Ottomans would con-

---

[32] George of Trebizond, *Collectanea Trapezuntiana: Texts, Documents, and Bibliographies of George of Trebizond*, ed. John Monfasani (Binghamton, NY: 1984), 495.

tinue to exist until the reign of a ruler whose name starts with the letter *mīm* (Ar. /m/), that is Mahdī. Then the Ottomans would conquer smaller Rome—that is, Constantinople—and also greater Rome (*al-Rūmiyya al-kubrā*)—that is the city of Rome. It is difficult to determine the real authorship of this text, but there is no doubt that the apocryphal text incorporated the material from the vast literary oeuvre of a fifteenth-century Syrian occultist named ʿAbd al-Raḥmān al-Bisṭāmī (*d.*1454), whose historical outlook and prophetic predictions became almost an imperial canon especially during the reign of Süleyman the Magnificent.[33]

Let us turn to another frequent topos in the apocalyptic narratives that circulated around the Mediterranean in the early modern period: the image of a messianic redeemer in the figure of a hidden king. From the dreams of the return of Dom Sebastian in Portugal and the *Encubierto* in Spain, to the sleeping king in Greece, people living in the Mediterranean projected their hopes of religious and political redemption onto figures that were expected to restore justice and order to the world. In the Iberian Peninsula, the figure of the Hidden King appeared in the work of the fifteenth century Franciscan monk Juan Alemany, whose apocalyptic visions included an uprising of Jews and Muslims, against whom the *Encubierto* (the Hidden One, a kind of messianic emperor) would appear and, supported by the New David (identified as the pope), would expel the rebellious infidels from the Iberian Peninsula.[34] After this initial victory, the *Encubierto* would march through Muslim lands until reaching Jerusalem, which he would conquer. With order restored, the *Encubierto* would be recognised as messiah by some Jews, and together with the New David, he would reign on earth until the definitive arrival of the End Times.[35]

The figure of the Hidden King appears in other fifteenth century texts, such as in the prognosticative corpus circulating in fifteenth-century Castile, attributed to the sixth/seventh century bishop of Seville, St. Isidore. The central message of these prophecies is the destruction of Spain. According to the purported St. Isidore, Spain's sins have resulted in God's wrath. God has therefore sent plagues upon her, such as the Muslim conquest and the presence of

33 Denis Gril, "L'Enigme de la Šaǧara al-Nuʿmāniyya fī l'Dawla al-ʿUthmāniyya, atribuee a Ibn ʿArabī", in *Les Traditions apocalyptiques au tournant de la chute de Constantinople*, ed. Benjamin Lellouch and Stéphane Yerasimos (Paris: 2000), 134; Fleischer, "A Mediterranean Apocalypse", 24, 28.
34 María Isabel Toro Pascua, "Milenarismo y profecía en el siglo XV: La tradición del libro de Unay en la Península Ibérica", *Península. Revista de Estudios Ibéricos* n. 0 (2003), 31.
35 Ibid.

Jews within it. However, in one of the texts, a bat (*verspertilio*), associated with the figure of the eschatological emperor, would be sent by God to kill all the mosquitos (Muslims), and rid Spain of all its enemies. In other texts attributed to St. Isidore the eschatological ruler is identified as the *Encubierto*, or hidden king.[36] The destruction of Islam in this particular text is reminiscent of an influential early text that circulated around the Mediterranean since at least the seventh century. The so-called *Apocalypse of Pseudo-Methodius* presents a vision of history in which a Roman emperor residing in Jerusalem would annihilate Islam and would be a witness to the second coming of Christ at the End Times. The whole edifice was built upon the Danielic schema of four successive universal monarchies.[37] The fifth monarchy would be reserved for the Emperor of the End Times. Thus, the expectation of the Last World Emperor who would unite Christendom against its enemies, so popular after the conquest of Constantinople in 1453, could be traced to Pseudo-Methodius.[38]

The myth of the hidden king also took root among Iberian Muslims and their descendants, who were forcibly converted to Catholicism in the early sixteenth century, and most commonly known as Moriscos. The presence of the *Encubierto*, or Hidden King in Morisco apocalyptic narratives offers a window into this shared nature of prophecy and apocalyptic ideas in the Mediterranean. As is well known, the idea of a hidden leader, the hidden imām, the *al-mahdī al-muntaẓar* (or the awaited Mahdī) is a key figure in Muslim apocalyptic thought, specifically in Twelver Shīʿism.[39] Twelver Shīʿīs believe that in the year 878 C.E. Muḥammad al-Mahdī, the twelfth-generation of the descendants of ʿAlī b. Abī Ṭālib, cousin and son-in-law of the Prophet Muḥammad, went into occultation (*ghayba*) and remains concealed until he returns to lead the community and to restore justice and order to the world. In the early modern Islamic world, the idea of a hidden leader was not always a matter of Shīʿī doctrine; in other words, it went beyond the issue of Alid loyalism, as Evrim Binbaş has recently argued. For example, in fifteenth-century Iraq, during the siege of the city of Baghdad by the Qaraqoyunlu, it was rumoured that the ruler of the city, who was killed during the siege, was in fact not dead but rather hiding, and was

---

36   José Guadalajara Medina, *Las profecías del anticristo en la edad media* (Madrid: 1996), 343–352.
37   Luis Vázquez de Parga, "Algunas notas sobre el Pseudo Metodio y España", *Habis* 2 (1971), 146.
38   Richard K. Emmerson, "Apocalyptic Themes and Imagery in Medieval and Renaissance Literature", in *The Encyclopedia of Apocalypticism*, vol. 2 (*Apocalypticism in Western History and Culture*), ed. Bernard McGinn (New York/London: 2000), 403.
39   Mohammad Ali Amir-Moezzi, *The Divine Guide in Early Shiʿism: The Sources of Esotericism in Islam* trans. David Streight (Albany: 1994).

expected to return to save the city.⁴⁰ Thus, the figure of the hidden leader, or hidden imām, surely must have been recognisable to Muslims and Moriscos in late fifteenth and sixteenth century Iberia. Given the likelihood of the Moriscos' familiarity with the Muslim myth, when they read the Christian prophecies circulating in the Iberian Peninsula since the late middle ages, they probably recognised the character and projected their hopes for a messianic redeemer onto the *Encubierto*. The Hidden King appears in two Morisco apocalyptic texts, known as *jofores* (from the Arabic root j-f-r, meaning prognostication). One of the texts purportedly derived from Muslim sources, while the other had been allegedly authored by none other than Isidore of Seville. The Morisco *jofor* is attributed to Muḥammad's cousin and son-in-law, ʿAlī ibn Abī Ṭālib, who purportedly predicted a Muslim reconquest of al-Andalus after its fall to Christians. The prognostication was discovered by the inquisitorial authorities of Granada in the aftermath of the Morisco rebellion in the Alpujarras mountains (1568–1570) among some papers that included two additional prophecies. The original was written in Arabic, and it was translated into Spanish by the Morisco Alonso del Castillo, a renown royal interpreter. Del Castillo shared these texts with a friend, the Spanish historian Luis del Mármol Carvajal, who included the prognostications in his chronicle of the revolt titled *Historia del rebelión y castigo de los moriscos del reino de Granada*. In the prophecy, ʿAlī ibn Abī Ṭālib foresees the conquest of al-Andalus by the Christians, and in particular the loss of Granada, which took place in 1492. According to ʿAlī ibn Abī Ṭālib, the Christians would subject the Iberian Muslim populations to cruel tortures, but then Muslims from the east would come to their brethren's rescue. In this prognostication the "Turks" (Ottomans) would come to the Iberian Peninsula and overtake it, "and the whole kingdom [of Granada] will return to the control of the house of the Messenger of God, and the law [Islam] will be exalted".⁴¹ In this apocalyptic scenario, the Hidden King appears to be a Muslim ruler who in turn would subject the Iberian Christians to all manner of punishments. Then the Ottomans "will march with their armies to Rome, and the Christians will not escape them, except for those who will convert to the law of the Prophet".⁴² This prognostication must have surely served as an incentive for

---

40   Evrim Binbaş, "The Jalayirid Hidden King and the Unbelief of Shāh Mohammad Qaraqoyunlu", *Journal of Persianate Studies* (forthcoming in Winter 2020). I thank the author for sharing a copy of the article before its publication.

41   My translation of the prophecy found in the edition prepared by Javier Castillo Fernández's edition of the text. Luis del Mármol Carvajal, *Historia del rebelión y castigo de los moriscos del reino de Granada*, ed. Javier Castillo Fernández (Granada: 2015), 150–155.

42   Ibid.

the Moriscos to continue their struggle during the Alpujarras revolt. The apocalyptic scenario of this prognostication resonates with the Christian prophecies discussed above—that is, the possible conquest of Rome, and the destruction of Christians, the conversion of the world to one law and the eradication of all other laws—yet in this case the general conversion before the End Times would be to Islam. This reveals on the one hand, the markedly Islamic character of these Morisco *jofores*, while on the other, it underscores the fluidity of cultural exchange at the level of prophetic knowledge and the impossibility of fixed confessional adscriptions to the individual topoi that made up this knowledge. Also, note the markedly Mediterranean flavour of this apocalyptic vision. The action takes place in a Mediterranean context where the three Abrahamic religions are in close contact with one another. In the particular case of the Iberian Peninsula, by the fifteenth century Christians had conquered all of the Iberian territory from Muslims, except for the Naṣrid emirate in Granada, and Jews and Muslims constituted an ethno-religious minority living under Christian rule. Large tracts of lands surrounding the Mediterranean, however, were in Muslim hands, including Jerusalem, which—according to many Christian apocalyptic scenarios since the eleventh century—had to be liberated. The close and intense contact between Muslims, Christians, and Jews featured prominently in this and many other apocalyptic narratives, as is made evident by most of the apocalyptic prophecies and prognostications discussed in this introduction.

The second Morisco *jofor* to feature the figure of the Hidden King, one attributed to St. Isidore with the title of *Plaint of Spain*, is part of a manuscript in Aljamiado—that is, using Arabic script to render Romance languages. The manuscript includes other apocalyptic prognostications that foretell the fate of the Iberian Muslim community, the Christian conquest of Iberia, the forced conversion of Muslims, and their subjection to Inquisitorial authority. Most prognostications also present a scenario in which the Iberian Peninsula will once again be in Muslim hands. Like the original (Christian) versions of the prophecy, the Aljamiado rendering of Isidore's *Plaint* is not so favourable to the Moriscos. Partially rewritten for a Muslim audience, the *jofor* describes St. Isidore as the excellent doctor of Spain, who extracted the prognostication from a "very old book titled Secret of the Secrets of Spain".[43] The learned saint describes Spain as a "sheep without a shepherd, a body without a head, a widow without a husband, or people without a leader", after having forsaken its Lord.

---

43 My translation. Paris, Bibliothèque Nationale de France (BnF), Ms. 774, fols 294ʳ–301ʳ. For an edition of the text, see Mercedes Sánchez Álvarez, *El manuscrito misceláneo 774 de la Biblioteca Nacional de París: Leyendas, itinerarios de viajes, profecías sobre la destrucción de España y otros relatos moriscos* (Madrid: 1982), 246–249.

Spain will be reduced because of her sins, but then "the renewal of the law will begin" after "a powerful snake arises in the East, which will surround the ancient city of Constantinople". Everything will be chaos, until the New David emerges by the calling of the *Encubierto* (Hidden King), and then all Jews and Muslims will be wiped out from Spain, and he will conquer North Africa as well. This particular *jofor* might seem surprising, foretelling as it does a terrible outcome to a Morisco audience. However, the rhetorically powerful images of the destruction of Christians by an "Eastern" *serpiente* might have provided comfort to the Moriscos, while the suffering of the Muslims might have served as warning to those who depart from the path of God. Moriscos also adapted the famous *Vade mecum in tribulatione* of Jean de Roquetaillade, which they rendered in Aljamiado, precisely because of its message of the destruction of the Church and the promise of an Ottoman conquest of Rome.[44] Arguably, Moriscos would read these Christian prophecies with a critical eye, distinguishing between favourable and unfavourable announcements, perhaps discarding the latter as misguided interpretations of an unfaithful author, while taking the former as proofs that served to ratify their own prophetic beliefs (that even Christian doctors had foretold). These appropriations also served to engage in surprising acts of subversion against their persecutors' discourse. For example, in the Morisco version of Roquetaillade's *Vade mecum* the Antichrist who comes to punish the sinful clergy is named "Fatimí", Faṭimī being the North African name for the Mahdī.[45] The prophecy explains how this "Fatimí" would also conquer Spain. To the Moriscos reading or listening to this prophecy, then, the Christian Antichrist could be none other than their awaited messiah.

The examples presented in this brief historical overview—whether the co-option of the apocalyptic discourse for the articulation of the imperial program of rulers, or to express the religious or political aspirations of subjects—illustrate the existence of an early modern Mediterranean apocalyptic phenomenon. This apocalypticism can only be fully deciphered in terms of a "connected history", where one trend would not have developed the way it did without the other trends—that is, without competition, but also the deep cultural understanding, between Christians, Muslims and Jews. This connected

---

44 My translation. Madrid, Biblioteca National de España (hereafter BNE), Ms. 5305, fols 61ʳ–67ᵛ. For an analysis, edition, and transcription of the text, see Gerard Wiegers, "Jean de Roquetaillade's Prophecies among the Muslim Minorities of Medieval and Early Modern Christian Spain: An Islamic Version of the Vademecum in Tribulatione", in *Transmission and Dynamics of the Textual Sources of Islam*, ed. Nicolet Boekhoff-van der Voort, Kees Versteegh, and Joas Wagemakers (Leiden: 2011), 229–247.

45 BNE, Ms. 5305, fols 61ʳ–67ᵛ. For an analysis, edition and transcription of the text, see Wiegers, "Jean de Roquetaillade's Prophecies".

history is one of unity in diversity taking place in a multi-cultural environment and an intense inter-confessional context that fostered contact, exchange and confrontation at the same time, and as part of the same historical horizon. If the characteristics of this apocalyptic culture, as I have described them, seem similar to those that historians nowadays use to refer to the Mediterranean as a cultural and historical region (fluid, interconnected, conflictual and intensely negotiated at all levels of social and political exchange), it is because the prophetic phenomenon mirrored it like no other. The early modern Mediterranean Sea looked exactly like the prophecies it dreamt.

CHAPTER 5

Sebastianism: A Portuguese Prophecy

Jacqueline Hermann

Introduction

The texts, selected to present some Portuguese prophetic writings, are the work of Dom João de Castro (c.1550–c.1628). There are few studies about this character, immortalised in Portuguese History as the "future apostle of Sebastianism", according to historian João Lúcio de Azevedo.[1] A little known figure, Dom João de Castro has been studied by several authors.[2] None of these, however, answer questions I consider essential to the understanding of Castro's life, which he turned into a crusade in order to defend his belief in the return of Dom Sebastian, alive, from the Moroccan sands. That defence fuelled the messianic wait for a 'Hidden King' and the flourishing of Sebastianism between the end of the sixteenth and the beginning of the seventeenth centuries.

The messianic Sebastianist phenomenon arose in Portugal after the Lusitanian defeat in North Africa, on 4 August 1578, at the Battle of Alcacer Quibir. The battle saw a Muslim army of over 150,000 men confront some 22,000 Portuguese soldiers. Part of Portugal's nobility and male population were allegedly killed or imprisoned by the enemy. They were led by their young king Dom Sebastian, who either died during the battle, or disappeared and had to hide his identity to escape prison and dishonour.[3]

The expectation of the return of relatives, as well as of the king himself, generated hope in all corners and among diverse social groups, that the 'Desired', as he was called from birth, might be alive. But, while in the streets and homes there was a growing hope, at the Palace the dynamics were different: since the throne might not be vacant—"the king is dead, long live the king"—the last male member of the Avis lineage became the King of Portugal. Cardinal

---

1 João Lúcio de Azevedo, *A evolução do Sebastianismo* (Lisbon: 1984), 29.
2 See Martim de Albuquerque, "O valor politológico do sebastianismo", in *Estudos de Cultura Portuguesa*, 2 (Lisbon: 2000), 293–326; Miguel D'Antas, *Os falsos D. Sebastião*, 2nd ed. (Odivelas: 1988), 155–195 and 199–239; João Carlos Gonçalves Serafim, "Don João de Castro (c.1550-c.1628). Um resistente que se tornou profeta", in *Via Spiritus* 6 (1999), 121–140 and *D. João de Castro, "O Sebastianista". Meandros de vida e razões de obra*, 3 vols (Porto, 2004).
3 For an analysis of the rise of Sebastianism in Portugal see Jacqueline Hermann, *No reino do Desejado*. A construção do sebastianismo em Portugal, séculos XVI e XVII, (São Paulo: 1998).

Dom Henrique, who had been regent during Dom Sebastian's minority,[4] was a sick and old man when he took over the crown, after confirmation of the King's death and subsequent shipment of the corpse.[5] His reign was very disturbed: beside managing the consequences of the defeat and negotiating the release of noble captives, he acted as a moderator in the dispute for the throne, which started as soon as the news of the tragedy was spread. Dom Sebastian was not married, leaving the kingdom without direct heirs, which fuelled rivalries between the various branches of the royal genealogy. Among these, three candidates rapidly imposed themselves:[6] Philip II of Spain, Dom Sebastian's uncle; the Duchess of Braganza, cousin of the Desired, and the unexpected Dom Antonio, Prior of Crato, the nephew of the Cardinal Dom Henrique.[7]

Philip II was the strongest candidate, either by family ties—Dom Sebastian's mother was the Spanish king's sister—or by military might, but he had always faced the King Cardinal's veiled resistance since his ascension would represent the submission of Portugal to Spain. The Duchess, the Cardinal's favourite, had against her the fact of being a woman as well as the lack of support from the high nobility, partly allured by the Castilian king. And finally, Dom Antonio, himself a former captive released from Alcacer Quibir, announced his candidacy as soon as he arrived in Portugal in October 1578. From the beginning, he faced the hostility of his uncle and king, with whom he had old disagreements. Son of the well-remembered Prince Dom Luis, who had died in 1555, he came to

---

4 Dom Sebastian was proclaimed king in 1557 after the death of his grandfather, Dom John III. Being only three years of age at the time, Portugal was ruled by two regents until 1568: from 1557 to 1562 by the queen and mentor of the boy king, Dona Catherine, and, from 1562 to 1568, by Dom Sebastian's great uncle, Cardinal Dom Henrique. About the period of regency, see Maria do Rosário de Sampaio Themudo Barata de Azevedo Cruz, *As regências na menoridade de D. Sebastião. Elementos para uma história estrutural*, 2 vols (Lisbon: 1992).
5 There was much controversy about the corpse sent from Morocco to Portugal. Confirmation of the death of the ruling king was necessary for the succession, but the spreading news about the lack of a single eye witness to the king's corpse fuelled the rumours and hopes that the king might be alive and would return, along with his missing relatives. See José Maria Queiroz Velloso, *D. Sebastião (1554–1578)*. 3rd ed. (Lisbon: 1945), 337–420.
6 For a summary of judicial debates about the succession, see Mafalda Soares da Cunha, "A questão jurídica na crise dinástica", in *História de Portugal*, ed. José Mattoso, 3 (Lisbon: 1993–1994), 552–558.
7 Cardinal Dom Henrique, despite being a clergyman and advanced in years, tried to obtain a release from his vows in Rome in order to marry, but never had any answer to his query. See Antonio Brásio, "O problema do casamento do Cardeal-Rei", in *Memórias da Academia das Ciências de Lisboa*, Classe de Letras, XII (Lisbon: 1981), 81–127; José Maria Queiroz Velloso, *O reinado do Cardeal D. Henrique. A perda da independência* (Lisbon: 1946), 93–130; Jacqueline Hermann, "Um papa entre dois casamentos: Gregório XIII e a sucessão portuguesa (1578–1580)", in *Portuguese Studies Review* 22/2 (2014), 3–38.

frequent the palace, treated with the deference due to his exalted rank, but was always reluctant to follow the religious life imposed upon him and followed up by his father and the Cardinal. But the main obstacle to his candidacy was his illegitimacy, which he tried to overcome by all means, proving that the marriage of his father and mother, a Christian convert, had occurred around forty years before.[8]

It was during that enterprise of Dom Antonio, Prior of Crato, that Dom João de Castro entered the stage. Son of Dom Alvaro de Castro, he descended from a family that became famous in the sixteenth century from the so-called Eastern Conquest. His grandfather was the celebrated Dom João de Castro (1500–1548), Viceroy of India, at a time of Portuguese dominance of the region.[9] But, despite bearing an illustrious surname, our author was one of the four bastard children of Dom Alvaro and, as it seems, he neither received financial support nor the attention of his father. At the Court of Dom John III (1521–1557), Dom Alvaro endured some difficult times, but he recovered during Queen Catherine's regency (1557–1562), when he was commissioned to negotiate Dom Sebastian's marriage to Marguerite of Valois with the French Court. During the reign of Dom Sebastian (1568–1578), Dom Alvaro came back to prominence, since he was alongside the King on the expedition to Tangiers, in 1574, which was considered as one of the preparatory stages for Alcacer Quibir.[10] Dom Alvaro died between 1575 and 1577, according to different authors, but it is not certain if he was present at Alcacer Quibir.[11]

Little is known about Dom João de Castro's life before his adhesion to the party of Dom Antonio, which appears in his own work some time prior to the described events. Perhaps because of lack of further information, his biography is not discussed by the above-mentioned historians. All of them reproduce the

---

8   No research has been conducted about Dom Antonio, Prior of Crato since the work of Mário Brandão in 1940s and 1950s Coimbra and Dom Antônio Rei de Portugal. *Documentos de 1582 a 1598* (Coimbra: 1947); José de Castro, *O Prior do Crato* (Lisbon: 1942); J.M. Queiroz Velloso, *O interregno dos governadores e o breve reinado de D. Antônio* (Lisbon: 1953) and Joaquim Veríssimo Serrão, *O reinado de D. Antônio, Prior do Crato*, I (1580–1582) (Coimbra: 1956). For a discussion of the political trajectory and the royal project of Dom Antonio, Prior of Crato, see Jacqueline Hermann, "An Undesired King: Notes on the Political Career of Don Antônio, Prior of Crato", in *Revista Brasileira de História*, 30/59 (2010), 141–166 (http://dx.doi.org/10.1590/S0102-01882010000100008).

9   Dom João de Castro was the fourth Viceroy of India, where he arrived in 1545 after taking part in the North African campaigns. He died on his way back to Portugal, in 1548.

10 On Dom Alvaro de Castro, see João Carlos Gonçalves Serafim, *D. João de Castro, "O Sebastianista"*, 33–40.

11 According to João Carlos Serafim, Dom Alvaro died in 1575. To Queiroz Velloso, the probable date is January of 1576, cf. *D. Sebastião*, 211.

tearful and miserable version created by Castro,[12] which was intended to evoke feelings of abandonment and suffering. After spending his first years in the care of a nanny, he went to live with his paternal grandmother until, at the age of thirteen, he entered a monastery in Sintra, near Lisbon. For four years he lived an "almost religious" life, until he left the monastery to study at the University of Evora, where he lived a vagrant's life, "tattered and patched".[13] In 1578, after the defeat at Alcacer Quibir, he joined Dom Antonio's supporters. He was at the Battle of Alcantara in August 1580, when the "Anthonists" were defeated by the troops of the Duke of Alba in Philip II's service. Before that, Dom Antonio would have been acclaimed king by his partisans, on 19 June 1580, thus precipitating the Spanish military invasion of the kingdom, which had been under siege since March 1579. Cardinal Dom Henrique had died in January of 1580, without any judicial resolution for the matter of the succession. The kingdom was ruled by a Governors' Board,[14] until Philip II was sworn in as Philip I of Portugal, at the Courts held at the city of Tomar in April 1581.

Defeated and persecuted by the Spanish troops, Dom Antonio and some of his followers fled the kingdom, seeking support from Spain's main enemies—France and England—for the Prior of Crato's royal project. However, neither wanted to get involved directly. Instead they relied on intermediaries such as corsairs,[15] thereby weakening Dom Antonio's project and creating internal tensions in the group. Dom João de Castro broke definitively with the Anthonists and from 1587 or 1588[16] distanced himself from their cause, when Dom

12   Lisbon, Biblioteca Nacional de Portugal [hereafter BNP], Códice 4388, Fundo Geral, "Obras de D. João de Castro, 'Dos nove Portugueses que procuraram em Veneza pella liberdade d'El Rey Dom Sebastião nosso Senhor' ", livro 5.
13   *Dos nove Portugueses*, apud Martins de Albuquerque, "O valor politológico do sebastianismo", 305.
14   The Board was composed of Dom Jorge de Almeida, Archbishop of Lisbon, Dom João de Mascarenhas, officer from the Exchequer, Francisco de Sá de Meneses, Chamberlain of the deceased king, Diogo Lopes de Sousa, Governor of the Civil Household and Dom João de Telo Meneses, former ambassador to Rome.
15   In the years 1582–1583, Dom Antonio tried to settle in the Azores and Terceira Islands, which were Portuguese possessions. In 1585 Dom Antonio sought support from England. In 1589, he tried to return to Portugal, backed by the English Fleet, led by the famous English corsair Francis Drake and by John Norris. Insufficient ammunition and above all lack of Portuguese support to the Prior of Crato resulted in retreat. See on that matter João Pedro Vaz, *Campanhas do Prior do Crato. 1580–1589. Entre Reis e Corsários pelo trono de Portugal* (Lisbon: 2004). For an analysis on the quest for foreign support to Dom Antonio's cause, see Jacqueline Hermann, "Politics and Diplomacy in the Portuguese Succession Crisis: The Candidacy of Don Antônio, Prior of Crato (1578–1580)", *Giornale di Storia* 13 (2014) (www.giornaledistoria.net, accessed on 20 December 2015).
16   Dom João de Castro's main criticism was the lack of financial soundness of Dom Antonio's

Sebastian's case "began to glitter for him". These initial impressions appear in the text that ushered in, so far as we know, his "career" as interpreter of prophecies from countless and diverse origins. *Of the Fifth and Last Future Monarchy*,[17] published in 1597, contains João de Castro's first written explanation of his "conversion", and may for that reason be regarded as the origin of the Sebastianist cause.

This text, which remains unpublished to this day, forms the basis of the other two selected works for this chapter. According to Gonçalves Serafim, Castro worked on what he called a "treatise" for ten years and conceived in it his thesis about Dom Sebastian's survival and return as a monarch chosen by God to unite and rule the Catholic world. The idea of a Fifth Monarchy which would succeed the Babylonian, Persian, Macedonian and Roman ones according to Daniel 7 is there,[18] mixed with messianic notions of long and lasting circulation on the entire Iberian Peninsula. Possibly, the lasting Jewish presence in the region contributed to that, as well as the persecutions leading to the prohibition of Judaism first in Spain and afterwards in Portugal.[19] In this work Castro already mentions and defends the prophetic character of some verses or 'trovas' attributed to a lowly born man, a shoemaker by trade, named Gonçalo Annes Bandarra. To Castro, however lower than the true biblical prophets consecrated by the Holy Scripture, Bandarra was a true prophet since, despite his little knowledge, he foresaw the torments endured by Portugal and its complete restoration with the return of the Hidden Prince, incarnated as Dom Sebastian.

The second selected text is the *Discourse of the Life of the Always Welcome and Arisen King Dom Sebastian*, first published in Paris in 1602.[20] In it, Dom João de Castro retells the story of Dom Sebastian, from his birth until the battle of

---

"subjects", complaining about marching ragged and starving, having "no shirt, no socks, no shoes", João Lúcio de Azevedo, *A evolução do Sebastianismo*, 31.

17 BNP Codice 4371, Microfilme F.7745. *Da Quinta e última Monarquia futura, com muitas outras coisas admiráveis dos nossos tempos* (Paris: 1597). The author has added some parts, between 1601 and 1606.

18 See *Da Quinta e última*, fol. 18.

19 After living for centuries in the Iberian Peninsula, the Jews were expelled and Judaism forbidden in both countries, between the end of the fifteenth century and the first half of the sixteenth. In Portugal, the Tribunal of the Inquisition was created in 1536 and began to act in 1540. In that context, there was an increase of apocalyptical and messianic projections in Portugal, as indicates Maria José Ferro Tavares, "O messianismo judaico em Portugal, 1ª metade do século XVI", *Luso-Brazilian Review* 28/1 (1991), 141–151.

20 *Discurso da vida do sempre bem vindo, e aparecido Rey Dom Sebastião nosso senhor o Encoberto desde seu nascimento até o presente: feito e dirigido por Dom João de Castro aos três Estados do Reino de Portugal: convém a saber ao da Nobreza, ao da Clerezia e ao do povo* (Paris: 1602), facsimile edition (Lisbon: 1994).

Alcacer Quibir. His attachment to both weaponry and religion would mark the fate of the last Crusader King of modern times. After the defeat, he allegedly ran away in disguise and walked across the world to purge his guilt. On the way, he approached a ragged hermit and avoided being recognised until he was called by God to come back and fulfil his holy mission of restoring the unity and supremacy of the Catholic Monarchy. In this work of João de Castro, the possibility glimpsed in *Of the Fifth and Last Monarchy*, seemed ready to materialise: in 1598, a man appeared in Venice claiming to be the king lost in Morocco—20 years after the battle, Dom Sebastian would have been 44 years old—and from then on Dom João de Castro strove to prove that he was the Hidden king predicted in Bandarra's trovas. He sought support from European courts and he went to Venice but, by the time he wrote his *Discourse*, the "king" of Venice, had already been imprisoned in Florence and afterwards transferred to Naples. The impostor, Marco Tulio Catizone, was sentenced to the galleys for life in 1602. Going to Spanish territory, he was murdered at San Lucar de Barrameda in September 1603. Dom João de Castro had been living in Paris since 1602, when his *Discourse of the life of Dom Sebastian* was published.

In the last selected text, *Paraphrase and Concordance of some Prophecies by Bandarra*,[21] Castro published what would come to be considered the first part of Bandarra's prophetic trovas, which formed the basis of his Sebastianist beliefs. He informs us that, since 1580, he had access to some verses while knowing others by heart, having read many different versions—to indicate that writings attributed to the shoemaker circulated clandestinely[22]—until he decided to organise them, according to the most accurate versions, in his opinion. From then on, the verses of the shoemaker Bandarra, who lived among converts when Judaism had just been banned, lost their Hebrew origin. In this process of rereading, their meaning was modified and Bandarra was turned into a Christian prophet and defender of the Catholic Universal Monarchy's unification.

From the brief biographical information available to us, it is not possible to understand why Dom João de Castro joined forces with Dom Antonio. The Prior of Crato belonged to the same generation as Dom João de Castro's father, Dom

---

21   *Paraphrase e Concordância de algumas profecias de Bandarra, sapateiro de Trancoso, por Dom João de Castro* (Paris: 1603). Facsimile edition by José Pereira Sampaio (Bruno), (Porto: 1901).

22   Bandarra was imprisoned in Lisbon by the local Inquisition in 1540 and left by "act of faith" in 1541. He was convicted for his free interpretations of the Holy Scriptures and was barred from writing and circulating them. Nevertheless, the verses attributed to the shoemaker continued do circulate and we will never know if the text we have today keeps any relation with that supposedly written by Bandarra.

Alvaro who, as we saw, had died before Alcacer Quibir. Despite their similar trajectories—Dom Antonio was also an illegitimate son and had lived under his father's protection—the Prior of Crato frequented the palace, he was close to the Cardinal, to Dom Sebastian and even to Philip II. His experience was therefore completely different from Castro's, which prevents us from knowing how and if they knew each other before 1578. Nor do we know why Castro did not go to Alcacer Quibir and only arrived in Lisbon after the battle. All the kingdom's men were convened and Castro reports that he had been at the University of Evora since 1568, the first year of Dom Sebastian's reign. These observations prevent us from understanding both the alliance established with Dom Antonio and the late discovered devotion for Dom Sebastian, which are determinant parts of "the apostle of Sebastianism's" trajectory. Whatever his reasons for embracing the Sebastic cause, he was undoubtedly the great architect of the rise and dissemination of a literate Sebastianism across Europe, where the expectation of the Hidden King's return resonated,[23] although without reaching the lasting roots found in Portugal and its colonial territories.

Dom João de Castro left numerous unpublished works, amounting to approximately 21 manuscripts.[24] After devoting himself to the literary world, he remained active until his death around 1628. A gentleman of bastard nobility, he received religious initiation, involved himself in political causes, although we do not know for certain why. Later, he also left politics to dedicate himself to a Hidden King and to an imaginary universal monarchy. Like many of his contemporaries, he mixed prophecy and politics and he spent his last days in solitude and poverty, waiting for Dom Sebastian to recognise the high services he had given him.

All the texts are orthographically updated and, as far as we know, there is no edition in English.

---

23 See on this matter, Yves-Marie Bercé, *Le Roi caché. Sauveurs et imposteurs. Mythes politiques populaires dans l'Europe moderne* (Paris: 1990).
24 This text has a new edition by João Carlos Gonçalves Serafim, *A Aurora da Quinta Monarquia (1604–1605)* (Porto: 2011).

1   **Dom João de Castro, *Of the Fifth and Last Future Monarchy With Many Admirable Things of Our Times* (Paris: 1597)**[25]

Chapter 1

Although writing about the last Monarchy of the world
and on to which nation it will fall, by chance.
Of the Prince who must find it and of the time it will be established.
It is an arduous task for the present,
being the most odious matter to Potentates,
Ridiculous to the huge slaughter of faith,
unbelievable to the corruption of customs
and very difficult, above all,
to clarify, since it is yet to come.

Nonetheless, I will not refuse the task, opposing myself to accidents;
moved by concern for the great downfall
God's church suffers in spiritual matters,
and the flood brought in upon it by a cruel enemy
of Christian name: coming to cover it, in these calamitous times,
with the plague of Christian abominations
(...)
Notwithstanding the great unwillingness of men,
God's grace is more powerful and His mercy always bountiful
to restore them with incorruptible and timeless gifts.
I will spread (...) the news
to the living, who, until our final times
never knew or ever will know
(...)
how it would be the Catholic Church
Roman and Greek, united as one, for many years,
ceased all the schisms;
(...)
Ecclesiastic foundations reformed (...);
The primitive Church resurrected;

---

[25] The original texts presented in this chapter are very long. Only the most important parts are therefore reproduced here. Passages that have been edited out are marked with an ellipsis (...).

the abominable and infernal Mahometan sect, as all enemies
of the Christian name, destroyed by shame;
The Gospel promulgated around the World and Satan banished.
(...)
Who will not be
thrilled, lifting their spirits,
(...)
filling Heavens with graces
and incenses of prayers ....

Chapter 2

First, the main points promised;
I will briefly set some foundations,
as necessary dispositions to our end.
Warning from the beginning that the same exactitude
is not required in all sentences and treaties of things;
(...)
since it is all about the future,
which only God knows about:
it cannot be shown by syllogism and demonstration
as matters of other nature: but (...) by wisdom
and divine secret, each one must be content with
clarity, shadows, or signs, as order and custom
from God without words.
He always used this way of choosing men,
endowing some of them with His holy spirit of prophecy,
as prophets sent by Him;
(...)
In that way, He many times prophesies through one man, without him knowing,
even seeing things diverse
from the Spirit. Those who come first are
the canonical prophets of the Holy Scripture,
whom God used to disclose so many secrets of His
to all peoples and nations, and for all times,
even the last of His coming,
although it happens so covertly and secretly,
and without much assistance

(...)
Thus it is necessary appealing to saints
as God's servants and friends, to whom
He appears and communicates his decisions. He also
chooses others to disclose the future, although
He does not make them as reliable as the former,
(...)
neither are they liked as prophets;
(...)
Of ones and others we will make use
of this discourse, with
the modesty required for that matter,
that requires all the considerations,
not only the frailty of
the time of faith, almost disabled today,
but also, the style in which,
the divine wisdom acts
and discloses things to men, maintaining them at the discretion
of His deep judgement.
(...)

Chapter 3

(...) And it will happen in the last days (says the Lord), I will pour
my Spirit over all flesh, and as prophesied
your sons and your daughters and your youths
will have visions, and our elders will have dreams
and truly in those days, over my servants
and my maids, I will pour from my Spirit
and they will prophesy (...). He testified the same
in many places, the same Acts many times,
and to great number of faithful He has given the gift of prophecy,
creating countless prophets.

(...)
No one must deny what is clearer than noon:
that God, after that
incomprehensible flood of graces, on Pentecost Day,
through the entire primitive Church, since then until
our times, has come back to us, with

His graces, restoring our faith
in the prophecies,
with the gift of intelligence
(...)
For that reason, the militant Church neither was
nor would be devoid of prophecies, about
its future: following heavenly routes
in so troubled and dangerous passage.

5 (...)
The Lord will never do anything without prior
revelation through the Prophets, his servants.

Chapter 4

Of the number of particular graces of this
kind He has sent us, I will do a brief recount
of some servants of His (not all of them, since it would require more space),
    which I will use in this treatise: since He chose them
as means to reveal His projects
for these times. One of them was the Venerable
Abbey Joachim,[26] who was born more than

6 four hundred years ago: a holy man, endowed with
copious gifts of Prophecy, or the Spirit
of Intelligence (...). He prophesied
endless things of all the nations of the world:
or, to say it more properly, he clarified what was
obscurely prophesied in the Holy Scriptures,
Many remarkable things said by him
already happened. Writers of those times
cite Abbot Joachim respectfully,

---

26   Abbot Joachim of Fiore (c.1132–1202) was a mystic and priest who was afterwards considered a prophet. He was a Cistercian friar, but left the orders to live as a hermit in Fiore, Calabria, attracting disciples, due to his visions of the Apocalypse. The chiliastic aspects of his work thrilled ensuing generations and "Joachimism" caused a deep impact during the thirteenth and fourteenth centuries. Moreover, it was considered one of the pillars of Portuguese Sebastianism. See H.R. Loyn (ed.), *Dictionary of the Middle Ages* (Rio de Janeiro: 1997), 223.

ascribing to him the gift of prophecy
in what he excelled those days: leaving,
in subsequent years (…)
proof of many things he predicted (…)
and today, in great part, we witness (…)

Chapter 5

For the future relevance, I wanted to
order this particular chapter, as one of the ensemble's rejects.
Firstly, in Portugal and Castile, there were current
prophecies from Saint Isidore, Archbishop
of Seville,[27] dating from more than a thousand years:
there is no doubt about them, except about the date they will be fulfilled.

All of them promise a great Prince
and Lord, who shall be Monarch: known only
as the Hidden (…),
and the main particular sign
given of him is an iron letter in his name.

(…)
Monarch, marked as hidden
I will refrain from talking about those of Portugal, who, although
they have not the same authority, do not seem to have
a different spirit. On the contrary, they show, if well considered,
the same divine source, from which they all shone forth (…)
(…)
Since, there will be no one who, admitted
by all of them, does not confess that God revealed in that last
world, many more things in particular and in general
and even clearer as regards
the future Monarchy, to a single Portuguese,
and not to all of them (…)
(…)
Circa 1570, a plebeian was born, shoemaker well
Illustrious by his virtues and nobility of heart, esteemed (…) by High

---

27   Saint Isidore, Archbishop of Seville (c.560–636).

Lords, Clergymen and persons of many letters and religion.[28]
He, who, besides sanctity, possessed the gift of prophecy, among other graces,
prophesying countless things to that Kingdom (...),
many of which (...) happened,
and he still is considered truthful today,
due to many witnesses of sight and word,
in whose hands are kept and maintained his prophecies.
(...)
Due to such prophecies, disclosed to the said Queen[29] and to
other persons, about many revelations he had about that
Kingdom, and about King Dom Sebastian, before he went to Africa,
Bandarra was taken to the Inquisition

9ᵛ of Lisbon, to be questioned about what his Spirit
revealed on the subject of the Kingdom's future.
(...) officials of the Holy Office questioned him many times,
and the only thing he declared: "that God revealed those things to him,
and ordered that he disclose(d) them", every time he was called to the Table,
he repeated them, without contradicting himself.
Finally, after many days in prison, he died in confinement,[30]
And it happened to King Dom Sebastian and to Portugal
all the misfortunes he had prophesied, remaining to be seen
the bonanzas and ventures promised to take place afterwards (...)
(...)
Leaving great prophesied mysteries,
commonly known by all as The Trovas of Bandarra,
since that was his nickname, and the prophecies are in Portuguese

---

28 Dom João de Castro wrote his papers about Bandarra from memory, many years after his first contact with the shoemaker's trovas. He showed no sense of chronology and focussed instead on Bandarra's ideas about the Hidden King. See note 33.

29 Dona Catherine of Habsburg (1507–1578), queen and widow of Dom John III (r.1521–1557).

30 Here, Castro is completely mistaken, from the year of Bandarra's prison to the end of the trial, including the possible interference of Queen Catherine in the case. Gonçalo Annes, alias Bandarra, was imprisoned on the first action of the Courts of Inquisition in Portugal, which had been created in 1536. This activity was initiated in 1540. Bandarra was convicted in 1541 for giving a "free interpretation of the Holy Scripture", having been banned from continuing to divulge his verses. All the same, written copies allegedly penned by the shoemaker of Trancoso kept circulating, both within and outside Portugal for several centuries. In this text, which is summarised here, Castro says that the trovas flourished fifty or sixty years beforehand. Since he was writing in 1597, these dates seem to be more in accordance with the ones of the Inquisition trial.

verse, properly called trovas.[31] Neither was he able to read
nor write,[32] the one who composed these trovas
so exquisite in their genre, that no Portuguese poet
of renown (...) would be able to
equal their perfection. Since there is no word excessive
or out of place (...) they [the words] are
very easy and fluid, of the most excellent language
(...), adorned by a thousand figures of eloquence,
in such way, that in such a man,
coming from the place he came and (...) one of the
most ignorant of the kingdom
they speak well for him.

(...) 10
Just the spirit in which he wrote them (...), they were much
divulged in handwriting by all in Portugal;
since they were most obscure
(...)
but also esteemed, due to certain
divine opinion which they believed to see in them,
(...) they did so many transcriptions: that by
inaccuracy of translators who committed mistakes,
according, more or less, to the thoughtfulness of those who transcribed them,
many copies containing words
changed by others, with many transposed verses
(...)
Nevertheless, there were many originals
from careful people, which maintained the purity
and were faithful to the original writing.

Among many other things he prophesies, the most important
describes the Monarchy to be (...): he speaks very clearly

---

31   Trovas are Portuguese verses inspired by popular medieval poems. They generally consist of a succession of sentences, either printed or composed orally.
32   Here the author is once more mistaken, since there are testimonies that supply us with evidence of Bandarra's ability to read, but also note his difficulty with writing. That may be the reason for these trovas, which may have been written by a shearer named Hector Lopes, who was Bandarra's neighbour in Trancoso. See de Azevedo, *A evolução do sebastianismo*, 26.

about the kingdom of Portugal and the great ventures
that would be given to it; he prophesies the tribulations of the Church;
the total destruction of the Mohametans and of all the infidels:
the conquest of the World and Portugal's triumph
in its partition by the conquerors, as well as many other secrets
(...)
When King Dom Sebastian
was defeated in Africa[33] (...), the referred prophecies,
although obscurely, seemed to consider him
alive but hidden: such opinion began to be followed by the people
who cared for the King's good: for that reason both the prophecies
and the evidences disclosed by those who were
in the battle, fitted in so well that, finally, the doubts
about the King being alive were dissipated and
people trusted the trovas of Bandarra.

When that notion began to spread,
and Cardinal D. Henrique became the heir to the Crown,[34]
since the rumour was not favourable to him,
he took advice from some councillors and prohibited the trovas,
to be read or possessed by anyone (...)

I will not abstain (...) from mentioning a
very remarkable thing. These trovas, which neither had
anything against the Faith, nor against the customs,
on the contrary, they promised greater goods to the
Kingdom, the Catholic Church and all Christendom, were,
nevertheless, forbidden.[35]

---

33 Dom Sebastian was defeated in North Africa on 4 August 1578 at the Battle of Alcacer Quibir.
34 After the defeat in Africa, Cardinal Dom Henrique became the last surviving member of the House of Avis. He occupied the throne of Portugal from 1578 until his death in January 1580. However, he was by then an old and sick man. Consequently, this was a period of heated dispute over the succession. And the ultimate victor of this battle was Philip II of Spain.
35 Gonçalo Annes, alias Bandarra, as noted previously, was imprisoned on the first action of the Courts of Inquisition in Portugal, and convicted in 1541 for giving a "free interpretation of the Holy Scripture".

Chapter 6

Two difficulties disquieted me very much, (...) on this
matter: firstly, if such things will happen, and if,
they are to be believed
how we will know when they will take place?
(...)

I must warn that, in this Treatise, I will not speak about
anything, if not with the utmost reliability, such
as I found it, done in all possible verification of its
authority and purity, and with all my strength.
(...)
And I will not accept less,
for passion or some affection,
but always keep the truth before my eyes,
without flattery or hate, universal respect for the Motherland,
or particular taste, I will interpret the Scriptures,
I will relate the prophecies; I will pass on my judgement,
according to the talent of knowledge given to me and in
grace (...)

It is already time for us to enter this real work, following
the custom of Portugal, where, it is common
to set the first stone of some magnificent constructions,
(...)
I have not found so beautiful and precious, in Heaven or Earth, for the foundation of the fifth future Monarchy, than

God's words, explained and declared by His
Spirit, from Daniel's mouth to the First Monarch
Nebuchadnezzar[36] (...). That lord
was laying in his bed, one night, when he saw
that dream so commented in Daniel, chapter two
(...)
For better understanding of this, I will make reference to

---

[36] The Prophet Daniel dreams and reveals the mysteries to Nebuchadnezzar, King of Babylon. Dan. 2:45; 7:14.

two opinions concerned with it.
The first (...) affirms
for those four parts of the statue until (...)
going from the Four Monarchies to the Romans.
(...)
The second opinion is singular,
by the Venerable Abbot Joachim[37] (...)
about Jeremiah, who says that the golden head
of the Statue was the Kingdom of Babylon;
the silver chest and arms, the Kingdom
of the Greek; the belly and thighs of metal, the
Kingdom of the Roman; and the iron legs, the Kingdom of the Mahometans.
(...)

19 Daniel: by the time of the kingdoms' division,
God in the Heavens, conceived a kingdom, which never
will be destroyed or yielded to other people.
(...)
God, the Almighty disclosed to the King the things that will come.
And the dream is true and its interpretation accurate.

Thus, it has been proven, unfailingly, that the Christian people
destroyed and annihilated all the
neighbouring potentates, enemies of the Holy
Church, ruling the Universe, for many years.
Thus, although it did not yet happen to
Christendom and the dream is true, and the interpretation
accurate, all in faith, there is no way to deny

20 the coming of the fifth and last future Monarchy. (...)

28 Bandarra of Trancoso speaks clearly and at length
about this Monarch, his
conquests, his victory over the Turks, extirpation of
Mahometans and infidels, with the universal triumph of the Earth. (...)

---

37 See note 26.

Chapter 11

Since there must be a Monarchy and a Prince
as its overlord, we will discuss in the most
humble way, suitable to so heinous matter,
from what Nation shall this Monarch be, whatever
the number of different opinions; each one
having his own, according to what
they learnt. (…)

The most common opinion, among Writers,
about this Conqueror, states that he must be French;[38]
they say that, based on many prophecies and ancient notions
which strengthen his conclusions and
with much fundament. (…)

I say more, as a maxim not to be found in the Scriptures,
than the Fifth Empire and the last Monarch
with his successors, which guarantees what
I have summarised (…)

Chapter 12

(…) And I also say that the nation where will be born
so great a Prince is the Portuguese, since he is
Portuguese and the true King of Portugal.
(…)
The lord who does not have it all, He is not
the prophesied one, and even if today all
Christian Kings and
Princes of Royal Houses have some Portuguese blood, through which
many prophecies could be complied with, it is not enough
to descend, in some way, of the Portuguese stem
(…)
Therefore, they clearly say He must be a

---

38 At this time, the French King was considered by Castro to be the most Catholic King in Europe despite Felipe II's title of "The Catholic King". Castro was probably in France at this time.

Portuguese natural, a true King, in particular
of the Kingdom of Portugal. And most of all (...)
prophesied Bandarra, to whom God disclosed more of
His Spirit than to a natural of the land, He
would endow with the greater graces of State and glory
as He never did or will He ever do.[39] (...)

Chapter 13

47ᵛ (...)
Because, there was no one, and never would be, to testify his death,
Or witness his last moments. (...)
Indeed it is a very mysterious thing that,
since the King was so loved and well surrounded,
no one could be found at his side on his death
or his imprisonment or, for that matter,
at the last moment of his fate.

Chapter 14

54 (...)
The World be aware, want it or not, that this great Prince,
so prophesied, shall be Monarch
of the whole Universe, extirpating
all the damned sects and wrongful triumph of
the Ottoman House and of all infidels.
(...)
All the lords united to this Lord
after his apparition
will have thousands and thousands of ventures; on the other hand,
those who oppose him will disappear alongside their domains. (...)

66 This is what this great prophesied prince will do,
having for principal and blessed sign (...)
life's goodness and sanctity, much exaggerated by prophecies

---

39 At this moment, the author cites the Trova, which begins with the verse "Strong name is Portugal". This was later reproduced in *Paraphrase e Concordância de algumas profecias de Bandarra*, which is included below in this chapter.

(…). King Dom Sebastian was, until his disappearance, one of the most virtuous (…)
Princes of his age (…).

Chapter 16

King Dom Sebastian, by my accounts,   80
(…) appeared before one begins to count (…)
in which year would be this wonder,
and I think firmly and infallibly that this will come in 98,[40]
and I have this opinion for sufficient reasons
in matter of such uncertainty (…)

Chapter 18

(…) This treatise, not very clear, I wrote in 1597,
and so it has many errors to fix
and many things to add.

---

[40] Presumably 1598. Castro wrote or published in the previous year, when the news of the appearance of a possible Dom Sebastian in Venice, had still not spread. Might he know what was being plotted? For this passage, the author did countless and odd calculations to reach the number 98. He included some calculations from the first edition and it is probably also the case here with this prediction.

2 *Discourse of the Life of the Always Welcome and Arisen King Dom Sebastian, Our Lord, the Hidden, From His Birth to the Present; Written and Addressed by Dom João de Castro to the Three Estates of the Kingdom of Portugal: As Follows: The Nobility, the Clergy and the People* (Paris: 1602)[41]

1 Chapter I: Of the causes that originated this discourse

Since men depend on the report of things for all their authority; since I consider a case so remarkable as the appearance of King Dom Sebastian; his release and imprisonment in Venice, as well as in Florence in his time of Hiding,[42] only and still in his Kingdom and African journey, so false reports, not only coming from enemies and maleficent writers, but also disseminated by friends and the Portuguese; ones for pure envy and great cruelty; others for having insufficient information about the substance and points of the events; for one single case of our times, a single venture not expected of the Kingdom of Portugal (...).

2 (...) I have decided (since it is up to me more than to any other to do so, since each one judges with his own mind) to take the pen and write briefly, when the subject permits, about the appearance of King Dom Sebastian, our lord, and what more has succeeded since his birth, to serve God's glory, firstly (...) for this reason I have not ventured on this discourse only as one who deals with Lords, Nobles, Clergymen and the People of Portugal, with whom I could excuse many baubles, as house matters that they also know, but also with Foreigners (...) leaving the longer narrative of his kingdom and disappearance | to 3 when the Most Merciful and Omnipotent releases him from the place where he is now, returning him as determined.

Chapter II: Of King Dom Sebastian's birth and the peril the Kingdom were in then.

As Your Graces know well, King Dom John, third of the name and fifteenth of Portugal, married Prince Dom John, his son of sixteen or seventeen years of

---

41 Reproduction facsimile (Lisbon: 1994).
42 This part refers to the case of a false Dom Sebastian, who appeared in Venice in 1598. Dom João de Castro was directly involved in this, believing the pretender was the Portuguese king who had disappeared in Morocco. He sought support of other exiled Portuguese as well of European Courts. Later, the pretender was revealed to be the Calabrian Marco Tulio Catizone. He was the last of four fake candidates claiming to be King Dom Sebastian: in 1584, there was the fake of Penamacor, a border region of Spain; in 1585 there was the fake of Ericeira, in Portugal, and in 1594, the fake of Madrigal, at that time in Spain. For a history of those cases, see Miguel D'Antas, *Os falsos D.Sebastião*, 83–95.

age, in 1553, to the Infanta of Castile, Dona Joana, daughter of the Emperor Charles V, but that Prince died in January of the following year, leaving the Princess pregnant. Until the successor's birth, the Kingdom would live in a State of fearful anguish, always followed by misrule. Since the Portuguese Courts had conceded to King Dom John and to his wife, Queen Catherine, when they married their daughter, Princess Mary to the King of Castile, Philip II[43] (...) their marriage agreement, read as follows: if King Dom John died without a legitimate male successor, the throne of Portugal would be given to Princess Mary's sons. My pen refused to write in shame of such ruling and my hands were shaking in astonishment of that time, as if forgetting the present. (...)

(...) At last, labour pains came to the Princess, at midnight and, soon after, on 20 January 1554, she gave birth to King Dom Sebastian, naming him after his birthday Saint, in remembrance of the grace received. And all the people, gathered at the Palace backyard, expecting in fear and hope, heard through the windows, news of the Princess' deliverance of a son. And with bouts of joy, everybody took the news around the city, which was occupied with processions, all the time. (...)

The Portuguese had never seen so fair and bright an hour, as there was that night. Worthy details of Your Graces' memories to be compared to these times wonders, thanking God for them (...) and hoping from Him, through King Dom Sebastian greater ones.

Chapter III: How King Dom Sebastian was raised to the throne, succeeding King Dom John, his grandfather. And of his upbringing, virtues and hopes he has given.

When the said Lord was four-years old, he was proclaimed King, on the death of King Dom John, his grandfather.[44] The Regency was granted to Queen Catherine, the King's grandmother who would raise him and rule for him. She ruled for some years and left the regency to Cardinal Dom Henrique,[45] uncle of the

---

43 Prince Philip, a Spaniard and a Habsburg, married Princess Mary, a Portuguese of the Avis dynasty in 1543. In 1545 their first son Don Carlos was born. Princess Mary died after the birth. It is important to note that in 1543 Philip was not yet King of Castile. Only in 1556 did he receive the title from his father, Charles V. The Emperor abdicated the throne of Castile and Philip succeeded him in 1556.

44 As previously mentioned, Dom João de Castro was not attentive to dates. In fact, Dom Sebastian was sworn king of Portugal at the age of three in 1557. This was the year of the death of his grandfather, King Dom John III, whom Dom Sebastian succeeded to the throne.

45 During Dom Sebastian's minority, Portugal had two regents. Between 1557, when Dom

5 Prince, his father, who reared the King in his minority, raising him in | all virtues, roles and royal conditions; telling him, since childhood, a thousand victories, by his vassals, and conquests of great kingdoms and empires, and each one at a time, to expand his opinions, as he was growing in years.

At fourteen years of age, he took the sceptre and began to rule, not only justifying the good hopes placed on him, but also surpassing them during his period of ruling. (…) He was highly Christian, who feared God, much zealous of the Catholic religion, ardent in its expansion, very devout to the divine cult, patron of clerical orders and most obedient to the Roman Church. He ruled the Kingdom with extreme justice, defending it equally for the powerful and the weak (…). He equipped it with weapons and military skills, having profound esteem for warriors and knights. Neither could he tolerate cowards, nor would he give less favour to plumes than to blades. (…). Finally, God endowed him with extraordinary natural and politic gifts, as the foundations for the achievement he would make. He was so honest and restrained that he was a wonder of a man. (…) Sober? As a most holy Prince could, eat-
6 ing sparsely (…), | abstaining from wine (…), enemy of all sorts of delights, although he was a prosperous and young King, the most handsome of the Kingdom.

Was there a single place, where one would not praise his valour and dedication? In such bodily vigour, who compares to him? (…). Perfect in all jousts, feasts, military training and horsemanship he was so fond of (…). Such was the fame of his royal perfections that all Kings, Princes and foreign Lords would love him, considering him, as one of the Princes of his time, who had eyes for the future. (…)

Chapter v: Of how King Dom Sebastian was raised and prepared to war and a few military feats of his time

8 As King Dom Sebastian was growing into manhood, while ruling the Kingdom, his virtues like beautiful rays encompassed all parts of Christendom. (…). He was growing in age, but even more in greatness of spirit and, although a youth, he was mature in his habits, keeping company with his elders and having much
9 fun with them. (…). And since during his upbringing, his | keepers were most inclined to weapons and physical exercises, (…); he was fed since a small boy with the glory of Africa's conquest. (…). And that fire burnt high with lessons

---

John III died, and 1562, Dona Catarina, the Queen, was the regent. After that, until 1568, the Cardinal Dom Henrique was the regent. In 1568, at fourteen years of age, Dom Sebastian came to rule the kingdom.

and tales of the Kings, his ancestors, as he knew about their miraculous victories and the feats of vassals who helped them win in Portugal, Africa and the East. (...) | (...) It seems God wanted him since the early days of his government, waiting with such feats against the Infidels, for an unknown time when He had plans to turn him into a lethal blade against Mahometans. But, since His ways are impenetrable, He wanted as punishment to Portugal's sins, as well as proof of His foundations, that Dom Sebastian would become so driven to war to the point of forgetting all prudence.

11

Chapter VI: How King Dom Sebastian went for the first time to Africa. And three of his remarkable thoughts.

And so nurturing in his chest the African venture, he called from several parts of Europe,[46] many Portuguese soldiers in the service of foreign Princes. Soldiers experimented in weaponry to bring modern military tactics that would help maintain his vassals well trained when needed. (...). This way, his venture's dissemination was inexorable and forged by youthful dreams.

Thus disposed, he decided to reform three chivalrous militias of which he was the Great master, with new ordinations (...), convening a meeting with the Orders Commanders and showing them his royal and knightly frame of mind, his sainted zeal against Mahometans, as well as his firm intent to cause their complete destruction. (...)

12

At his arrival in Tangier, the King saw the strength and cavalry of the Moors and began to be disappointed by that brief experience and judged advisable to hasten his comeback to the kingdom. (...). Thus, giving the impression that his voyage had the single aim of seeing places in Africa, he returned in the same year [1574], his reputation more shaken than his finances, while satisfying his exploring appetites.

The King was assaulted from three thoughts, each one likely to occupy such a great Monarch. The first one was fame and glory (...).

---

46   It is impossible to know whom Dom João de Castro refers to. Castro wants to convince his audience and does not compromise with the truth. This text was a construction after his adventure with Dom Antonio and it is not credible because Castro himself was in Portugal but did not go to the battle in Morocco. I have never discovered why. The meaning of Dom Sebastian's expeditions before the Alcacer Quibir remains controversial. It seems that the expedition to Morocco was always planned, but it is not easy to prove. In August 1574, Dom Sebastian was in the Algarve, in the south of the kingdom. In September and October, he was in Ceuta and Tangier, in northern Africa. These expeditions were considered preparatory to Alcacer Quibir. However, Dom Sebastian was only involved in the succession dispute of Morocco in 1576, after local successive disputes.

13 The second was of Catholic zeal and its increase for the love of, as if there were no other, the same enterprise. (...). The third thought was the least powerful of the three: to enlarge his Crown; since he was not greedy and avaricious, usually twin vices. (...)

Chapter VII: Of the origin of Sheriffs, Kings of Africa, and the change that provoked King Dom Sebastian's journey

Returned from Tangiers, King Dom Sebastian still had the burning warrior fire that never let him rest, always increasing, and decided to equip and form a
14 powerful army; he eventually | engaged it on the occasion of the Moors' disputes (...) and to further improve their destruction, it happened that Mullah Mahamet, King of several Berber kingdoms, was defeated and stripped of them, by Mullah Maluco,[47] his uncle, the wars between them, beginning in 1575. Thus, finding what he desired, The King decided to make war, and his decision was reinforced by the danger of the Turks entering Africa (...)
17 (...) Abdala Sheriff died and left as successor Mullah Hamet, his son. Afraid of him, Maluco's other brother, also named Mullah Hamet, escaped carrying a great amount of money, to Algiers, where he rules today. (...)
18 (...) finally, as the fighting was totally adverse to the Sheriff (Mullah Hamet), he was forced to forsake his kingdoms and seek refuge (...) from there writing to King Dom Sebastian, asking for help. (...)

Chapter VIII: How King Dom Sebastian decided to hasten his journey to Africa, meeting, for that end, with the King of Castile, in Guadalupe.[48]

When King Dom Sebastian received the Sheriff's embassy and saw all his wishes attained, he considered his enterprise done and rekindled his war-like intentions with that resolution. In 1575, he travelled to Guadalupe, in order to

---

47 Local disputes in Morocco involving the Catholic kingdoms began in 1576, when Moulay Mohammed Al-Motaou Kikil died and left his brother, Moulay Malik, or Maluco, in power. The son of Al-Motaou Kikil, Mullah Mahamet or Hamet, did not accept his uncle's choice and decided to seek the help first of Spain, then of Portugal, to wage war in Morocco. Philip II had already made an agreement with the uncle of Mahamet and sent him to Dom Sebastian. The Portuguese king then decided to organise the battle of Alcacer Quibir.

48 Guadalupe is a place in Spain where Felipe II and Dom Sebastian met to define the Spanish aid to the Portuguese expedition to Morocco. At the same meeting, Dom Sebastian reported on his desire to marry Isabel Clara Eugenia, the eldest daughter of the Spanish king. Philip II, who never agreed to this marriage, said that after the African expedition they would discuss it. As we know, Dom Sebastian disappeared in battle.

have talks with his uncle, King Philip II, about his journey to Africa and marriage to the Infanta, the eldest daughter of that king. Both he and the King of Castile were surrounded by the most important lords of their kingdoms. (...) And so | they agreed on the journey to Africa and the Infanta's marriage;[49] however, the King of Castile and his Council advised King Dom Sebastian not to make war *per se*, but to send his captains. Since His Highness was taken by the unquenchable fire that burnt inside him, they insisted that they agree with him, to some extent. King Philip promised fifty ships and five thousand soldiers to help him, in 1577, and the King came back content to the Kingdom. Being there, when he asked Castile about the promised help, he just received excuses and delays, as well as discouraging words from the Duke of Alba[50] about both the journey and the enterprise. (...)

King Dom Sebastian, despite the broken promises, neither gave up nor weakened in his intent. On the contrary, he decided to go ahead, even without help, as is natural in youths, and ordered the release of military funds for the purchase of ammunition, warfare and provisions, acting well beyond his experience and age, but below what was required by so arduous conquest. (...)

(...) They left Lisbon on 24 June 1578 with a handsome fleet of eight hundred vessels, either armoured or not, although some say they were two thousand and two hundred. (...). When the King's ship arrived in Tangiers, where the Sheriff was, the latter visited him and both hugged, with many courtesies and kingly words. Dom Sebastian told the Sheriff about his personal efforts to bring warfare and vassals to help him to retrieve all his losses. (...)

The King landed and soon after embarked to Arzila,[51] taking the Sheriff with him; after their arrival, he ordered his people to disembark and occupy the field outside the City, with him as his young Captain, lacking just experience, which is no gift of age (...).

Chapter IX: How King Dom Sebastian decided to invade Africa and to face Mullah Maluco, against whom he fought.

King Maluco was gifted with much royal perfection and, when he heard of King Dom Sebastian's arrival in Barbary, commanded his kingdoms to stop all rebellions and gather the best people of all regions. The King, our lord, who before

---

49 The marriage was never truly agreed upon. Philip II promised to consider the matter after the battle. See note 48.
50 Fernando Álvarez de Toledo y Pimentel (1507–1582), Duke of Alba, Commander in Chief, of the Spanish Army.
51 Moroccan city.

leaving Portugal decided to lay siege to Larache[52] from the sea, changed his mind, when in Africa, wishing the glories of a conquest by land, in which to prove his valour and weapons. (...)

23 And as he did not know the hour of the battle, since they decided to go by land, he commanded the army, on 29 July of the same year, to march towards Alcacer-Quibir and to make provisions for five days. (...)

Thus he marched for five days, having poor knowledge of the route and the enemy's territory, until, arriving on the 2nd of August at Huadma Chafim River, he received warning of King Maluco's arrival with his powerful army. Having heard the news, Dom Sebastian, unruffled, called a meeting with the Sheriff and his Captains, among (...) ours there were many different opinions (...)

24 (...) and finally, after many discussions, they agreed on His Highness' wishes to go ahead and fight the enemy and that decision was as pleasant to him as it would be a victory. (...)

On the 4th of August 1578 the battle began, between nine and ten in the morning, after both kings assembled in their positions. And since I have not yet described Mullah Maluco's, I will do it briefly now. The Moorish King brought forty-five-thousand riding lancers, five-thousand horse-riding shooters, all fine men, as well as the infantry. Beside them, in the same the field, countless peasant Moors, some on horseback, some on their feet (...) amounting, according some historians, to the unbelievable number of one hundred and fifty thousand. (...)

25 Maluco disposed his Field in a semi-circle, in an infantry belt, with three large sections of shooters, foot soldiers, Andalusian and renegades (...)

When the Moors saw our army approaching, they began to close the circle, intending to surround and divide our army. And so they did, bringing forth many of his followers in huge battle cries.

King Dom Sebastian, seeing the enemy troops move into formation, tried to organise his battalions (...)

26 (...) but so fast was the charging Moors from all parts, there were no time for the Portuguese regiments to take their posts. While the field was being organised, King Dom Sebastian made a speech, worthy of his valour and his royal person, to the Lords, Colonels and Captains (...)

The Moors, when they saw our men going towards them, formed a semicircle and our men, disorderly, went towards the middle of the enemies, who then uncovered their artillery, causing much damage to ours, much inferior and soon

27 defeated. (...) |

---

52 Moroccan city.

When King Dom Sebastian saw his men disrupted, with the invincible courage of an angry Lion, as if he alone would be able to take the victory from the enemies, charged against them, many times, on horseback, witnessed by the ones who escaped, as the entire world commented. And when, one of his captains advised him (...) to save his life, he answered that he would do so by dying. Finally, after many changes of horses, (...) wearing too many spears and blades, he rode one last time to the circle of enemies. But no one saw his killing or imprisonment. (...)

As regards the Portuguese, they never had given such proof of valour, obedience and loyalty as then, since many important lords, noblemen and knights even having clear knowledge of their certain death, due to the disorderly whims of a young warrior, had chosen to perish instead of having any kind of rebellion, mutiny or | cowardice. (...). About ten thousand of ours died, of the enemies, at least double died (...). 28

Chapter x: Of the corpse that was supposed to be King Dom Sebastian's and of a digression about Portugal.

Mullah Hamet, who succeeded his brother, King Maluco, on the second day after the battle, ordered that to be brought from the battlefield, a nude corpse with seven wounds, supposing it to be King Dom Sebastian, as he was led to believe. The corpse was seen and recognised by some noblemen, captured in battle. They confirmed what the Moor wished; although they did not truly identify the King's remains, they were so deformed, due to wounds and decay, caused by heat and climate. Some did that by precaution for, if the King was supposed dead, he would not be hunted, and also to expedite their own liberation. (...)

Let us leave the battlefield now and go back to Portugal, which, after many years of prosperity (...) in 1569, God visited with the lethal blow of Lisbon's Plague.[53] Still not content with that blow, He sent a second one of hunger and after that (...), to avoid a third one: many heavenly signs and prodigies seen in our provinces announce everything fallen on us, including monstrosities in women and animal's deliveries (...). until the Supreme Justice, seeing our evil obstinacy and disregard for His admonitions in particular, wanted to give us a public admonition, and taking the world as witness, sent an appalling Comet,

---

53 Lisbon was hit by the plague in July 1569. The epidemic lasted for about a year and records indicate that about 60,000 people died from it.

in November of 1577, causing terror to all. (...) And no one dares to laugh at this or say it is a natural thing, since God uses His creatures as He wills (...)

30 He not only alerted us in this manner, but also in a clearer way (...). Coming to that, He made great revelations to a few of His servants (...), unveiling the huge evils that would come, such as Africa's perdition, the Captivity of Portugal and all the rest.[54] (...)

Finally, as we ignored it, triumphant in our sins, The Most Righteous determined to call us to judgement in a foreign land, in the face of Barbarians, His enemies, and Mahometans, where He judged us, as the world knows, afterwards taking His judgement to Portugal before our first enemies, who have taken us for neighbours, friends and relatives, with whom we used to work together and help as they were our own.[55] (...)

Great sins we committed, since The Lord, so merciful, showed no mercy to us. (...)

31 What did God give us, since the beginnings of this Kingdom of Portugal, and does He want it still? And I do not know what we owe Him more. If the uncountable graces given since its foundation,[56] increase and maintenance for many years? Adorned by so many and beautiful joys, or by His memory of it, to punish and teach? (...) And since the infinite wisdom always chose the weak and unprepared of the world to confound them, He did the same to Portugal, determined to create there the greatest Monarchy ever founded or to be founded on Earth. And so, in our times, He decides to defeat and extinguish Empires and domains of all infidels. (...) And with God's help all opponents will be destroyed. (...)

32 (...) I want to justify, as a man to all men, how, despite all the punishments they have suffered, the Portuguese are, in general, much better than many

---

54 The captivity of Portugal was the way Castro referred to Portugal's submission to the Kingdom of Spain, from 1580. After two years of a hard fight for succession, Philip II was proclaimed King of Portugal and its dominions, succeeded by his son and grandson until 1640.

55 Portugal defeated Castile at the Battle of Aljubarrota in 1385, consolidating its independence and starting the Avis dynasty, which ended with the Portuguese Crown's submission to Spain in 1580. Since the 15th century, a lasting marriage policy between the two Iberian kingdoms tried to unite the neighbours, first under Portuguese leadership and afterward under the Spanish. The ties of kinship of the two kingdoms' Royal houses were undeniable: Philip II, Dom Sebastian's uncle, brother of his mother, Dona Joana of Habsburg (1535–1573).

56 The author refers to one of the foundation myths of the Kingdom of Portugal, the Ourique Miracle. In 1139, during a battle against the Moors, Christ allegedly appeared to Afonso Henriques, afterwards first King of Portugal, in a miraculous explanation for the Portuguese victory over a larger number of Muslims.

nations of Christendom. And not only while they had a King, but also until the beginning of their punishment (...). However, speaking in general, they are good Christians and most fine Catholics, God-fearers, guardians of the Faith, obedient to their priests, men of justice, of truth and of their word. (...)

Chapter XIII: Of the beginning and original means of disclosing that King Dom Sebastian was alive and He would reappear

I take the first hoe to the foundation of King Dom Sebastian's building. (...)

While in Paris (...), Dom João de Castro, having curiosity about prophecies and revelations, became interested in the case of King Dom Sebastian. When he fully dedicated himself to it, he clearly understood that this Lord was alive and he would return. (...). But God, who had guided him to it, more and more, enlightened his mind (...), and so, from that time on, and always loudly, with no whispers or contradictions, he announced Dom Sebastian was alive and he would return, along with his destiny and many other things, according to the prophecies. And if never, until that time, had he cared for the King, alive or dead, from that time on he did not care for what was said against him (...), fulfilling the task | God had chosen for him, being given the Scriptures spirit and knowledge of what would come, not only to the Kingdom of Portugal, but to many others.

Chapter XV: How Dom Sebastian appeared in Venice, in 1598

During the course of the month of June 1598, when the peace was agreed between France and Castile,[57] with all ceremonies; when the Portuguese here lost all human hopes, God, Who, in such extremes, usually manifests himself to those He kept Himself from, ensured a letter of Venice arrived in Dom João's[58] hands, at the beginning of the following August (...), telling about a despicable man, who arrived on that land, saying he was Dom Sebastian alive, but mockingly said. (...) after that one, another came, from Pantaleon Pessoa, chamberlain of the Lord Dom Antonio,[59] | arrived from a pilgrimage to Jerusalem and wrote at length about his conversations with the abovementioned man, who swore to be King Dom Sebastian alive and soon to be seen (...). And on the course of the conversations it seemed that he was really the King. (...) Since

---

57 The Peace of Vervins, signed in May 1598 between Philip II of Spain and Henry IV of France, after years of religious wars.
58 The author is beginning to refer to himself in the third person.
59 The Prior of Crato, who died at Paris in 1595.

the beginning of the good news to the end, Dom João always did his duty of writing and communicating to his friends and also to his foes, that the man was an envoy of King Dom Sebastian. As the news broke everywhere, to the astonishment of some and mockery of others, the Most Christian King[60] and other important people were informed that King Dom Sebastian appeared in Venice, being His Majesty very joyous of the Court, although the news had not been confirmed. As the news spread in Paris, the evil weighing on them too, knowing what the future would be, began to dispute the Prince's great destiny (...) | Dom João de Castro, who never believed the man of Venice to be the King, but just his envoy, although maintaining he had been liberated from prison, thought there were stratagems by that Lordship[62] to keep the true King hidden. The reason for his belief was a letter addressed to a very important lord of this Court, telling him that the man from Venice was King Dom Sebastian (...). That lord conveyed the news to the Court and to the Portuguese who talked to him. And so he persisted in his opinion, until he was disillusioned in Venice, by several pieces of prophecies, which caused him to believe that the King would come from India or the Ethiopian coast, where he was imprisoned. In the meantime, in Paris, where he was, he accomplished his given task, encouraging good men, in hopes of what they would see and discrediting falsehoods. (...)

(...) As Dom João de Castro could not remain at the French Court, due to false information brought to His Most Christian Majesty, he left, at the beginning of winter of the same year (1599) for England, with the help of close friends. When he arrived to the Most Serene Queen's[63] Court, he talked to some of her main councillors, telling them about the case, hoping they would present the case to the Queen and that she would intervene with Venice's government to make the prisoner be seen and examined. (...) Above all, he thought that if Her Majesty joined forces in such an enterprise, it would be proved that King Dom Sebastian was alive, but there were no proof that he was | the prisoner or another one in hiding, having no reason to his remaining in prison, to be punished, if he was not the King. The Queen sent her thanks, but said it was not convenient for her, to tangle herself in such uncertain and impossible questions, otherwise she would be mocked by Kings and Princes, but if any of them decided to do

---

60   King Henry IV of France.
61   There is an error in the page numbers. This one appears again as 53, but should read "55".
62   Due to King Philip III of Spain's pressure on the Government of the Most Serene Venice, the pretender king was arrested, but not handed over immediately to the Castilians. That would only take place in 1602, the date of this edition of *Discourse of the Life of* [...] *Dom Sebastian* by Dom João de Castro.
63   Elizabeth I, Queen of England from 1558 to 1603.

so, she would be willing to join them. Hearing that, Dom João decided to pursue the matter and, at the beginning of the following year, travelled to the Netherlands, where he talked to a man of the Parliament (...) proposing the same as he had in England, begging intervention by the Most Christian King and the Most Serene Queen (...) they responded (...) almost in the same way, using the timing as an excuse (...). With that answer, Dom João returned to Paris, where, after days, he received, from Bordeaux, letters by Friar Stephen of Sampaio[64] and his companion, (...) arrived from Portugal and going to Italy. If the friar went to (...) Paris, he would serve King Dom Sebastian better (...). But, as he seemed to think he did not need anyone and the signs he was taking to the domain would be enough to deliver The King (...) (...) he neither wanted to come to Paris (...), nor invite anyone to Venice. Due to these two mistakes, he managed to render a disservice to His Highness (...) and finally (...) ended by handing him over | to his enemies, destroying God's work and the resurrection of Portugal. (...)

Dom João de Castro, (...), decided to verify in person, if the prisoner was Dom Sebastian, (...) leaving Paris for Venice, where he arrived on the 28th of July 1600. There, as Friar Stephen informed him of the events (...), Castro said (...) according to the news of France and letters of that domain, it seemed to him that there was another one hidden, the true King. Thus, he decided to investigate thoroughly, and so he did for the eight following days, afterward coming to the conclusion that there was no other man but the prisoner (...), and for that prisoner's characteristics, Castro clearly saw that he was the true Dom Sebastian.

Chapter XVI: Of how King Dom Sebastian disappeared, of his time of hiding and how he reappeared

Concerning the little known truth about King Dom Sebastian, I will inform Your Graces, since the Battle of Africa, until the present. For that matter, I will use neither things I have heard, nor uncertain reports, but only words from the King's mouth and those written by his hand. (...)

King Dom Sebastian, on the day of the African Battle, coming so near to loss of life and liberty, escaped wounded (...). As he felt more affronted by defeat than by the loss of his kingdom, he did not want to rule or appear in front of his acquaintances and posing as a commoner, the King went to explore the

---

64 Friar Stephen of Sampaio, another supporter of the cause of Dom Antonio, Prior of Crato, exiled in Europe. He allegedly travelled incognito to Portugal to obtain information about Dom Sebastian's bodily marks in order to confirm whether the man imprisoned in Venice was the Portuguese king.

world, with his companions[65] (...) If the great and famous kings and captains of the Earth would return to life today to judge this Prince, they would, doubtless, find him deserving of many thousand kingdoms due to the greatness of his opinion, his invincible spirit and his royal honour, never surpassed by any of them. (...) when walking the world, he fought many wars (...), in which he suffered | many wounds, mainly during the Persian wars against the Turks. He travelled all of Europe, many parts of Asia and some of Africa, visiting Prester John,[66] and other inland kingdoms. And as he was insatiable for seeing and exploring the world, never (...) being tired, the time came in which, undeceived and bored of it, touched by God, he decided to leave it and to have a pious life of penance, in remote regions, until the end of his days. For that purpose, he chose the company of a holy hermit,[67] with whom he spent some time, enjoying the virtues of a lonely life, as all foreigners, who see and talk to him, testify. God, Who had hidden him to learn until the due time, sent him visions and revelations telling him to leave that life and to rule his kingdom, unveiling mighty secrets (...). As he found it very difficult to leave that life, for his spirits and resolution, and mainly by thinking that they were the Devil's illusions to distract him and deflect him of that perfection, he did not follow God's commands. Until the Lord, most tired of that, appeared to (...) the holy hermit, his companion, showing His displeasure with such disobedience and ordering him to advise the King (...), conveying God's orders to him (...) to return to the world and rule his kingdom. Thus, constrained (...) The King decided to obey, with a heart full of regret from leaving that life and the holy company (...). So, he took his leave of the holy man, who, among other things, told him to be wary of his friends, who would be cause (...) of pain and deception, as the ones caused by the two clergymen.[68] The king left those remote regions for Sicily and decided to present himself to | the Supreme Pontiff.

(...) obeying to God's command, he was on the way to present himself to the Supreme Pontiff, when headed to Sicily, and if he was in Tuscany, as he says,

---

65   The king supposedly ran away with the Duke of Aveiro, the Count of Redondo, Count Sortelha and Christopher of Távora, all of whom were present at the battle.

66   King of a legendary kingdom within the heart of infidel lands, located sometimes in Africa, sometimes in Asia; he would be joined by European monarchs in order to defeat the Muslims.

67   Like the other false Dom Sebastian, the character of a hermit is present. In this case, the King met in his path one kind of holy man, a person who has withdrawn to a solitary place for a life of religious seclusion. He was a popular man, not someone recognised by the Church.

68   Castro believes the King was betrayed by Friars Stephen and Christopher and handed to the authorities of Florence, who were allied to Spain.

he did not need to be there, on the way to Rome. When we found His Highness imprisoned in Florence, we embarked from Livorno to France, we did (...) inquiries into the matter and we found that, almost at the same time as the King's apparition, disappeared from that area (...) a hermit, supposed to be Portuguese or Spanish, said to be a holy man, a bearer of miracles and remarkable virtues. An Italian priest told me they were unable to understand him, because he did not speak Italian well. And he was blond. Nowadays, the King is no longer blond and speaks and writes well in that language, even composing poetry. (...)

(...) The King arrived to Sicily, in 1597, or at the beginning of the following year, and sent an Italian to Portugal bearing letters to some lords, letting them know of his apparition and arrival. The messenger went to that kingdom and delivered the letters to their recipients (...)

(...) In Sicily, the said Lord embarked on one of His Sanctity's ships and went to Rome, determined to make himself known, but when he was on his way, he was robbed, while sleeping, by some foreign servants. And since they took even his clothes, he needed to beg for some rags to cover his person. I ask of Your Graces that you ponder deeply on God's procedures with this King, whom He led through the world, kept from many dangers, and finally took from the solitary life of a hermit, sending him back to his kingdom to serve Him. (...). When the unfortunate Lord found himself in such a miserable state, knowing that he would not be seen or believed, in that guise, he crossed Italy as a beggar, poor in luck and in thoughts. And, as a pilgrim, passing by Our Lady of Loreto, the unfortunate Prince arrived in Verona, in the Venetian republic, where the infinite wisdom and providence, for such desperate misery awoke compassion in a local tailor, who gave him shelter (...), who then used the name of Dom Diogo. In order to avoid starvation, the king spent some time there; hearing word of His Sanctity's visit to Ferrara, he decided to go there and try talking to him. But the Devil, knowing his part in that Prince's demonstration, thwarted his plans, and made him go to Venice. He arrived there, in the month of June, bearing so little money (...), that he was taken to the poorest inn of the city. (...)

At that time, he had (...) declared in writing he was a King. The document was taken to the Senhoria,[69] from where the rumour has been spread. So, he unveiled himself as the true King Dom Sebastian, lost in Africa, in 1578, and from then on he never hid again. This amazing and unbelievable case astonished the Lords of that State, the entire city and the whole | world. (...) However, there were many who said they remembered King Dom Sebastian very well and that that man bore no resemblance to him. He was therefore an impostor

---

69   Supreme Authority of the Venetian Republic.

because of thousands of discrepancies, and above all because of the certainty of the death of King Dom Sebastian, confirmed by captive Portuguese lords, and his subsequent burial in Belém. (...)

In those circumstances, there was no one, noble or powerful, to publicly take his defence or protect him, with authority, soundness and substance, since no one was found worthy (...). God, Who was determined to raise that Prince, wanted through those infinite divine moves, to humble him, to avoid vanity in him, thus permitting his dedication, in wisdom and strength, to his Kingdom (...) and He allowed the Devil to disturb The King (...). And if I were able to tell in detail everything | that truly happened; how amazed Your Graces would be to know how he fell out of fortune and took no advantage of being alive. This suffices for the Incomprehensible glory.

Chapter XVII: How King Dom Sebastian was imprisoned in Venice

(...) The rumour was growing and men were divided in opinions, in huge bets, according to each one's humour (...). The Senhoria saw the increasing | movement and, fearing to lose its dominance in parts of the Kingdom (...), determined to close all their domains, and orders were sent to Padua's government to notify the so-called King Dom Sebastian to leave the city within three days and to leave the State within eight days. (...) the Spanish Ambassador disagreed, asking the Senhoria to imprison him, as a seditious impostor. In that, he was helped by Portuguese and Jewish merchants, who testified against him. (...)

The Venetian lords, torn between the respect due to a man who showed signs of being the King, albeit taken for dead for so much time, and the requests of the King of Spain backed by testimonials of the so-called King's errors, spent some time in perplexity. (...)

As he was jailed, many and greater falsehoods were laid against him, robbing him of all justice, during two years, and there were no Princes, Potentates or Lords (...) who wished to know the truth (...). The troubled King rested alone and forsaken by men (...), with no maintenance, eating leftovers from the other prisoners. In that period, he was interrogated by four judges of the Senhoria (...). When asked, he confessed to be the true King Dom Sebastian, giving them some particular signs, beginning from the journey to Africa, how God saved him and as he thought they intended to be just, he asked to be seen and recognised, if they did not think he was who he alleged to be. (...). But, as he perceived from their attitudes that they did not intend to make justice, but that they were just curious about his life's history, the King decided to remain silent and cease to answer them, and so he did. (...)

Calling this prison the Garden, 71
where nobody enters, or they cannot write,
or send messages. Nor are the prisoners
allowed to look outside. Here, where he stayed longer,
He endured very much contempt and mockery,
from some people,
but, by reason of his nobility, there were others (...)
who treated him well and gave him help and support,
and there were also people who respected and served him.
After he was taken to the prison, the Senhoria gave him the amount of five cruzados per month and some citizens of Venice, helped him all along, moved by charity and their notion of him being the true King, but, above all, for the amazing fame of his virtues, that went beyond the gaol, spread by guards and prisoners
Who had been released. (...)

The grieving Lord was forced to wear rotten clothes, 72
blackened by dirt, and he was afflicted by lice and lived in squalor.
His activity in prison was the same as it was in liberty: only prayers (...). He had visions while there (as God gives graces to His servants in places of suffering) and raptures, witnessed by other prisoners, who thought him dead or near dead, while enraptured.
He fasted almost the entire week, on Fridays and Saturdays he lived on bread and water and he only had meat on Sundays and Tuesdays, however not on a regular basis. On Wednesdays he always fasted.
(...)
Despite all abstinence, he was given incredible strength at the prison.
He confessed and communicated at all feasts and times he was allowed to (...).
Of the five cruzados he received per month, he spent the major part on masses, and asked to be remembered in the prayers of religious and honest people, trying to know through them, what were God's intentions for him (...)

Chapter XIX: How King Dom Sebastian continued to claim for justice and how he was released

Until this moment, I have not described The King, as I saw him, when he left 93
prison, and, briefly, I will do it now. He is of medium height, neither small, nor tall and broad in shoulders, although he was so thin, when he left prison, due to abstinence, that he was only skin and bones. The hair on his head had (...) grown, very soft, black or dark brown, like his beard, but since it was night, I

could not know for certain. His face is not much covered by hair. (...). A short and sparse beard, and a small moustache. He was not as handsome as before, so blushing and white. (...).

His forehead is large, not so firm as before, by lack of flesh (...). The colour of his eyes, because of the darkness, I cannot tell (...), they are neither small, nor big (...), so joyful and alive that they looked like stars. His cheekbones are high and very prominent due to his thinness. (...). A pointed nose, a little sharp. Mouth well formed, thin lips, the lower the fullest and more noticeable when he talked.[70] He left prison, much deaf in both ears. (...) He is short of trunk and taller on the right side, leg and arm. (...), bowed legs, very small feet and bedecked chest (...).

His little toe has a big wart. And he has another big wart on his back, as seen by other people. He suffers from a flux in his parts, but not so much as he was younger, and it does not render him impotent to procreate, as some evil men say.[71] (...). For many years he had not spoken Portuguese until that night (...), some very well spoken words, such as those foreigners are unable to pronounce and other mispronounced. But, by his way of pronouncing, soon everybody thought he was born in Portugal. His voice is not very clear (...).

His personal appearance is very serious. (...) and very strong. (...)

That same night, two Venetian citizens, for whom the King holds a deep gratitude, came to see him; he said many dignified words to them, in thanks for their help and promising to reward them, with rewards and graces he could not name, since he had not conditions to bestow them, at that moment. One cannot see any sign of greed or ambition in him, as he remembers his reign, just for the love of the service he comes to do for God and not by his desire to rule. (...). And if the Castilians, who have him in his hands today, could convince God to cancel His command to him, he would gladly resign his reign to them (...). Although they are his enemies, who have imprisoned and caused suffering to him, in spite of that, he confesses it is very difficult and grievous to shed Christian blood, making war to them (...)

---

70   A consistently emphasised characteristic of the Habsburgs, Dom Sebastian's maternal family. He had a full inferior lip. Dom Sebastian's portraits, from the sixteenth century, always show this particular facial feature.

71   Castro refers to the news, always disseminated by the Spanish, about a disease on Dom Sebastian's genitalia. That news has certainly influenced matrimonial projects intended for the desired, since it could mean incapacity to procreate. Without heirs, matrimonial alliances would be hopelessly compromised.

(...) And that nobody hinders his great work, since it comes from the Highest, otherwise they will suffer the wrath and indignation of God. (...)

Finally, to shorten the description of this Lord, he still has his moments of anger, but also of virtue and prudence, which make him come to his senses and wisely refrain. On the night of his release, he presented much peace of mind, as if he was not leaving that prison, and showed no other joy, but of being among his Portuguese subjects.

(...) And his greatness of soul was such that, while imprisoned, what he did most, through words and messages, was to send encouragements to his friends and Portuguese subjects, as if they were the prisoners. Finally, King Dom Sebastian shows no differences from the times when he was at the Lisbon Palace, besides those caused by age and suffering.

Chapter xx: Of the decision taken in order to save King Dom Sebastian and how it failed, leading to his imprisonment in Florence

(...) The King had to go to France and there were only three routes to there, one of which was through Germany, crossing the lands of his enemies the King of Spain's relatives, which was not convenient. Another route was (...) through the Alpine mountains, in the cold of wintery snows, and since the King was much weakened (...) to follow that route would have put his life and health in danger, since any newly released prisoner needed to remain abed for a few days (...). Besides, he added, time was very short and there were risks to his leaving (...) that State, in danger of falling back in the Senhoria's hands again. So, Castro thought the better route for the King would be to embark at Livorno, going from there to France, since the Grand Duke was French at heart, always favourable to the side of the King of France (...). To follow that route, it would be necessary to find a very loyal foreigner who could save him and none of us could go with him, since we were well known and flagged in that land of spies. (...)

After the King departed from Venice, we waited fifteen days for Dom Christopher,[72] who was unable to find money for himself and his entourage.[73] (...) |

---

72   Son of Dom Antonio, Prior of Crato, who joined the Portuguese who supported "the king of Venice".

73   One of the main difficulties of Dom Antonio and his partisans always encountered was raising funds to continue their fight against Philip II. They sought support from England and France, unsuccessfully. Dom João de Castro complained about this and mentioned this difficulty as one of the reasons for leaving Dom Antonio's group. After Dom Antonio's death in 1595, the Portuguese who tried to support the Venice case faced the same problem.

(...) we left for Florence on the 29th of the same month.[74] On the way, in Ferrara, we were told, at the inn, that the prisoner of Venice, the so-called King of Portugal had passed by that city. (...). From Ferrara we went to Bologna (...). Finally, we arrived in Florence and that same afternoon we heard how the Grand Duke,[75] on the night of the same day of our departure from Venice, ordered the imprisonment of the King of Portugal, our lord. (...)

Chapter XXIII: Of the resolution taken by the Portuguese after the Grand Duke's decision.

118 (...) After his imprisonment in Florence, much contradictory news circulated: it seemed to some that the Grand Duke would hand the prisoner over to the Supreme Pontiff to investigate judicially and to disengage the Christian Princes involved; others considered King Dom Sebastian's name so full of divine grace, released from great suffering, the Most Christian King, who were, due to exalted faith against the infidels, being his former fame and virtue a single work of God, he was so friendly with the House of Medici and, particularly, with Grand Duke Ferdinand (...) that he could rely on their protection. (...), judging by natural ruling considerations that the Prince would be sent to the Most Christian Pontiff, for the due respect to such Majesty and the Kingdom (...)

However, some believed that he would be imprisoned by the King of Spain, which really happened, when he was delivered by the Grand Duke, on the following month of April of 1601. King Dom Sebastian was taken to a castle in 119 Naples | where he is currently treated as a particular man, locked in a chamber and being shown to many who come to see him, from Portugal and Italy. I ask of Your Graces that they follow closely Castile's decisions in this matter that I present: if the King of Castile consider the prisoner an impostor and Calabrian, why, did he send him to the most distant of his European kingdoms, eighteen hundred miles away from Portugal, instead of sending him to that kingdom, where he could show him, to undeceive Your Graces, justify himself before all Christendom and pacify his Kingdom? Nevertheless, he has maintained the prisoner in Naples, for ten months, and might dispose of him soon. (...)

120 The 29th of December 1601, was the first anniversary of his imprisonment in Florence, by command of the Grand Duke Ferdinand (...), and according to prophecies, it may last for three and a half years or four. (...)[76]

---

74 29 December 1600.
75 Ferdinand I, Grand Duke of Tuscany, from 1587 to 1609.
76 Castro was not a good prophet: the Calabrian Marco Tulio Catizone was killed at San Lucar de Barrameda in September 1603.

Chapter XXIV: The Author concludes all the discourse

Foreseeing King Dom Sebastian 's future, God, Who does things ever so smoothly and intended to operate many wonders through him, noticing how unbelievable would the King's apparition be, due to its circumstances and timing, as well as to the huge changes in his looks and age (...), provided two solutions worthy of His wisdom, one divine, the other human, to approach the strong and the weak, | and through renewed work, make him be recognised by all.

Divine were the prophecies and revelations, first of Christ's life, and afterward, some clear, other obscure, with the remarkable events of the Prince's life. (...). Since what He wanted was dear to His heart and much needed to mankind, He chose King Dom Sebastian, by means of one out of two main instruments for that, enlightening, in that way, His incomprehensible statements (...). And since we were the first people to whom He promised supreme ventures, through a King, our countryman, very gracious to His eyes, so He chose the Portuguese, in our times (...) to point him, although the entire world have mocked him, the same way they did with the holy prophets. And in a treatise composed by me, in 1597,[77] I show through ancient and modern prophecies, that King Dom Sebastian was alive and that he should reappear in the year of 1598, to accomplish the main tasks God destined to him (...).

We proceed to the human solution provided by the Divine Providence, in order to identify King Dom Sebastian, in these times. He was gifted, since his mother's womb, with many remarkable signs[78] that no other man possesses them all. (...). For that purpose, He told King Dom Sebastian apart from other men, ordering them to notice those signs, since the King was little, keeping them as witnesses, until the present, even allowing the same King to fall in foreign hands (...)

And so, in a loud voice, when possible, I testify and assure that He is the true King Dom Sebastian, our Lord, as God is God, before Him and mankind, for His glory and their good. And, since Our Graces are Portuguese of deep faith, who trust in God, either by belief or by Christian duty of giving credit to words so

---

77 *Of the Fifth and Final Future Monarchy, With Many Admirable Things of our Times*. See the first text presented in this chapter.
78 Nothing about these signs can be verified. A king would not allow himself to be seen without clothing except by those who deprived him of his intimacy. In the case of Venice, among the many fanciful stories, was that one of the supporters of the Venice case went to Portugal to obtain information about these "signs". The objective was to prove that the Calabrian Marco Tulio was Dom Sebastian.

127 clear and bright (…). And if, being weak, Your Graces put God's matters aside, could you not be persuaded (…)? Because as men | they cannot deny credit to King Dom Sebastian's testimonial, who in his time of ruling, never was accused of breaking his word or lying. He, who affirms to be sent by God to rule his people and accomplish great feats. Higher testimonial there will not be, since it comes from a King, and a Portuguese King, and so truthful King, and holy King, and since the promise comes from the King of Kings, the supreme truth. How could Your Graces doubt it? (…). And according to the prophecies, in some way through them, you will be freed by weapons, lashing out at Castile; and as it was also prophesied, through this Prince, all Christian Princes will be united in friendship. That understanding depends on the concordance of time; everything could be true. (…)

From my discourse to Your Graces, do not you see that this flourishing nation so esteemed by all the others in the world started from the year of 1578 to be seen in a different way and today is the most vile and despised?

128 (…) If Your Graces only knew the great ventures this Lord has prepared (…)

Because this holy King misses his people so much that no other thing interests him. (…) Search the entire world (…) neither among the dead nor among the living or those to come, only him.

129 He is the promised great Emperor, cited in the Scriptures, and prophesied for so many years (…), so endearing to God, the ever-welcome King, our so desired Dom Sebastian, the Hidden One (…).

Thus, Lords, how do you not see it? If his hour comes soon and the Hidden King appears, the promise will be fulfilled and King Dom Sebastian, our Lord, will take the place of the great Holy Roman Emperor (…)

Long live the Motherland and its generous hearts, which no other have respected but their God, their King and their honour, leaving to their descendants all they received from their ancestors. Long live the ever-welcome King Dom Sebastian, our Lord. (…)

130 (…) Finally, this great King will comfort our ancestors' bones; he will release them of their past captivity, clearing their shame and taking their hearts' sorrows. (…)

And so I serve to the present, as much as I can, since I have had for so many years great desire of serving them, which I did not fail and God will ratify now. I hope Your Graces and the Three Estates of this Kingdom, who deserve everything, will accept this discourse.

3   Dom João de Castro, *Paraphrase and Concordance of Some Prophecies by Bandarra, Shoemaker of Trancoso* (Paris: 1603)[79]

A short reasoning from the Author about Bandarra and his work;

In the name of the Holy Spirit, who continually sprinkles with His gifts the Earthly Paradise of His Militant Church: the lesser of them not being the gift of prophecy with which, since the Beginning of Time, he founded in men the real knowledge of God, conveying to them his countless secrets: and in them persisting, men will not lack anything until the End of Times.

(…) participating, in recent times, Bandarra, our natural, has announced so many ventures that barely fit in human faith, as in the Kingdom of Portugal (…). His name was Gonçalo Anez, alias Bandarra, a shoemaker, born in Trancoso, who is believed to have died in 1560, and to have prophesied these occurrences in 1540. Chosen by God, Who does not despise the humble, He gave him the gift of prophecy, with which he prophesied the conquest of the Holy House and all the Earth: a universal promulgation of the Gospel, the universal triumph of Christendom over all the Church's enemies; promising to King Dom Sebastian and to his Kingdom of Portugal the best part. It reveals the highest mysteries of the said Lord, of their own, of foreigners and of peace and general unison among Christian princes, against the infidel, as well as dignified things from those who will accomplish them, as it will be clearly seen as this treaty progresses. And although many other prophe|sied the same, no one spoke so clearly, so copiously in the King and Kingdom of Portugal, as him, to whom, it seems, as a Portuguese, have fallen greater revelations of the said ventures.

And although Bandarra's are not prophecies of faith, since they are not canonical, they still are of the greatest temerity, (…) considering all the reasons for which they originated from the Holy Spirit, albeit without authority. (…) There are many ancient and modern prophecies by many and various saints and pious persons of diverse times and nations, guarded and worshipped by our ancestors as such, that contain in substance the same as Bandarra's, without any repugnance between them, thus one can see that all of them come from the same Spirit and deserve equal worship. (…) | (…) so called by all,

---

79   The first edition of this text is from 1603. The version used here is the facsimile edition by José Pereira Sampaio (Bruno: 1942). A new edition of this text appeared in 2018, edited and organised by João Carlos Gonçalves Serafim (Porto: 2018).

Bandarra's Trovas contain the Prologue and the Dream, prophesying in two humble styles of Portuguese Trova, Redondilha and Broken verse or Caesura,[80] commonly used in his time. Such trovas are (...) in so beautiful terms, figures and development that even the most famous poets of Portugal were not able to match him in the same verse (...). Although, since there are infinite translations of them to this day, they are full of errors, and this is due to many causes; firstly because they were made by idiots, who have no certainty when translating, and | for the high quantity of copies mainly scattered in Beira,[81] where people usually were neither educated, nor attentive to writing. Besides, since they were so obscure and not revered as prophecies, being addressed just as curiosity or secret mystery, the errors made were not considered (...), some translating them by half, others taking verses and words and putting others in their places, or transporting them as their own will, without intending to refine them, since scholars and opinionated men had not given them any importance, taking them as nonsense. (...). Due to these causes, they are poorly written, with three main types of errors. Firstly: many translations lack entire sessions of the Trovas, while in all of them many rules and words are missing. Secondly, and possibly most importantly: some verses and words have been imposed. Thirdly and finally: the great difficulty to their comprehension resides in their relocation, causing | extreme obscurity clouding their understanding. (...)

4ʳ

4ᵛ

I saw them, for the first time, in the year of 1509 [i.e. 1579?],[82] derived from Beira, and afterwards, by my judgement, the best written and accurate prophecies to be found in the Kingdom. Since I did not understand anything of them, I have enjoyed very much the reading and had all of them in memory, by their order, for some time, having lost their written version in Alcântara, when we were vanquished by the Duke of Alba. Later, neglecting them due to the

---

80 Redondilha: four-verse *stanza*, in which the first verse rhymes with the last, and the second with the third. *Caesura*: syllable put at the end of a word in a verse to serve as the beginning of the immediately following one.
81 Beira was one of the six Portuguese districts at the time, corresponding to the Kingdom's central region.
82 The date is incorrect, since Dom João de Castro had not yet been born; nor did the Trovas exist at that time. As Castro affirms himself, they must have been written in 1540 and possibly even before, maybe by the end of 1520 or the following decade. Thus, he possibly meant 1579, when he already was part of the group that supported Dom Antonio, Prior of Crato, in the succession to the Portuguese throne. This possibility seems to be confirmed by his next declaration, on the Battle of Alcântara, in August of 1580, when Dom Antonio was defeated by Castilian armies, led by the Duke of Alba.

changes in the Kingdom, I came to forget many and their order, (...) remaining (...) sentences and ideas to which I was never able to find a good translation. (...) I found eight or ten versions; they were so wrong and different themselves, that they have inhibited me, to this date, to take up my pen to write this work.

However, | I decided, in Paris, today, the fourth of June, 1603, (...) to thank God and serve Him with the talent of Spirit, of some insight about the future or for our times, which will not derive of small glory upon those zealous for His affairs (...)

Cutting short, from the start, the Devil's ploys, through his members who discredit theses prophecies by mocking them, are making ridiculous interpretations to discredit their sympathisers. They do not haunt me, detractors who kindled but did not honour the clarity. But, if the Lord gives me life and strength I will accomplish, with His favour, the task I begin now, putting them in order, by the greater | purity they show, with declarations and concordances suitable to the unburied talent.

Now, I will interpret just some, not putting them in order, but according to purposes, mentioning some concordances between them and other prophecies, ancient and modern, in my composition of a treatise (...). Understand that this was opinion and not science, without de-meriting to what is considered well said. The same way we see in supreme comments on the Holy Scripture, where not all writers' opinions are well received, but the good ones deserve to be followed | (...) submitting all my words to the Holy Roman Catholic Church's correction as well as the pious and wise men.

Prologue

Most Illustrious Lord
So perfect in virtues,
You might be chosen,
By every Legislator.
God gave you so much grace,
Seldom found in your kind,
Very wise Patriarch
Shepherd of noble people.
I decided to describe
My cobbler workshop,
Seeing by Your Lordship
The result of my seam.
That I want to interweave

In this work that I offer:
For you know all I know,
And what more I can do.
(...)
My work is very safe,
Since it is made of strap:
Someone who thinks it ugly,
Understands not the sewing
I make work that lasts,
And I go beyond the surface:
I know well the leatherwork
Convenient to the Creature
(...)
I am always busy
In doing my work well:
If I lived in Lisbon
I would be much esteemed
Content I am and well paid
To make a single patch:
Although some come to slander,
Do not touch the shoe

I am also an official,
I know a little about cork:
I do not see justice
Made to every one
Since now out of anyone
With no letters they make Doctors:
I see many judges
Who do not know good or bad.
(...)
I also know how to burnish
Any bow and ornament:
Bachelors, Prosecutors
It goes on and on
And when the litigants
Ask counsel from them,
Since they lack the coins,
They will not be heard.

It must be well shaped
The large chapins[83] made:
The lineage of noblemen
By money is traded.
I see too much mixture
With no Chief to rule:
How do you want to see the cure
If the wound is festered?
(...)
As in the tanneries
Leather turns and turns,
So are the great revolts
Now in all the Clergy
Because they use tyranny,
And worship the monies;
Churches are slums
(...)
I am also an official
Sometimes I stitch the edge
And I know well how to earn
The gain and the wealth.
If a mocker comes
To ask me any question:
I will tell how to gather
The needle and the thimble

Part 2: Bandarra's Dream

(...) Of some remarkable things from King Dom Sebastian, prophesied by Bandarra

A new King will be born
What new name he shall have:
This King who shall be born,
From land to land will walk
Many people shall die for him.

---

83   A particular sort of high-heeled shoes.

Strong name is Portugal
A name so excellent:
King of the West Cape
The most important of all.
No one compares to you
King of such merit;
Not to be found, I believe,
From the West to the East.

Portugal[84] is a whole name,
A manly name, if you will?
The others are of women,
Like the iron without edge.

And if not? Look, first
Portugal has the border
[...]
Portugal has the Flag
With Five Quinas[85] in the middle:
As I see and believe
He is the leader
He will rise to summit
(...)
And will be King of herds
Which come from long runs.

In the following prophecies Bandarra points to King Dom Sebastian and some particularities much glorious of his.

This so excellent King
Whom I resolved to defend stubbornly,
He is not of bad breeding
But a relative of high kings.
And he comes from the highest seed
From all four branches
All Kings of the highest rank
From the East to the West.

---

84   In Portuguese, Portugal is a masculine word.
85   Heraldry: escutcheons with bezants.

This one has such nobility
As never seen in a King;
This one defends the law
For nobles and commoners alike.
And so leads His Highness

All the ports and travels,
Because he is Lord of the ways
Of the Sea and its richness

The wounds of the Redeemer,
The Saviour's wounds,
Are the weapons of our King;
Because He defends the law
And the people
Of the Almighty King Creator.
No King, no Emperor,
And no great Lord
Ever had such signal
Only you, good Portugal
For being loyal,
And loving the people.
(...)

Of the times when Dom Sebastian should appear; and Portugal should change his natural King

In thirty-two years and a half
There will be signs on Earth;
The scripture does not fail,
And tells the entire tale

One in three comes adorned
Showing great danger,
Of whip and punishment
To people I do not name

Before the eight will end
This era that we have,
Many great things we will see

As never we have seen nor read,
Have not heard nor will hear.

Yet the desired time
Has arrived:
Already eighty are accounted for
And resumed
(…)

A new King is raised
And acclaimed
His flag already appears
Against the wandering,
Prolific vultures
That these pastures have enjoyed.

How King Dom Sebastian shall rule over the Kingdoms of Barbary where He was lost; how it will fortunately open in Africa a door that will cause the ruin of Mahometans; and how the House of Mecca will be taken and all the Turks, Moors and Infidels will be destroyed forever.

(…)
A great Lion will rise,
And let out a huge roar:
His roar will be heard
And will astonish all.
It will run and walk
And will cause much harm,
And the African Kingdoms,
All of them, will be dominated
(…)
Do not fear the Turk, not?
At this time
Or the great "Moorishness",
That has neither Baptism,
Nor Chrism,
Second of confirmation
Final by declaration
With this intent
I call them animals, with no manners,

They who do not have commands,
Are animals, with no reason.

Of the Holy House's restoration; of the prophecy of the Lord Dom Antonio; of some secrets to come and two prophecies against Castile

The House that is desired,
Will have its door open,
Despite the Dead Beast,
Soon it will be taken.
The vine will be pruned
All cleaned with the trimmer
And the one that gives sour wine,
With fire will be burnt.
(…)
In honour to such Victory
There will not be much sadness:
Instead we sing with glory,
Always keeping the memory,
Approving the Scripture,
Since accomplished the task:
And in others we clearly see,
Since everything is ascertained,
To the Lord of the Heights
With joy, a thousand graces.
(…)

Of some remarkable things to come to King Dom Sebastian, Represented by the Lion

Thus the Lion is clever,
Very alert.
He already is on his way,
To early take from the nest.
The Pig, and more, this is certain,
Will run across the desert
From the Lion and his roar
Showing it is wounded
By this good hidden King.
(…)

Of the release from prison; of imperial dignity, of, at last, King Dom Sebastian's canonisation; and of concord and unison among Christian princes, most dignified wonders among the prophesied, with confirmation of these prophecies.

Leave? Leave this Infant
Still walking?
His name is Dom Foam:
He will have the Flag
And the Banner,
Powerful and triumphant.
The news will reach him instantly
From the conquered lands,
That is bestowed,
And declared
By his King, from that moment.

The Kings will be contestants,
Four of them, no more
All of them the main leaders
From the West to the East.

Other Kings much content
Having him as ambassador,
And only by his lordship,
Not by gifts or presents.

He will cease all mistakes,
Peacemaker to the entire World,
Of four kings, the second
Will triumph.
On him will be such memory
For being guardian of the Law
To honour this King
Triumph and Glory will be given.

From everything said here
Mark well the prophecies:
And ponder on the origins
Daniel and Jeremiah.

You will find that those days
Will bring great news,
New Laws, varieties.
A thousand fights and disputes.

CHAPTER 6

"Hopes of Portugal" by Antonio Vieira: 17th-Century Portuguese America, a Luso-Brazilian Fifth Empire and Prophetical Views of History

Luís Filipe Silvério Lima

Introduction[1]

In 1659, the Jesuit Antonio Vieira (1608–1697) wrote a letter addressed to his confrère, André Fernandes, Bishop of Japan and confessor to John IV's widow and queen regent of Portugal, Luisa de Guzman (1613–1666). Entitled "Hopes of Portugal. Fifth Empire of the World. The first and the second life of King John IV", it contained an extensive prophetic-based argument explaining why the late king, John IV (d.1656), should resurrect to lead the Portuguese kingdom to the Fifth (and Last) Empire of the World. This kind of prophetical and miraculous reasoning among clergymen, or even men of letters, was not uncommon in the early modern period, rather the contrary—and not only in the Portuguese Empire and its conquests, but in almost any part of early modern Christendom.[2] However, what makes that particular letter noteworthy is both its global dimension and its centrality in Vieira's and Luso-Brazilian messianic ideas.

Allegedly written by Vieira while sitting in a canoe navigating in an Amazonian river, the letter was sent from Maranhão, in Portuguese America, not to

---

1 This research was supported by the National Council for Scientific and Technological Development (CNPq) research grant 309704/2015-4.
2 As Sanjay Subrahmanyam has shown, this millenarian ideology was pervasive, ranging from Europe to Asia in early modern empires and monarchies, and operating as a common currency in both Christendom and Islam. Sanjay Subrahmanyam, "Sixteenth-Century Millenarianism from the Tagus to the Ganges" in *Explorations in connected history: from the Tagus to the Ganges* (Oxford: 2005), 102–137. See also: Michele Olivari, "Milenarismo y política a fines del quinientos: notas sobre algunos complots y conjuras en la monarquía hispánica" in *En pos del tercer milenio*, Adeline Rucquoi et al. (Salamanca, 1999), 137–160; Matt Goldish, *The Sabbatean Prophets* (Cambridge, MA: 2004); A. Azfar Moin, *The Millennial Sovereign. Sacred Kingship and Sainthood in Islam* (New York: 2012); Nachtan Wachtel, "Theologies Marranes. Une configuration millénariste", in *Des Archives aux terrains* (Paris: 2014), 465–505; Brandon Marriott, *Transnational Networks and Cross-religious Exchange in the Seventeenth-century Mediterranean and Atlantic Worlds* (Farnham, Surrey: 2015); Andrew Crome (ed.), *Prophecy and Eschatology in the Transatlantic World, 1550–1800* (London: 2016).

Edo, the capital of Japan, but to Lisbon, the "head" of the Portuguese Empire, where Fernandes resided at the time as he was never officially consecrated Bishop of Japan by Rome. From the midst of the Amazon rain-forest to a never installed bishopric in the East Indies, talking about the Portuguese imperial destiny to convert the world while fighting the Spanish crown, "Hopes of Portugal. Fifth Empire of the World" imagined a project that articulated local and global dimensions, intertwining the Jesuits' missionary experiences in Portuguese America with diplomatic and political calculations in Europe.[3] All of that, amassed with prophecies upon which Vieira erected his historical-political interpretation for the Portuguese kingdom and the Christendom.

In this introduction, I will seek to highlight some central aspects for the understanding of "Hopes of Portugal" and, at the same time, to place it in the broader context of both Vieira's own prophetical work and the millenarian milieu in the Portuguese Empire. However, one should have in mind that rather than talking about Brazil and Maranhão, the two states of the Portuguese domain in the Americas, this source deals with an imperial vision of the conquests as part of a bigger eschatological plan. From that vantage point, the Americas were a secondary though crucial stage of a play which would end at the Old World theatre. In this sense, to properly read "Hopes of Portugal" one must understand it as part of the early modern Portuguese (if not Iberian) prophetism, and not necessarily as an example of an incipient or inaugural "Brazilian" messianism.[4] Notwithstanding, as I will try to point out at the end of this text, Vieira's writings and ideas were crucial for eighteenth-century messianic hopes which would foresee the head of the Fifth Empire in the Edenic landscapes of the New World.

Maranhão, Brazil, Portugal, the Americas, and the World

In the mid 17th century, what is today known as Brazil was constituted by two different administrative divisions. In 1549, the Portuguese crown had created

---

3   Lauri Tähtinen, "The Intellectual Construction of the Fifth Empire: Legitimating the Braganza Restoration", *History of European Ideas* 38/3 (2012), 415–416.
4   Brazilian scholars have tended to understand early modern messianism in order to explain contemporary "rustic" messianic movements, such as late 19th-century Canudos' and early 20th-century Contestado's Wars. For a critical perspective and innovative interpretations of the so-called "rustic messianism", see Cristina Pompa, "The Missionary Roots of Rural Messianic Movements: Seventeenth to Nineteenth Centuries", in *Visions, Prophecies, and Divinations. Early Modern Messianism and Millenarianism in Iberian America, Spain, and Portugal*, ed. Luís Filipe Silvério Lima and Ana Paula Megiani (Boston: 2016), 74–90.

the State of Brazil and established its capital in the city of Salvador of Bahia, which was in many ways the centre of the Portuguese dominions in the South Atlantic. However, in 1611, to fight the French occupation in the northern parts of its American domains, Lisbon constituted the State of Maranhão; in 1654, in an attempt to expand the actual control of the territory during the disputes with Spain, it changed it to the State of Maranhão and Grão-Pará, though keeping the "head" of the State in the city of São Luís of Maranhão, originally founded by the French in 1612.[5]

Vieira, a royal preacher and king's adviser raised in Salvador, but at the time back in his native Lisbon, was sent to São Luís in 1653 as the Superior of the second attempt to found a Jesuit mission in Maranhão. As a sign of both Vieira's prestige in the court and the Jesuit's importance within the Portuguese Empire and colonial project, Vieira arrived with a Royal Charter signed on 21 October 1652, which conceded great power and full jurisdiction over the natives and missions to the Jesuits. Moreover, it put the colonial, civil, and military administration of Maranhão under the Jesuits'—and hence Vieira's—supervision.[6] Because of the broad jurisdiction granted by the Charter, Vieira's power in some ways rivalled the Maranhão governor's, and years later his confrère João Felipe Bettendorf described him as the "spiritual governor of the souls".[7] While the governor was sympathetic to the Jesuit mission, this superposition of powers did not pose problems regarding the relations between the order and the civil administration. However, the missionary work sometimes collided with the interests of the Portuguese colonists, who saw the exclusive "government of the Indians" by the Society of Jesus as a menace to their survival.[8]

Maranhão and Grão-Pará's economy was mainly based on the exploitation of the indigenous population workforce, rather than of African slave labour as in most of Brazil state's plantations, and the Jesuit campaign against the

---

5 Antonio Filipe Pereira Caetano, "'Para aumentar e conservar aquelas partes ...': Conflitos dos projetos luso-americanos para uma conquista colonial (Estado do Maranhão e Grão-Pará, séculos XVII–XVIII)", *Revista Estudos Amazônicos* VI:1 (2011), 3–9.
6 Dauril Alden, *The Making of an Enterprise. The Society of Jesus in Portugal, its Empire, and Beyond, 1540–1750* (Stanford, California: 1996), 220–226, 487–490.
7 João Felipe Bettendorf, *Crônica dos padres da Companhia de Jesus no Estado do Maranhão* Apud Geraldo Mártires Coelho, "A pátria do Anticristo: A expulsão dos jesuítas do Maranhão e Grão-Pará e o messianismo milenarista de Vieira", *Luso-Brazilian Review* 37/1 (2000), 21.
8 About the complex relationship among the settlers, the governor and crown officials, and the Jesuits, as well as about Vieira's attempts to use the apostleship as a political tool to mitigate conflicts, see Rafael Chambouleyron, "Uma missão 'tão encontrada dos interesses humanos'. Jesuítas e portugueses na Amazônia seiscentista", in *Vieira. Vida e Palavra*, ed. Silvia Azevedo and Vanessa Ribeiro (São Paulo: 2008), 29–53.

enslavement of tribes (though accepting if not encouraging African slavery and the Atlantic slave trade) became a reason for recurrent conflicts between the priests and the settlers.[9] From the Jesuits' standpoint, as stated by Vieira in sermons and letters,[10] the conversion of the Amerindian heathens was instrumental for the fulfilment of Portugal's destiny as the defender of the Catholic faith. Therefore, they should be left to the supervision of the priests to save their souls through conversion—but also to work in (and for) the Jesuit "aldeias", as they were accused by some colonists.[11] Eventually the local interests prevailed, and, despite Vieira's efforts towards the colonial society and within the Portuguese court, and maybe a sign of his declining influence in Lisbon, the Jesuits were expelled from Maranhão in 1661.[12]

More than moved by any (anachronistic) humanitarian or egalitarian notion, Vieira's defence of the indigenous population's freedom was part of an

---

9   Rafael Chambouleyron, "'Ásperas proposições': Jesuítas; moradores e a Inquisição na Amazônia seiscentista no tempo de Vieira, missionário", *Revista Lusófona de Ciência das Religiões* 13–14 (2013), 94–96. For the slave trade's centrality in the Portuguese Atlantic economy, see Luiz Felipe de Alencastro, *O Trato dos Viventes* (São Paulo: 2000), for Jesuit's and Vieira's views about African slavery (as well as their justification for it) 180–187. For Indian slavery and workforce in Maranhão and Grão-Pará, see Rafael Chambouleyron, "Indian Freedom and Indian Slavery in the Portuguese Amazon (1640–1755)", in *Building the Atlantic Empires: Unfree Labor and Imperial States in the Political Economy of Capitalism, ca. 1500–1914*, ed. John Donoghue and Evelyn P. Jennings (Leiden: 2016), 54–71.

10 For instance, see Vieira's "Sermão da Epifania", which Thomas Cohen regards as "the most important sermon on Brazilian society that Vieira ever preached": Antônio Vieira, "Sermão da Epifania", in *Sermoens do P. Antonio Vieira da Companhia do Jesu*, vol. 4 (Lisbon: 1685), 491–549; Thomas Cohen, *The Fire of Tongues. António Vieira and the Missionary Church in Brazil and Portugal* (Stanford, California: 1998), 99. For more examples, see also: Alcir Pécora, "Vieira e a condução do Índio ao Corpo Místico do Império Português (Maranhão, 1652–1661)", *Sibila* (24 March 2009) (http://sibila.com.br/mapa-da-lingua/o-padre-vieira/2703, accessed on 18 July 2018).

11 "Aldeias" were a Jesuit institution that "regulated Indian policy (...), devised (...) to protect the Indians from settler attacks. (...) Under the Aldeia system, the Indians could not refuse to come to live in the settlements, for if they did, colonial law determined that a just war could be waged against them. Once in the Aldeias, the Indians were granted civil liberties such as equality before the law, but if they refused to join the settlement or elected to flee from one, they lost not only their civil liberties but also their natural liberty, and could thus be captured as slaves." Aware of the settler's dependence on an indigenous workforce, Vieira tried to mitigate the conflict by proposing that the "Aldeados" (the indigenous people living and working in "Aldeias") worked half of the year for the settlers upon the "Aldeados" receiving some form of wage. The settlers were not willing to compromise and did not accept the deal. José Eisenberg, "António Vieira and the Justification of Indian Slavery", *Luso-Brazilian Review* 40/1 (2003), 91–92.

12 Concerning the colonists' strategies for the Jesuits' expulsion, see Chambouleyron, "Ásperas proposições", 97–103.

imperial vision according to which the Jesuit Order and the Portuguese Empire would conquer and convert the world "to the greater glory of God".[13] Vieira and the Jesuit missionaries in Maranhão understood their work as part of a Catholic project; in Vieira's particular case, a project with millenarian, imperial tones and with a pursuant defence of the Portuguese dynasty of Braganza against the Spanish Habsburgs during the Restoration wars (1640–1668). For Vieira, the conversion of the Indians, the mission in Maranhão, the Portuguese America, or even the slave trade, all of it should be considered as part of a Divine plan in which the newly restored Portugal (and the Society of Jesus) would have a central role.

Although central for the conversion of the globe, the Portuguese mission and conquest of the Americas would only be significant as far as they were a decisive factor to sustain the Portuguese Empire and help the fights of the Braganza Crown.[14] In this sense, the Americas were an important part—but not the centre—of an Empire. However, this empire had a triple dimension in time: a present and embodied one, which was constituted by the "parts" (*partes*) of the Portuguese domains coordinated around its "head" (*cabeça*), the crown; a future and desired one, which would be formed by a Christianised world led by the Portuguese monarchy; and a past and promised one, in which both of the former were prophesied in the very foundations of the kingdom. It was the future and prophesied imperial dimensions that should ultimately conduct not only the interpretations of prophecies but also the politics regarding the Americas.[15] However, to fulfil the promised and glorious destiny, the

---

13 "Ad maiorem Dei gloriam", the Jesuit motto. For the debates about Amerindian and African slavery and the Jesuit missionary plan, see José Carlos Sebe Bom Meihy, "A ética colonial e a questão jesuítica dos cativeiros índio e negro", *Afro-Asia* 23 (2000), 9–27.

14 In a text known as "Papel Forte" (Bold Paper), Vieira, for instance, suggested to John IV that Portugal should sell Pernambuco, in Northeast Brazil, to the Dutch Western Company, instead of trying to fight and expel the Dutch from the Brazilian Northeast. Vieira's argument was that since Portugal was fighting against Spain in Europe and against the Dutch in the Eastern parts of the Empire, it would be an error to maintain too many fronts; hence, it would be wiser to cease fire and seek peace with the Dutch Republic, enemy of the Spanish crown too, in order to guarantee the independence of the Portuguese crown under the Braganzas. Once the Spanish enemy was defeated, Portugal could resume its path to defeat the Infidel and the Heretics (i.e. the Dutch) and regain all the lost territories in the name of Christ. "Parecer que deu Padre António Vieira sobre se entregar a campanha de Pernambuco aos holandeses, em 21 de outubro de 1648, para efeito de se ajustarem as pazes: ao qual comummente chamam o 'Papel Forte'", in António Vieira, *Obra completa*, t. IV, v. I (Lisbon: 2013), 68–112.

15 I am following João Adolfo Hansen's interpretation on Vieira's conception of time, prophecy, and politics. Among Hansen's many texts, see João Adolfo Hansen, "Prefácio. A Chave dos Profetas: Deus, Analogia, Tempo", in Vieira, *Obra completa*, t. V, v. I, 11–56.

actions in the present should respect and follow strict calculations, according to what was coined as a Catholic "Reason of State" by which the prudent should seek foremost to maintain the integrity of the head and its parts.[16] To complete the prophecies, it would not be sufficient to wait; it was necessary to act prudently, that is, to weigh the opportunities as well as to seize the occasion, as suggested in Alciatos's emblem "In Occasionen".[17] In an expanded globe, the cardinal virtue of prudence had to ponder situations in all corners of the world, and not only within the Old World Christian courts and against their enemies in the Near East or North Africa. Christian politics had gained a global connected perspective, and its desired apocalyptic outcome, the final victory of Christendom over the infidels, had to include regions and populations not discussed before by evangelical exegesis and the Classical tradition.

Notwithstanding the importance of the New World in this broader scenario and its decisive role in shifting interpretations of prophecies and even traditions, Portuguese America played a crucial but still auxiliary and supporting position in Vieira's imperial drama. The struggle with the Portuguese settlers about the heathens certainly had a part in a broader strategy aimed at the necessary conversion of all the peoples in the globe to Christendom, but it was not the main act of the plot. In other words, even the prophecies which had been seen, written or interpreted in the Americas dealt more with the greater destiny of this final Empire (or even of the Portuguese Empire), than with the particular one of the Americas. Because of new and more comprehensive knowledge of the different peoples and places in the globe, the colonisation of the New World did indeed change the perspective of old European and Christian prophecies,[18] but as far as Vieira's thoughts were concerned, the central

---

16　Luis Reis Torgal, *Ideologia Política e Teoria de Estado na Restauração*, vol. 2 (Coimbra: 1981), 135–232; João Adolfo Hansen, "Razão de Estado" (1996), *Artepensamento: ensaios filosóficos e políticos* (https://artepensamento.com.br/item/razao-de-estado/, accessed on 12 December 2018); João Adolfo Hansen, "Educando Príncipes no Espelho", *Floema* 11:2 (2006), 133–169. For the reception of Machiavellian "Reason of State" in Portuguese America, see Dossier "Translation of Machiavelli from Portuguese India to Brazil", *Tempo* 20 (2014), especially: Rodrigo Bentes Monteiro and Vinícius Dantas, "Machiavellianisms and governments in Portuguese America: two analyses of ideas and political practices". *Tempo* 20 (2014), 1–26; Luciano Raposo de Almeida Figueiredo, "Brazilian Machiavellians: dissimulation, political ideas, and colonial rebellions (Portugal, 17th–18th century)", *Tempo* 20 (2014), 1–24.

17　Andrea Alciato, Diego Lopez, *Declaracion magistral sobre las Emblemas de Andres Alciato* (Najera: 1615), fols 299–301.

18　Luís Filipe Silvério Lima, "Between the New and the Old World: Iberian Prophecies and Imperial Projects in the Colonisation of the Early Modern Spanish and Portuguese Americas", in *Prophecy and Eschatology in the Transatlantic World*, ed. Crome, 36–46.

and final stage of the prophecies remained the Old World. The head of the Last and Fifth Empire would still be Europe, or more precisely, Portugal. Vieira, however, would take a while to formulate his millenarian plan.

Vieira's Fifth Empire

Born in Lisbon in 1608, a six-year-old Antônio Vieira went with his family to Salvador of Bahia, where his father had secured a position as a registrar. Educated at the Jesuit College of Bahia, Vieira entered the Society of Jesus against his parents' wishes. At Bahia's College, Vieira soon became a teacher even before his ordination, and from the pulpits of the Jesuit church, he started to gain respect and fame as a gifted preacher in the capital of the State of Brazil. In 1641, when the news of the coup of 1 December 1640, the Restoration of Portugal and the acclamation of John IV arrived in Salvador, the governor of Brazil Jorge de Mascarenhas, first Marquis of Montalvão, decided to dispatch a greeting committee to Lisbon. He wanted not only to pledge his loyalty to the new king, but also to dismiss any doubt about his possible allegiance to the Spanish and former Portuguese king, Phillip IV. Vieira joined the Brazilian entourage, most certainly because of his preaching skills, and crossed the Atlantic once more to return to the long-departed Lisbon.[19]

After being ill-received in Portugal because of a general distrust about where the governor's fealty indeed lay, Vieira quickly overcame the situation, gained John IV's trust and marvelled the court with his sermons full of support for the Braganzas' cause. On 1 January 1642, he preached a sermon ("Sermão dos Bons Anos") at the Royal Chapel in which, despite the current war against the most powerful European monarchy, Habsburg Spain, he promised not only "good years" (*bons anos*) to the realm but also the prompt consummation of all the Divine promises to Portugal. Since the foundation of Portugal as a kingdom during the 1139 Battle of Ourique, Christ would have elected it as his personal Reign

---

19   The biographical details presented here and below heavily rely upon the classic biography of Vieira by João Lúcio de Azevedo. João Lúcio de Azevedo, *História de António Vieira* (1918; repr. Lisbon: 1992), 2 vols. For a more recent biography, see Ronaldo Vainfas, *António Vieira* (São Paulo, 2011). In English, see Charles R. Boxer, *A Great Luso-Brazilian Figure: Padre Antonio Vieira, S. J., 1608–1697* (London: 1957); Dauril Alden, "Some Reflections on Antonio Vieira: Seventeenth-Century Troubleshooter and Troublemaker", *Luso-Brazilian Review* 40/1 (Summer, 2003), 7–16; Cohen, *The Fire of Tongues*; Ana Valdez, *Historical Interpretations of the "Fifth Empire": The Dynamics of Periodization from Daniel to António Vieira*, S.J. (Leiden: 2011); Mónica Leal da Silva and Liam Brockey, "Introduction" in *António Vieira: Six Sermons* (Oxford: 2018), 1–31.

and Empire and the Portuguese as the new people of God. The Restoration with John IV would be the first step to finally complete the destiny of the kingdom. Not only was Vieira assuring the rightfulness of John IV's cause against the Spanish Habsburgs' claims in the sermon, he was also aiming at the hopes of the Sebastianists who were still waiting for the "Desired" and "Hidden one", Sebastian I, lost in action in the Battle of Ksar El-Kibir (1578).[20] To Vieira and John IV's supporters, it was instrumental to convert a well-established and rooted belief built around the return of King Sebastian into a prophetic dynastic discourse that granted legitimacy but moreover invested the House of Braganza with all the hopes of Portugal. To achieve this, they needed to rearrange a body of prophecies, visions, signs, and their interpretations, organised during decades to prove the necessary and imminent return of King Sebastian. For that, they sought to look for new foundations and arguments.

As John IV's personal counsellor, Vieira was dispatched to several diplomatic missions in France, Italy, and the Netherlands from the mid-1640s until the early 1650s. It was the perfect opportunity to consult libraries and to talk with several men of letters and of the clergy about his prophetical ideas regarding Portugal. In France, he managed to establish a network of Braganza supporters around the embassy of the future Marquis of Niza, Vasco Luís da Gama, through which they exchanged books and information within the Republic of Letters.

The circle around the Marquis of Niza's embassy produced many of the foundations of a providential if not messianic-based support for the Braganza dynasty. For instance, it was under Niza's patronage that the first version of the 16th-century *Trovas de Bandarra*, called the "Bible of the Sebastianists", gained an (allegedly) complete printed edition, in 1644 at Nantes. These prophetic *Trovas* (quatrains) written by a 16th-century cobbler, Gonçalo Anes Bandarra (c.1550–1556), were widely circulated by oral transmission and manuscript copies throughout the Portuguese Empire, though its author was prosecuted by the Portuguese Inquisition in 1541 and it was also later included in the Portuguese *Index* in 1581. Its verses about a "Hidden" and "Desired" king were promptly interpreted as referring to Sebastian I after his alleged disappearance in North Africa.[21] However, the Nantes edition not only stated that the promised "Hidden one" was John IV and not Sebastian I, but it also changed some passages to favour a pro-Braganza interpretation.[22] While abroad either

---

20 Antônio Vieira, "Sermão dos Bons Annos" in *Sermoens do P. Antonio Vieira da Companhia de Jesu*, vol. 11 (Lisbon: 1696), 399–431.
21 On Bandarra's trovas and Sebastianism, see Jacqueline Hermann's chapter in the present volume.
22 João Lúcio de Azevedo, *A Evolução do Sebastianismo* (1918; repr. Lisbon: 1984), 40–45, 48–

in diplomatic or commercial affairs, the Braganzas' supporters wrote texts in Portuguese to defend John IV's cause, but they also corresponded and met with many men of letters and many Jews (and former New-Christians) of Iberian origin. One of them was Menasseh Ben Israel (1604–1657), a well-known rabbi of the "Portuguese Nation" of Amsterdam and main source on Jewish lore for many Christian scholars.

Vieira met with Menasseh in 1648, while he was in the Netherlands serving John IV both as a diplomatic emissary, seeking ways to end the Dutch-Portuguese war in Pernambuco, Brazil, and as a mercantile agent, trying to buy boats—perhaps to fight the same Dutch along the Brazilian shores. None of the missions reached a favourable outcome, but his encounter with Menasseh would have some significance for Vieira's millenarian project. During their meeting in Amsterdam, the Jesuit and the Rabbi discussed the apocalyptic outcomes of their times and whether the Jews scattered through Europe and the world would be converted to the Catholic Faith in the Last Empire to come or not. According to Vieira, confronted with infallible arguments, Menasseh would have revised his position and eventually agreed with the Jesuit's view about the necessity of the Jewish people's acceptance of Christ as the true messiah. The hypothesis of the Jewish acceptance of the Final Kingdom to-come was a key piece in Vieira's argument to weaken the Holy Office's persecution of the New-Christians and to seek the support of the Judeo-Portuguese merchant network to finance the Restoration, although neither achieved their intended success.[23] On the contrary, his contacts with Jewish rabbis and merchants in the Netherlands and his defence of New-Christians would be later used by the Inquisition as one of the grounds to prosecute him.

82; José Van Den Besselaar, *Sebastianismo—uma história sumária* (Lisbon: 1987), chap. V–VI; Jacqueline Hermann, *No Reino do Desejado* (São Paulo: 1998), chap. 4–5; Luís Filipe Silvério Lima, "O percurso das *Trovas* de Bandarra: circulação letrada de um profeta iletrado", in *O Império por Escrito. Formas de transmissão da cultura letrada no mundo ibérico (séc. XVI–XIX)*, ed. Leila Algranti and Ana Paula Megiani (São Paulo: 2009), 441–452.

23 About Vieira's contacts with Menasseh and the Portuguese-Jews, see António José Saraiva, "António Vieira, Menasseh ben Israel e o Quinto Império" in *História e utopia* (Lisbon: 1992), 75–107; Anita Novinsky, "Sebastianismo, Vieira e o messianismo judaico" in *Sobre as naus da iniciação*, ed. C.A. Iannone (São Paulo: 1998), 65–79; Florence Lévy, "La prophétie et le pouvoir politico-religieux au XVIIe siècle au Portugal et en Hollande: Vieira et Menasseh Ben Israel", in *La prophétie comme arme de guerre et des pouvoirs*, ed. Augustin Redondo (Paris: 2000), 433–446; Valmir Muraro, *Padre António Vieira. Retórica e Utopia* (Florianópolis: 2003), 129–176; Lúcia Helena Costigan, "Judeus e Cristãos-Novos nos escritos de letrados do Barroco espanhol e de Antônio Vieira e Menasseh Ben Israel", in *Diálogos da Conversão*, ed. Lúcia Helena Costigan (Campinas: 2005), 123–154; Nachman Falbel, *Judeus no Brasil*, (São Paulo: 2008), 121–133 (chap. "Menasseh Ben Israel e o Brasil").

For many authors, Vieira would have formulated the notion of a Fifth Empire for the first time in the midst of these intense diplomatic, courteous, and political activities to defend and legitimise the Braganza dynasty.[24] According to his most important biographer, João Lúcio de Azevedo, Vieira would have started the draft of his *História do Futuro* (*History of the Future*) circa 1649 as a first attempt to define what the "Last Reign of Christ on Earth" would be.[25] In this sense, his prophetical-political plan was resulted from the effort of legitimising John IV's rule and transforming the Sebastianists' belief into a "Joanista" belief.[26] The very use of a different denomination, the Fifth Empire, instead of the more widely known notion of Fifth Monarchy[27] could be seen as evidence of this effort to detach the cause of the Braganzas' supporters from that of the Sebastianists. One should remember that in the early 17th century, the Sebastianist João de Castro had written dozens of tracts, treatises, and commentaries in which he tried not only to defend the cause of Sebastian of Venice, but also to establish the ground for a Portuguese Fifth Monarchy. Castro's efforts summarised and organised a plethora of Iberian and Portuguese prophecies under the light of a fifth-monarchist plan by which Portugal would be the head of this last, final, and Catholic empire.[28] Vieira's writings, though not quoting Castro's, most certainly benefited from—if not directly used—the Sebastianist's construct. However, Vieira's Fifth Empire would gradually assume a global dimension, less abstract in terms of a prophesied conversion or conquest of all parts of the world, and more solid in terms of the significance of the practical and concrete experiences of the colonisation and missionary efforts among the "strange peoples" predicted in some Portuguese prophecies.

Whether Azevedo's hypothesis is correct or not, the fact remains that there are not many—if any—manuscripts or printed texts from this period in which

---

24 See, for instance, Silvano Peloso, *Antônio Vieira e o Império Universal. A Clavis Prophetarum e os documentos inquisitoriais* (Rio de Janeiro: 2007), 49–80.
25 Azevedo, *História de António Vieira*, t. I, 155–157.
26 In 1951, Eduardo D'Oliveira França argued that this "joanismo" became the ideology of the Restoration and assumed the form of a "messianismo brigantino" (a messianism of the Braganza dynasty). Eduardo D'Oliveira França, *Portugal na Época da Restauração* (1951; repr. São Paulo: 1997), 250–259. For views derived from this hypothesis: Torgal, *Ideologia Política*, vol. I, 296–341; Lima, *Império dos Sonhos*.
27 For early modern cases of Fifth Monarchy projects, see Bernard Capp, *Fifth Monarchy Men* (London: 1972) esp. "Conclusion"; Luís Filipe Silvério Lima, "Prophetical hopes, New World experiences and imperial expectations: Menasseh Ben Israel, Antônio Vieira, Fifth-Monarchy Men, and the millenarian connections in the seventeenth-century Atlantic", *AHAM*, XVII (2016), 359–408. For a genealogical perspective of Fifth Monarchy ideas, see Valdez, *Historical Interpretations of the "Fifth Empire"*.
28 See Jacqueline Hermann's chapter about João de Castro's works in this volume.

Vieira employed the term "Fifth Empire" or more concretely dealt with what it should be. His sermons and letters preached or written during this time indeed averred the providential events of the Restoration and the divine election of Portugal in the struggle against Spain; however, they did not explicitly mention a Fifth Empire to come as a motive for it in the way his later writings would do.[29]

For Thomas Cohen, the 1650s mission in Maranhão and Grão-Pará would be the turning point which allowed Vieira to transform a dynastic effort into a global eschatological expectation. Vieira's Fifth Empire was the result of reflections upon the Portuguese Empire drawn from "the hardship of the Maranhão Mission." Based on that strenuous and constant struggle as the Superior of the Jesuit mission which involved actual evangelisation work among the indigenous population, he was able to understand how profoundly "Scripture, missionary enterprise, and the apostleship of the Portuguese nation were interwoven."[30] The Fifth Empire was thus the outcome of Vieira's missionary experience and his embracing of the Jesuit (imperial) universalism which modified and broadened a prophetical defence of the Braganza dynasty. Written during that period, "Hopes of Portugal. Fifth Empire of the World", his first known prophetical tract, is hard evidence of that.[31]

Not long after the Jesuits' expulsion from Maranhão and Vieira's return to Portugal, the same "Hopes of Portugal" was used as evidence for the Inquisition opening a case against him. Indeed the return to court was not very gleeful for Vieira. After a coup in 1662 that put an end to the regency of John IV's widow, Luisa de Guzman, Vieira lost royal favour with the ascension of Afonso VI, son of John IV, sympathetic neither to his father's former supporters in general nor to Vieira's plans, advice, and causes in particular. At the same time, the political disputes within the court, the unappealing image of Afonso VI as a weak ruler, and setbacks in the Restoration wars gave rise to a feeling of dissatisfaction towards the Braganza dynasty which strengthened the old Sebastianist "sect", as Vieira called it.[32] Expelled from the court, defending a cause that no longer had much popular appeal, and lacking support even inside the Society of Jesus after his downfall in Maranhão, Vieira became an easy target for the Inquisition, his

---

29 About the Fifth Empire's presence in Vieira's sermons, see Jacqueson Luiz da Silva, "Arquitetura do Quinto Império em Vieira", PhD dissertation (Campinas: 2007).
30 Cohen, *The Fire of Tongues*, 150.
31 Thomas Cohen, "Millenarian Themes in the Writings of Antonio Vieira", *Luso-Brazilian Review* 28/1 (Summer, 1991), 23–26. See also: Coelho, "A pátria do Anticristo".
32 Besselaar, *Sebastianismo*, chap. VI. For Vieira's derogatory remarks on the Sebastianists' beliefs, see Vieira, *Obra completa*, t. I, vol. II, 516–517.

long-term adversary. And "Hopes of Portugal", with its pervasive authoritative use of popular prophecies, namely of Bandarra, its prediction of the miraculous resurrection of John IV, and its evocations of a universal conversion of the Jews under an earthly Fifth Empire to come, presented a solid ground to start an Inquisition trial.[33]

Summoned in 1663, Vieira spent the following four years—some of them incarcerated—defending himself against accusations of heresy, of being "suspected of Judaism" and of writing a paper, "Hopes of Portugal", denounced as "fatuous, damnatory, scandalous, injurious, sacrilegious, offensive to pious ears, erroneous."[34] Impelled by the urgency of answering all the Inquisitors' charges of heterodoxy, he organised his defence to address and counter the questions made by his judges—starting by answering the objections made to "Hopes of Portugal" but evolving into a more comprehensive vindication of his interpretation the Fifth Empire. Confined, isolated and without access to libraries, Vieira managed to write hundreds of pages that constituted his defence, the "Representações", as well as many other unfinished manuscripts with the Fifth Empire's justification as the main theme. The orthodoxy of his Fifth Empire as a valid Catholic reading of Daniel's five monarchies and the Portuguese prophecies was the core argument of all of those texts. For Adma Fadul Muhana, it was during this time that Vieira was able to finally systematically write about his Fifth Empire project, and he only did it because he was motivated by the Inquisitors' accusation. Moreover, his texts about the Fifth Empire—for example, the later yet unfinished versions of the *História do Futuro* and *Clavis Prophetarum*—were derived from his defence and they kept similarities if not the same rhetorical structure from his answering to the Inquisitor's questions.[35] In other words, it would have been due to the Inquisition trial that he at last developed his own millenarian and messianic theory. If Muhana's hypothesis is true, and it does sound likely, one could see some irony in it. Vieira's messianic justification was one of the arguments—if not the main

---

33 For analyses of Vieira's trial, see Alcir Pécora, "O processo inquisitorial de Antônio Vieira", in Iannone, *Sobre as naus da iniciação*, 49–64; Adma Fadul Muhana, "O processo inquisitorial de Vieira: aspectos profético-argumentativos", *Semear* 2 (1998), 9–19; José Pedro Paiva, "Revisitar o processo inquisitorial do padre António Vieira", *Lusitania Sacra* 23 (2011), 151–168.

34 "Suspeito de Judaísmo", "fátuo, temerário, escandaloso, injurioso, sacrílego, *piarum aurium* ofensivo, errôneo". Adma Fadul Muhana (ed.), *Os Autos do processo de Vieira na Inquisição: 1660–1668* (São Paulo: 2008), 313.

35 Muhana, "O processo inquisitorial de Vieira"; Adma Fadul Muhana, "Introdução", in *Os Autos do processo*, 20–26. Cf. Alcir Pécora, "O Processo Inquisitorial de Antônio Vieira", 58–61.

one—for his being prosecuted and accused of heresy, and on the fringe of being a judaiser; and at the same time, it was because of the Inquisition charges that he saw himself compelled to define his interpretation—and his later prophetical writings built on it.

Irony aside, on 23 December 1667 the inquisitors convicted him of heresy, condemned all his prophetical propositions, and reinforced the prohibition of Bandarra's *Trovas*. He received the sentence of reclusion and silence. A few years later, he managed to have his imprisonment suspended, and in 1669 he was authorised to travel to Rome under the false pretence of advocating the canonisation of Jesuit martyrs. In the Holy See, using his oratorical skills once more, he acquired fame, and through his prestige at the Papal court he eventually received a Papal Brief which put him directly under Rome's jurisdiction and thus far from the Portuguese Inquisition's grasp. Holding this brief, he returned to Lisbon, but not to find the prestigious place he was hoping for in the court of the new king, Peter II (Afonso VI's brother). Maybe for this reason, maybe for another, Vieira went back to Salvador, Bahia, where he spent his final years. There, he dedicated himself to prepare his sermons for printing and to write the *Clavis Prophetarum*, the Key of the Prophets. He considered the *Clavis* as his masterpiece, in which he would discuss the "Last Reign of Christ on Earth", one of the names of the Fifth Empire. At his demise at the age of 89, in 1697, 11 volumes of the *Sermoens* had been printed, and one was launched the following year. The *Clavis* was neither completed nor printed.

Rather than driven only by the Restoration efforts or a response to the Sebastianists, Vieira's Fifth Empire heavily relied upon his Amazonian and American experience that later assumed a more solid basis as a theological-historical-prophetical project, ironically due to the Inquisition prosecution. These two contexts—the missionary experience in Maranhão and the inquisition trial in Coimbra—transformed a political, dynastic messianic defence into a universal, global, imperial millenarian plan. And "Hopes of Portugal" is the link by which one may connect both contexts.

"Hopes of Portugal"

The original letter written by Vieira and sent to the Bishop of Japan, André Fernandes, has not survived.[36] Actually, we should speak of the letters, because there were two versions of the letter—as Vieira himself indicated in the text

---

36 During the Inquisition's proceedings, Vieira declared that he destroyed the autograph first

of the second and known version. It seems that Vieira had sent a first letter through São Luís do Maranhão postal services, while allegedly navigating an Amazonian river near Camutá, and this was a revised and updated version, probably written around November 1659. Still, the date signed at the end of the second version remains 29 April 1659. In the letter from November, Vieira possibly just added some remarks to actualise his interpretations of Bandarra. The reasons for doing that are not completely clear, but one can infer some motives from a mention of this second version of "Hopes of Portugal" in a letter to the regent queen, Luisa de Guzman. On 28 November 1659, he wrote to the queen:

> To the Bishop Confessor, I have sent another paper of bigger effects, as I want to call it despite the fact that it only carries hopes; so assured are my faith and certainty on these hopes. This paper will prostate itself before Her Highness' feet, embarrassed and fearful, asking to be accepted, because it has already been offered and was not accepted.[37]

As one can infer from a letter written and sent to the queen on the same day as the first copy of the "Hopes" (29 April 1659), Vieira had indeed great expectations about this paper, and had even assumed that it could help the queen to fight against the Jesuit's enemies at the Court.[38] These letters show us that the "Hopes" of April 1659 was not well received in Lisbon, and Vieira tried to modify and improve it in order to (re)gain the queen's favour and a good reception at the Court, and thus by sending another version to the Bishop of Japan on 28 November 1659, together with the second letter to the queen.

This second version is the one that was brought to the Inquisition's attention and the one that André Fernandes, the recipient of the letter, delivered on 15 April 1660.[39] There are two copies of the November "Hopes" in Vieira's proceedings, one of them probably used by the inquirers ("qualificadores") to qualify Vieira's heretical propositions and to give grounds to open the case against him. In spite of any attempts of censorship, "Hopes of Portugal" had a widespread circulation. A sign of this is that "Hopes of Portugal" is possibly

---

       version of the manuscript as it was full of revision marks right after he knew the clean copy arrived in Lisbon. *Os Autos do processo*, 75.

37   Vieira, *Obra completa*, t. I, vol. II, 260. "Ao Bispo Confessor envio outro papel de maiores efeitos, que assim lhe quero chamar, posto que só leva esperanças, tão segura é a certeza e a fé que nelas tenho. Vai este papel prostrar-se aos reais pés de Vossa Majestade, corrido e temeroso de ser aceito, porque já foi oferecido e não aceitado."

38   Vieira, 254.

39   José van den Besselaar, *Antônio Vieira. Profecia e polêmica* (Rio de Janeiro: 2002), 38.

the prophetical text by Vieira with the largest number of early modern handwritten copies known today. Just at the National Library of Portugal, there are 11 copies, 10 from the late 17th century or 18th century.[40] Regardless of its broad circulation, it was printed for the first time only in the 19th century when the Inquisition no longer existed.[41]

The genre of "Hopes of Portugal" poses another set of questions, an aspect discussed both in his Inquisition trial and in contemporary studies about Vieira. Though presenting the basic elements of a letter (Addressee, Salutation, Conclusion, Signature, Date, etc.), the subject and the structure may more likely suggest a tract or a small treatise than a missive in some passages. At some point, Vieira called "Hopes" a "papel" (paper). Defining text as a "papel" could be a clue for the reader to understand the discourse as a proposition of something. In early modern lettered practices, a paper might refer to any kind of miscellaneous writing, but not unusually did it identify a written discourse produced for presenting arguments or intervening in a debate or dispute.[42] Whereas Sebastianism was rising again as the main prophetical interpretation in the late 1650s and early 1660s, one may read the paper "Hopes of Portugal" as belonging to a prophetic polemical genre, and therefore rhetorically produced to dispute the messianic hopes with the Sebastianists. However, in his defence before the inquisitors, he argued that it was merely a letter to be read and seen only by the bishop and the queen. Either a paper or a letter—or maybe both, "Hopes of Portugal" was certainly a controversial text.

The full title, "Hopes of Portugal. Fifth Empire of the World. The First and the Second Life of King John IV. Written by Gonçaliannes Bandarra", has also provoked some discussion and interpretations in the literature and has some noteworthy aspects. The first aspect is the expression "Hopes of Portugal" which could evoke Menasseh Ben Israel's *Esperança de Israel*, printed in Amsterdam in 1650 and translated and printed in London as *Hope of Israel* in the same year. The hypothesis, defended by António José Saraiva among many others,[43] has interesting implications as one can suppose the effects of the 1648 discus-

---

40   José Pedro Paiva (ed.), *Padre António Vieira. 1608–1697. Bibliografia* (Lisbon: 1999), items 679–689. There are four copies at the National Library of Brazil. Luiz Felipe Baêta Neves Flores (ed.), *Padre Antônio Vieira. Catálogo da Biblioteca Nacional* (Rio de Janeiro: 1999), items 753, 846, 857, 868.
41   António Vieira, *Obras Inéditas* (Lisbon, 1856), t. II, 83–131.
42   Among Vieira's own writings, one famous example is the aforementioned "Papel Forte" (Bold Paper). See note 14.
43   António José Saraiva, "António Vieira, Menasseh ben Israel e o Quinto Império"; Novinsky, "Sebastianismo, Vieira e o messianismo judaico", 73–77; Costigan, "Judeus e Cristãos-Novos", 140–141.

sion between Menasseh and Vieira upon the latter. However productive that hypothesis may be, the similarity between the titles could be hardly seen as a definitive proof that "Hopes of Portugal" was inspired by *Hopes of Israel*. Hope was a common concept as well as a recurrent word within early modern apocalyptic literature, particularly within millenarian texts.[44]

A second noteworthy aspect is the first occurrence of the term "Fifth Empire" as an explicit denomination of Vieira's messianic projects—although the term did not occur in the rest of "Hopes of Portugal" beyond the title. The third aspect, which may lessen the significance of the second, is that it is not known when the title was given (or even who titled it), and one could further wonder why a letter should have received such a title. Also, presenting a title— and not a short description of the letter elements, as was usually done in copies of letters—could be another proof of the mixed genre of "Hopes of Portugal". For instance, in the copy in the inquisitorial proceedings, the title is presented on a separate sheet, centralised in the page, written in capital and carefully designed letters, the usual elements of a frontispiece of a manuscript treatise (and not the ones of a letter).[45]

The fourth and last aspect is that Gonçalo Anes Bandarra appears in the title as the writer of "Hopes of Portugal", and not Vieira, who signed his name at the end of the letter. As providing some guidance to the reader on how to interpret the paper, this attribution of shared authorship entails both an argument of authority (*auctoritas*) and evidence of the contemporaneity of Bandarra's vision. In terms of an attribute of authority, not only does the authors' duplicity demonstrate the early modern plastic notion of authorship, but it also entails a twofold rhetorical effect. On the one hand, Vieira posing as a mere glossator of Bandarra's authority evoked the commonplace of "affected modesty" deployed to gain the benevolence of his interlocutor (the *captatio benevolentiae*). On the other, the superposition of authorship circularly reinforced the foundation and argument of the paper: Bandarra was a true prophet. Hence one should believe in what Bandarra had prophesied. Therefore one should consider him as an authorised authority. And finally, one should be convinced of the validity of Vieira's arguments since they were based on this established authority.

---

44 Luís Filipe Silvério Lima. "Aproximações para uma história do conceito de Esperança nas expectativas milenaristas do século XVII", *O que nos faz pensar* 26/41 (2017), 75–106. About the idea of Hope in the title, see Vieira's explanation in *Livro anteprimeiro da História do Futuro*, ed. José Van Den Besselaar (Lisbon: 1983), 28–30. Cf. Ana Valdez, "Making of a Revolution: Daniel, Revelation and the Portuguese Restoration of 1640", *Oracula* 9/14 (2013), 10–11, 13–14.

45 I tried to reproduce, though partially, the lay-out of the title page in the translation. About the implications of the title page, see Peloso, *Antônio Vieira e o Império Universal*, 25–27.

In terms of the prophecies' contemporaneity and temporality, the action of displaying the name of Bandarra in the very title, but signing it with the name of Vieira and dating 29 April 1659 at the end of the letter, reminds the reader that Bandarra had talked in the past about events in his future that were happening in Vieira's present. According to the title, Bandarra had written the "Hopes of Portugal" which would be fulfilled in John IV's "first" and "second life", and this points out not only that the text would be based on Bandarra's predictions but also that his predictions would happen at a particular moment: the Portuguese Restoration. The superposition of temporalities, derived from the inner quality of the prophecy as a revelation of the Divine eternity, required a complex sewing into the fabric of the text—textual sewing. Since Vieira was writing about what Bandarra had already written about future times, he had to mix several verb tenses—past, present, future—when interpreting Bandarra's *Trovas;* he had to retell and interpret some of Bandarra's prophecies using the present tense, others, the past, and the most important ones, the future. In a sense, while Vieira was composing "Hopes of Portugal" as an interpretation of a prophetic destiny, Bandarra, as a herald of the times to come and an authority of the Divine prophecies, was as alive as John IV, the deceased king who would be resurrected. History, as a mere mirror and effect of God's eternal will, could be written in the past, in the present, and in the future.[46]

"Hopes of Portugal" Reception and Vieira's Fifth Empire Further Impact

Besides the immediate reception by its recipients, André Fernandes and Queen Regent Luisa, "Hopes of Portugal" was read by the inquisitors and might have been read by members of the Portuguese court just after its arrival in 1659. More significantly, it stirred up some debate within the lettered and millenarian circles of 1660s Lisbon too. Produced in the same year (1661), two anonymous Sebastianist responses criticised Vieira's interpretation of Bandarra by, on the one hand, emulating an ironic if not Pyrrhonic tone, though, on the other, vigorously defending the Sebastianist position. So far as is known, only a Lisbon merchant of Flemish origin, Nicolas Bourey, came out in defence of Vieira's interpretation. Bouray composed his "To the incredulous of John IV's

---

[46] One should remember that Vieira did indeed write a *History of the Future*. There is a partial English translation of *History of the Future* in António Vieira, *The Sermon of Saint Anthony to the Fish and Other Texts* (Dartmouth: 2009), 77–106.

resurrection" in late 1660 while imprisoned, possibly for debt. Bouray's paper managed to circulate outside the prison walls perhaps through the same ways by which "Hopes of Portugal" had entered them. It swiftly ended up at the Inquisition palace in Lisbon, and Bouray was summoned by the inquisitors in April 1661. However, he was dismissed with no further charges after his testimony, as someone earnest in his beliefs but whom no one would take seriously.[47]

Aside from the responses to "Hopes of Portugal" in the 1660s Sebastianist debates, there was a more indirect yet pervasive reception of Vieira's paper. If one pays attention to Sebastianist manuscripts produced in late 17th century and throughout the 18th century, one will notice the presence of the term "hope" in Sebastianist titles. If this is not something unexpected in prophetical writings, as mentioned previously, this recurrence gains significance when one realises that many of these titles were attributed to Vieira. In this Vieira's Sebastianist "apocrypha", expressions such as "Hopes in King Sebastian", "Hope of King Sebastian", or "Hope of King Sebastian's coming" abounded; and in some cases, they were linked to Vieira's "Hopes of Portugal" by notes in the margin or in the Sebastianist texts' introduction. The evocation of "Hopes" title could be read as a strategy to legitimise and identify the Sebastianist "apocrypha" as valid interpretations of Vieira's Fifth Empire.[48]

In a sense, Vieira became the authority (*auctoritas*) on prophetism (and paradoxically on Sebastianism too), and his name and writings (whether legitimate or spurious) were like a synonym to the prophetical genre in the late 17th century and well into the 18th century. His Fifth Empire managed successfully to coin the bulk of imperial expectations for Portugal and to organise the providential discourse about the Portuguese Empire's future and destiny. Nevertheless, it was adapted and employed according to the (wider or lesser) interest of the successive Braganza rulers and their supporters, of the Sebastianists, and also of Vieira's detractors. It was even used as one of the excuses to justify the expulsion of the Jesuits in 1759, in the midst of the Enlightenment-inspired reforms led by the future Marquis of Pombal. From this enlightened but still conspiratorial perspective, "Hopes of Portugal" would be a deception

---

47 Besselaar transcribed, edited and presented the two Sebastianist papers and Bouray's paper together with his edition of "Hopes of Portugal". Besselaar, *Antônio Vieira*, 109–274.

48 Luís Filipe Silvério Lima, "Um 'apócrifo' de Vieira: discursos sebastianistas, leitura de impressos e circulação de manuscritos (séc. XVII–XVIII)", in *Poderes do Sagrado. Europa Católica, América Ibérica, África e Oriente portugueses (séculos XVI–XVIII)*, ed. Jacqueline Hermann and William Martins (Rio de Janeiro: 2016), 53–83.

to incite fanaticism, and Vieira would be the real author of Bandarra's *Trovas*, a mere forgery created by him as part of a bigger Jesuit plot to seize power while maintaining Portugal in the realm of superstition.[49]

However, the case of most interest for the present discussion is the interpretation of Vieira's Fifth Empire by Pedro de Rates Henequim, illegitimate son of a Dutch diplomat, who sought fortune in the Americas. Henequim's interpretation allows one to envision how the ideas presented on "Hopes of Portugal" and later on developed on *History of the Future* and *Clavis Prophetarum* had an impact on the Portuguese American scene. In the first half of the 18th Century, the discovery of gold mines in Minas Gerais, central Brazil, allowed some long unseen opulence in the Portuguese Empire, now under the rule of John V, grandson of John IV. Engaged in the gold rush, Henequim came to Brazil in 1702 and found himself impressed by its landscape and richness. While reading Vieira's prophetical works in the hills of Minas and combining them with his own cabbalistic and esoteric exegesis, he imagined a Fifth Empire with an even more central place to the New World. Henequim agreed with Vieira's imperial plan for the Portuguese Empire, and on the decisive role of the Brazilian Jesuitical mission, but he transferred the stage of the last act of human history from Portugal to the Americas: Brazil would be the head of the Fifth Empire. As a place of the end but also the start of world history, Henequim identified hidden signs that the Brazilian forests would have been the original location of the biblical Paradise. Eden's rivers were actually the great Portuguese American rivers, the Amazon and the São Francisco; the trees of Life and Knowledge were banana trees, in whose leaves Adam inscribed messages to his descendants, the Amerindians. In 1722, Henequim went back to Portugal to spread his word in the court, and in Lisbon, he was listened to by crowds in the streets. With fame as a visionary and popular support increasing, boldness also rose, and thus he proposed that prince Immanuel, John V's younger brother, should rise up against his sibling and king and flee to Brazil to start the Fifth Empire there, as Emperor of South America. Without any success, a riot was even planned in Minas to enthrone the new emperor. As a result, Henequim was arrested as a traitor and eventually denounced to the Inquisition as heretic because of his

---

49   José Seabra da Silva. *Deducção Chronologica e Analytica* (Lisbon: 1768), 204–208 (about Vieira forger of Bandarra), 229–230 (about "Hopes of Portugal" and Vieira ill-intended interpretation of Bandarra), cf. *Provas da Primeira Parte* (Lisbon: 1768), Divisão IX, 179–181, 213–214, 222–225, 230; "Edital da Real Mesa Censória de 10 de junho de 1768" in *Colleção das leys, decretos y alvarás, que comprehende o feliz reinado Del. Rey Fidelissimo D. Jozé o I*, t. II (Lisbon: 1770), 83–86. See Lima, "Um 'apócrifo' de Vieira", 53–54, 81–83; José Eduardo Franco, Bruno Cardoso Reis, *Vieira na Literatura Anti-Jesuítica* (Lisbon: 1997), 42–56.

Fifth Empire interpretation. Not as fortunate as Vieira, he was burnt at the stake on 21 July 1744.[50]

Far from being a mere anecdote,[51] Henequim's case shows the entanglements among the colonial reality, an Edenic perception of the New World, the imperial expectations, and the ubiquitous presence of Vieira's Fifth Empire. Henequim had contact with Vieira's prophetical texts in Minas Gerais and found there a propitious space to discuss them and develop a new version of the Fifth Empire, one founded in Brazil. But Henequim's hopes were no longer the ones of Portugal.

---

50 The most comprehensive study is Adriana Romeiro, *Um visionário na corte de D. João V* (Belo Horizonte: 2001). The Inquisition sentence was transcribed and edited by Pedro Tavares in his *Pedro Henequim. Proto-mártir da separação (1744)* (Lisbon: 2011), 73–119. Plinio Freire Gomes edited some of Henequim's writings in his book *Um herege vai ao Paraíso. Cosmologia de um ex-colono condenado pela Inquisição (1680–1744)* (São Paulo: 1997), 154–171.

51 A similar trial had occurred in the late 16th-century Peru, where Spanish Dominican Francisco de La Cruz was part of an apocalyptic upheaval and he argued that the millennial kingdom would take place in Peru. He was prosecuted by Lima's Inquisition and was sentenced to death by fire on 1 April 1578. For a comparison among La Cruz's, Vieira's, Henequim's, and other millenarian cases regarding the Americas, see Wachtel, "Theologies Marranes". See also: Adriano Prosperi, *America e apocalisse e altri saggi*, (Pisa: 1999), 16–18; Olivari, "Milenarismo y política", 146–150. La Cruz's trial proceedings were published in: *Francisco de la Cruz, Inquisición, Actas* (Madrid: 1996).

1. Hopes of Portugal.*
Fifth Empire of the World.
The First and the Second Life of King John IV.
Written by Gonçaliannes Bandarra.⁵²

My Lord, Bishop of Japan,⁵³

Your Lordship tells me about prodigies of the world and hopes of happiness for Portugal. Your Lordship says to me that all of them refer to the coming of

---

* Translation by Verônica Calsoni Lima, revision and footnotes by Luís Filipe Silvério Lima (English revision by Maria Rita Corrêa Vieira, whom we would like to thank). The translation was based on two editions of the "Esperanças de Portugal": Adma Fadul Muhana (ed.), *Os Autos do processo de Vieira na Inquisição: 1660–1668* (São Paulo: 2008), 39–70; José van den Besselaar, *Antônio Vieira. Profecia e polêmica* (Rio de Janeiro: 2002), 49–108. Muhana's and Besselaar's lessons are from two different manuscripts—neither of them the autograph, which is lost. Besselaar edited the copy transcribed in Vieira's Inquisition trial proceedings (Lisbon, National Archives "Torre do Tombo", Tribunal do Santo Ofício, Inquisição de Lisboa, Proc. 1664, "Processo de Padre Antônio Vieira", First part, fols 5–21). Muhana transcribed a copy existing in a volume of the General Council of the Holy Office's books, which most likely is the copy used by the inquisitors to build their case against Vieira (Lisbon, National Archives "Torre do Tombo", Tribunal do Santo Ofício, Conselho Geral, liv. 266, fols 289–316). The other copy, from the trial proceedings, can be accessed online: http://digitarq.arquivos.pt/details?id=2301562. Many of the notes were based on Besselaar's edition and commentaries.

52 Antônio Vieira (1608–1697), or some copyist, wrote in the title that "Gonçaliannes Bandarra" (and not him) was the author of "Hopes of Portugal". Gonçalo Anes Bandarra (c.1500–1556), a cobbler from a small Portuguese village, Trancoso, wrote several prophetical quatrains, known as *Trovas de Bandarra* in the first half of the 16th century, for which he was prosecuted and convicted by the Inquisition of Lisbon in 1541. The *Trovas*, one of the main themes of "Hopes of Portugal" as we will see, has had a tremendous impact in Luso-Brazilian history and culture and, in the early modern period was interpreted as prophetical evidence of the imperial and divine destiny of Portugal. It was one of the key elements both for Sebastianism and for the defence of the new Braganza dynasty. They became the source for the Sebastianist and for a broader Portuguese and Luso-Brazilian messianism until the 19th century (for more information about Bandarra, Sebastianism, and the *Trovas*, see introduction to "Hopes of Portugal" and Jacqueline Hermann's chapter in this volume). Posing as a mere interpreter of Bandarra's prophecies, Vieira put himself in the role of a glossator of an "authority" (*auctorictas*) more than author of the paper. About this aspect and the possible textual and readership implications, see the introduction.

53 The Jesuit André Fernandes (1607–1660) was nominated Bishop of Japan by John IV in 1649. However, André Fernandes was never consecrated as bishop since Rome would not recognise the new Braganza dynasty until 1668, when Portugal and Spain eventually signed a peace treaty. John IV also chose him to be his son's confessor and afterwards his own too.

King Sebastian,[54] about whose coming and life I had already said to Your Lordship what I believe.[55] Lastly, Your Lordship commands me that I provide some greater clarity about what I had repeated so many times to Your Lordship concerning the future resurrection of our good lord and master King John IV.

The matter is too wide and not appropriate for writing en route as I am doing, afloat in a canoe in which I have been sailing to the river of the Amazons,[56] to send this paper by another that will reach the ship that is in Maranhão[57] preparing to depart to Lisbon.

---

54 Like many of Vieira's correspondents, André Fernandes believed that Bandarra's *Trovas* referred to King Sebastian's return. He was what was called a Sebastianist, i.e., someone who believed that Sebastian I (1554–1578) would return to lead the Portuguese kingdom and that the prophecies circulating in the Portuguese Empire were about his return. Although Vieira, on several occasions, mocked what he called the "seita" (sect) of the Sebastianists, he still tried to dissuade his Sebastianist interlocutors of their reading— and to defend his position when challenged by them. See Antônio Vieira, "Carta 223. A D. Teodósio de Melo" [10/8/1665] in *Obra Completa*, t. I, vol. II (Lisbon: 2013), 516. Reading Vieira's letters of the late 1650s and 1660s, it seems, however, that Vieira's interpretation of Bandarra was the weaker position amid the prophetical interpretations in the Portuguese Empire, mainly pervaded by the belief of the Sebastianist "sect". As matter of fact, Besselaar points out that a significant increase of Sebastianist texts occurred after the death of John IV, with a new succession crisis and, most of all, the delay in the fulfilment of the promised Imperial future with the Braganza dynasty. The proximity of the ominous year 1666 would also create a sense of urgency in the apocalyptic expectations which were not met in the figure of the new Braganza king, Afonso VI, John I's son. Van Den Besselaar, chap. VI. For Vieira and the Sebastianists, see Eduardo D'Oliveira França, *Portugal na Época da Restauração* (1951; repr. São Paulo: 1997), 250–259; Jacqueline Hermann, *No Reino do Desejado* (São Paulo: 1998), chap. 4; Lauri Tähtinen "The Intellectual Construction of the Fifth Empire: Legitimating the Braganza Restoration", *History of European Ideas*, 38/3 (2012), 413–425. About Sebastianism and its sources, see also Jacqueline Hermann's chapter in this volume.

55 "sinto". In early modern Portuguese, the verb "sentir", feel, could mean "to opine, to think, to be of opinion, to give one's opinion or judgement". Antonyo Vieyra, *A Dictionary of the Portuguese and English Languages*, vol. 1 (London: 1773), s.p., "Sentir". In fact, this was sentir's first meaning in Antonyo Vieyra's *Dictionary* as well as in the famous Bluteau's *Vocabulário*. Nowadays the most recurrent usages of "sentir" (to feel something with our senses, to have feelings about something ...) appeared after this now archaic use. Rafael Bluteau, *Vocabulario portuguez & latino*, vol. 7 (Coimbra: 1712–1728), 590, "Sentir". The same occurred in English. See "feel, v.", *Oxford English Dictionnary* online (hereafter OED Online) (http://www.oed.com/view/Entry/68977?isAdvanced=false&result=2&rskey =venqqb&, accessed 08 March 2018).

56 "Rio das Almazonas", i.e., the Amazon river. Here, Vieira used an old form of the river's name, which refers to the alleged presence of the Amazons, the mythical female warriors, in the region.

57 Maranhão probably refers to the capital of the State of Maranhão and Grão-Pará, São Luís

To summarise everything to one fundamental syllogism, I would say:
- Bandarra is a true prophet;
- Bandarra prophesied that King John IV shall do many things which he has not yet done, nor can he do them but by resurrecting;
- Therefore, King John IV shall be resurrected.

These three propositions only, I will prove; and it seems to me they will suffice for the greater clarity wished by Your Lordship.

Proving the consequence of this syllogism

Correctly gathering the consequence of this syllogism is a matter of clear and evident reasoning:[58] if Bandarra is a true prophet, as it is proposed, it follows that his prophecies shall infallibly be fulfilled and that King John shall do what Bandarra has prophesied about him; and as King John cannot do these things being dead, as he is, it follows—with the same infallibility—that he shall be resurrected. This inference is not only a matter of reasoning, but also of faith. Abraham inferred it and so Saint Paul confirmed it when he clarified Abraham's reasoning at the moment in which God had ordered Abraham to sacrifice and kill Isaac about whom the same God had made many promises that had not yet been fulfilled. *Fide obtulit Abraam Isaac* (says Saint Paul), *cum tentaretur, et Unigenitum offerebat, qui susceperat repromissiones, ad quem dictum est. "Quia in Isaac vocabitur tibi semen": arbitrans quai et a mortuis suscitare potens est Deus.*[59]

(also known as São Luís of Maranhão). Founded by the French in 1612 to be the centre of the Equinoctial France, the settlement was conquered by the Portuguese armies in 1615, and in 1621 it became the capital of the newly created State of Maranhão (later State of Maranhão and Grão-Pará).

58 "discurso". As Besselaar points out, "discurso" more properly means reasoning in this passage, evoking a now rare and archaic use of the term (see first and second meanings of "discourse" in *OED*: "discourse, n.", *OED Online*). In Bluteau's *Vocabulário*, the first meaning for "discurso" is "uso da razão, *Rationis usus*" ("use of reason"), followed by "ato da faculdade discursiva" ("the act of discursive faculty") and by its description as a "Termo Dialéctico" ("Dialetic term"): "terceira operação, ou (...) gráo de operação do Entendimento (...) por meio delle vai a razão correndo de uma proposição para outra (...)" ("third operation, or level of operation of Understanding by which reason courses from one proposition to another"). Bluteau, *Vocabulario*, vol. 3, 245.

59 Heb. 11:17–19. "By faith Abraham, when he was tried, offered Isaac: and he that had received the promises, offered up his only begotten son; (To whom it was said: In Isaac shall thy seed be called.) Accounting that God is able to raise up even from the dead." All the biblical quotations in English are from the Douay-Rheims Bible (1899 North American version), unless otherwise stated.

Therefore, when Abraham was on his way to sacrifice Isaac in whom God had promised much still-not-fulfilled happiness and his house's succession to him, Abraham pondered: "God promised me that Isaac shall be the foundation of my lineage; God orders me to kill the same Isaac: therefore, if God does not repeal his decree, and if Isaac indeed dies, it follows that God shall resurrect him". This was Abraham's conclusion, this is mine after King John IV's death, as it was already when His Majesty was in the great danger of Salvaterra,[60] in which I so many times and so continuously repeated, and afterwards preached that, either the King should not die, or, if he does, he should be resurrected; so I said in his life, so I preached in his obsequies,[61] so I believe and hope; and so shall believe and hope as an infallible consequence, all that have Bandarra as a true prophet, which is what I will show now.

Proving the first proposition of the syllogism

The true proof of men having prophetic spirit is the success of the things prophesied by them; so does the Church prove in the canonisation of saints, and so do the same the canonical prophets, who are part of the Sacred Scripture. Apart from the principles of faith, there is no other proof of the truth of their revelations or prophecies but the demonstration of having been fulfilled what they had prophesied so many years before.

God Himself provided this rule to know the true from the false prophet: *Quod si tacita cogitatione responderis—Quomodo possum intelligere verbum quod Dominus non est loquutus? Hoc habebis signum, quod in nomine Domini propheta ille praedixerit et non evenerit, hoc Dominus non est locutus.*[62] In chapter eighteen of Deuteronomy, God promised the Hebrew people that he would give them prophets from their nation. Because it was not unusual for false prophets' arising among the same people, and because it was difficult to recognise which of them were the sent-by-God and true ones, the same God

---

60   In 1654, John IV felt gravely ill when visiting the village of Salvaterra, in Portugal, where there was a royal palace. As he returned to Portugal from the State of Maranhão and Grão-Pará, Vieira comforted the queen and, after the king's recovery, preached a thanksgiving sermon with messianic tones.

61   See Antônio Vieira, "Sermão das Exequias do Augustissimo Rey D. João IV" in *Sermões varios, e tratados ainda não impressos*, vol. 15 (Lisbon: 1748), 280.

62   Deut. 18:21–22 ("And if in silent thought thou answer: How shall I know the word that the Lord hath not spoken? Thou shalt have this sign: Whatsoever that same prophet foretelleth in the name of the Lord, and it cometh not to pass: that thing the Lord hath not spoken, but the prophet hath forged it by the pride of his mind: and therefore thou shalt not fear him.").

provided as a safe rule in order to know one from another whether what they had prophesied succeeded or not: "If what the prophet says does not succeed, take him as false, and if what he says succeeds, take him as a truthful one and sent by Me."[63] Therefore, it cannot be denied that Bandarra was a true prophet, because he wrote and prophesied many years ago so many precise, minute, and particular things, which we have seen all fulfilled with our own eyes; from which I will briefly point out here a few which will suffice. All of them presented in the same form and within the same order they were written.

Firstly, Bandarra prophesied that, before the year 40, it should rise in Portugal what he calls "great storm" (which was the rising of Évora)[64] and that the intents of this storm should be other than what was showed, because truly they were to rise all the Kingdom, and that storm should be soon tamed, and then all should be silent, and the risen ones would not have followers or someone who animated them, as it followed. That is what those verses mean:

> Before the forties close,
> A great storm will arise
> Of which attempts,
> That it will soon be tamed,
> And they will take the road
> Silently,
> They will not have who lash them.[65]

Be warned that these verses shall be read between parentheses, because they do not make sense with the immediately next three verses which tie with the ones above; and these keep carrying on the story with the ones that follow afterwards—such an ordinary style in the prophets as well known by the ones who read it.

Yet Bandarra prophesied that there shall come a time when the Portuguese (who had a king and kingdom while he was writing) shall desire a change

---

63 This is not part of Deutoronomy, but it was shown as a logical consequence of the biblical narrative.

64 Between August and November 1637, popular riots against the Spanish rule, the "alterações" (disturbances) or "levantamento" (rising) of Évora took place in the capital of the Alentejo, Évora, and became one of the most important and serious revolts against Phillip IV and his viceroys before the Restoration of 1640.

65 Cf. Gonçalo Annes Bandarra, *Trovas do Bandarra Apuradas e impressas, por ordem de hum grande Senhor de Portugal. Offereçidas aos verdadeiros Portugueses, devotos do Encuberto* (Nantes: 1644), 35, stanza 86 (from now on *Trovas*, followed by the stanza number).

of state and long for a time to come; and that the fulfilment of this desire and this time shall be in the year 40; and in this year 40 there shall be a king, not old, but new, not introduced by himself, but raised by the kingdom; and not with the title of defender of the country, as some wanted, but with the title of king; and that this king shall take up arms and raise his flags against Castile, which for a long time had desired and eventually conquered the kingdom of Portugal. This is clearly said in the verses of the same *Dream*:[66]

> Finally the desired time
> Has come,
> According to what the clasp binds together;[67]
> The forties are already coming,
> Which it has been invoked
> By a Doctor[68] already gone.
> The new king is arisen,
> He already makes a shout,
> He already looms his flag
> Against the breeding griffon,

---

66 In the 1644 edition, Bandarra's *Trovas* were divided in three "Dreams".
67 "segundo firmal assenta". In his "Representações" presented as his defence to the Inquisition, Vieira interpreted these same verses and said that "Firmal" meant a firm and imutable decree of God ("he o decreto firme & imutavel de Deos"), Antônio Vieira, *Defesa perante o tribunal do Santo Ofício*, vol. 1 (Salvador, Brazil: 1957), 55. However, a more common meaning of "firmal" (and maybe more suitable to the verses' context as well as to Vieira's interpretation in "Hopes") was a clasp, a latch of a horse halter ("são as pontas do cabresto, que se atão nas argolas das ilhargas"), or a brooch or clasp to fasten or tighten a piece of wardrobe, a belt, etc. ("Peça com que se prendião os golpes dos vestidos antigos. (...) broche") Raphael Bluteau, *Vocabulario*, vol. 4, 129, "firmal"; Antonio de Moraes Silva, *Diccionario da lingua portugueza*, vol. 2 (Lisbon: 1813), 36, "firmál".
68 In "Representações", Vieira said that the "Doctor" in the verse would refer to Isidore of Seville (560–636) and that Isidore would have named the "Desired Time" in his prophecies. However, Vieira was not quoting the Bishop of Seville's actual writings but rather pseudo-Isidore's prophecies which had circulated in the Iberian Peninsula since the late 14th century. These prophecies in verses were one of the main sources for the "Hidden One" myth ("Encubierto", in Spanish, or "Encoberto", in Portuguese) and had a noticeable influence on Bandarra's *Trovas*. Vieira, *Defesa perante o tribunal do Santo Ofício*, 55. About the "Encubierto" or "Encoberto": Pablo Pérez García and Jorge Antonio Catalá Sanz, *Epígonos del encubertismo. Proceso contra los agermanados de 1541* (Valencia: 2000); Sarah Nalle, "El Encubierto revisited: Navigating between visions of Heaven and Hell on earth", in *Werewolves, Witches, and Wandering Spirits*, ed. Kathryn A. Edwards (Kirksville, M.O.: 2002), 77–92.

> Gluttonous and greedy,[69]
> That has enjoyed such pastures.[70]

The griffon very appropriately means Castile, because kingdoms distinguish themselves by their arms, and the griffon is an animal made of a lion and an eagle, which greatly symbolises with the eagles and lions such principal parts of Castile's coat of arms. And he calls it, with the same propriety, "breeding griffon", because, by births and marriages, Castile was able to inherit so many kingdoms and states as it has nowadays—and that was also the title by which Castile entered Portugal.

Bandarra prophesied yet: that the new king shall be from the House of the Infant;[71] that he shall be named John, that he shall be happy and fortunate; and that he shall promptly receive news from all the Conquests (called "prized lands" by Bandarra) which would declare themselves for the new king, and from thenceforth they would be his steady supporters. All of this has been fully witnessed, and also all about the hope of everybody and of the same king have I heard him telling many times. The verses are in the same *First Dream*:

> Get out, get out, this
> fortunate Infant!
> His name is Sir John.[72]

---

69 "Lagomeira". "Lagomeira", here translated as greedy, was not a common word in Portuguese, even in the 17th century. Other Bandarra's commentators before Vieira tried to explain its meaning, such as Jesuit João de Vasconcelos, in his *Restauração de Portugal Prodigiosa* (1643). For João de Vasconcelos, the term had been used to describe a cow that never stops grazing and keeps eating grass in any place. João de Vasconcelos, *Restauração de Portugal prodigiosa* (Lisbon: 1643), 124–125. Vieira presented another explanation in his defence in the Inquisition trial, saying that "logomeira" (or "langomeira") was a term from Bandarra's region which meant gluttony. Vieira, *Defesa perante o tribunal do Santo Ofício*, 57. Both authors pointed out that the adjective was used prophetically by Bandarra to qualify the Spanish Crown's hunger for power and lands.

70 *Trovas*, 87.

71 Infant ("Infante" or "Infanta") is a title given to Portuguese and Spanish royal princes and princesses who are not the heir apparent.

72 "Dom João". In other versions of the *Trovas*, it was written "Fuão" instead of "João". "Foão" (or "Foam", "Fuão", "Fuam") was used when a person was unknown or you did not know the name of a person ("fulano" in current Portuguese). These versions were considered the most reliable by the Sebastianists, who understood that Dom Foão should be read as King Sebastian. Vieira and other Braganza supporters strongly disagreed with this interpretation and rejected all the versions with "Foão" as poor copies (Vieira, *Defesa*, 58; for more Braganza supporters' sources, see José Van Den Besselaar, "Dom Foão ou Dom João?" in *Antônio Vieira*, 402–404). In his 1918 *A Evolução do Sebastianismo*, João Lúcio de Azevedo

Take and carry the pennon
Glorious and triumphant
News shall come in an instant
From those prized lands,
Which are declared
And affirmed
For the King now on.[73]

He prophesied yet more, and with prodigious circumstances: He said that in the aforementioned "prized lands", or Conquests, there shall be two viceroys at that time, something that never happened either before or after. One of them (who was the Marquis of Montalvão)[74] shall be acute,[75] and the other (who was the

---

seemed to partially agree with Vieira and the brigantines. He said that in handwritten letters as "F" and "J" could be misread, and it was possible that at some point "Dom João" was read as "Dom Foão", which if not favouring the Sebastianist claim at least would not present an interpretative problem for them. João Lúcio de Azevedo, *A Evolução do Sebastianismo* (1918; repr. Lisbon: 1984), 43–44. However, as Eduardo D'Oliveira França and others have pointed out, it is quite likely that the shift from "Foão" to "João" had taken place during the early Restoration years as an attempt to reinforce John IV legitimacy and popular support to the Portuguese throne. França, *Portugal na Época da Restauração*, 251. Notwithstanding, if "Dom Foão" was indeed Bandarra's first option, it might indicate a taste for irony: "Foão" was someone without a name, who could be anybody, a regular and common person, a nobody, a commoner; whereas the honorific "Dom", derived from the Latin "Dominus", indicated nobility, a (sur)name, distinction, up to the point to be used as title of kings.

73 *Trovas*, 88.
74 Jorge de Mascarenhas (1570–1652), first Marquis of Montalvão, had been governor of Mazagão, now El Jadida, (1615–1619) and Tangiers (1622–1624), in Morocco, and of Algarve, before being nominated first Viceroy of Brazil in 1639 by Phillip IV (III of Portugal). When the news about the 1640 Restoration reached Salvador, capital of the State (or vice-reign) of Brazil, he promptly dispatched a ship to Lisbon with a greeting committee formed by his son, several local authorities and priests, including Antonio Vieira. Nevertheless, because of his successful career during the Iberian Union and his family's support for the Spanish Habsburgs, he was accused of being part of the pro-Spanish party and lost his office in Brazil, returning to Lisbon as a prisoner. Eventually, he managed to prove his loyalty to the new dynasty of Braganza, gained prominence over John IV and became the head of the Ultramarine Council in 1643. His good position within the court did not last, though. Accused again of supporting the Habsburg claims to the throne, he was arrested once more in 1644, now losing all the titles too. One more time, he managed to be freed, to receive his titles back and to gain the royal favour. But not for long. Denounced once again for treason, he was arrested in January 1649, and died in prison on 31 January, 1652. See Lorrain White, "Dom Jorge Mascarenhas, Marquês de Montalvão (1579?–1652), and Changing Traditions of Service in Portugal and the Portuguese Empire", *Portuguese Studies Review* 12/2 (2004–2005), 63–83.
75 "agudo". In 17th-century Portuguese, the word "Agudo" might be more properly translated

Earl of Aveiras)[76] shall be stern and hairy. The first would not be remanded, or kept in the government, i.e., he would be removed from it. Bandarra declared yet: he should be called Excellency, and the motives for him being removed would be suspicions of infidelity. But this infidelity should not be in his shield, as truly it was not at that time, because he, as the same Bandarra said, was the means for the King's acclamation in Bahia[77] and in all Brazil, since he sent the orders for King John to be acclaimed. On the contrary, the Earl of Aveiras would put some difficulty and resistance to the King's acclamation in the State of India, and that State, with great desire and impetus, and freed from the viceroy's restraints, was to acclaim him, as it did. The verses say in the same *Dream*:

> I do not find him to be remanded,
> The Acute,
> His being the instrument;
> I do not find (as I feele)[78]
> The Excellent[79]

---

as "Witty", as the concept of "agudeza" in Portuguese or Spanish (or "accutezza", in Italian) corresponded to the early modern English notion of "wit" (or "witze", in German). However, "agudo" (as acute) could also denote having a slim, sharp shape; another meaning used by Vieira to make Bandarra's "Agudo" concur with Marquis of Montalvão's character, as explained further in "Hopes".

76 João da Silva Telo e Meneses (c.1600–1651), First Earl of Aveiras, was vice-Roy of India (the eastern domains of the Portuguese Empire) between 1640 and 1645.

77 Bahia was how the Captaincy of the Bay ("Bahia") of All Saints was known, today part of the state of Bahia in northeast Brazil. Captaincies were administrative divisions and hereditary fiefs of the State of Brazil. Bahia was one the most important and richest captaincies of Brazil and, until the mid-18th century, it was the seat of the capital of Governorate General of Brazil, later State of Brazil. It was located in the city of São Salvador da Bahia de Todos os Santos (Saint Saviour from the Bay of All Saints), founded in 1549 as capital of the Governorate General. In this passage, "Bahia" is a metonym for Salvador of Bahia as head of the State of Brazil, where Vieira resided at the time of John IV's acclamation (1640). About the indistinctness between Salvador and Bahia as "heads" of Brazil, see Pedro Puntoni, *O Estado do Brasil* (São Paulo: 2013), chap. 2 "'Como coração no meio do corpo': Salvador, capital do Estado do Brasil"; Cf. Guida Marques, "'Por ser cabeça do Estado do Brasil'. As representações da cidade da Bahia no século XVII", in *Salvador da Bahia: retratos de uma cidade atlântica*, ed. Evergton Sales Souza, Guida Marques and Hugo R. Silva (Salvador: 2016), 24–30.

78 "segundo sento". We used "Feele", an archaic form of "feel", to indicate the difference between Bandarra's use of the older form of the verb "sentir", "sento", and the 17th-century (and now) more recurrent form, "sinto", in Portuguese.

79 "Excelento". "Excelento" is a word apparently created by Bandarra. It would be the masculine form of the adjective "Excelente" (Excellent), though here used as a noun. Vieira commented on Bandarra's wording below when he interpreted the meaning of the verses.

> To be false in his shield;
> But I think that the Woolly,
> Very circumspect,
> Will pluck the cat,
> And will make it to wall the rat,
> Of his belongings,[80]
> Leaving it all naked.[81]

Because this is Bandarra's most difficult quatrain,[82] and it is the one that no one could ever make sense, I want to comment upon it verse by verse, for a better understanding.

"I do not find him to be remanded": Everyone who governed the Portuguese garrisons in the conquests were remanded or detained in there, because the King conserved them in the same posts. Marquis of Montalvão was the only one Your Majesty ordered to be withdrawn from his post because of his sons' escape and of the marchioness's inclinations.[83] And because of that Bandarra says he does not think he is remanded.

"The Acute": Anyone who has met the Marquis knows how well the word "acute" fits him, because of the natural smartness in all his actions and accomplishments, and yet in the features and body movements; but more than everything in the inventing, tracing, trading, introducing himself, etc.

"For his being the instrument": In many parts[84] the people were the instrument of the acclamation, and not the ones who ruled. In Brazil the Marquis of Montalvão was the instrument of the acclamation, which he did execute with great prudence and dexterity, because there were in Bahia two thirds of Castilians and one third of Neapolitans, who could sustain the interests of Castile or, at least, cause rampages.

---

80 "Fato". According to Vieira (see his explanations further in the text), "fato" could mean both clothes as things, properties.
81 *Trovas*, 89.
82 "trova". "Trova" refers both to a ballad composed by a troubadour (and by extension, a poet) and to a (usually four-line) rhymed stanza which characterises this genre of poetry.
83 After the Restoration, Marquis of Montalvão's eldests sons, Pedro de Mascarenhas and Jerônimo de Mascarenhas, fled from Portugal to Gibraltar on 7 February 1641 and declared allegiance to Philip IV. His wife, well known for her pro-Spanish sentiments, was accused of having influenced their sons' defection and was imprisoned in the castle of Arraiolos. See White, "Dom Jorge Mascarenhas, Marquês de Montalvão (1579?–1652)".
84 Parts ("Partes") of the Portuguese Empire.

"I do not find (as I feele)": Notice the "as I feele", or "as I feel"[85] (here Bandarra is already speaking with some doubt about the fidelity of the Marquis, which he vouched in this place).[86] It is certainly a fact that the Marquis had been loyal for a long time; the way by which he ended the verse showed that he was not always loyal.

"The Excellent": He calls him Excellency for being a marquis and viceroy, since he was the only viceroy and the only marquis who has ever governed Brazil;[87] but Bandarra saw all these circumstances. But why does he not call him "Excellent" instead of "Excellency"? Undoubtedly he utters this so disused masculine form so that one could infer its difference from the feminine—as if he had said: Be aware that the fidelity of what I say belongs to the husband, and not to the wife; to the "Excellent", and not to the "Excelenta",[88] as he explains as follows.

"To be false in his shield": Since Bandarra was puzzled by the fact that the Marquis was ousted but not remanded, as he was the instrument of the acclamation, it seems it was enough to say he was not false; But he added: "in his shield", because at the same time he saw the Marquis's loyalty in the acclamation, he also saw his wife and sons' infidelity, as if he said: False, not in his shield, but in his wife's and in his sons'.[89]

"But I think that the Woolly": The earl of Aveiras was very hairy and bearded, as we all saw. He had too much hair in the eyebrows, in the ears, inside and outside the nose, and only inside of the eyes he did not have hair, although the beard got very close to them. And I heard from his nephew, the earl of Unhão, D. Rodrigo,[90] that his uncle had as much wool over his body as sheep. That is why Bandarra calls him "Woolly".

"Very circumspect": Only when he went to India for the second time, he was not.[91] But in his speech, in his silence, in his walk, in his trade, and in all his

---

85 "note-se muito o 'segundo sento', ou 'segundo sinto'." See note 78.
86 We decided to translate "lugar", "lugares", when referring to passages in a text, literally as "place", "places", also because of the relation with the rhetorical notion of "locus", "locis", a now obsolete meaning of the term in English. See "place, n.1, 7.c", *OED Online*.
87 At least, until 1659. In 1684, Antônio Luís de Sousa (1644–1721), Marquis of Minas, was appointed governor of Brazil.
88 "Excelenta" would be the feminine form of "Excelento". See note 79.
89 See note 83.
90 Rui (or Rodrigo) Teles de Castro (?–1671), second Earl of Unhão. In 1651, Vieira delivered the funeral sermon of Rui Teles de Castro's father, the first Earl of Unhão. Rui is another form for Rodrigo.
91 Vieira was probably referring to the fact that João da Silva Telo e Meneses died on his way to India to assume the position of Viceroy of Portuguese India for the second time, in 1651.

actions, inside and outside, there is no doubt that the Earl of Aveiras had those traces by which the World calls the men circumspect; and that is how the King defined him even when he did not commend him.

"Who will pluck the cat, And make it to wall the rat": The cat means the State of India, which wanted to acclaim the new King publicly as soon as the acclamation news arrived to Goa from Portugal. However, the Viceroy plucked it, because he curbed the people's and soldiers' impulse, shutting himself inside the Palace to consider, as having a circumspect temper as he had, what he should do in such a great matter. That was the only reason for the delay, or waiting for the acclamation in Goa. This is explained by the walling for the rat by the cat, meaning the waiting or delay,[92] in which the cat seems to be in doubt whether he is going to attack or not.

"Of his belongings, Leaving it all naked": as if disgusted by him, Bandarra concludes against the earl, saying he would leave the State of India denuded: because he brought from India plenty of goods,[93] which in India is properly called belongings,[94] as in Italy it is called "roba".[95] I based myself upon the lesser opinion of Bandarra about the earl of Aveiras to say to His Majesty, when the King made him viceroy of India for a second time, that I was greatly surprised at the fact that His Majesty elected as viceroy of India a man about whom Bandarra spoke so badly. The results proved indeed that it could not have been well succeeded.

---

92 Using a recurrent strategy in his texts, Vieira sought to provide more evidence for his interpretation by indicating a phonetic similitude between words. "Murar/muro" (walling/wall) are phonetically close to "mora" (a legal term that indicates a malicious and ill-intended delay in a payment); therefore, Vieira might say, this points out the correct understanding of the term in the verses and reveals the historical event to which it was referring. Though whimsical to our view, Vieira's understanding (and use) of phonetics was embedded in the Thomistic-Scholastic assumption that analogy and homology were a necessary result of a common First Cause, God and his act of creating the world. By having the same original cause and being the effects of divine creation, not only did it mean that all things were analogous by having the same attribute, but it also meant that they participate in His will, though at different hierarchical levels. In this act of will, any part of the Creation, regardless of how small it was, would have a role and a place. As part of this Divine plan, the language was not arbitrary, but rather a result of the Creation. Hence, the names of things reflected their essence as things created by God (being a reflection of God), and the words expressed a substance in their oral sound, as well as in their written form. In this world understood as reflection of its Maker, the phonetic proximity of words should be read as hints of His plan and a way to try to reach His veiled design.
93 "fazenda".
94 "fato".
95 Vieira played with multiples meanings of Portuguese "fazenda" (wealth, goods, estate, property, fabric), and Italian "roba" (stuff, things, clothes).

All these verses I have been referring to are continuous, and in them it is described the success of the King's acclamation in the Kingdom and in the conquests, with all their circumstances. Then it follows immediately next, in the same First Dream:

> Fear not, the Turk,
> In this season,
> Neither his great Moorism,
> That did not know the baptism,
> Neither the Christening;
> He is cattle in confusion.[96]

These verses contain an admirable circumstance of prophecy, because not only Bandarra prophesied and declared the things that shall be, and the time when they shall be, but also the times and conjunctions in which they shall not be. Bandarra's main subject is the war that the King shall make against the Turks, and the victory that he shall achieve. And for us not imagining that this enterprise should be soon after the people's acclamation of the king, Bandarra warns, and wants us to warn, that the Turk's enterprise was not for the time of the acclamation, but for another time, and for another season, long after. And for this he says that in this new season the Turk can be without fear: "Fear not, the Turk, in this season", etc.[97]

To this negative prophecy about the Turk, another negative one is added about the Pope, by which Bandarra implies that the Pope would not recognise the King,[98] until after the Turk crosses the Church's lands. So clearly say and imply the verses of the *Second Dream*:

> The new King is awaken
> He already makes shout,

---

96 *Trovas*, 90.
97 It is not clear in this passage if Vieira referred to the fear of an Ottoman invasion or to the Ottomans' fear of a war against the Portuguese. Bandarra's verses seemed to refer to the fact that the Portuguese or Christians do not need to fear the Ottomans, but the verse "Não tema o Turco, não" (which we have translated "Fear not, the Turk") could be read as "The Turk shall not fear". As Vieira went with this latter meaning, we opted for putting comas, as if in a vocative, to maintain the ambiguity explored by Vieira in his interpretation. Some pages below, Vieira's reading turns more explicit.
98 Vieira was probably referring to the fact that, at that time, Rome, a strong ally of Habsburg Spain, had not yet recognised the new Portuguese dynasty. This would not happen until the peace treaty of 1668 by which Spain accepted Portugal's independence, putting an end to the Restoration Wars.

> His cry already resounds,
> Levi already gives him the hand,
> Against the rambunctious Shechem.[99]

This couplet will be explained later. For now, it is enough to say that Levi is the Pope, and Shechem, the Turk; and when Shechem disturbs the lands of the Church, Levi will give the hand to the new king, who will already be awaken at this time. What one shall regard in this verse is the word "Already": "Levi already gives him the hand", through which Bandarra implies that the Pope has not wanted to give a hand to the new king up to this point. In fact, none of the three Popes—Urban, Innocent, and Alexander—[100] wanted to give a hand to him up until today, not recognising him, although they were requested by the King, by the clergy and by the people, through so many sorts of embassies.[101] Many times I said to the King, especially when he sent me to Rome,[102] that the Pope would not give bishops to us;[103] and when there was news that he had already given or wanted to give them, I have always laughed about it whether my being in Portugal or in Maranhão. Witnesses of this are all those who have many times heard me saying that the Pope would not give us bishops, but the Turk would.

---

99   *Trovas*, 99.
100 Urban VIII (r.1623–1644), Innocent X (r.1644–1655), Alexander XVII (r.1655–1667).
101 Until 1659, there were four Portuguese missions to Rome trying to receive the Holy See's recognition. In 1641, an official embassy led by the Bishop of Lamego was sent by John IV to the Papal court, but failed to be received by Urban VIII due to the Spanish influence in Rome. Worried about the effects of the broken relations in the Portuguese church, particularly regarding the confirmation of new bishops, the Portuguese clergy sent, in 1645, the prior of Cedofeita as their proxy to request the newly seated pope, Innocent X, to consider the acceptance of the new dynasty, without, however, any success. In 1649, the three States of Portugal gathered in the "Cortes" (the parliament representing the People, the Nobles, and the Clergy) unsuccessfully petitioned Innocent X for the recognition of Portugal's new sovereign through the Portuguese Church's agent in Rome, friar Manuel Álvares Carrilho. After Innocent X's death, another attempt was made and the experienced Portuguese ambassador Francisco de Sousa Coutinho was sent by the king. Though Coutinho had been granted an audience and had apparently been well received by the new pope, Alexander XVII, he did not achieve Portugal's intended goal. José Pedro Paiva, "A igreja e o poder" in *História Religiosa de Portugal*, ed. Carlos Moreira Azevedo, vol. 2 (Lisbon: 2000), 158–163.
102 In 1650, Vieira was sent by John IV to Italy to find a bride for the prince and heir apparent, Theodosius.
103 With the broken relations with the Holy See, all the possible new Bishop nominations made by John IV could be considered void since the pope would not recognise the new king's power to do so and therefore would not confirm the newly appointed bishops.

The fact of Our Lord Infant Afonso's being our king[104] and the fact of Joane Mendes de Vasconcelos'[105] being governor of our arms[106] have also been prophesied by Bandarra. About the Infant, he said:

> I see an Infant climbing
> On the top of all the timber.[107]

Everybody, as a natural consequence, imagined that and waited for the Prince Theodosius, who has been in Heaven, to be the one who should have succeeded the King, his father, and for him to be the one who should have climbed on the top of all the timber, according to the turnings of what Bandarra has called the "triumphant wheel".[108] Yet, the one was the Infant Afonso, God save him, because it was written so. Many times the King, Your Lordship, and that very Prince heard me say that Bandarra had not a word to say about the latter.

About Joanes Mendes, he says:

---

104 Afonso VI (1643–1683) was not the heir-apparent, hence the title Infant Prince. His elder brother, Theodosius, was raised to be the heir of John IV, but he died of tuberculosis in 1653 at the age of 19. Afonso was appointed as the heir in the Courts of 1653, although the rumours of his mental instability and paralysis from a childhood illness made many in the reign suspicious of his capability of becoming king. When John IV died in 1656, he was acclaimed king, but since he was only 13 years old (as well as considered by many unfit to reign), his mother, queen Luisa de Guzmán, assumed the regency and became the Portuguese ruler *de facto*. In the following paragraph, Vieira would insist on the opposition between Infant and Prince, as a way to highlight what he then thought was the correct interpretation of Bandarra's verses.

105 Joane Mendes de Vasconcelos, son of the writer and nobleman Luís Mendes de Vasconcelos (1542–1623), came to Brazil to fight against the Dutch armies in 1625, and stayed as a military commander until the Restoration of 1640. Returning to Portugal, he was soon named "Mestre de campo general" (a general-officer rank) in 1643, reached the position of "governador das armas" (governor of arms, see note below) in 1652, and was appointed governor of the province of Alentejo in 1658, at the time in which he led the unsuccessful 1658 Siege of Badajoz. Because of the defeat in Badajoz and under suspicion of treason, the Regent Queen ordered that him to be stripped of his rank, arrested and brought to justice in Lisbon. Eventually, he was acquitted. Concerning Joane Mendes de Vasconcelos and his military campaigns during the Restoration, see Luiz de Menezes (Conde da Ericeira), *História de Portugal Restaurado*, vol. 2 (Lisbon: 1751), 54–76, 92–137, 233–235.

106 During the Restoration War, Governor of Arms ("Governador das Armas") was a general responsible for the army of each one of the six provinces of Portugal (Entre-Douro e Minho, Trás-os-Montes, Beira, Estremadura, Alentejo, and Algarve). Mendes de Vasconcelos was Governor of Arms of Trás-os-Montes between 1652 and 1656.

107 *Trovas*, 149.

108 This quotation refers to verses in the same stanza of Bandarra's *Trovas:* "I see a high Engine/ In a triumphant wheel", *Trovas*, 149.

I see, rising, a frontier captain[109]
Of the Kingdom, from behind the hill,
Desiring to wage war,
The striven cavalier.[110]

When it was known in Maranhão that the Castilian was upon Olivença and that the earl of S. Lourenço was governor of arms,[111] I wrote to Your Lordship[112] that I had said in front of many ecclesiastic and secular people that Joane Mendes de Vasconcelos was the one who should lead all the military enterprises, basing myself on this same couplet and reading him as the "frontier captain (...) from behind the hill", because he was the captain of Trás-os-Montes.[113]

This whole paper,[114] with the same procedures by which it has been so far exposed here, I wrote at the end of April of this year, as may be seen in its first copy that, right after, I had it sent through Maranhão.[115] Now that I have heard that Joane Mendes de Vasconcelos was not only removed from the war, but arrested,[116] it seems that my conjecture about the explanation or the accom-

---

109   "fronteiro". Until the mid-17th century, a "Fronteiro" was a captain responsible for a garrison on the frontiers.
110   *Trovas*, 152.
111   Martim Afonso de Melo, second Earl of São Lourenço, was three-times governor of arms of Alentejo (1641, 1657, 1659). In this passage, Vieira was referring to Melo's second term as governor of arms of Alentejo, at a moment during which the frontier and garrison town of Olivença was besieged and eventually conquered by the Spaniards. The Spanish crown kept Olivença until the peace treaty, signed at Lisbon in 1668.
112   That letter has not survived.
113   Trás-os-montes is a mountainous region in north-eastern Portugal and its name literally means "beyond the mountains".
114   It is worthwhile noticing that Vieira called his text "paper" and not "letter", because this could tell us the actual textual genre of the source. In early modern lettered practices, a paper ("papel") might refer to any kind of miscellaneous writing, but not unusually did it identify a written discourse produced for presenting arguments or intervening in a debate or a dispute. See the introduction for more.
115   Vieira had sent a first version of the paper through São Luís do Maranhão postal services, and this is a revised and updated version, probably written around November, 1659. Still, the date signed at the end remains April 29, 1659. As we may infer from the following sentences, Vieira added some remarks to actualise his interpretations of Bandarra. From some letters sent by Vieira, we deduce that the first version of "Hopes" was not well received in Lisbon; thus, Vieira rewrote some passages to gain the Queen's favour and a good reception in the Court, sending another version to the Bishop of Japan on 28 November 1659. Muhana, *Os Autos do processo de Vieira na Inquisição*, 70 (note 1). For the other letters, see Vieira, *Obra completa*, t. I, vol. II, 254, 260. The passages of the letters are quoted in the introduction.
116   Joane Mendes de Vasconcelos was arrested after his defeat in the 1658 Siege of Badajoz.

modation of these verses was wrong. I will easily concede this error and admit that Bandarra talks about another frontier captain from Trás-os-Montes, or, as some tells us nowadays, about the earl of São João.[117] Here comes such an honorable fame from his endeavours and knighthood that "striven cavalier" is a title which quadrates well with him. However, should someone wish to insist on the first meaning given to the verses, one can find in themselves the solution and say that what I was saying before the news about the retreat from Badajoz was known here. I was saying—and I have many eyewitnesses of it—that, if the surrender of the hold were not achieved, the application and aptness of the verses would not be undone. On the contrary, they would be better construed, because the words "Desiring to wage war" do not signify effects, but desires. Thus, in a certain fashion, the verses seem to prophesy that the enterprise would stop only in desires, albeit gallantly manifested desires. Here one should also notice the expression "to wage war", which is proper of besieging strongholds and not of defeating armies.

And about the couplet which follows after this, talking about the same subject:

> This will be the first
> That shall put the pennon
> In the head of the dragon,
> Will fully overthrow it[118]

It is a prophecy and promise of future, which can be either the Castle of Lisbon[119] or any other part, because it speaks manifestly about the war against the Turk, as it will be seen more clearly ahead. Bandarra says that the same frontier captain he saw going out of the Kingdom behind the hill will be the one, whoever he is, who shall put the pennon in the Turk's head, which is Constantinople, and that shall completely overthrow and defeat the Turk.

This is what I am saying, and this is what it seems to me to be. That is a protestation of not being my intention to take from anyone the right to go over these verses, as over all those by Bandarra, and far less the right to transfer them to somebody else, which is what you see the most in our kingdom.[120]

---

117   Luís Álvares de Távora (1634-?), third Earl of São João da Pesqueira and, after 1669, first Marquis of Távora.
118   *Trovas*, 153.
119   Joane Mendes was incarcerated in the Castle of Lisbon. See notes 105 and 116.
120   Vieira might be referring not only to the different interpretations about these particular verses but also to the very belief that the saviour Hidden King announced in Bandarra's *Trovas* was not the late John IV, but still Sebastian I.

All that has been said is about things in which we have more palpably seen the fulfilment of Bandarra's prophecies so far. If well distinguished and counted, we will find more than fifty already-fulfilled prophecies, apart from infinite other things upon which they depend, and with which they are involved. And all of these things, Bandarra knew and foresaw, and with such individuation of time, places, names, people, features, modes and all other detailed circumstances, as it seems that he could see them in a clearer light than the very eyes that have seen them afterwards. And, as all these events were fully contingent and dependent upon human liberty, and upon as many liberties as many were the men, republics, governors, cities and states of all the Kingdom and its conquests, it follows that with no science, neither human, nor devilish, nor angelical, Bandarra could conjecture the minimum part of what he said. Even less could he affirm it so surely, write it so truly, and individualise it so minutely, and this is something he regards in his work's prologue, when he says: "I sew tight with no hump".[121] Hence, it was supernatural, prophetic and divine light that enlightened the understanding of this illiterate and humble man, so that God's wonders that the world was to see in Portugal in these recent times might also have that prominence of all great divine mysteries, which is to have been prophesied long ago.

Surely, there will be those who will doubt about some of the explanations I have given to the referred texts, though so clear and current. However, for the intent that I want to prove—Bandarra's prophetical spirit—it will suffice those that everyone confesses and those that do not admit any doubt, which are a great part of the ones mentioned.

If not, I ask: who said to Bandarra, at the time of King John III, that a successor to Portugal would be lacking, and that the crown would go to a foreign king? Who told him that the "farrowing Griffon" or Castile, by means of a childbirth, that was the one of Philip II, son of the Infant Empress Isabel, would possess Portugal? Who told him that the desired time for redemption of this captivity would be the year of forty? Who told him that the restorer would be a new and risen King? Who told him that this King shall be called John, and that he would be happy and a descendent of infants? Who told him that the Conquests would promptly recognise and accept him, and thenceforth they would stay steady, with not one of them hesitating or retreating? Who told him that one of these Conquests would be governed by a very stern and hairy man then? And that the one who would govern the other Conquest would be called Excellency, and that he would be "acute"? And that, being the instrument of the

---

121 *Trovas*, "Dedicatória", stanza 7.

Acclamation, he would be ousted because of suspicions of infidelity, and that this infidelity would not be in his shield? Finally, who told him that the Pope would not accept this king, and that an Infant would succeed the crown, and not the Prince, his first-born? It is certain that only God could say and reveal all these futures to Bandarra. And with the same certainty it ought to be considered and affirmed that Bandarra was a true prophet.

Now there still remains to be seen whether or not Bandarra prophesied anything about King John that has not yet been fulfilled. That is the second foundation of our consequence.

Proving the second proposition of the syllogism

The things that Bandarra prophesies about what King John has not yet worked but what he shall work, are so great, so extraordinary, and so prodigious that, as if what has already happened does not possess anything for admiration, your prophet starts the narrative about them with this prologue:

Second and Third Dream

Oh, who could have said
The dreams that man dreams!
But I fear that I will feel
Such a shame
If no one wants to believe me about them.[122]

That, My Lord Bishop, is a prophecy of what today we see: Bandarra shall be accosted and ashamed by the opinion of many, until the marvellous works of King John IV, our lord, conquer the faith for his prophet's verses, since the first part of them has already deserved our esteem.

Bandarra says firstly that the King will go out for conquering the Holy House, making himself his lord, leaving the Kingdom devoid of everything, because he shall take with him all there is of men who can take up arms. Thus the beginning of the *Dialogue of Balls*[123] starts:

I see, I see, I say, I see,
Now that I am dreaming,

---

122 *Trovas*, 106, cf. 94.
123 "Diálogo dos Bailos". "Bailos" is an old form of "Bailes" (Balls).

> King Ferdinand's seed
> Making a great void,
> And going out with grand desire,
> And leaving his vine,
> And saying: "This house is mine,
> Now that here I see myself".[124]

He calls the King "King Ferdinand's seed", because John IV is the fourth grandson of King Ferdinand, the Catholic,[125] such a well-known and celebrated king in those times. And that this departure be to Jerusalem, and this house of which he speaks be the Holy House, it will be clearly seen in everything that follows.

Bandarra goes further yet. He says that this journey will be by sea, and that its effect will be the taking it away from the Turk by the King, with great easiness and almost without resistance. *Second Dream*:

> I saw a grand Lion running,
> And making its trip,
> And taking the wild Pig,
> In the passage,
> Without any defence.[126]

"Wild Pig" is the Turk, as the same Bandarra declares in many places. In the *Third Dream*[127] he speaks of the same wild pig and of the same trip, and he says this:

---

124 *Trovas*, 17–18.
125 John IV was the third great-grandson (hence, "fourth grandson") of Ferdinand of Aragon, the Catholic Monarch, by his father's lineage. John IV's father, Theodosius II, Duke of Braganza, was the first born of Catherine of Braganza, one of the contenders for the Portuguese Crown in 1580 after Sebastian I's death. The Duchess of Braganza was daughter of the Infant Duarte of Portugal. The Infant Duarte was son of Mary of Aragon, Queen Consort of Portugal, married to Manuel I of Portugal, and daughter of Ferdinand II of Aragon and V of Castile.
126 *Trovas*, 94.
127 In the 1644 *Trovas* edition, the following stanzas are part of the "Second Dream". As we shall see, those are not the only differences we will find when comparing Vieira's quotations to the 1644 edition. Discrepancies in quotations were not unusual in early modern cultural practices. Moreover, when one was dealing with a well-known text of which, notwithstanding, printed copies were scarce and rare, as was the case of Bandarra's *Trovas*. Therefore, it is likely that Vieira was either using a manuscript copy of the *Trovas* (with some textual differences) or even citing some passages by heart, employing the often used mnemonic techniques of the early modern art of memory.

> The Lion is already roaring,
> And desiring
> To run after the wild Pig
> And take it on the passage.
> Good trip,[128]
> It goes thus declaring[129]

And in the same *Third Dream:*

> This king of grand perfection,
> With fury,
> Will pass the salty sea,
> In a bridled but not
> Saddled horse,
> With people of grand valour.
>
> He says that he will help,
> And he will take
> The ones who are in sadness.
>
> About him tells the Scripture,
> That he strives,[130]
> That the field will dump.[131]

The peoples[132] of whom he speaks here, that, he says, will be in sadness and will be helped by the King, are the People of Italy. They will be oppressed by the Turk's weapons which are going to make great cruelties against them, as Salutivo[133] largely describes and as Bandarra also does in *Dialogue of Balls.* In

---

128 The 1644 *Trovas* edition does not contain this verse.
129 *Trovas,* 107.
130 "Que se apura". This verse does not exist in the 1644 edition.
131 *Trovas,* 104–105 (with a different division in stanzas).
132 "gentes".
133 Salutivo refers to the Franciscan Friar Bartolomeo Cambi (1558–1617), better known by his religious name Bartolomeo Da Salutio (rendered sometimes as Salutivo or Salúcio in Portuguese). Born in Tuscany, Cambi entered the Orders of the Friars Minor in 1575 and rapidly became famous for his apocalyptic sermons, which stirred both intense responses from the population and deep concerns from the authorities. His prophetical and mystical writings were read around Europe, and one of his ascetic pamphlets, *La Sette Tube,* was translated and printed in English in 1626, under the title *The Seaven Trumpets of Brother*

the *Dialogue*, Bandarra starts with Venice, which will be (or is already) the first to suffer with the Turk's invasions, and will spend its treasures in this war:

> Also, to the Venetians,
> With the riches they have,
> The King of Salem will come,
> Will judge them as mundane.[134]

He calls the Turk "the King of Salem", because the Turk is today lord of Jerusalem, which is also called Salem in the Scripture.[135] And, continuing the description of the cruelties that the Turk will make in Italy, he says after the verses above:

> The wolves have already entered[136]
> By packs in the mountains,
> They have flayed the cattle,
> And many have been wolfed down,[137]
> Making a great deed.
>
> The Chief Shepherd[138] gets enraged
> And gathers his sheepmen,

Bartholomevv Saluthius of the Holie order of S. Francis; Exciting a Sinner to Repentance. A Worke Very Profitable for the Salvation of All Such Soules, as are Bound With Sinne. Now Lately Translated Out of the Latin, Into the English Tongue, by Br. G. P. [George Perro] *of the Same Order and Obseruance* (At S. Omers: 1626). For Campi, see Adriano Prosperi, "CAMBI, Bartolome" in *Dizionario Biografico degli Italiani*, vol. 17 (Rome: 1974), 92–96 Besselaar, "Notas complementares: 4. Bartolomeu de Salutio", in *Antônio Vieira*, 316–319.

134 *Trovas*, 20.
135 Vieira was probably referring to Psalm 75:3 (in the *Vulgata*; 75:2, in King James Bible) in which Zion and Salem are referred to as places where the name of God is known and revered, in the same verse. For this reason, sometimes Salem was read and identified with Jerusalem.
136 "Já os lobos são entrados". In the 1644 edition of Trovas, it is "Ia os lobos saõ aiuntados", meaning "the wolves are already toghether" or "the wolves are already assembled".
137 "alobegados". Besselaar suggests that "alobegados" means 'devoured by wolves'.
138 Chief Shepherd ("Pastor Mor") might refer to the "Princeps pastorum" of 1Pet. 5:4. We opted to translate "Pastor Mor" as "Chief Shepherd" following King James version of 1Pet. 5:4 ("And when the chief Shepherd shall appear, ye shall receive a crown of glory that fadeth not away") and not Douay-Rheims, in which "Prince of the Shepherds" is literally translated from the Latin Vulgate version.

> Awakens his company,
> Succours his pasturers.[139]

The Chief Shepherd is the Pope that, by seeing Italy and still Rome in this grip, will call the Christian Princes who are his sheepmen or the lords of his sheep and will awaken his company which are the Catholics. And one should note the words: "awakens his company", because it truly seems that the Christian princes are sleeping, because after so many years that the Turks have been making war against Christianity in Italy, they are so distracted as if they were sleeping. To the Pontiff's cries, the Christian Princes will answer and, amongst them, the famous King of Portugal. This, Bandarra repeats and declares in the *First Dream*, also prophesying the ruin of the Ottoman Empire, the end of the law of Muhammad and the destruction of the House of Mecca:

> The moon[140] will go down[141]
> According to what is seen in it,
> And so those who have loyalty with it,[142]
> Because the tax[143] is no longer.
> It will be opened that box,[144]
> Which until now was closed,
> And it will forcibly surrender
> Wrapped in its band.[145]

And by declaring who the Author or the instrument of everything will be, he continues:

---

139   *Trovas*, 22–23. The 1644 *Trovas* renders Bandarra's verses quite differently than Vieira's version.
140   Probable reference to the Crescent as symbol of Eastern and Islamic monarchies and, more particularly, of the Ottoman Empire.
141   "dará grã baxa". "Dará grã baxa" would more properly translate as will greatly dismiss or discharge, but we prefer to maintain the double meaning of "baixa" (down) by which one can describe both a movement of decline and the moon-set.
142   "ter lei com ela". An old usage of "lei" (law) was "lealdade" (loyalty), therefore the expression "ter lei com" (literally have lawn with) means "have loyalty to". See João Ribeiro, *Frases feitas. Estudo conjetural de locuções, ditados e provérbios* (1908; repr. Rio de Janeiro: 2009), 67.
143   Tax ("Taxa") meaning "A price-list, tariff (...) *Obsolete. rare.*" "tax, n.1". *OED Online*.
144   According to Besselaar, the box was a reference to the Kaaba.
145   *Trovas*, 77.

> A grand Lion will arise
> And will give great roars.
> Its shouts will be listened;
> They will awe everyone.
> It will run and bite
> And will make many great damages,
> And in the African kingdoms
> It will subjugate all.
>
> It will enter, very brave,
> It will happen anyway.
> Of wooden horses,
> The sea will be seen full.[146]
> It will pass along and shout.
> In the Land of Promise
> It will arrest the old Dog,
> Which walks very waywardly.[147]

From this, it becomes well understood from which passage is the one that Bandarra has said that the Lion will take the "wild Pig":[148] it is undoubtedly that part of the sea between Italy and Constantinople, which happens to be the mouth of the Adriatic sea and the Archipelago. So that the Turk, forced by the Christian army, shall run away and withdraw from Italy to his lands, and in this retreat or passage shall be defeated. This will present no difficulties, if not rather easy for anyone who has knowledge of the site; because, as that whole sea is a wood of islands, one can settle ambushes there or, better saying, will settle them there. Because so says the same Bandarra in the same *Ball*:

> After being already noticed,
> And the mountains taken
> By very wise men,
> Very well chosen shepherds,
> Who know well the sheepfolds,[149]
> Will put in the crossroads

---

146 These four first verses of the stanza are missing from the 1644 edition.
147 *Trovas*, 78–79.
148 It refers to *Trovas*, 107: "The lion is already roaring,/ And desiring/ To run the wild Pig/ And take it on the passage." For Vieira's commentary of these verses, see above.
149 "malhadas": tents or shacks where the shepherds used to rest with the herd.

> Snares, steel traps,
> Watchtowers on the roads,
> And will hold crossbows at night
> With very fast shots.[150]

Not only shall the King do that by using his army, but, Bandarra says, he in person shall hit the Turk. First Dream:

> Already the Lion is awake,
> Very alert.
> Already awakened, it carries on.
> It will soon take the Pig
> Out of the nest; and this is for sure.
> It will run away through the desert
> From the lion and its roar;
> It shows that it goes hurt
> By this good Hidden King.[151]

And though the Turk being hurt shall go away, Bandarra says that he shall surrender and subject himself to the King after this retreat. *Dialogue of the Balls*:

> Oh lord, take unto you the pleasure,
> That the grand wild Pig
> Already comes from its own will
> Meddles in your power,
> With its ports and passage.[152]

Notice the verse "with its ports and passage" which confirms that the passage that he speaks about is the sea and islands between Italy and Constantinople.

Bandarra goes further: surrendered the Turk, his lands will be shared amongst the Christian Princes who go to this war, and Constantinople will belong to the King. In the same *Dialogue of Balls*:

> Play the great flute,
> Gather all the flock,
> And I, as your Shepherd,

---

150   *Trovas*, 23–24.
151   *Trovas*, 66.
152   *Trovas*, 66.

> With so much love,
> We will share the gain.
> Everything is subjected to us,
> Hills, valleys, and shepherds;
> Rest, oh Dancers,
> That no strangers will enter here.[153]

And right below:

> Alas, before more extremes
> Dance Ferdinand and Constance,
> And since we see everything,
> For the good that we want to him,
> He shall be the master of the dance.[154]

Constance means Constantinople, and Ferdinand means the King: and one clearly sees that his dancing with Constance and his being the master of the dance means that Constantinople shall be his, and that he shall have the greatest place of all in this partition.

Do not raise, however, doubts about the name of Ferdinand, because the names of the figures[155] of this Dialogue are supposed names and not their proper ones. And as the people who formed the same dialogue are called Pedro, João, André, Garcia,[156] etc., those not being the names of the Princes who shall

---

153   *Trovas*, 36–37.
154   *Trovas*, 43.
155   "figuras". "Figuras" could refer to the characters of the dialogue, as human yet fictional persons, but also to the figural meaning of the names evoked in Bandarra's prophecy. Being prophetic figures of something, they (pre)announce in a figurative and covered fashion what will be fulfilled in the future. About the literary, prophetical, and historical operation of figure and fulfilment, see Erich Auerbach, "Figure", in *Scenes from the Drama of European Literature* (Minneapolis, MN: 1984), 11–76.
156   We have not translated the names as we have been doing until now, because it is instrumental for Vieira's interpretation that the names remain in Portuguese. Below, the verses to which Vieira was referring to:
       "FIGVRAS DO SONHO.
       Virá o grande Pastor
       Que se erguera primeiro,
       E fernando tangedor,
       E Pedro bom bailador,
       E Ioaõ bom ouelheiro.
       E despois hum Estrangeiro,

go to the conquest of Jerusalem (because those are not customary names for foreign Princes), the name of Ferdinand is not the King's proper name, but a supposed one.

But if there is anyone who wants to insist (without any reason though) that this is the proper name of the conqueror king of the Holy Land, it can be easily said that the King—in his resurrection or in his ascension to the Empire—will take the name of Ferdinand; and, if so it is, we will say that Saint Anthony left the name Ferdinand in S. Vicente de Fora,[157] so that King John take it. And in this name change or appendage (as the King may well add the name Ferdinand to the name John), it would be also corroborated that tradition which says that "the Hidden one will have the name of iron";[158] because in the parts

---

> E Roduaõ, que esquecia,
> E o nobre Pastor Garçia,
> E Andre mui uerdadeiro:
> Entraraõ com a [a]legria."
> *Trovas*, 26–27.

157 Fernando or Ferdinand Martins de Bulhões was Saint Anthony's name before joining the Franciscan Order in 1210. São Vicente de Fora is a Franciscan cloister in Lisbon (see note 216).

158 Vieira was quoting a verse of a prophecy wrongly attributed to Isidore of Seville in early modern Iberia: "El Encubierto tendra en su nombre letra de hierro". However, the interpretation of what a name with an iron letter ("tendra en su nombre letra de hierro") would mean varied according to the chosen "Hidden one" ("El Encubierto"). A Portuguese exile during the Iberian Union and supporter of the cause of the false king Sebastian of Venice, João de Castro presented an intricate explanation for the iron letter in the first printed (although incomplete) version and commentary of Bandarra's *Trovas*. Basing himself on other interpreters, Castro stated that iron letter was a reference to the design of the metallic spring-loaded serpentine used to ignite fire or gunpowder ("fozil de ferir fogo"), which had a format similar to an S or more precisely a B. King Sebastian was called Bastian ("Bastião") as a child and, even after his coronation and "disappearance", the common people kept calling him king Bastian. Hence, the more precise reading of the iron letter should be "B", as in Bastian for King Sebastian. João de Castro, *Paraphrase et concordancia de algüas propheçias de Bandarra: çapateiro de Trancoso* (1603; repr. Porto: 1942), 116–118. Later in 1626, another Portuguese exile, the *converso* Jacob Rosales, alias Manuel Bocarro Francês, said that B was indeed the iron letter but only because the Hebrew word for iron was Barzel (BRZL, without the vowels). But instead of pointing a prince or even attributing the "iron letter" to pseudo-Isidore's prophecies, he astonishingly concluded that the letter was referring to his own family and lineage. Bocarro's grandfather, N. Rosales, would have been the first to discover this kabbalistic relation between the Hidden One and the word and element Iron, and, since then, the Rosales family would have been the herald of the "Hidden One" for the following generations. Thus, the Iron Letter would represent the letters of his family name, Be(n) Rosales (son or descendent of Rosales), which, if one only counts the consonants, would read BRSL, i.e., Barzel/Iron. Francisco Moreno-Carvalho, "A Portuguese Jewish agent of the Philips and a Sebastianist: the strange case

of the Levant, where this enterprise shall be, Ferdinand is called Ferrante,[159] as Jacob, Jacques. It is also possible to say: as Bandarra called the King an Infant because he is the grandson of Infant Duarte,[160] he would also call him Ferdinand, because he is the seed of King Ferdinand, as we have said above. But without resorting to any of that, the easiest and more natural way is just to say that the name Ferdinand in this Dialogue is a supposed and not a proper one, just like the others.

After the King has been made Lord of Constantinople, he will be elected emperor, with a fair election, not a rigged one, says Bandarra:

> The kings will be concordant,
> Four will be, and no more,
> All the four, the most principal ones
> From the Ponent to the Levant.
> The other kings will be very content
> To see him as Emperor,
> And will consider him as Grand-Lord
> Not by rewards, nor gifts.[161]

These kings are four who will be found in the war against the Turk, and the kings, recognising that all the victory is due to King John, will give him the imperial crown as a reward for it. And the King has been made emperor of Constantinople says Bandarra, with great authority, that he will be named as Grand-Lord, because in his lands entitles the Turk himself Grand-Lord, and in Italy is given the same name to him.

And that the whole victory should be granted to the King, said the same Bandarra in the *Second Dream*:

> Of the four kings, the second
> Will take all the victory.[162]

---

of Rosales/Manuel Bocarro", in *Visions, Prophecies, and Divinations*, ed. Luís Filipe Silvério Lima and Ana Paula Megiani (Leiden: 2016), 168, 172–173.

159   "Ferrante" contains the root of the word *Ferro* (Iron in Portuguese).
160   John IV's mother, Catherine, Duchess of Braganza, was the daughter of the prince Infant Duarte, son of king Manuel I, who married Isabel of Braganza. About the term "infante" and the genealogical links of John IV to Infant Duarte and Ferdinand of Aragon, see note 71.
161   *Trovas*, 73.
162   *Trovas*, 95.

Calling the King "the second" in this occasion could well be because he would have taken the name of Ferdinand, and therefore he would be Ferdinand II. But one could also possibly call him "the second" because the kings of Portugal truly have the second place among the Christian kings, the first place belonging to France's or Spain's indecisively, who are still vying in front of the Pontiff, who has never wanted to decide it. It also can be "the second" for his having the second place in this enterprise, as general of the sea that he shall be, the first having the king who shall become the general of the land. At last, it will be possible to call him "second" because of any other accident for which the time will more easily give an interpretation than we can make a guess about it at this present moment.[163]

Crowned as emperor, says Bandarra, the King will come back victorious with two pennons, which must be one of the King of Portugal and the other of the Emperor of Constantinople:

> With pardons[164] and prayers
> He will go strongly armed,
> In them, he will give Saint James[165]
> In the turn, he will make later.
>
> He will enter with two pennons,
> Among furry Pigs,
> With strong arms and shields
> Of his noble vassals.[166]

---

163   Accident in the Aristotelian-Thomistic sense, i.e., the actions, elements or characteristics that are secondary to the substance of things. More specifically in a theological-historical-prophetical perspective as was Vieira's, accidents were the actions and events which were not possible to determine through human guessing or deduction since they were only subsidiary to the Divine plan (as a result of the First and Final Cause). Hence, when one was analysing the figurative and veiled language of prophetical predictions, one could only uncover all the specific meanings and individual facts of a prophecy after the predicted outcome had eventually happened.

164   "perdões". Pardons ("Perdões") as the remission of the punishment of sins, an indulgence, the royal pardoning of a crime, and the legal document that granted pardon or indulgence. "Perdão". Bluteau, *Vocabulário*, vol. 6, 410; "pardon, n.1 (and int.)". *OED Online*.

165   "Dará neles Santiago". This verse could refer to San James' Spanish epithet, "Matamoros", i.e., the Moor-slayer, hence, the expression "dará neles Santiago" could mean "he will strike them [the Moors/Turks] with or as Santiago [Matamoros]".

166   *Trovas*, 80–81. "Infanções", here translated as "vassals", is a medieval nobiliarchical title granted by the Portuguese kings for the mid-level aristocracy. In early modern Portugal, it was progressively replaced by the term "fidalgo" (literary son of someone), which even-

These "furry Pigs", with which the King will enter, will be the pashas and captains of the Turks; and in his return, he will bring them and put them in front of himself in his triumph. Finally, Bandarra says that the same king shall introduce to the Supreme Pontiff the ten Tribes of Israel,[167] which in that time shall go out and appear in the world for the awe of the whole world.

At the beginning of the *First Dream*, Bandarra introduces two Hebrews, one called Dan, and the other called Ephraim.[168] They come to talk to the Chief Shepherd, who is the Supreme Pontiff, and, to be introduced to him, they ask for admittance to Ferdinand, who represents the King as we have already said. And so they say in manner of dialogue:

Ephraim: Say, sir, can we
Talk to the Grand-Shepherd?[169]

---

tually became a general word for nobleperson or a person not belonging to (or desiring to differentiate from) the popular and lower elements of society. A possible (though perhaps inaccurate) translation would be "gentry", but "infanções" implies specific and well defined rules of service to the Portuguese sovereign which the more general (and controversial) English "gentry" would not.

167 According to 2 Kings (16:6–7, 22–23), ten of the twelve tribes of Israel were expelled from their kingdoms by the Assyrians and never returned as a divine punishment for their sins. In IV Ezra (or 2 Esdras in Catholic tradition) (13:39–47), the Ten Tribes appeared crossing over the waters and gone to a distant country; they would remain there until the "latter time" when God would allow their return to Jerusalem. Ezra's passage had been read as a prophecy about the reconquest of Jerusalem, the reunion of the Tribes and the subsequent end of the world since the Middle Ages, but it gained new layers of interpretation with the discovery of new and unknown lands and the enlargement of the globe. About the Lost Tribes, see Zvi Ben-Dor Benite. *Ten Lost Tribes: A World History* (Oxford: 2009).

168 When commenting on these verses of Bandarra, António José Saraiva said that Ephraim was a term used for collectively referring to the Lost Tribes and its mention would be one of the many biblical and apocalyptic remarks in the *Trovas* which stirred the New-Christian communities' hopes for the coming of the Messiah in sixteenth-century Portugal. Antonio José Saraiva, "Antonio Vieira, Menasseh ben Israel, et le cinquième empire", *Studia Rosenthaliana* 6 (1972): 28–30 (Translated as "António Vieira, Menasseh ben Israel e o Quinto Império", and published in António José Saraiva, *História e utopia* (Lisbon: 1992), 79–82). In the Bible, Dan and Ephraim were descendants of Jacob, and two of the twelve tribes of Israel appeared named after them (for Dan, see Gen. 30:6; Num. 1:12; for Ephraim, see Num. 1:32; 13:9). Dan was son of Jacob, and Ephraim was son of Jacob's son Joseph (along with Manasseh). However, neither Dan nor Ephraim appeared among the tribes "of the children of Israel" listed in the Christian book of Revelation (Rev. 7:4–8). This aspect about Ephraim (and Dan) would maybe be a sign of a message more orientated towards a judaiser audience and, hence, it could also confirm Saraiva's hypotheses about the *Trova*'s partial Jewish prophetical foundation and its completely New-Christian ambivalent tone—though with different evidence.

169 "Grão-Pastor".

> And from here we promise you
> Rich jewels that we bring,
> If you want to take them from us.
>
> *Ferdinand:* Jews, what shall you give him?
>
> *Dan:* We will give him great treasure,
> Plenty of silver, plenty of gold
> That we have brought from overseas.
> You will make me great mercy
> By giving me a sight of him.
>
> *Ferdinand:* Enter, Jews, if you want to,
> You may well talk to him,
> That inside you will find him.[170]

Not a word does Bandarra declare about the place where it shall happen, whether in Jerusalem or in Rome, when the King goes there, or in Portugal, when the tribes come. Wherever the place that it happens, this will be one of the great wonders, or yet the great of the greatest ones which was ever seen or heard in the world. Thus, the same Bandarra ponders it in one of his answers in which he returns to prophesy the tribes' appearance:

> Before these things were
> (From this age that we have talked about),
> We will see very great things,
> That those who had lived had not seen,
> [That] we have neither seen nor heard.
>
> The prisoner will leave
> From the new people who come
> Of this tribe of Reuben,
> Son of Jacob, the first
> With everything else he has.[171]

The place, however, where Bandarra fully treats this matter is in his *Third Dream*. He spends all of it with the portentous description and narrative of

---

170 *Trovas*, 82–84.
171 *Trovas*, 134, 135.

the coming and the appearance of this people, using a style that is much more elevated than usual. Representing that he was dreaming, so says Bandarra:

> I was dreaming with great pleasure,
> That the dead were resurrecting,
> And that all of them were getting together
> And were being reborn again.[172]
> And that from behind the rivers
> Were coming the ones who were once hidden.
> I was dreaming that they had left,
> Out of that prison.[173]

In chapter 37 [of the Book of Ezekiel], when the prophet Ezekiel is literally speaking about the same restitution of the ten tribes (as it is clearly seen from the next three chapters),[174] he calls this restitution resurrection; because until now these peoples have been in this world as if they were buried and entombed, since nobody has known about them. Following this same sentence of Ezekiel, Bandarra says that he "was dreaming with great pleasure that the dead were resurrecting", and he declares and promptly explains it by saying that he was dreaming that those who have been hidden behind the rivers have walked out of their prison. That is because when the ten tribes disappeared, they crossed to the other side of the Euphrates river, and since then 'til now, no one has ever known about them.

Bandarra goes further, and describing in particular how each of the ten tribes has come or will come, he says:

> I saw the tribe of Dan
> With grinning teeth
> And very torn
> By the Dragon's Serpent[175]

---

172 "E tornavam a renascer".
173 *Trovas*, 110–111.
174 Of the Book of Ezekiel.
175 Following the 1644 edition of the *Trovas*, Besselaar opted for "Serpente e Dragão" (Dragon and Serpent) instead of the manuscript's "Serpente do Dragão" (Dragon's serpent). He pointed out that this probably was a quotation from the book of Genesis (49:17): "Let Dan be a snake in the way, a serpent in the path, that biteth the horse's heels that his rider may fall backward".

And I also saw Reuben
With great voice of many people,
Who came very content
Singing Jerusalem:

"Oh, that who already sees Bethlehem,
And this mount of Zion!
And sees the Jordan river
For cleaning himself very well!"

And so I saw Simeon,
That surrounded all the parts,
With flags and banners
Nephtalim and Zabulon.

Gad came as captain
Of this people I am telling you about.
All came by horse,
Without any footman among them.[176]

Let the learned-persons notice that among these captains or heads of the tribes, there is no mention of the names of either the tribe of Judah, or of Levi, or of Benjamin—being the first two ones, the former, the royal, and the latter, the sacerdotal—because these three tribes are the ones that stayed. About the properties by which Bandarra describes them, I will not detain myself with commenting upon, because it would be something wider and out of my intent. For the major part, they are taken from the dignity of the persons, from the etymology of the names, and from the blessings that Jacob gave to his sons.[177] I only warn that Bandarra's telling that "all come by horse, without any footman", is taken from the prophet Isaiah, in chapter 66, in which he says these words: *Et adducent omnes fratres vestros de cunctis gentibus donum Domino in equis, et in quadrigir, et in lecticis, et in mulis, et in carrucis, ad montem sanctum meum Hierusalem, dicit Dominus.*[178] And in the same chapter, a little above, the aston-

---

176 *Trovas*, 112–116.
177 See Genesis 29–30, 48–49.
178 Isa. 62:20. "And they shall bring all your brethren out of all nations for a gift to the Lord, upon horses, and in chariots, and in litters, and on mules, and in coaches, to my holy mountain Jerusalem, saith the Lord".

ished prophet of the same unprecedented prodigy that was writing, shows his admiration: *Quis quadivit unquam tale, et quis vidit huic simile? Nunquid parturient terra in die una, aut parietur gens simul? Quia parturivit et peperit Sion filios suos!* "Who has ever seen or listened to such a thing?", says the prophet, "By any chance, will the land give birth in one day, or will a whole nation be born? Because that way Zion will give birth, and thus, its children will be born!"[179] The joys of this parturition will be of Portugal; the pains, some may say to whom they will belong.

Bandarra continues with the entrance of his pilgrims, and introduces an honoured elder who got out from the middle of that company to talk to him. And he asked him, among other things, if he was one of the Hebrews they came to seek. And this is what Bandarra says he replied:

> "Everything you ask",
> I answer this while asleep,
> "Lord, I am not from this people
> Neither do I know them.
> But according to the signs
> You came from the foreign people,[180]
> That God put, by His commandment,
>
> In these eastern parts:
> Many are desiring
> That the peoples be put together;
> But others, very cautious,
> Are fearful of it.
> They fear that in the flock
> Come this giant Goliath,
> But as they see Enoch and Elijah[181]
> Yet they are rejoicing."[182]

---

179 Isa. 66:8. Cf. Douay-Rheims "Who hath ever heard such a thing? and who hath seen the like to this? shall the earth bring forth in one day? or shall a nation be brought forth at once, because Sion hath been in labour, and hath brought forth her children?".
180 "povo cerrado". One of the meanings of cerrado in Bluteau's *Vocabulario* refers to a foreigner who does not speak a language well.
181 According to some interpretations, Enoch and Elijah were the Lord's two witnesses mentioned in the Book of Revelation (Rev. 11:1–14), and they would return before the End of Times.
182 *Trovas*, 119–122.

The giant Goliath signifies the Antichrist here, and, as such a great interpreter of the Scriptures, Bandarra says that there are many persons (who are considered wise) who fear the coming of the Ten Tribes and the conversion of the Jews because they believe that, when it happens, the end of the world will have already arrived, and that we will already be in the time of the Antichrist. However, between one thing and another, many hundreds of years will pass,[183] as it appears in the same Scriptures, in which Bandarra says (and says well) that he saw his dream figured and found many paintings or figures of it. And it is truly so: the Hebrew people's restitution to their homeland through the knowledge of Christ[184] is the most frequent and repeated thing in the Prophets among the many they had written. Let us listen to Bandarra, right after the elder asked him if he believed in one God only:

> I wanted to answer him
> And to touch him with the Law:
> However at this moment I woke up
> And I had great pleasure.
>
> And after I was awaken
> I went to see the Scriptures
> And I found many paintings,
> And the dream, figured.
>
> In Ezra[185] I saw it painted,
> And also in Isaiah
> That shows us in these days
> the foreign people getting out,
> Which soon I went to seek;
> Gog, Magog and Ezekiel,
> The Weeks[186] of Daniel
> And I started to look at them.[187]

---

183 This is a clear mention of the millennial kingdom—something that the inquisitors would later question Vieira about during his trial. For the Inquisition evaluation of this remark and Vieira's interpretation of the stanzas above, see *Os Autos do processo*, 95–97.

184 "por meio do conhecimento de Cristo". That is: by converting to Christianity. The universal conversion (especially Jewish and Amerindian populations) was a central aspect for Vieira's conception of the Fifth Empire—and one that put him against the Inquisition in Portugal and the settlers in Brazil and Maranhão.

185 The apocryphal IV Ezra (or 2 Esdras in the Vulgate Bible). See note 167.

186 Seventy weeks of Daniel (see note 285).

187 *Trovas*, 125–128.

The curious ones may do the same, and they will have much to look at, to see, and to admire, mainly in the three chapters of Ezekiel which above I have quoted. As for this matter of the Ten Tribes, I would only say for closure that they shall also submit themselves to the unbeaten Five Shields[188] of Portugal and shall receive our great monarch as their king too. So the same Bandarra says in the quatrains before the *Dreams*:

> Portugal has the flag,
> With five shields in the middle,
> And according to what I hear and believe
> It is the forefront
> It has the crest of the Five Wounds
> That was given to him in the Calvary,[189]
> And he will be the king of the herd
> That comes from the long race.[190]

To the victory over the Turks and the reduction of the Jews, will follow the extirpation of the heresies thanks to this glorious Prince too. Bandarra, in the final quatrains:

> I see a great king arise,
> All blessed,
> And he will be so thrived
> That he will defend the flock;
> He will protect the law

---

188   "quinas". The five "quinas" (small shields aligned to form a cross) were the central part of the arms of Portugal. They represent the five wounds of Christ as a figure of the Saviour's apparition to the first Portuguese king, Afonso I (D. Afonso Henriques), before the battle of Ourique in 1139. This miraculous and mythical episode would be the foundation of the Portuguese kingdom and a sign of the imperial destiny of Portugal and its nation as God's chosen kingdom and people. Concerning the Miracle of Ourique, see, among others: Carlos Coelho Maurício, "Entre o silêncio e o ouro—sondando o milagre de Ourique na cultura portuguesa", *Ler: História* 20 (1990), 3–28; Ana Isabel Buescu, "Vínculos da Memória: Ourique e a fundação do reino", in *Portugal: Mitos revisitados*, ed. Yvette Kacere Centeno (Lisbon: 1993), 11–50; Luís Filipe Silvério Lima, *Império dos sonhos* (São Paulo: 2010), chap. 3.

189   As the place where Christ was crucified, Calvary is probably a reference to Afonso I's vision of Christ in Ourique, since he would not only have appeared crucified but would also have given his wounds as a coat of arms to the Portuguese king and the newly founded kingdom of Portugal.

190   *Trovas*, 70.

> From all the heresies,
> He will overthrow the fantasies
> Of the ones who protect I do not know what.[191]

And below, summarising everything:

> All will have one love,
> Both gentiles and pagans,
> As Jews, and Christians,
> Never having an error,
> They will serve only one Lord,
> Jesus Christ who I name.
> All will believe that had already come
> The Anointed Saviour.[192]

To this universal knowledge about Christ, Bandarra says will follow the universal peace so promised and sung by all prophets of the world. It will crown everything, and it will be under only one Shepherd and only one monarch: our most happy King, God's instrument for all these ends of His glory. Bandarra says in the *Second Dream*:

> He will take away all the scum,
> There will be peace in the whole world.
> Of four kings the second
> Will take all the victory.
> That memory will be his,
> For being keeper of the Law,
> By the arms of this King
> They will give him triumph and glory.[193]

Because all this triumph and all this glory will be of Christ and of his Five Wounds, which are the King's arms. One should notice that never does Bandarra mention anything as frequently as these Five Wounds of Christ and these arms of Portugal—to which virtue, he always attributed the wonders about he writes. And he does so that it does not occur to any mind of any king of Europe—or of the world—that he could be the subject of these prophecies.

---

191   *Trovas*, 150–151.
192   *Trovas*, 156–157.
193   *Trovas*, 95–96.

Thus, summarising everything that was said, and leaving aside another future and not yet fulfilled things prophesied by Bandarra about King John, the ones of most importance and consequence are seven [in number]: 1st, That he will leave his Kingdom with all his power and will sail to Jerusalem; 2nd, That he will rout the Turk in the passage from Italy to Constantinople; 3rd, That he will, by his own hand, hurt the Turk, who will surrender to him; 4th, That he will become lord of the City and Empire of Constantinople, of which he will be crowned Emperor; 5th, That he will return victorious to his Kingdom with two pennons; 6th, That he will introduce the miraculously appeared Ten Tribes of Israel to the Pontiff and to Christ's faith; 7th, That he will be the instrument of the whole world's conversion and universal peace, which is the ultimate end for which God has chosen him.

And all of these things remaining for King John to do, and being certain that he shall do them because it is so prophesied, it seems that the foundation of our second consequence is well founded.

But Your Lordship will rightly ask me: and where do I prove that this king about whom Bandarra speaks is King John IV? I answer that I prove it with the same Bandarra in two places, which are for me rather evident. The first place, in the quatrains right before the *Dreams*, in which it is said:

> This very excellent King,
> From whom I got all my resolve,
> He is not from a gluttonous stock,[194]
> But cousin and relative of princes;
> It comes from very high seed,
> From all sides of his family tree,[195]
> All kings of the highest grades
> From the Levant to the Ponent.[196]

---

194 "casta goleima". The old meaning of the Portuguese word "casta" (as "caste" in early modern English usage) was primarily stock, breed, or stem of people or a family. According to Bluteau's *Vocabulário*, "Casta" corresponded to the Latin word *genus* as lineage or *gens* as family. Bluteau, *Vocabulário*, v. 2, 183, "Casta", see "caste, n.". *OED Online*. For "goleima", see note 198.

195 "todos quatro costados". It can be roughly translated as all the four sides of one's lineage, that is, maternal grandparents and paternal grandparents. It means that a person was a true Old Christian noble and had no commoner or "infected blood", according not only to aristocratic rules but also to Iberian laws of purity of blood against New Christians and Moors.

196 *Trovas*, 56.

Consequently Bandarra says that the matter and the theme, or the resolve of his prophecies is only one "This very excellent king from whom I got all my resolve";[197] and from that it follows—effectively and evidently—that the matter and the theme of the said prophecies is King John IV, because it is something assured and seen by everybody's eyes that all the past prophecies are fulfilled in King John IV, as it is shown in the first proposition of this syllogism. Therefore, if the matter of Bandarra's prophecies is only one king, and if King John is mentioned in the matter of the past prophecies, it clearly follows that he is the matter of the future ones too. Because if the past prophecies were fulfilled in King John, but the future ones were supposed to be fulfilled in another king, it would follow that Bandarra's theme and matter were not one king only, but two.

Someone may say that this king about which Bandarra talks is not a king in particular, but the King of Portugal in general, and even if these prophecies are to be confirmed partly in a king and partly in another, they are always confirmed in the King of Portugal. There was no shortage of people discussing or fancying that notion, but God wanted the same Bandarra to explain himself. And in this same quatrain, Bandarra declares that he does not talk about the king of Portugal in general, rather in particular: about such person, about such individual, son of such parents and such grandparents, and from such progeny, as here he describes. He says this king is not from a gluttonous stock, because King John does not descend from the house of Habsburg; and he calls the house of Habsburg a gluttonous stock, because the one who eats too much is called "gluttonous",[198] and the Princes of the House of Habsburg, as all Germans, are

---

197 "com quem tomei minha teima". Vieira uses a phonetic approximation between "tema" (theme) and "teima" (obstinacy, resolve) to say that Bandarra was talking about his prophecies' themes or subjects in this verse. We tried to maintain this ambiguity translating "teima" as resolve, and stressing its less used meaning of solution, answer.

198 "goleima". As far as we have researched, the word "goleima" does not have many occurrences in the early modern Portuguese beyond Bandarra and his commentators. However, Bandarra's 17th-century interpreters did not agree about its origin and meaning. In his effort to support the Sebastian of Venice, João de Castro wrote in his commentary of Bandarra's *Trovas* that being from the "casta golleima" meant being of Black or Moorish origin ("casta golleima: que significa a de negro ou de mouro"), "races" considered "infamous" and "low" ("raças tidas por baixas e infames"), and therefore, by metonymy, representing all kinds of lowness. King Sebastian always kept himself away from anything that was low, hence, he was not from "casta golleima". Castro, *Paraphrase*, fol. 45. Produced at the beginning of the Restoration wars, Jesuit João de Vasconcelos's arguments in his *Restauração de Portugal Prodigiosa* partially agreed with Castro's. Vasconcelos stated that "de casta goleima" refers to someone from low and humble origin ("casta Goleima he o mesmo que geração baixa, & humilde"), but his explanation for the etymological reason

famous for eating too much. He goes further and says that this king is a cousin and a relative of kings,[199] because King John was neither the son nor the grandson of kings, as all kings commonly are, but he was a cousin and a relative of kings only: he is the King of Castile's cousin, the King of France's cousin, the Emperor's cousin, and relative of other kings of Europe. Even though he is not any king's son, Bandarra says he comes from a very high seed from all sides of his family tree: which is the Infant Duarte, son of King Emmanuel and Queen Mary, son of the Catholic Kings. From these two grandparents the King is a descendent of the greatest kings that ever existed in the Levant and in the Ponent, because he is a descendent of the kings of Portugal, Castile, and Aragon, which were the greatest kings in the Ponent, and of the kings of Naples and Sicily,[200] which were the greatest kings in the Levant.

Whereas it is true that Bandarra in his prophecies talks about such a king in particular, about such a person, and about such an individual, and whereas it is also true that this king, this person, and this individual is King John IV, as it is proved by the individuating signs and by the personal qualities by which the same Bandarra describes this king; it follows, as infallible consequence, that, as well as the prophecies about what went by were understood as belonging to this king, so the prophecies about what will come are to be understood as belonging to him too. And in conformity with this, Bandarra called his matter very gallantly as "resolve" and not "theme", because, after speaking about one king, leaving that one and speaking about another one, it was not maintaining

---

provided another flavour to the word. "Goleima" would be an adjective derived from the name Goliath, the biblical giant, and the giants were known by the Romans as sons of Earth ("filhos da terra") and as Earth is the ground (in Portuguese, "terra" has both meanings), they are low (as the ground), thus having a low origin. The irony of giants being low was not missed by Vasconcelos, who ends up quoting verses from the "Satyrist" ("o Satyrico"), Juvenal. Gregório de Almeida [i.e., João de Vasconcelos], *Restauração de Portugal Prodigiosa*, vol. 3, [27]–28. Yet a different explanation was provided by Homem de Mello in *Resorreiçam de Portugal e Morte Fatal de Castella*, although still as part of the same Restoration efforts of a prophetic defence of John IV's claims. Mello stated that "Goleima" was a corruption of the word "Goths" ("godos"), therefore, being from "casta goleima" meant descending from the Goths, from which John IV did not. Fernaõ H. de Figueiredo [i.e. Homem de Mello], *Resorreiçam de Portugal e Morte fatal de Castella* (Nantes: 1650), 65.

199 In Besselaar's edition, there is one clause more (here in italic): "Diz mais que é este Rei primo e parente de reis, *a qual propriedade admiravelmente está demonstrando a pessoa del-Rei D. João, porque toda a maior nobreza que Bandarra podia dar a el-Rei D. João era ser primo e parente de reis*", Besselaar, *Antônio Vieira*, 83.

200 The Kingdom of the Two Sicilies was formed the Kingdom of Sicily and the Kingdom of Naples, united by King Afonso V of Aragon in 1442, and was incorporated into the Spanish Crown by the Catholic Monarchs in 1501 under the title "King of Both Sicilies".

his resolve about the one,[201] as he says: "This very excellent King, From whom I got all my resolve." Truly, after the King was dead and buried, still saying that he shall go to Jerusalem to conquer the Turk seems upon too much of a resolve[202] but this is Bandarra's resolve.

The second place is stil more evident and clear in a certain way, because it talks about King John calling him by his own name. Bandarra keeps talking about the arms of Portugal, the Five Wounds of Christ, and, after putting Portugal's arms before all other kingdoms', he says the following in the *First Dream*:

> The arms, and the pennon,
> And the banner,
> Were given as a reminder
> Of the victory
> To a King, holy man;[203]
> He succeeded King John,
> By possession,
> The Calvary[204] as flag.
> He will take it as crest,
> Will clean the path
> Of all the Land of the Dog.[205]

The "King, holy man", to whom the insignia of Christ's passion were given as arms as a reminder of the victory was King Afonso I. These same arms of passion (which he calls Calvary) succeeded King John in possession to be his flag. And what will King John do with this flag, with these arms, and with this Calvary? "He will take it as crest, will clean all the course to the Land of the Dog." As a result, King John who was like the second founder of the Kingdom of Portugal, as he restored it after it had been lost,[206] and who succeeded King Afonso I in the possession of the Kingdom and of the Holy Wounds arms, this King John, and not another, will take these insignia of the passion of Christ as his elm's crest. This same King John, and not another, will be the one who will clean all

---

201 "teimar com um".
202 "demasiado teimar".
203 This verse is different in Muhana's lesson ("A um santo varão"), in Besselaar's ("a um Rei, Santo varão"), and in the 1644 edition ("A hum Santo Rey barão"). We follow Besselar's edition because the next paragraph in both Hopes of Portugal's copies quotes the expression "King, holy man" at its very beginning.
204 See notes 188 and 189 above and Vieira's explanation bellow.
205 *Trovas*, 93.
206 It was commonplace within the Restoration literature to compare the 1640 separation of Spain to the 1139 miraculous foundation of Portugal, reading the latter as a figure of the

the course to the Land of the Dog,[207] restoring the Holy Land and freeing the ways to it, occupied by the Turk.

All the successes promised to this king are divided in two main parts by Bandarra: the first one contains the successes of the acclamation in Portugal; the second contains the successes of the conquest of the Turk and the Holy Land. And to make it clear that both one and another namely belong to King John, Bandarra says that the King is called John when talking about the first one in the beginning of the *First Dream*: "His name is John." And when talking about the second at the end of the same *Dream*, Bandarra also says that he is called John:

> He succeeded the King John,
> By possession,
> The Calvary as flag
> He will take it as crest, etc.

And one should notice the expression "by possession", because the possession of the Kingdom was that one to which King John succeeded, whose right to it he always had, as the same Bandarra says:

> Praise this man[208]
> From the heart,
> Because he is the King by right.[209]

---

former and regarding the former as the fulfillment of the latter promises. This analogical and historical operation was completed by establishing a further relation with the 1363–1365 interregnum (also called the Crisis of 1363–1365 or the Revolution of Avis), in which John, the Master of Avis, later John I, defeated the Castilian interests in the Portuguese crown and started a new dynasty which would rule until the death of Sebastian I. By comparing Afonso I, John I, and John IV, the Braganza supporters established, through figural interpretation, three foundations of the Portuguese kingdom, each one confirming the vows made by Christ in Ourique and reassuring the prophetical mission and providential existence of John IV's reign at the same time. The Portuguese arms played a central role in this prophetical and reflective operation as both a proof and a constant reminder of the divine foundation(s) of the kingdom. See Lima, *Império dos sonhos*, chap. 3.

207   "Dog" ("Cão") was a common derogatory term to call Muslims, as it was a word used to refer to the Devil too. For this and other derogatory expressions, see João Adolfo Hansen, *A Sátira e o Engenho: Gregório de Matos e a Bahia do século XVII* (São Paulo: 2004), 399–400.

208   "Louvemos este varão". We opted to translate "varão" as man (and not knight), following Richard Fanshaw's 1655 translation of the first verse of Luís de Camões' *The Lusiad*: "Arms and the Men above the vulgar file". Luís de Camões, *The Lusiad, or, Portugals Historicall Poem* (London: 1655), 1. In the 1644 Trovas, it reads "Baraõ" instead of "varão".

209   *Trovas*, 101.

Such right, affirmed and confirmed by Bandarra, is a new and clear sign of being King John IV the subject about which the prophecies talk; because, if King John's right were to be acknowledged and well-received by all, as it happens with King Sebastian's and other kings' rights, it would not be necessary for Bandarra to say that he was the "King by right." However, because King John's right is doubted and discussed, Bandarra does state that he is truly king by right. And, because of this same right, which everyone professed by mouth when they acclaimed the King, was still by some denied with the heart;[210] to them, Bandarra casts the stone when he says: "Praise this man—from the heart".

Those words that we have already repeated, "Fear not the Turk, not, in this season",[211] also prove that the same King John about whose acclamation Bandarra spoke is the one who shall go conquer the Turk. Bandarra does not say to the Turk not to fear King John, but not to fear him in this season, because in this season the King would only be the restorer of Portugal, and in the expected season he shall be the conqueror and destroyer of the Turk, and he shall make him fear.

The same is clearly demonstrated with the combination of two places or verses, one from the *First Dream*, the other from the *Second Dream*. The verse of the *First Dream* says: "The new king is arisen"; and talks about the past acclamation, of the year 40, as proved by the outcome. The verse from the *Second Dream* says: "The new king is awake", and talks about the future journey and conquest of the Turk, for which the new King shall wake up, as the following verses prove:

> The new King is awake
> He already shouts,
> His cry already resounds,
> Levi already gives him the hand,
> Against the rambunctious Shechem[212]

Shechem is the Turk who is the Turk who shall behave unrestrainedly[213] throughout Italy and the Church's lands. From that, one clearly gathers that

---

210 According to Besselaar, Vieira was alluding to the 1641 attempted coup against John IV.
211 Vieira inserted another "not" into these verses that he had quoted before. Cf. note 96.
212 *Trovas*, 99.
213 "se há-de desmandar". Bluteau, *Vocabulario Portuguez & Latino*, vol. 3, 155: "desmandarse. Alargarse mais do que he razaõ, como fazem os criados, que excedem os limites da ordem, & mandado de seus Senhores. Estendese a significaçaõ desta palavra a outros generos de excessos."

one prophecy and another, that one about the past as this about the future, both refer to King John, because the one who was risen is the new King, and the one who shall be awaken is also the new King: "The new king is risen",[214] "The new king is awake."[215] And do not let the verse "Levi already gives him his hand" pass without notice, because it proves the same since that "already" is relative. Who says "already gives him his hand" supposes that before he did not gave it to him, or that he did not want to give it to him: so, that king, to whom the Pope shall give the hand later, is the same to whom he did not give it, neither wanted to give, who is King John IV.

I have promised to prove this glorious conclusion with two places by Bandarra, and I have already proved it with six. To shorten the arguments and close this reasoning, which is the key of all this paper, with an irrefragable demonstration, I therefore say:

> That King is the one who shall conquer and overcome the Turk, etc., is the one in whom all the individual signs and differences are found and with which, in all his prophecies, Bandarra portrays him;
>
> King John IV, who is is today buried in S. Vicente de Fora,[216] is that one in whom all these individuating signs and differences are found, missing none;
>
> Therefore, King John IV is the one who shall conquer the Turk, and whom all the prodigies of this fatal quest belong to and wait for;

And that all those individuating signs and differences may be found in King John IV, I prove it evidently with a general introduction, in which I am going to discourse on all of them.[217]

Bandarra says that this king is the seed of King Ferdinand: and that King John is the seed of King Ferdinand, as it was said. Bandarra says that his King is a new king, and King John is a new king, because he was never a king before. Bandarra says this king shall have risen as such in the year 40, and King John was risen king[218] in the year 40. Bandarra says this king is happy and very fortu-

---

214 *Trovas*, 87, v. 7.
215 *Trovas*, 99, v. 7.
216 The Franciscan church of São Vicente de Fora is located in Lisbon and is the royal pantheon of the Braganza dynasty.
217 The arguments presented by Vieira are partially in the dedication of the 1664 *Trovas* edition. *Trovas*, "Aos Verdadeiros Portvgvezes, devotos do Encvberto", s.p.
218 "há-de ser levantado", "foi levantado rei". By "ser levantado", Vieira here meant the act of enthroning a monarch. Early modern Portuguese rulers were not crowned or consecrated, they were acclaimed by the people and sworn during the "Cortes" (the three States of the

nate, and King John was the happiest during all his reign. Bandarra says that the name of this king is John, and King John, before and after being king, always had this name. Bandarra says that the Portuguese conquests and territories would declare for this king soon, and they would be firm by him, and King John was recognised as king in his conquests soon, and all persevere in the same fidelity. Bandarra says that his king would raise his flags and make war against Castile, and King John, in the sixteen years that he governed, always made war against the Castilians. Bandarra says that this king is very excellent: and the King John was endowed with many excellencies, moreover he was only Excellency while Duke of Braganza.[219] Bandarra says this king is not from a gluttonous stock, and King John is not from a gluttonous stock, as we have already explained. Bandarra says that his king is a cousin and a relative of kings, and the King John is a cousin (and no more than a cousin) of three kings of Europe, and a relative of the others. Bandarra says that this king comes from a very high seed, the King John came from the kings of Portugal, whose title is: "Very High and Mighty".[220] Bandarra says that his king descends from the kings from the Levant to the Ponent: and the King John descends from the kings of Portugal, Castile and Aragon, who are kings from the Ponent, and the kings of Naples and Sicily, who are kings from the Levant. Bandarra says that this king has a good captain as a brother and that the brotherhood is not known,[221] and the King John is brother of Infant Duarte,[222] a very good captain, as we know, yet we do not

---

kingdom meeting). The act of acclamation was also called "levantamento" (in the sense of lifting or elevating), since the people of Portugal lift, raise or elevate someone to be their new king when acclaiming this person. In the 1644 *Trovas* edition's dedication, both "aclamação" and "levantamento" were used as synonyms when commenting upon these verses of Bandarra: "este Rey serà acclamado e aleuantado" (*Trovas*, s.p.). Throughout "Hopes of Portugal", Vieira mentioned several "levantamentos" that happened in the Portuguese domains after 1 December 1640 as proof of John IV's prophetical election. Notwithstanding, in Bandarra's verse "O Rei novo é levantado", the first meaning would probably be "risen", in the sense of got up, ascend and also appeared.

219 John IV was Duke of Braganza from 1630 to 1645, styled as John II of Braganza. His eldest son and heir-apparent, Theodosius (1634–1653), was named Duke of Braganza as Theodosius III on 27 October 1645. The Portuguese formal treatment for a Duke or Duchess is "Vossa Excelência" (Your Excellency).
220 The Portuguese sovereigns were to be addressed by this formula: "Ao Mui Alto e Poderoso Rei" or "A Mui Alta e Poderosa Rainha" (To the Very High and Mighty King or Queen).
221 Vieira refers to these verses, not quoted in his "Hopes of Portugal": "Este Rey tem hum Irmaõ/ Bom Capitaõ./ Naõ se sabe a irmandadẽ?", *Trovas*, 102, v. 1–3.
222 Second-born of Theodosius II, Duke of Braganza, and brother of John IV, Duarte (1603–1649) left Portugal in 1634 to serve Emperor Ferdinand III and to join the Catholic forces in the Thirty Years' War. After the Restoration of 1640, Phillip IV asked his cousin the Emperor to arrest Duarte for treason, with success. Despite all the Portuguese diplomatic efforts to get him released, he died in prison in 1649.

known if the King is as good a captain as he is a brother is.[223] Bandarra says that his king or this monarch is from the lands and county:[224] and the King John is from the county land, because he is natural from Vila Viçosa.[225] Bandarra says that his king is a law-keeper, and that he praises the justice,[226] and King John praised the law more than anything else, and he left only that recommended to the King,[227] God saves him, in his will.[228] Bandarra says, or supposes, that this king shall not be received by the Pope until a certain time, and none of the three Pontiffs had received King John until the time of his death. Bandarra says, or supposes, that not all of the people who acclaimed this king with the mouth would follow him with the heart, and it is certain that, after the acclamation, some did not follow King John with their hearts, at least those whom he had the heads taken off. Finally, Bandarra says that God made this king the most perfect and with no flaws,[229] and who can doubt that after King John is resurrected he shall be a perfect man and shall show himself to have been made and perfectly made by God? Moreover, a man without flaws cannot be a man of this world, but rather has to be of the other.

In the same fashion, Bandarra says that his king is a good hidden king, because in King John God has placed many parts and qualities of a good king to the highest degree, which so far have been hidden and will be later discovered. One piece of a good king which we desired and found missing in King John, at the time God made him, was for him being a very great warrior and inclined to the arms, and this military and warrior spirit will be discovered in the King

---

223 "Posto que ainda não sabemos quão [seu?] irmão é el-Rei em ser bom capitão". Besselaar interpreted this very obscure passage as meaning that it was not known if John IV was equal to his brother, Prince Duarte, in battle.
224 "terras e comarca". Another unquoted passage: "Ser das terras, e comarqua,/ Semente del Rey Fernando." *Trovas*, 103, v. 9–10.
225 Vila Viçosa was the seat of the Dukes of Braganza, where the Ducal Palace was located. Though the palace of one the most powerful houses of the Iberian Peninsula, Vila Viçosa was known to be a remote and bucolic place, up to the point that, during the Iberian Union, *Corte na Aldeia* (Court in the village) was the title of courteous dialogue written by Francisco Rodrigues Lobo and dedicated to the House of Braganza. Francisco Rodrigues Lobo, *Corte na Aldeia*, ed. José Adriano da Fonseca (Lisbon: 1991), 52–53, see França, *Portugal na Época da Restauração*, 105–116.
226 Another unquoted passage: "Este, tem tanta nobreza,/ Qual eu nunca ui em Rey:/ Este, goarda bem a ley/ Da justiça e da grandeza." *Trovas*, 71.
227 That is, Afonso VI, John IV's son.
228 Besselaar identified a passage in John IV's will in which one reads: "remind him [Alphose VI] to seek to excel, among all his virtues that I hope he will have, in the ones of equality of justice". Apud Besselaar, 89, note 248.
229 *Trovas*, 148: "Resolui o meu canhenho/ Sobre este forte Baraõ,/ Naõ lhe acho nenhum senaõ,/ Dizer delle muito tenho."

with notable wonders on the war against the Turk, when, after his armies flee and rout, the world will see the Turk surrendered at King John's feet and hurt by the King's very sword.[230] This is the evidence[231] of what Bandarra says:

> He shows that he goes hurt
> By this good Hidden King.[232]

showing that this part of being a good king that he seemingly lacked was hidden within him. Oh! how much was hidden in that subject, King John! King John was hidden within himself. Some of the King's most noticed accidents were just a natural cover and disguise with which God had hidden in the King what He would like to perform through him, that his marvels thus be even more marvellous.[233]

Now, the curious people might read all of Bandarra's prophecies, those which contain already-passed successes as well as those which promise the future ones. In all of them, you will not find any individuating differences nor personal qualities and signals of the prophesied monarch beyond those that we had here faithfully referred, which all are proper to the person of King John IV. They fit him all so naturally and without any violence, that one may clearly see that Bandarra had King John in front of his eyes, and not someone else, in order to depict him with colours so alive and so properly his. It is evidently shown and demonstrated that our Lord King John IV, who is in the grave, is the fateful[234]

---

230 In Besselaar's lesson is "by his very hand".
231 "Energia" (energy) here refers to the rhetorical notion of "energeia", the vigorous efficacy of proof and evidence acquired by vividly putting something in front of one's eyes ("evidentia", evidence) through the use of images.
232 *Trovas*, 75.
233 As explained in note 163, Vieira used the term "accidents" ("acidentes") in the scholastic sense, i.e., characteristics not intrinsically related to the substance of the being. Accident follows the also Aristotelian-Thomistic term subject, which denominates the essence of a thing, without its accidents. The substance of John IV would be only revealed in the prophecies and in the fulfilment of his and Portugal's destiny. The subject, John IV's real essence designed by God, would not be defined by his accidents (for example, not being a "good captain" as his brother was), rather would be only completely uncovered in the fulfilment of his and Portugal's destiny. By this contrasting relation between accident and subject within John IV's image as the late king and the king to be, Vieira drew a parallel between being the Hidden King yet to be un/dis-covered, having hidden qualities to be uncovered and the very notion of divine prophecy regulating human history by the complementary pair of figure and fulfilment.
234 "Fatal". Translated as "fateful", "fatal" in the original was used in the sense "of fate" ("do fado"). For the importance of this word and its variants in Vieira's writings, see Carlos Alberto de Seixas Maduro, *As Artes do Não-Poder. Cartas de Vieira: um paradigma da retór-*

king of whom Bandarra speaks in all his prophecies, both those which have been already fulfilled and those which yet remain to be accomplished.

If King John IV is, with such evidence, the one who shall perform all the marvels that we left prognosticated along all this discourse, and if this same King John is today dead and buried, it is not just love and nostalgia, but reason, understanding, and obligation that urge us to believe and to hope for his resurrection. To believe the contrary would be ignorant and witless, as Saint Augustine names those who seeing one part of the fulfilled prophecies do not believe in the other. It pains me not to be able to quote his words, which are excellent.[235]

Here might the unbelievers (if there are any yet) consider how many men have been resurrected in this world, not only Christians, but heathens,[236] and for very ordinary purposes. Almost in our days, Francis Xavier alone resurrected 25.[237] If God in all ages, as in our own, has resurrected so many men, even heathens, for particular purposes, why for such a universal and extraordinary end, the biggest that ever happened in the world as it is the recuperation of the Holy Land, the destruction of the Turk, and the conversion of all the heathendom and Judaism, will He not resurrect a religious, pious, Christian man? A man, who, when king, did know how to be humble, which is the quality that God seeks more than any in those He wishes to make an instrument of his wonders, without noticing any further human imperfections and weaknesses in him, as it was seen in David?[238] King John shall resurrect beyond any doubt, and his resurrection will be the easiest way to conciliate the respect and obedience

---

ica epistolar do barroco (Lisbon: 2012), 306–307 (though one could have some reservations towards the somewhat nationalistic tone of his remarks regarding "fatal" and "fatalidade").

235 According to Besselaar, Vieira was possibly referring to the following passage: "Stultus est enim qui non vult credere pauca quae restant, cum videat tam multa impleta esse" Augustine, *Exposition on Psalms*, 62, 1 in *Patrologia Latina*, 36, 748. As Thomas Cohen pointed out, Vieira's remark of not being able to identify the exact passage is "a reminder of Vieira's limiting circumstances in the Brazilian backlands" but also exemplifies Vieira's position regarding the hierarchy between scholarship and his prophetical interpretations. Thomas Cohen, *The Fire of Tongues* (Stanford, CA: 1998), 130–132.

236 "gentios". According Bluteau, "Gentio, pagão" (heathen). Bluteau, *Vocabulário*, vol. 4, 57.

237 Among the miracles attributed to Saint Francis Xavier, there is the resurrection of many people, especially newly converted Christians, during his mission in Asia. For some examples, see the hagiography written by the Jesuit João de Lucena in 1600, before Xavier's canonisation: João de Lucena, *História da Vida do Padre Francisco de Xavier* (1600; facsimile ed. Lisbon: 1952), 109, 207, 887. Like Besselaar, we have not identified from which source Vieira got this exact figure of resurrections.

238 Cf. Psalm 30:8: "I will be glad and rejoice in thy mercy. For thou hast regarded my humility, thou hast saved my soul out of distresses."

of all nations of Europe. They shall follow him and militate under his flags in this enterprise, and, because being so proud and haughty, they would never do that in any other way if they were not obligated by this heavenly signal, realising all of them that they are not obeying a king of Portugal, but a captain of God.

> Ma verrà da Lisbona
> Chiara e illustre persona,
> la cui fama risona
> in tutta parte e lido.
> Nel mondo dà gran grido[239]

says Salutivo,[240] prophesying the medicine with which God shall help from Lisbon to Rome, destroyed by the Turk. And what is this "great cry" that shall resound throughout the whole world, if not saying that the King of the Portuguese has been resurrected? To this cry, or this shout (as Bandarra calls it), the same whole world will answer in order to see, to admire, to venerate and to follow the resurrected and miraculous king. And this stupendous prodigy, seen with the eyes, will be what will open the doors to the faith and fulfilment of all the others.

Against all this discourse there remains only one objection, which could weigh against any understanding, and it is the following: if Bandarra's main and utter subject and theme, or resolve (as he says),[241] are prophesying King John's prodigious successes, and among these successes and prodigies, the one that seems the biggest and the most incredible of all is that the King shall be resurrected; why did Bandarra not talk about his resurrection? I do answer and say: yes, Bandarra did talk about it, and he did talk in the most proper and ordinary terms by which the prophets usually talk about this matter.

Calling death "sleep" and the resurrection "awakening", is such an ordinary speech in the prophets that there is no need for quoting places. David, prophesying the resurrection of Christ, said in his name: *Ego dormivi et soporatus sum, et exurresi.*[242] And the same Christ, prophesying or promising Lazarus's resurrection, used the same terms: *Lazarus amicus noster dormit, vado ut a somno*

---

239 But there will come from Lisbon/Clear and illustrious person,/Whose fame resounds/Through all parts and shore./In the world he gives great cry.
240 About Salutivo, see note 133.
241 "o seu tema ou sua teima (como ele diz)". See note 197.
242 Psalm 3:6: "I have slept and taken my rest: and I have risen up."

*excitem eum.*²⁴³ Bandarra thus talks about the resurrection of King John, and so he says in the *Second Dream*:

> Finally, the desired time
> Has come,
> According to what the clasp binds together,
> The forties are already passing,
> Which has been evoked
> By a Doctor already gone.
> The new King is awake
> He already makes a shout,
> His cry already resounds,
> Levi already gives him the hand
> Against the rambunctious Shechem
> And, for what I have read,
> And known well,
> The dishonour of Dinah
> Will be avenged,
> As it was promised.²⁴⁴

This couplet's first seven verses are so similar to those other seven which referred to the King's acclamation that in many copies they appear scratched or incomplete, since they were assumed to be the same ones. Thus I had suspected, having compared some of the aforementioned copies, and I did finally verify it in a very old volume of manuscripts²⁴⁵ belonging to Doctor Diogo Marchão Temudo,²⁴⁶ to whom I communicated about this thought of mine in

---

243 John 11:11: "Lazarus our friend sleepeth; but I go that I may awake him out of sleep." Besselaar pointed out that Vieira misquoted the Vulgate passage, probably because he was citing by heart: "Lazarus amicus noster dormit *sed vado ut* [instead of only "vadum ut", Besselaar's lesson, or "vado ut", Muhana's] a somno exsuscitem eum." Besselaar, *Antônio Vieira*, 92, note 174.
244 *Trovas*, 99.
245 "cartapácio". Vieyra Trasmontano's *Dictionary* translated "cartapácio" as: "a stitched book, or any parcel of writing put together", Antonyo Vieyra, *Dictionary*, "Cartapácio, s.m", s.p. More specifically, "Cartapácio" usually refers to a mixed manuscript volume or miscellaneous manuscript copies bound together, or to use Bluteau's definition: "livro de mão, em que se escrevem várias matérias" ("handwritten book, in which several subjects are written"). Bluteau, *Vocabulário*, vol. 2, 169.
246 According to Besselaar, the Diogo Marchão Temudo mentioned here was not the one with whom Vieira corresponded in the 1680s and 1690s, but his father and namesake. Both were active in the judiciary branch and, as far as one can infer from Vieira's letters, Sebastianists.

the year 1643. He took the volume from his library to check what I had said, and we found that both couplets were in it, and the latter was over-scored.[247]

From the comparison of these two couplets, and from the similarity and difference between them, it is clearly seen how King John shall have two lives and very different successes in any each of them. In both couplets it is said: "Finally, the desired time has come"; because there have to be two desired times: the first desired time was the Kingdom's restitution; and the second desired time is the one in which we are today, in which all desire and wait for the prodigious king, even though with different hopes. The first couplet says: "The forties are already coming"; and the second says "The forties are already passing"; because the term in the first couplet would have to be in the year 40, and the term in the second would have to be after this time was passed. The first couplet says: "The new king is risen"; the second says: "The new king is awake"; because the new king who in the year 40 was risen is the very same new king who, after passing this time, shall wake up from the sleep he was sleeping, i.e., he shall be resurrected. In both the couplets it is said: "[He] already makes a shout" because the same new king shall make two shouts: one great shout in his acclamation, and another greater one in his resurrection. These are the same words of Salutivo: "*Nel modo dà gran grido.*"[248] The first couplet says: "He already looms his flag against the breeding griffon"; and the second says: "His cry already resounds, Levi already gives him the hand, Against the rambunctious Shechem" because the acclamation of the new king was followed by the wars against Castile, in which time the Pope did not receive him, and because the resurrection of the new king shall be followed by the wars against the Turk, and then the Pope shall receive him and shall not only give him the foot, but also the hand.

Here one must notice how proper the story is and how appropriate it is an illiterate man who indeed seems to be guided by divine spirit. Prince Shechem, a heathen, dishonoured Dinah, Jacob's daughter, and, to avenge this affront, the two brothers of Dinah, Levi and Simeon, united themselves, and killed and

---

Temudo senior (1620–1659) had a rising career as a judge, and after being magistrate ("corregedor") in the Madeira Islands and judge ("desembargador") in Porto, reached one of the most prestigious and highest positions in the legal system, "Desembargador do Paço".

247 José Alberto Tavim sees this passage as one example in many of Bandarra's *Trovas* circulation and its profusion of manuscripts and copies. José Alberto Tavim, "Revisitando uma carta em português sobre Sabbatai Zvi", *Sefarad*, 67/1 (2007), 171–172. One could also wonder about the libraries and collections in which *Trovas's* copies were. Finally, it is also interesting to notice that, according to Vieira, the episode took place prior to the publishing of the 1644 Nantes edition of the *Trovas*, which was proposed as the official version of the *Trovas* according to the Braganzas' supporters.

248 In the world, he gives great cry.

destroyed Shechem with all his people.[249] Then Bandarra applies this past story to the future successes with extreme accommodation, because Shechem is the Turk, Dinah is the Church, Levi is the Pope, Simeon is the King. And in the same fashion that Levi joined Simeon to vindicate Dinah from the injuries done by Shechem, the Pope shall unite with the King to vindicate the Church from the injuries the Turk will do. The same Bandarra alludes to these when he says in his answers:

> As my count adds up,
> The text shall be fulfilled,
> First, Lord, in Rome.[250]

First, the Turk shall come to Italy and to Rome, and then the King shall be resurrected. In another place of the text, the same Bandarra talks about the resurrection of the King, under the same metaphor of the awakened one, and under the same circumstances of the Turk. So he says in the quatrains before the *Dreams*:

> The Lion is already awake,
> Very alert;
> It has already woken up, walks its way,
> And it will soon take off, from the nest,
> The Pig; and it is very certain.[251]

In such a manner that, when the King (which is the Lion) wakes up and is resurrected, it will be after the Pig (which is the Turk) makes a nest in Christian lands. And Bandarra says he will soon take it off from its nest, because the war will be very brief, not as the very long and lasting ones which attempted to conquer the Holy Land without effect. And because this effect and this haste seemed to be a difficult and unbelievable thing, he adds, to leave no doubt about it: "and it is very certain". Thus, Bandarra says in two places of the text that the new king will be resurrected under the metaphor of awakening: "The new king is awake"; "And the Lion is already awake, Very alert, It has already woken up."

In both these places, Bandarra says he will awake and be resurrected to make war against the Turk and to beat him. From this effect, one evidently gathers that waking up means being resurrected because, as the new king is dead, as

---

249 Genesis 34.
250 *Trovas*, 130.
251 *Trovas*, 75.

he is in the present, he cannot wake up but by being resurrected, and as he has to make war against the Turk, he cannot go unless by being resurrected.

With the same clarity, although also through metaphors, I find the resurrection of the King prophesied by Bandarra in another two places.

In the Scriptures, the resurrection is explained by the word "arise". This term was used by the Angel when he announced the resurrection of Christ: *Surrexit, non est hic*.[252] The same term was used by Christ when he resurrected the widow's son: *Adolescens, tibi dico, surge*.[253] And the same was used by David when he was prophesying the resurrection of the same Lord: *Surge, Domine, in requiem tuam*,[254] etc. Because in the same way that "to lie" means "to be buried" (that is why we write "Here lies someone" on the graves), "to rise" or "arise" mean "to be resurrected". And by this fashion Bandarra says, in two great texts, that King John will be resurrected. The first text, in the quatrains before the *Dreams*, says:

> A great lion will arise,
> And will give great roars,
> Its shouts will be heard;
> They will amaze everyone, etc.[255]

The second text, at the end of the quatrains, says:

> I see a grand king arising,
> All blessed,
> That he will be so thrived
> That he will defend the flock, etc.[256]

Here must one notice that, from the consequences of these very texts, one clearly gathers that in both of them the meaning of the "arising" is "resurrecting", because in both of them the effects of the King's resurrection follow the "arising". In the first text he says that "[he] will arise", and that "[it] will amaze everyone", because there cannot be anything that amazes the world more than seeing the King of Portugal resurrected, after being dead for so many years. And then the next verses continue by saying what he shall do against the Turk, and

---

[252] Mark 16:6 ("he is risen, he is not here").
[253] Luke 7:14 ("Young man, I say to thee, arise").
[254] Psalm 131:6 (in Douay-Rheims, 131:8, "Arise, O Lord, into thy resting place").
[255] *Trovas*, 78.
[256] *Trovas*, 150.

how he shall enter into the Promised Land, etc., which is the final purpose why God shall resurrect the King. In the second text, concerning the passage "he will arise all blessed",[257] which is the proper quality of a resurrected man, Bandarra says that "he will arise to defend the flock", which is Christ's flock, to which the resurrected king will help and defend against the wolves, that, as it is said by the same Bandarra, will be tearing apart the same flock in Rome and in Italy. Thus, in four conformable places of the text, Bandarra explicity says that King John IV shall be resurrected, using the terms by which the prophets typically talk, and using the same terms by which David prophesied Christ's resurrection.

In this same sense and with the same clarity spoke Saint Methodius,[258] whose words have been much vitiated on the Sebastianists' papers,[259] and I

---

257 Vieira changed and adapted Bandarra's verses here and in the following quotation.

258 The Church Father Methodius (?–ca. 311) was the bishop of Olympos in Lycia, Asia Minor, and wrote several dogmatic and ascetic dialogues. Among the writings under his name, there was an apocalyptic history which had great circulation and influence especially in medieval Western Christendom as it partially moulded medieval eschatological ideas. As such, it was included in the first printed collection of Patristic works in the Sixteenth and early Seventeenth Centuries, and it eventually had a significant impact on early modern Iberian messianic interpretations. The apocalyptic history, however, was not actually from Methodius, but from an unknown 7th-century Christian author (possibly a cleric), and the text is nowadays referred to as *Apocalypse* of Pseudo-Methodius. Pseudo-Methodius. *Apocalypse. An Alexandrian World Chronicle*, ed., trans. Benjamin Garstad (Cambridge, US: 2012); José van den Besselaar, "A Profecia Apocalíptica de Pseudo-Metódio", *Luso-Brazilian Review*, 28/1 (Summer, 1991), 5–22; Besselaar, *Antônio Vieira*, 348–354.

259 "cartapácios dos Sebastianistas". Quotations of Pseudo-Methodius indeed appeared in several prophecies' compilations and commentaries, whether Sebastianist or not. Among the Sebastianist papers, the one attributed to Portuguese Friar José Teixeira is an interesting example not only because it quoted the very same passage of "Hopes of Portugal" but also because of its broader circulation. Teixeira's text was translated and printed in French and eventually in English at the very beginning of the 17th century. The French edition was called *Adventure Admirable* and was published as part of the campaign for the Sebastian of Venice at Paris in 1600. It was promptly translated and printed in London as *The Strangest Adventvre That Ever Happened*. The passage in the English version is slightly different from Vieira's though: "S. Methodus Bishop and Martyr. lib. 6. cap. 28. *Expergiscetur Rex in furore tanquam homo à somno vini, quem existimabant homines tanquam mortuum esse. Hic exiet super filios Ismael à mari Aethiopum, &c.* Vide *Biblioth. Patrum*, fol. 526. primae Lutet. Paris. Editionis. In English thus. There shall a king awake in great furie, like a man out of a slumber of wine, whom men shall repute to haue bene dead. He shall goe out against the sonnes of Ismael towards the Aethi[o]pian sea, &c." [José Teixeira], *The Strangest Adventvre That Ever Happened: Either in the ages passed or present. Containing a discourse concerning the successe of the King of Portugall Dom Sebastian* (London: 1601), 33. The same passage was cited again in the "Jardim Ameno", an important prophetic compilation handwritten between 1635–1643. However, "Jardim Ameno"'s authors did just partially transcribe the Latin quotation, although fully rendering it in Portuguese: "Prophecia de S. Metho-

read them in the *Biblioteca Antiga dos Santos Padres*,²⁶⁰ which is in the library of the College of Santo Antão,²⁶¹ and they follow like this: *Expergiscetur tanquam a somno vini quem putabunt homines quasi mortuum et inutilem esse.* The saint speaks about a Prince who shall win and smite the Turkish Empire in future times, and says: "He will awake, like a man out of a slumber of wine, the one whom men have imagined that, as being dead, was useless".²⁶²

By saying that "he will awake, like a man out of slumber of wine" he wants to signify the indomitable value and effort, the rush, the resolution, and the exceptional activity with which the just-resurrected King will dedicate himself to the arms, to the provisions, to the war, and especially to the execution of revenge against his and Christ's enemies, in such a way that he will seem

---

dio Bispo de Antiochia. *Expergiscet[u]r Rex in furore magno. &c.* Quer dizer. Despertara hum Rey cõ grande furor como de uinho, aquem os home*n*s tinhão por morto, este hira sobre os filhos de Ismael do mar de Etiopia." Lisbon, National Archives "Torre do Tombo", Manuscrito da Livraria, Cód. 774, fol. 11ᵇ. For other examples, see Besselaar, "A Profecia Apocalíptica de Pseudo-Metódio"; Besselaar, *Antônio Vieira*, 348–354.

260   According to Besselaar, Vieira was referring to the Bigne's *Magna Bibliotheca Veterum Patrum et Antioquorum Scriptorum Ecclesiasticorum Collectio*, but the expanded and modified edition printed in Cologne between 1618 and 1625. As in most cases here, Vieira was quoting by heart, and reminding us that, Besselaar points out that the Jesuit slightly misquoted the Pseudo-Methodius text. However, what has called Besselaar's attention was not this perfectly understandable (if not impressive) citation by heart, though with some minor changes, but the fact that Vieira made a not so precise translation in order to accommodate the Pseudo-Methodius passage to his purposes as shown below. Besselaar, "A Profecia Apocalíptica de Pseudo-Metódio", 13. One should also notice that the passage quoted and translated in *The Strangest Adventure* and "Jardim Ameno" is quite different from the Latin passage transcribed by Vieira. As we have not compared the *Magna Bibliotheca*'s different editions, we cannot say whether this discrepancy came from the editions or was indeed a Sebastianist corrupted version, as Vieira stated. See note above.

261   The College of Santo Antão, in Lisbon, was the first Jesuit college and see in Portugal.

262   As Besselaar says, Vieira changed the meaning of "quasi mortuum et inutilem esse" when rendering it to Portuguese. He ignored the "quasi" and what could be read as an analogy, impression or possibility (almost dead, as if dead) was translated as a certainty: "como morto, era inútil" (as being dead, was useless). This alteration of the meaning did not go unnoticed at the time. One of the papers written to contest Vieira's "Hopes" explicitly mentioned the "quasi mortuum" mistranslation, and there is a chance that Vieira was aware of this criticism since he addressed the question in his "Representações" when defending himself during his Inquisitorial trial. Besselaar, "A Profecia Apocalíptica de Pseudo-Metódio", 13–14; Besselaar, *Antônio Vieira*, 181–182, 352–353. It is curious though that the same mistranslation and emphasis on the certainty of death were also made in both *Adventure*'s and "Jardim Ameno"'s translations of Pseudo-Methodius. See notes 259 and 260. Our translation was based on the English version of Methodius quotation in *The Strangest Adventvre*, 33.

like in furore.²⁶³ In this same way, David described Christ as victorious against Death and Hell in the day of his resurrection: *Et excitatus est tanquam dormiens Dominus, tanquam potens craputalus a vino: et percussit inimicos suos in posteriora; opprobrium sempiternum dedit illis.*²⁶⁴ And so, finally, it will be completely understood Saint Isidore's celebrated prophecy, which has been so twisted and violated in so many writings: *erit Rex bis pie datus*.²⁶⁵ God already gave King John IV to us by his mercy once, and for the same mercy he will give him to us one more time, and so he will be mercifully given twice: one time in his restitution to the Kingdom, another in his restitution to life; and one when acclaimed, another when resurrected.

And, to avoid that my interpretation of Bandarra seems a singular one, I want to bring forward here the very ones who were believed and were given the title of prophets by those who have stolen their truths from them. Friar Bento,²⁶⁶ in his prophecies, says:

---

263   The mention of a furore was neither in the passage nor in the translation provided by Vieira, nor was it in the Cologne's *Magna Bibliotheca* edition of Pseudo-Methodius's *Apocalypse*—Vieira's source according to Besselaar. However, it was explicitly mentioned in both *The Adventures* and "Jardim Ameno" transcription and translation of Pseudo-Methodius. From this and other evidence showed in the notes above, it is quite likely that Vieira had had access to several versions of the text (both first-hand and second-hand) and was mixing them when quoting the Pseudo-Methodius passage by heart—either on purpose or not.
264   Psalm 77:65–66 ("And the Lord was awaked as one out of sleep, and like a mighty man that hath been surfeited with wine./ And he smote his enemies on the hinder parts: he put them to an everlasting reproach").
265   This passage attributed to Isidore of Seville appeared among the pamphlets printed in Paris and London to support Sebastian of Venice's cause. [José Teixeira], *The True Historie of the Late and Lamentable Adventures of Don Sebastian King of Portugall* (London: 1602), C2–C2ᵛ. In 1688, writing from Salvador, Brazil, Vieira added one more name to the prophecy's authorship, the Sybil Cassandra. According to him, the vision would have been transcribed by Friar Zacharias, founder of the Franciscan convent in Alenquer, Portugal, and found in the same convent. In that manuscript, both Isidore and the Sybil would appear as having prophesied that "reinará hum Rey duas vezes piamente dado" ("a King two times piously given will reign", in Latin "regnabit Rex bis pie datus"). Vieira's 1688 Latin transcription of the prophecy was, albeit, a little different from the one in "Hope"'s ("erit Rex bis pie datus") and the one in the sebastianist *True Historie* ("Occultus Rex, bis pié datus"). Antônio Vieira, *Palavra de Deos Empenhada, e Desempenhada* (Lisbon: 1690), 256–257, see also: Besselaar, *Antônio Vieira*, 479–481.
266   "Frade Bento", literally, Benedictine Friar. In other texts, Vieira attributed this passage to the "Ermitão de Monserrate", "Rocacelsa", and "Rocacelsa, Ermitão de Monserrate", and in several 17th-century manuscripts, the prophecies appeared under the various names of "Frei João de Rocacelsa", "Juan de Rocacelsa", "Ermitão de Monserrate, Monge de Aragão", "Religioso da Ordem de São Bento", "Rocatalhada", besides the ones used by Vieira. Not

Pero viviendo verá
quien viviere: un gran León
muerto resuscitará.²⁶⁷

And the Carthusian,²⁶⁸ in his own prophecies:

Veo entrar una Dama
con armas en el Consejo,
y que resuscita el Viejo,
debaxo de la campana,
con su barba larga y cana.²⁶⁹

---

finding further information about it, Besselaar assumed, as João Lucio de Azevedo did before him, that this Juan de Rocacelsa existed and probably was an Aragonese Benedictine friar, influenced by the 14th-century Joachimite millenarianism that generated the pseudo-Isidore prophecies. Besselaar, *Antônio Vieira*, 355–360. However, it is quite likely that Rocacelsa (or in its Castilian and Catalan variants, Rocatallada, Ribatallada, Peratallada) was a corrupted version of the name Jean de Roquetaillade or Rupescissa (1310–c.1370), a French Franciscan friar known for his alchemical treatises and Joachimite visions. Roquetaillade's prophecies and texts circulated in the Iberian kingdoms (even among the Muslim communities under the name of "Juan de Rokasia"), and probably his name (or some variant of it) was borrowed—as was common in early modern cultural practices—to confer authority to a new body of prophecies written in the late 15th century. About Rocacelsa/Rocatalhada and Rupescissa in the Iberian world, see Karl Pietsch, "The Madrid Manuscript of the Spanish Grail Fragments. I", *Modern Philology*, 18/3 (1920), 147–156; Karl Pietsch, "The Madrid Manuscript of the Spanish Grail Fragments. II", *Modern Philology*, 18/11 (1921), 591–596; Lima, *Império dos Sonhos*, 179–183; Gerard Wiegers, "Jean de Roquetaillade prophecies among the Muslim minorities of medieval and early-modern Christian Spain: An Islamic version of the *Vademecum in Tribulatione*", in *The Transmission and Dynamics of the Textual Sources of Islam*, ed. Nicolet Boekhoff-van der Voort (Leiden: 2011), 229–247. Concerning Roquetaillade, see Marjorie Reeves, *The Influence of Prophecy in the Later Middle Ages. A Study in Joachimism* (Notre Dame, USA: 1993), 224–228, 324; Leah DeVun, *Prophecy, Alchemy, and the End of Time: John of Rupescissa in the Late Middle Ages* (New York: 2009).

267 But who lives will see/ Who live: a great lion /Once dead, will resurrect.
268 The Carthusian refers to a Castilian Carthusian monk called Pedro de Frias. He would be responsible for collecting and rendering in verse the prophecies about the "Hidden One" (the "Encoberto", "Encubierto"), falsely attributed to Isidore of Seville. Under Frias' or Isidore's name, several prophecies in Spanish circulated in early modern Portugal, and some of them were possibly known and used by Bandarra in his dreams about the "Hidden One". Besselaar, *Antônio Vieira*, 324–329; Lima, *Império dos Sonhos*, 150, 179–180, 195.
269 A Lady enters/ With the arms in the Council/ And resurrects the Old man,/ Under the bell,/ With his large and white beard.

Thus, these two authors, whose prophecies are held in the archives of modern antiquity, either talking by their own spirits or—which I believe—by interpreting Bandarra's, both prophesied or understood that: the fateful king has to die and be resurrected before he works on his prodigious deeds by which he shall ascend towards his long awaited monarchy.

And for not leaving the Carthusian's couplet's without explanation, as it has things worthy of comment, it is possible that Portugal or Christendom would be under such a pressure that obligates the royal and virile spirit of our lady the Queen[270] to walk into the council[271] with arms. The King's resurrection "debaxo de la campana"[272] is well explained by the Church of São Vicente de Fora, where he rests; the fact of being so close to the Holy Sacrament, *quod est semen resurrectionis,*[273] does not require divine Mystery.[274] Only in the epithet of "old" and in the "large and white beard", one could still make remarks. The King is not a youngster anymore, and compared to the new and young king[275] we have today,[276] he is old. And if the hair gets whiter in the grave, I see that the King can resurrect with a white, very white beard, considering my own hair, even my being four years younger [than John IV]. However, it seems to me that this beard is fake, and that this prophetic poet painted our King's resurrection aiming at King Sebastian's age, whom he was expecting; and, as he painted the resurrection of one and the beard of the other, it does not come as a surprise that the portrait would be less adjusted in this part.

And since we have touched on these old matters which last so long, I will only tell Your Lordship that Bandarra said no word about King Sebastian. On the contrary, all of his words undo that hope, from the beginning until the end, because the king that he described is composed by contradictory proprieties entirely, that altogether disagree with King Sebastian's image. And if not, let us deduce it in a way contrary to the past one. This king about whom we are talking, Bandarra calls him "new and young king"; and King Sebastian is such an

---

270   The Queen Regent Luísa de Guzmán (1613–1666), John IV's widow.
271   "entrar em conselho". "Entrar em conselho" could mean both entering in the Council (of State, for instance) or reaching an agreement.
272   "Under the bell".
273   "It is the seed of resurrection". According to Besselaar, this passage is a quotation of Cornelio A Lapide's works.
274   "não carece de Mistério". That is: it does not need the intervention of the Divine mystery to explain it. Mistery, in theology, is a hidden reality that is not accessible through human perception or knowledge, only through divine revelation.
275   "rei novo". Vieira is playing with the ambiguities between "novo rei" (a new king) and "rei novo" (a new king but also a young king).
276   Afonso VI was only fifteen years old at the time.

old king that at the age of three he began to be king. About this king, Bandarra says "his name is John"; and King Sebastian has another name and such a different one. This King, Bandarra names him "Infant"; and King Sebastian was never an Infant, because he was born a Crown Prince, after Prince John [Emmanuel], his father.[277] About this king, Bandarra says "he is very fortunate and happy"; and King Sebastian was utterly unhappy and the reason of all of our unhappiness. To this king, Bandarra says: "get out, get out"; and to King Sebastian, all the Kingdom said: "do not get out, do not get out".[278] About this king, Bandarra says "he is not from a gluttonous stock" or the house of Hapsburg; King Sebastian had Charles V's blood. About this King, Bandarra says he is a seed, a cousin and related to kings; King Sebastian was grandson of kings, on his father side, and of emperors, on his mother's. About this king, Bandarra says "he has a good captain as a brother"; and King Sebastian did not nor could have a brother because neither Prince John nor Princess Joanna, his parents, had another son. About this king, Bandarra says he "is from lands and county": and King Sebastian is not from any county, because he was born in Lisbon. About this king, Bandarra says he would make war against Castile in the beginning of his reign; and King Sebastian never made war against Castile. About this King, Bandarra says he "praises justice"; and King Sebastian praised strength and bravery. About this king, Bandarra says the Pontiffs shall not give him the hand in a certain time: and King Sebastian received great favours from the pontiffs of his time, Paul IV, and Pius IV and V.[279] About this king, Bandarra says "he found flaws in him": and King Sebastian would not be lost, if he had not gone to Africa: see whether this was not a great flaw. Finally, to not tire us with more proofs of such a clear thing: with the exception of King Sebastian's being "seed of King Ferdinand", Bandarra's whole text does not mention any other thing about the King's signals or qualities which can be accommodated, not even far, to King Sebastian.

The others ones, which the Sebastianists call prophecies, are forged and modern papers made at the sounds of time and unmade by the same time which has demonstrated the complete opposite about everything. Even that much celebrated text, *Cujus nomem quique apicibus scriptum est,*[280] which the

---

277   Sebastian was born heir-apparent, when his father, John Emmanuel, son and heir of John III, died two weeks after Sebastian's birth. When his grandfather John III died in 1557, he was acclaimed king at the age of three, under the regency of his paternal grandmother, Catherine of Austria, and afterwards by his great-uncle, Cardinal Henrique. Therefore, as he was the heir of the Crown since his birth, he did not receive the title of Infant, given only to royal princes and princesses who are not heir-apparent. See note 71.
278   I.e., to get out to fight in North Africa where Sebastian I died in the battle of Ksar-El Kibir.
279   Paul IV (1555–1559), Pius IV (1559–1565) and Pius V (1566–1572).
280   "Whose name is written with five apices". Prophecy attributed to the Sibyls.

same Sebastianists accomodate to the five-syllable name of *Sebastianus*, is so far from being in favour of their hope but rather it is a miraculous confirmation of ours. Apices are neither syllables nor letters, but just little dots put over the letter *i*. Thus, Christ's text says or assumes: *Jota unum aut unus apex*.[281] And which is the name with five apices or five little dots over the letter *i*? The following name will answer: "joannes iiij". And I say no more.

But I am seeing that Your Lordship holds me and tells me: *Dic nobis quando haec erunt*.[282] Firstly, I answer: *Non est nostrum nosce tempora vel momenta quae Patter posuit in sua potestate*.[283] However, as this answer is so disconsolate, I will also say what my conjecture has achieved or imagined about this topic. I believe that within the age of sixty[284] all this great tragicomedy shall be represented in the theatre of the world. I am basing myself on five of Bandarra's texts: three are very clear, and two, more obscure, though very notable. In the *Third Dream*, referring to Ezekiel's prophecies and Daniel's hebdomads,[285] Bandarra says:

> I found in his counting,
> According to what here is represented,
> That Gad as Hagar,
> That all shall be over,
> Saying: "it closes the seventies".[286]

And if Gad, who are the Jews, and Hagar, who are the Hagarenes or Turks,[287] shall perish as sects when the year of seventy closes, which is the whole comedy's end, it follows that its acts shall be represented throughout the sixties. Bandarra confirms the same in his answers, talking about the same prophecies:

---

281 "one jot, or one tittle shall". Matt. 5:18.
282 "Tell us when shall these things be?" Matt. 24:3.
283 "It is not for you [in Vieira's quotation, *nostrum*: us] to know the times or moments, which the Father hath put in his own power." Acts 1:7.
284 "era do sessenta", i.e., the 1660s.
285 In the Book of Daniel (Dan. 9), the angel Gabriel reveals to Daniel the meaning of the 70 years of desolation in the vision of Jeremiah (Jer. 25:11–12, 29:10) with a cryptic message of the 70 weeks (week—hebdomad), interpreted as the description of the historical phases until the messianic reign of the Saints in Jerusalem. Ana Valdez, *Historical Interpretations of the "Fifth Empire"* (Leiden: 2011), 79–85.
286 *Trovas*, 128.
287 Hagarenes, i.e., the offspring of Hagar. Hagar was the servant of Sarah that bore Abraham's child and his firstborn, Ishmael, the father of the Ishmaelites (Genesis 16; 21). Hagarenes or Ishmaelites was used as a broader denomination for the Muslims (even the non-Arabs as the Turks or the Persians).

> And after they [the prophecies] have entered
> Everything will be known;
> Those who arrive in the sixes
> Will have as much as they wish,
> And one God only will be known.[288]

Bandarra calls it the age of "the sixes" because is the age of [1]660, and that the sixes appear twice, and in [1]666 they appear three times, which is a very noticed and a very notable number in the Book of Revelation.[289] And with no doubt there is plenty of what is to come and to see in these sixes, because Bandarra says that those who arrive in these sixes "will have as much as they wish". In the *Second Dream*, he says:

> And in these sixes
> You shall see astonishing things.[290]

And soon he repeats the same below:

> From six to seventy,
> That it had been calling,[291]
> Of the king that shall come to free.[292]

Therefore, all these three or four places of Bandarra's text show that this age of [1]660 is the determined time for the fulfilment of his prophecies and the prodigies promised in them.

And if someone says that this number of six or six hundred may belong to another century and not to this one, I answer it may not; because we already have the year 40 for warrantor, which evidently was from this century, and not from other, and it was over this year 40 that Bandarra was placing his counts. One time, he says: "Before the forties arrive";[293] another time: "The forties are already coming"; and another time: "The forties are already passing"; and afterwards, he speaks about these forties in the sixties and seventies.

---

288 *Trovas*, 132.
289 Rev. 13:18: "Here is wisdom. He that hath understanding, let him count the number of the beast. For it is the number of a man: and the number of him is six hundred sixty-six."
290 *Trovas*, 100.
291 "que se amenta". "Amentar" can be translated as called, mention, named.
292 *Trovas*, 101.
293 Vieira had not quoted this specific verse, but a similar one: "Before the forties close" ("Antes que cerrem quarenta"). This verse does not appear in the 1644 *Trovas*.

One gathers even more confirmation about this conjecture in the other two texts that I have promised to present. I called them dark texts, and I could have also called them sad texts. The first is one from the ending quatrains, and Bandarra says:

> I see forty and one year,
> By the running of the planet,
> By the grazing of the comet,[294]
> That demonstrates being of great harm.[295]

In the year [1]618, the latest and the most famous comet which our age has ever seen appeared for the whole world. Its figure was of a perfect palm; its colour was bright; its magnitude was as the sixth part of all the hemisphere; its site was in the East; its course was always in front of the Sun; its duration was for almost two months.[296] I saw it in Bahia, and Your Lordship should also have seen it.[297] And from then on there was no other comet, at least this notable; Caussinus talks about it in his book *De regno et domo Dei*[298] in three passages, attributing

---

294 Vieira inverted the 1644 *Trovas* sequence of "Comet" and "Planet": "Pello correr do Cometa,/ Pello firir do Planeta."
295 *Trovas*, 144.
296 Between 1618 and 1619, three comets crossed the skies; one of them, extremely bright, known as "The Great Comet of 1618" or "Cysat's Comet", was the one Vieira was referring to. Those comets sparked several observations, commentaries, and interpretations because of their astronomical importance as well as for their alleged eschatological and astrological impact in the history of kingdoms and empires. In some cases, both aspects presented themselves together. The millenarian, physician, and astrologer Manoel Bocarro Francês, alias Jacob Rosales, wrote a pamphlet about these comets published at Lisbon in 1619, in which he astronomically described the "Palm comet" ("Cometta Palma") mentioned by Vieira and astrologically predicted several events of turmoil based on the comets' appearance. Manuel Bocarro Francês, *Tratado dos cometas que apareceram em Novembro passado de 1618* (1619; facsimile ed. Lisbon: 2009). About the divinatory aspects of comets and astronomical observations in early modern Portugal and the Americas, see Luís Miguel Carolino, *Ciência, Astrologia e Sociedade. A teoria da Influência Celeste em Portugal (1593–1755)* (Lisbon: 2003), esp. chap. 5 (chap. 4 for Vieira's sermons); Carlos Ziller Camenietzki, "O Cometa, o Pregador e o Cientista: Antônio Vieira e Valentim Stansel observam o céu da Bahia no século XVII", *Revista da Sociedade Brasileira de História da Ciência*, 14 (1995), 37–52.
297 Vieira would have been about 10 years old at the time of the comet's appearance. André Fernandes, the Bishop of Japan, about 11.
298 Nicolas Caussin (1583–1651), French Jesuit. Caussin never wrote a book with this specific title, but two separate works, *Domo Rei* (1650) and *Regnum Dei* (1651), that were sometimes sold together, bound in one volume. *Domus Dei* was the treatise in which Caussin discussed the stars from a theological and philosophical perspective. According to Vie-

some effects to it, especially regarding Spain. It is about this comet, known by antonomasia as the comet of this age, that I understand that Bandarra speaks, because it was the comet of the century of his prophecies. Since the grazing of the said comet, the computation of the years' sums "forty and one year" at the end of this year or in the beginning of the next; because the comet, as it is said and I well remembered, appeared in the year [1]618, and, as Caussinus observes, the day in which it appeared was on the 27 November, and the day when it completely disappeared was on the 14 or 15 January, because one could hardly see it then. If we count since the day when the comet showed up, the 41 years are completed on the 27 November of this year of [1]659; if we count since the day when it disappeared, the same 41 years are completed on the 14 or 15 January of the next year, which is the year 60. About this year, Bandarra says "that demonstrates being of great harm", because the beginning of this noteworthy representation shall certainly be tragic and fateful, as its eves have been showing. In all the aspects, the second text agrees with the first one, except for the fact that the darkness of the computation is darker in it:

> ⌊In⌋ Thirty two years and a half,
> There will be signs on the earth,
> The Scripture[299] does not make mistakes,
> That here it is a full count.
>
> One of the three that comes in array
> Demonstrates great peril,
> There will be scourges and punishment
> For people I do not name.[300]

To shed light on, I suppose that "full counts" are perfect numbers that end in ten, such as 30, 40, 50, 60, 70, etc.; "no full counts" are the ones that do not improve to this number of ten, such as 31, 42, 53, 64, etc. This said and assumed, the first four verses talk about the King's acclamation, which occurred during the full count of the year 40, so celebrated by Bandarra, and having passed,

---

ira's testimony to the inquisitors, he met Caussin, probably in 1657, while on a diplomatic mission at the French court. Muhana, *Autos do processo*, 221–222.

299 Probably a reference to Luke 21:25: "And there shall be signs in the sun, and in the moon, and in the stars; and upon the earth distress of nations, by reason of the confusion of the roaring of the sea and of the waves."

300 *Trovas*, 97–98.

since the death of the last Portuguese king [until the acclamation], thirty-two years and a half, i.e., 61 years (because "thirty two" are 60, and "half two" is one).[301] And that amount of years has punctually passed from the death of the last king of Portugal, King Henry, who died in January [1]580, to the acclamation of King John IV, which was in December [1]640. So far, the explanation of this couplet runs easily. The difficulty resides in the following verses: "One of the three that comes in array/ Demonstrates great peril, etc." because the three years "that come in array" after the "full count" of the year 40 have already long ago passed, and we have seen neither these dangers, nor these scourges, nor these punishments. Thus, I say, "one of the three comes in array" does not mean one of the three years [of the 40s], as it was imagined, rather one of the three full counts which is immediately behind: that is, the three full counts after the year 40 are the year 50, the year 60, and the year 70, and one of these three full counts represents great peril. Now, what remains to be known is which of these three will be the one. As far as I can reach, I am convinced that it is next year, the year 60. And I prove it. These three full counts are the year 50, the year 60, and the year 70. It is not the year 50, because it had already passed; it cannot be the year 70, because, as it is said, everything shall be finished by then; thus, it must be the year 60. In this year, there will be scourge and punishment upon people who Bandarra does not name—which I attribute to a reverence to the Ecclesiastic State.[302] There will be scourge and punishment in Rome, there will be scourge and punishment in Portugal. And, albeit all must accept these scourges and punishments as they come from the hand that gives them and must seek to appease His divine justice so deservedly invoked, yet the Portuguese people must know (for no hardship might discourage them, how big it may be) that the same God who punishes them, loves them. Rather, because He loves them, He punishes them. So they must know that, after punishing and purifying them with this tribulation, He shall make them the chosen vessel of His glory.[303]

Out of Spain we will see everything that was prophesied in this paper; inside of Spain we will see that Portugal prevails and Castile perishes. Bandarra says in the final quatrains:

---

301 Vieira means thirty times two equals sixty, and half times two equals one.
302 "Estado Eclesiástico". Besselaar supposes that Vieira was referring to a possible punishment against Rome because of the Pope's non-recognition of John IV as the legitimate Portuguese ruler.
303 Vieira was alluding to Acts 9:15, "for this man is to me a vessel of election, to carry my name before the Gentiles, and kings, and the children of Israel."

> I see a human high king
> Raise his flag,
> I see, as through a sieve,
> The Griffon dying in the pipe.[304]

On effect of the successes, it is certain and very certain that I am not mistaken; on the counting of the times about which I am not so secure, I also presume that I shall not be mistaken. And if so it be, be ready, world, for seeing in these ten fateful years a representation of the biggest and most prodigious cases that the world has ever been seeing from the world's beginning to the present. In Spain, it will see the King of Portugal be resurrected, and Castile defeated and dominated by the Portuguese. In Italy, it will see the Turk savagely victorious, and afterwards him being routed and forced to run away. In Europe, it will see a universal cessation of arms among all Christian, Catholic, and Non-Catholic Princes; it will see the land and see the seething with armies and navies against the common enemy. In Africa and Asia, and in part of the same Europe, it will see the Ottoman Empire finished, and the King of Portugal worshiped as Emperor of Constantinople. Finally, for the amazement of all the peoples, it will see the sudden appearance of the ten tribes of Israel, disappeared for more than two thousand years, and their recognition of Jesus Christ as their God and Lord, in whose death they did not take part.[305]

This is the prodigious tragicomedy to which, in these ten years, Bandarra invites the whole world. But know, those who live, that, in the first scene of this great representation, all the theatre will swim in blood, in which the same world will almost drown, because the blood shall even cover the head. *Et Thybrim multo spumantem sanguine cerno.*[306]

Therewith, my Father and Lord, Your Lordship may consider me acquitted of the clarity that was requested, since one cannot speak clearer. And I may also consider myself departed from my prophet, who, dressed as a pilgrim, parts[307]

---

[304] *Trovas*, 145.

[305] The Ten Tribes would not have been in Israel when Christ was crucified, as they would have been scattered around the globe after their deportation from the Kingdom of Israel in the 8th century B.C.

[306] Virgil, *Aeneid*, VI, 87: "I see: and the Tiber foaming with much blood". This verse is part of the Sibyl's prophecy, which was recurrently mentioned in Portuguese (and Iberian) millenarianism.

[307] "despedido do meu profeta, que em trajo tão peregrino, parte". By a metonym, Bandarra, "my Prophet" ("meu profeta"), represents "Hopes of Portugal", since its subject is Bandarra's prophecies. By a metaphor, its path crossing the Atlantic is similar to a pilgrimage, and as a pilgrim, a letter has a characteristic "trajo" (a garb), the sheet of paper which involves it.

from Maranhão to Lisbon, taking his very own truth as warrantor of his fortune. So he says in the prologue of his cobbling, from which are all the verses I want to end with:

> All the time, I am busy,
> For doing my work well.
> If I had lived in Lisbon
> I would have been more esteemed.[308]

Esteemed, he will be, because he promises to be well received by many lords, though not by all of them (because his labours are not for all either):

> From my sewing, will come out
> So many works of labours,
> Which many lords will rejoice in
> To wear and carry them.[309]

He acknowledges that there will be those who like these rude verses and those who do not, but he also says that ones and others bring the cause within themselves: those who understand will like them, those who do not like them will be because they do not understand them.

> If someone wants to lace[310]
> Ribbons upon a rude work,
> One who had good manners
> Will rejoice in seeing it.[311]

And below:

> My work is rather sturdy[312]
> Because it is made with leather straps,

---

308 *Trovas*, 15th quatrain from the "Dedicatória".
309 *Trovas*, 5th quatrain from the "Dedicatória".
310 "Se quiser entremeter". In the 1644 edition, it reads "E quero entremeter" (I want to lace).
311 *Trovas*, 6th quatrain from the "Dedicatória".
312 In Muhana's lesson of "Hopes of Portugal", one reads: "A minha obra é grosseira", that is, "My work is rude"; but in Besselaar's version, on the contrary, one reads: "A minha obra é mui segura", that is, "My work is very solid" or "very safe". We opted for "sturdy" to find a meaning between the two versions.

> If to someone it seems ugly,
> One does not know about sewing.[313]

Finally, he supposes that there shall be glossators of his text, and I suppose there will be many more to my gloss.[314] But despite that, I will not say like he does:

> Even if you are rowing,
> Do not touch the shoe![315]

Only do I say about having said so much, that yet it is plenty about what I keep silent. Everything have I learnt from the same Master, who did not doubt to say about himself:

> I know how to cut, how to measure,
> Even if it does not seem so to you,
> I have all by heart,
> If I want to use it.
> And those who want to gloss it
> Have a good look at my work,
> And they will see that I still have
> Two ropes to put together.[316]

God guards Your Lordship for many years as I wish and as this Christianity needs.

Camutá,[317] on the way to the river of the Amazons, 29 April 1659.[318]

---

313   *Trovas*, 11th quatrain from the "Dedicatória".
314   As Besselaar remarks, this passage indicates that, despite claiming the contrary to the inquisitors, Vieira was indeed expecting to have a broader readership than only the Bishop of Japan and the Regent Queen. Besselaar, *António Vieira*, 37–38.
315   *Trovas*, 16th quatrain from the "Dedicatória".
316   *Trovas*, 13th–14th quatrains from the "Dedicatória".
317   Then a small settlement near Belém, on the mouth of Tocantins river, Camutá was named after an indigenous group that lived in the region. The Franciscans were the first to Christianise the Camutás in 1620s, followed by the Carmelites and eventually by the Jesuits, who—Vieira among them—established a mission in 1655. Camutá is today's Cametá, city in the State of Pará, in Brazil.
318   About the date and the two versions of "Hopes of Portugal", see note 115.

CHAPTER 7

Prophecies in Early Modern Spain: Deceit, Scandals, and the Spanish Inquisition

Monika Frohnapfel-Leis

Introduction

This chapter aims to contribute to the phenomenon of prophecies in early modern Spain, especially in terms of their social potential, as well as concerning the difficulty in distinguishing true from false prophesies. After some general introductory remarks concerning prophecies and dreams in the early modern period in general, and in Spain in particular, I would like to present two extracts of primary source material.

In the 16th century, dreams and percipience were often understood as linked with one another. Insight itself was defined as divination and was practised by compilation and classification of the signs that, to a certain extent, became manifest in things and which served as a reference to a deeper reality. By interpreting these signs, prognostications could be formulated. This was a notion and an expression of an ancient and biblical heritage, which tended to analyse the past and the present, and predict the future. It can be understood as a form of coping with the unknown and uncertain future and therefore a way of coping with contingency.

The following hierarchy of different modes of revelation can be distinguished: firstly, on the lowest level, nightly dreams while sleeping; secondly, daily visions while being awake; thirdly, ecstasies; and fourthly, miracles.[1] This line-up illustrates that insight in the early modern period was seen as a chain, connected through meanings ranging from dreams over visions and ecstasies to wonders. This hierarchy, as well as the demarcation between the natural and the supernatural, soon caused debates and nourished the discourses concerning the classification and assessment of revelations and oneiric phenomena.[2]

---

1 Claire Gantet, "Zwischen Wunder, Aberglaube und Fiktion. Der Traum als politisches Medium in Frankreich, 1560–1620", in *Traum und res publica. Traumkulturen und Deutungen sozialer Wirklichkeiten im Europa von Renaissance und Barock*, ed. Peer Schmidt and Gregor Weber (Berlin: 2008), 307–326, here 308.
2 Ibid., 309; María Jordán Arroyo, "Francisco Monzón y 'el buen dormir': La interpretación teo-

In order not to lose the orientation within the numerous forms of prophecies it is necessary to differentiate between collective and individual forms of prediction. "Collective" is understood as a form of prediction without an individual addressee. By contrast, "individual" forecasting means answering very personal questions given by single persons to individuals. In this pattern, prophecies can be considered as an appearance of collective divination, even if they address the king, for instance. Examples for prophecies as collective forms of divination are those given by people preaching in the street or from the pulpit; maybe prophetic dreams and almanacs range between them. Examples of individual forms of divination would be the conjuring of spirits or practicing crystallomancy, chiromancy, pyromancy, hydromancy, geomancy, etc.

In early modern Europe, prophecies were a frequent instrument for announcing a new monarch or a new regime and for consolidating support for it. In Spain, royal births were often celebrated as the fulfilment of ancient prophecies, similar to those of older medieval traditions. Those prophecies claimed that the future monarch was destined to complete the work of the so-called "Reconquest".[3] But prophecies could also be used as a political and ideological weapon by opposition movements and radical groups in order to establish religious standards by which to judge a secular regime.

Prophetic dreams were also a popular genre in 16th-century Spain. In spite of all the moral warnings concerning their doubtful reliability, most Spaniards were utterly fascinated by them, like most people in other parts of Europe. Generally, dreams were considered to have two different sources, a natural and a supernatural one. For the dreams' natural origin Aristotle's explanations were assumed, which explained dreams as a product of the mind's sensual perception while sleeping. Concerning the supernatural side, a diabolic or a divine origin was considered.[4] True prophecies were regarded as being inspired by God. By contrast, false ones and scandalous propositions were seen as being inspired by the devil.[5] Further, the assumption that a prophet did not utter his

---

lógica de los sueños en la España del siglo XVI", *Cuadernos de Historia Moderna* 26 (2001), 169–184. On mantic dreams in early modern times, see Andreas Bähr, "Furcht, divinatorischer Traum und autobiographisches Schreiben in der Frühen Neuzeit", *Zeitschrift für Historische Forschung* 34/1 (2007), 1–32.

3 Richard L. Kagan, *Lucrecia's Dreams. Politics and Prophecy in Sixteenth-Century Spain* (Berkeley: 1990), 3.
4 Kagan, *Lucrecia's dreams*, 35; Jordán Arroyo, "Francisco Monzón y 'el buen dormir'".
5 Serena Turri, "Il Tratado de la verdadera y falsa prophecía di Juan de Horozco: Una nota su Lucrecia de León", in *I racconti delle streghe. Storia e finzione tra Cinque e Seicento*, ed. Giulia Poggi (Pisa: 2002), 217–224, here 220; Kagan, *Lucrecia's dreams*, 35, 147.

own wisdom but spoke for someone else[6] had to be taken into account. So, the often decisive question was: whom did a prophet speak for? Or simply did the prophet speak for God or for the devil? It is rather unlikely that "the common people" knew the answer to the above question. But what they surely were aware of is that any kind of prediction was generally forbidden by the Spanish Inquisition. Nevertheless, predictions were very popular and prophesying persons normally found an interested audience.

In the wide field of controlling Christian orthodoxy the Spanish Inquisition was crucial. This institution's founding intention was to curb deviance. In this context, the so-called edicts of faith played a very important role in practical matters. Like a catalogue, they listed forms of deviant behaviour and heresy and were read out loudly during the visitation by an inquisitor, normally during High Mass on Sunday.[7] Each member of the community (of adults) was requested to participate in this mass or face excommunication and other forms of punishment by the Holy Office.[8] The central point of the edicts was that everyone, who had the slightest knowledge of any circumstance described in it, was obliged to tell the Inquisition in order to make a secret denunciation.[9] This meant that, in spite of the edict's normative character, its authority arose from the participation of "the people", from "below", because everybody was aware of the edict's content. Because later on I will talk about prophecies and scandals caused by them, and about dreams and visions, it makes sense to have a look at what the edict said concerning these topics. Concerning scandals, the edict determined:

> We make it known to you that before us the prosecuting attorney of the Holy Office appeared and made us a relation stating that it has come to his attention that many people have come from many diverse parts of this our district with little fear of God and in great damage to their souls and consciences and that they have scandalised the Christian people, contriving against the precepts of the Holy Mother Church and against what we

---

[6] Matthias Riedl, "Einleitung: Prophetie als interzivilisatorisches Phänomen", in *Propheten und Prophezeiungen—Prophets and Prophecies*, ed. Matthias Riedl and Tilo Schabert (Eranos, Neue Folge 12), (Würzburg: 2005), 9–16, here 9.

[7] Gustav Henningsen, *The Witches' Advocate. Basque Witchcraft and the Spanish Inquisition (1609–1614)* (Reno: 1980), 96; Stacey Schlau, *Gendered Crime and Punishment. Women and/in the Spanish Inquisition* (The Medieval and Early Modern Iberian World 49), (Leiden: 2013), 9f.; Geoffrey Parker, "Some Recent Work on the Inquisition in Spain and Italy", *The Journal of Modern History* 54 (1982), 519–532, here 523.

[8] Henningsen, *The Witches' Advocate*, 96.

[9] Ibid., 99.

have ordered [...]. Instead, they have given themselves over to the study of judicial Astrology, and they exercise this with mixtures of many other superstitions, making predictions by the stars and their aspects concerning future things, successes or other fortunes, or actions that depend on divine will or upon the free exercise of men [...].[10]

In the case study of María de la Concepción, we find the aspect of someone "scandalising the Christian people" as mentioned in the edict of faith as a result of contravening the Catholic Church's concepts of coping with the uncertain future.

The first example of primary source material I would like to present are five chapters selected from Juan de Horozco y Covarrubias' *Treatise of the Truthful and False Prophecy* [*Tratado de la verdadera y falsa prophecia*], which was published in Segovia in 1588. The question whether prophecies are of divine or diabolic provenance is the crucial point in Horozcos y Covarrubias' treatise. The author dedicates the whole book to this question; "false" and "truly" are keywords in this context. His main concern is to unveil deceit.

The second example consists of the trial records against a religious woman who was accused of agitating in the west Andalusia region near Seville by her predictions before the Spanish Inquisition at Seville in 1645. It is María de la Concepción,[11] whose foretelling during the 1640s caused disturbances in the wider region. What is especially remarkable about the case is the connection of statements concerning the future with social and political disturbance and the authorities' fear of it. Particularly interesting is the question as to what extent María's prognosticating activities had been tolerated and from which point on this no longer became possible. That the Inquisition was charged with this case is typical because any form of religiously deviant behaviour fell under its responsibility, and also any prophetic statements. María de la Concepción's activities serve as a typical example of street prophets in early modern Spain.

---

10   Edict of faith of 8 March 1616, edited by John F. Chuchiak, *The Inquisition in New Spain, 1536–1820. A Documentary History* (Baltimore: 2011), 111. This is an extract of an edict for México and other parts of New Spain, but it can be assumed, in my view, to have been valid also for the Iberian Peninsula.
11   Unfortunately, the trial acts tell nothing about María's year of birth or year of death, or how old she was when the trial took place.

Primary Source Material

1. Juan de Horozco y Covarrubias

Juan de Horozco y Covarrubias and his writing ought to have been quite well-known among his contemporaries. By contrast little is known about his life and the background of his works. Juan de Horozco y Covarrubias was born in about 1545 in Toledo to a family with a *judeo-converso* background and died in 1610.[12] Like his far better studied brother Sebastián, the famous philologist and author of *Tesoro de la lengua castellana o española* [*Treasure of the Castilian or Spanish Language*] (1611), the fist monolingual dictionary of the Castilian language,[13] Juan also held various ecclesiastic positions, some of them quite important like the one as canon at the Cathedral of Salamanca.[14] He also became a bishop, namely of Guadix in Andalusia.[15]

When he wrote his treatise *Tratado de la verdadera y falsa prophecia* [*Treatise of the Truthful and False Prophecy*] in 1588, he held the office of an Archdeacon in Cuéllar near Segovia, where the work was also published.[16] The treatise consists of two parts: part one deals with prophets and different forms of prophecies whereas part two deals with diverse types of divination. In both parts the author gives a lot of examples from the bible and from late antiquity. The version of the Biblioteca Valenciana (Generalitat Valenciana) which I chose to present here consists of 183 double-sided pages, i.e. the treatise is quite comprehensive. It is a sixteenth-century print and has not been edited yet to the best of my knowledge.

Within the treatise's sixty chapters, I am presenting five below, all from the first book. All demonstrate the difficulty discerning the true and the false prophecies; they describe the role of the devil in the context of predicting, his numerous forms of deception, and give a lot of examples. This is part of a wider theological debate happening in the period, and among those who

---

12 Jack Weiner, "El indispensable factótum Sebastián Covarrubias Horozco (1539–1613): pedagogo, cortesano y administrador", *Artifara* 2 (2003), sezione Addenda (http://www.artifara.com/rivista2/testi/covar.asp, accessed on 26 December 2017).

13 Juan Gutierrez Cuadrado, "Covarrubias y Horozco, Sebastián", in *Diccionario de Literatura Española e Hispanoamericana*, dir. Ricardo Gullón, vol. 1 (Madrid: 1993), 389.

14 Jack Weiner, "El indispensable factótum Sebastián Covarrubias Horozco" (http://www.artifara.com/rivista2/testi/covar.asp, accessed on 26 December 2017).

15 Gabriel María Verd Conradi, "Las poesís del manuscrito de fray Miguel de Guevara y el soneto *No me mueve, mi Dios, para quererte*", *Nueva Revista de Filología Hispanica* LXV (2017), 471–500, here 480.

16 See the author's denomination on the title page of the treatise.

participated were Horozco as well as Pedro Ciruelo (1470–1554), Francisco Monzón (d.1575), Martín del Río (1551–1608) and several others.[17]

The examples Horozco y Covarrubias cites are mostly taken from the Bible, like the accounts of the prophets of the Old and the New Testament. Others treat early Christian martyrs, historians and philosophers, or further influential figures of Church history. This wide range of topics does not only prove the author's extensive humanistic knowledge; it also shows that the examples' message was still very virulent and up-to-date in early modern Spain. All the topics Horozco treats show this: the problem of how to discern false and true prophets; the great numbers of feigned wonders and false sanctity, especially during the period after the council of Trent.

Although it must have been quite famous at the time, little is known today about the book's circulation and reception because to date it has not been well-studied.[18] As Segovia lacked a printing press so far, Horozco himself established one in order to have his works edited there. Thus, he was able to control the printing process of his books.[19] As far as I know it was never re-edited or translated. With Pedro Ciruelo he shared his interest in getting to know the world of superstition. While standing up against deceitfulness, in his treatise he defended the forms of true prophecy. Further, he admired Teresa of Avila (1515–1582), the famous nun and founder of the discalced Carmelites.[20] Maybe these were reasons why his book about prophecies was approved by the censors.

Horozco's treatise was allegedly inspired directly by street prophets like Lucrecia de León.[21] He seems to have watched the prophets' activities and their reception, when he recognised the potential influence of prophesying women and men on the religious elite.[22]

---

17 Their most important works in the context of prophecies and dreams were: Pedro Ciruelo, *Tratado de reprobación de supersticiones y hechizerías* (Alcalá de Henares: 1530) and *Tratado en el qual se repruevan todas las supersticiones y hechizerías* (Barcelona: 1628); Francisco Monzón, *Avisos Spirituales que enseñan cómo el sueño corporal sea provechoso al espíritu* (Lisboa: 1563); Martín del Río, *La magia demoníaca* (libro II de las *Disquisiciones mágicas*) (Leuven: 1599), cf. Jordán Arroyo, "Francisco Monzón y 'el buen dormir'", especially 178–180; Fabián Alejandro Campagne, "Witchcraft and the Sense-of-the-Impossible in Early Modern Spain: Some reflections based on the literature of superstition (ca. 1500–1800)", *The Harvard Theological Review* 96/1 (2003), 25–62, here 30–31, especially note 27.

18 Rafael Zafra Molina, "Nuevos datos sobre la obra de Juan de Horozco y Covarrubias", *Imago* 3 (2011), 107–126, here 109, 120.

19 Ibid., 110, 120.

20 Ibid., 109.

21 Kagan, *Lucrecia's Dreams*, 115. Kagan denominates Horozco's treatise as "an important anti-superstition tract", cf. ibid.

22 María V. Jordán Arroyo, *Soñar la historia. Riesgo, creatividad y religion en las profecías de Lucrecia de León* (Madrid: 2007), 16.

Lucrecia de León was one of those prophets who directly operated within a phenomenon that had come into popularity: prophetic dreams. The question whether dreams were signs or cause for past, present or future events was frequently discussed at the time.[23] It was a topic that was studied by the Madrid theologian and preacher Francisco Monzón, foremost in his famous *Spiritual Advices which Teach How the Corporal Dream Could Be Beneficial for the Spirit* [*Avisos spirituals que enseñan cómo el sueño corporal sea provechoso al espíritu*] (Lisbon: 1563).[24] Horozco was one of the people who seized the ideas of Francisco Monzón.[25]

2. María de la Concepción

We know very little about the life of María de la Concepción, my second case study. She was a religious woman and member of a third order. In Spain, the female members as Tertiary nuns were called *beatas*.[26] The rare pieces of information that have passed on derive from her trial before the Inquisition's court of Seville in 1645. The handwritten records are kept at the National Historical Archive [*Archivo Histórico Nacional*] in Madrid[27] and have never been published before.

María was tried because of the agitation and scandals she had caused with her prognostications. Unlike Lucrecia's example, there is almost nothing published about her case yet, as far as I know.[28] María was accused before the Holy Office of directly opposing the edicts of faith. Her predictions on the future scandalised the people causing trouble in the whole region. Unfortunately, the trials acts reveal nothing about her or the content of her predictions.

---

23 Jordán Arroyo, "Francisco Monzón", 169–184, here 170.
24 Ibid., 172. Regarding Monzón's year of death cf. ibid., 169.
25 Ibid., 180.
26 *Beata* is a synonym for a tertiary religious woman. Both "were lay women who chose to profess certain vows and live dedicated to religion, although outside the confines of a convent". Stacey Schlau, *Gendered Crime and Punishment*, 13; See also María Isabel Barbeito Carneiro (ed.), *Cárceles y mujeres en el siglo XVII. Razón y forma de la Galera. Proceso Inquisitorial de San Plácido* (Biblioteca des escritoras 21) (Madrid: 1991), 28; and Ángela Atienza López, "De beaterios a conventos. Nuevas perspectivas sobre el mundo de las beatas en la España moderna", *Historia social* 57 (2007), 145–168.
27 Madrid, Archivo Histórico Nacional [hereafter AHN], Inquisition 2061, Expediente 12.
28 Apart from my article: Monika Frohnapfel-Leis, "An enchantress, a saint and a prophetess. How religious deviance is described in Spanish Inquisition trials", in *Recounting Deviance. Forms and Practices of Presenting Divergent Behaviour in the Late Middle Ages and Early Modern Period*, ed. Jörg Rogge (Mainz Historical Cultural Sciences 34), (Bielefeld: 2016), 77–95, especially 89–93.

But because of their apparent impact they must have treated issues like general menaces, political crises, catastrophes, illnesses, hunger and war in a very insistent way. As we know from the records of the inquisitorial trial, María's case had been revisited by Don Augustin de Villaviçencio because there had been some irregularities and entanglements with employees of the tribunal of Seville. What he had to check was not the question of whether she had made predictions, but whether the mentioned employees actually had come to consult her in the village of Mairena, where she used to live. Two problems resulted in this context, and the first relates to the provocation of disturbances by telling the future to members of all social classes of Seville's surroundings. The Inquisition had known about María's activities in fortune-telling for some time. In fact, María had been admonished two or three years earlier, when the Holy Office reprimanded her. But it did not intervene until the scandals increased to a high degree and were notorious in the whole region. The increase was mostly caused by the visit of the Inquisitor in charge at her home. For the people as well as for the Inquisition's employees this was perceived as being very strange. The inquisitor and the secretaries had made a contribution to raise the scandal.[29]

Not only did she not stop performing her divinations and prophecies after the admonition, she also continued scandalising and causing social disturbances in the city and district of Seville. Countless people consulted her, not only those belonging to the lower classes—which, to a certain extent, would probably have been "normal"—but she was also sought out by "illustrious"[30] and noble persons. Thus, there seemed to be some kind of demand for her advising service, and for that intention people did not hesitate to come from a distance of more than twenty leagues[31] to her village of Mairena. The actual reasons for the consultations must remain unknown because the trial acts tell us nothing about them.

These facts are reflected in María's case, when it is mentioned that not only "common people" counted among her clients, but also persons belonging to the "illustrious" upper class. One of the witnesses refers to this in a very clear way: "the message came up to the tribunal that there were such disturbances caused by her actions and that people from all status, high and low, came to consult

---

29 AHN, Inq. 2061, Exp. 12, fol. 9ᵛ–10ᵛ.
30 AHN, Inq. 2061, Exp. 12, fols 4ʳ and 9ᵛ.
31 One league in the ancient Spanish system corresponds to 5,572.7 m, the distance one can walk within one hour. See "legua", in *Diccionario de la lengua española de la Real Academia Española* (http://dle.rae.es/?id=N5PoXDE, accessed on 2 September 2018). Thus, 20 leagues equate to 111,45 m or 11,145.4 km.

her and ask for her advice".[32] We can follow this opinion directly in the trial records, which mention that the *beata*[33] was supported and favoured by quite a number of "lordly people and of great authority" as powerful supporters.[34] Unfortunately, the names of these persons are not mentioned within the case files, but one witness stated: "Nobody dared to say anything of matter because the named *beata* was favoured and assisted by such illustrious persons and of such authority".[35]

The second problem was the Inquisitor's visit to Maria's: the Inquisitor Don Diego de la Fuente Peredo had decided to visit the accused *beata* together with three other Holy Office's employees, Athanasio Torres de Auila, Juan Lasso Cordero, and a staff member. They went over to Mairena in order to get an impression of this scandalous woman and consulted her. One of the trial's witnesses had seen them there and sent a note about it to the inquisition's prosecutor. He stated having been appalled by the Inquisition's employees visiting the *beata*, whom they would have been better prosecuting rather than consulting; even if it had been done for mere curiosity, since this would have fallen within their competence. In fact, interrogations of suspects normally took place at the Inquisition's rooms.

This visit had two consequences. Firstly, it seems to have publicised María's case, because afterwards the number of people seeking María's advice rose as well as the scandals. Her tendency to scandalise her clients with her predictions and to cause disturbances in the whole region seemed to be stronger than ever before.[36] This could certainly not have been in the Holy Office's interest. Secondly, it caused trouble among the inquisitorial staff: the colleagues of those who had joined the visit were very upset about it, because it contravened every inquisitorial custom. An inquisitor searching a suspect at her home almost like a client was perceived as equal to a tacit permission for continuing the criticised practice, here of telling the future, and consequently of her approval. In this way the inquisitor and the secretaries contributed to amplify the scandal.[37] According to the testimonies given by the Secreto's notary, Don Juan de la Vega y Davila, and the Fiscal of this Inquisition court, the licenciado Juan de Morales, the Inquisitor Don Diego de la Fuente Davila and the secretary Athanasio Torres had changed their behaviour after their return from Mairena:

---

32 AHN, Inq. 2061, Exp. 12, fol. 4^r.
33 See note 26.
34 AHN, Inq., 2061, Exp. 12, fol. 6^{r-v}.
35 AHN, Inq., 2061, Exp. 12, fol. 6^{r-v}.
36 AHN, Inq., 2061, Exp. 12, fols 4^v–5^r.
37 AHN, Inq., 2061, Exp. 12, fols 9^v–10^v.

they were described as being "frightened as never before".[38] Furthermore, while the secretary asked for his transfer to another tribunal the Inquisitor consciously avoided talking about the visit at all. This behaviour contributed to the public opinion that the *beata*'s answer to the men's questions had not been the desired one or at least, more generally, not a good one and—what certainly was more important—that they indeed believed in her predictions.[39]

Conclusion

In early modern Spain prophecies were part of the daily reality, at every social level. The providers of these services as well as their clients often had very different social backgrounds. As a form of practical faith, the Spanish Inquisition also supervised prophecies. But it seems as if the institution admitted them to a certain extent.

Juan de Horozco's treatise is a good example of the discourses regarding the difficulty to distinguish true from false prophecies, which also concerned other early modern Spanish authors like Pedro Ciruelo, Martín del Río and Francisco Monzón. It mirrors the contemporary learned discourse regarding the devil's role in the context of deceit and superstition, reflecting them by examples deriving from the Bible. At the same time, Horozco's treatise is a pleading for the true prophecies inspired only and directly by God. Presumably it was received only in the scholarly circles of theologians and others as well as within the Inquisition courts.

In contrast to Horozco and his theoretical book, the religious woman María de la Concepción offers a practical example of performing prophecies in early modern Spain. She can be seen as an outstanding example of the variety of different possibilities for telling the future as a method of coping with the uncertainty of one's individual future. Although unique, at the same time her experience can be considered as being unexceptional because prophecies in early modern Spain represented an everyday phenomenon, even though the practice was illegal.

Regarding María de la Concepción's social background, this seems to have aligned with the majority of her clients: the sparse information that we have about this figure suggests that like many of them, she belonged to the "common people". Unfortunately, we do not know how she became a prophetess or

---

38   AHN, Inq., 2061, Exp. 12, fols 8^r, 10^v.
39   AHN, Inq., 2061, Exp. 12, fols 2^r, 8^r–9^r, 10^v.

whether she claimed to have experienced revelations. Probably it was her fame that contributed to her being an expert in predicting. But what we know from the trial acts is that also members of the "illustrious" upper class, of Seville's nobility, came to ask for her advice in coping with the uncertainty of their own individual future. María could continue her activities for quite a long time before the Inquisition started to intervene and prosecute her in trials. The scandals, which came along with her prognostics, included a great social potential and risk of uprisings. The turning point in the authorities' attitude towards her was the unofficial and irregular visit of the Inquisition's employees, which not only contributed to the raising of scandals, but also seems to have signified the crossing of an absolutely intolerable prohibition.

A far better studied foretelling woman, though, is the aforementioned Lucrecia de León, a young woman living in the last third of the 16th century in the new capital of Spain, Madrid, with connections to the court. She claimed to be having prophetic dreams, which some powerful supporter transcribed and published. Soon she had a great number of followers. In the beginning, her dreams were quite harmless, but as time went on, their content became more critical and painted a very dark and gloomy future for Spain, all owing to King Philip's incapacity to reign in a 'good' way. According to Lucrecia's dreams, the king had lost popularity within his realms at the time because of his domestic and foreign politics. Actually, many Spaniards must have felt insecure about various menaces like the second Moorish rebellion of the Alpujarras 1568–1570, Spain's enemies France, England, the Moors of North Africa, and the Turks preparing to invade the country, or the Armada's defeat. Prior to this, the extensive and expensive building activities on Philip's palace and monastery El Escorial must not have pleased everyone.[40] Such dreams and prognostications circulated among Madrid's population and nourished a climate of civil disturbance, as they touched upon central concerns of the people.[41]

---

40   Kagan, *Lucrecia's dreams*, 71, 76, 81, 90–94, 105, 107, 124–127. For the Alpujarra rebellion, see John Huxtable Elliott, *Imperial Spain 1469–1716* (reprint London: 1969), 228–234.

41   Her case is very well studied. See for instance Kagan, *Lucrecia's dreams*; Jordán Arroyo, *Soñar la historia*; Roger Osborne, *The Dreamer of the Calle de San Salvador. Visions of Sedition and Sacrilege in Sixteenth-Century Spain* (London: 2002); Antonio Fernández Luzón, "Profecía y transgresión social. El caso de Lucrecia de León", *Historia Social* 38 (2000), 3–15.

1   Juan de Horozco y Covarrubias, *Treatise of the Truthful and False Prophecy* [*Tratado de la verdadera y falsa prophecia*] (Segovia: 1588)

Treatise of the Truthful and False Prophecy
Made by Don Juan Horozco y Covarruvias
Archdeacon of Cuéllar in the Holy Church of Segovia

With Privilege
In Segovia
By Juan de la Cuesta
In the year 1588

[Extract][42]

First book

14ᵛ   **Chapter IIII. About the way to reveal the prophecies and about the certainty about them.**

To uncover these secrets and make their revelations public, has not always been
15ʳ permitted to the prophets, because | a lot of things which they revealed had been only for their own purpose, like Isaiah said about himself, my secret for me, and Saint Paul saw things which were not suited to be spoken out, and those who had secret revelations and talked to God, are also called prophets, as it is assured for Abraham, of whom it is well-known that he talked many times with God, and therefore he is called Prophet in the book Genesis, though he did not announce what God revealed to him. And by this way also Joshua,[43] whom Ecclesiastes[44] calls great among the prophets, as his name, for talking with God in such a regular manner. Maria, sister of Moses, and Aaron were called

---

42   Annotations, supposedly written by Horozco, are printed on the margins of each page. I have not reproduced them here.

43   The prophet Joshua is the author of the eponymous biblical book of Joshua. See Ernst Axel Knauf, "Joshua (Book and Person), I. Hebrew Bible/Old Testament", in *Encyclopedia of the Bible and its Reception* (*EBR*) *online*, vol. 14, ed. Christine Helmer [and others], 757–762 (accessed on 2 January 2018).

44   Together with the book of Job and the book of Proverbs, Ecclesiastes is considered to be one of the three Wisdom books in the Old Testament. It is also known under the book's title "Qohelet". William P. Brown, "Ecclesiastes, Book of, I. Hebrew Bible/Old Testament", in *EBR*, vol. 7, ed. Hans-Josef Klauck [and others], 274–278 (accessed on 2 January 2018).

prophets in the Exodus, for having talked with God, as it is said in the Book of numbers.[45] The other prophets did what God told them to do while publishing their predictions, sometimes with deeds, like the prophet Hieremias[46] who enclosed himself with wooden chains. And usually it was to publish with words and with writing what God served to be revealed. And concerning the aspect of certainty one cannot doubt that what God had said to become that would fulfil itself, and the fact, that there had been | many prophecies containing menaces like the one of Jonah,[47] who by the order of God published that they had to destroy the city of Nineveh, and afterwards God forgave the inhabitants of Nineveh because of the repentance they made, in which they understood that the prophet Jonah had certainty about the destruction of the town like the sentence against them was given because of their vilification, but he was not sure whether those vilifications would change by their repentance. And this was what happened to Isaiah[48] when he announced to King Hezekiah his death sentence, which according to his faults would be a certain illness, but when he turned to God he converted the execution of the sentence and he conceded him fifteen years of life, and it is an infallible rule that in the prophecy of menace, and this one is of menaces, God knows well what has to be, and regarding him there is no mutability of his divine will, which always understands the threat, but there is compensation, but in which is prophecy, like the knowledge of God, and his eternal order there is no removal, nor cannot be, | what the divine Chrysostom[49] teaches us, like these words. The prophecy,

---

45   Horozco writes "Maria", even though "Miriam" is meant here. See Num. 12:2.
46   The prophet Jeremiah was born about 650 B.C. in Anatot near Jerusalem to a family of priests. He predicted among other things the 70 years of exile of the Jewish people (Jer. 25:1–14). Gabriele Wulz, "Jeremia", in *Calwer Bibellexikon*, ed. Otto Betz, Beate Ego and Werner Grimm, 2nd ed., vol. 1 (Stuttgart: 2006), 639–641. See also the book Jeremiah in the bible.
47   The prophet Jonah lived in the 8th century B.C. He predicted the restitution of the kingdom of Jeroboam II. within its former frontiers. Werner Grimm, "Jona", in *Calwer Bibellexikon*, ed. Otto Betz, Beate Ego and Werner Grimm, 2nd ed., vol. 1 (Stuttgart: 2006), 682.
48   The prophet Isaiah made predictions concerning Israel's future and the arrival of diverse (last) judgements. See, for example, Isaiah 1:21–31; 9:7–20; 11:1–16; 24:1–23. For his account of King Hezekiah's illness and healing, see Isaiah 38:1–8.
49   St John Chrysostom (347–407 A.D.), bishop of Constantinople from 398 on, was a very productive writer, commentator of the Old and the New Testament, and an important person within his contemporary ecclesiastical circles. His sermons and writings were received widely during his lifetime up to the Renaissance period. See Hagit Amirav, "John Chrysostom", in *EBR*, vol. 5, ed. Dale C. Allison, Jr. [and others], 263–267 (accessed on 2 January 2018). So it is no wonder that St John Chrysostom is mentioned as a reference in Horozco's treatise.

which derives from prescience does not change itself, but according to the sentence of the works it changes itself while changing the cause, and therefore it changes itself according to the words, and not according to how it is understood. Saint Anselmo[50] says the same, although he divides what we have said concerning prescience, because he says that there exists a prophecy in which God acts without us, which is necessary to happen at any rate, and this is called predestination,[51] and another one says that it is prescience that our freewill is mingled with, and with the help of grace we will achieve the price, or justly defenceless left without grace we keep on following the tempest. This prophecy of menace has many causes and it was necessary for many aspects which we will mention later. And for understanding the extent to which a prophecy is full of threats or not, for the incidents it is necessary to understand that it cannot have any other rule, and for us it is only beneficial to improve our lives, for any occurrence. And before we go ahead, it is the normal way to reduce to three types of revelations by prophets.

16ᵛ The first, when by hearing or external seeing the objects present themselves because they are signs or figures of the things to come. The second, when they only show themselves in the comprehension. And the third, when they represent in the imagination, which is like a medium between the understanding and the external sensations. And considering prophecy in a more general way, Bede[52] divides it in three ways. The first is, when what is to come shows itself by figures or similarities represented as the most ordinary. The second when it shows itself in living pictures which are the deeds, like Abraham's sacrifice, which was a representation of Christ. The third is the one which is manifested by words, as the prophets' sayings are and the psalms of David.

---

50 Probably Saint Anselm of Canterbury (1033–c.1121), a Benedictine monk and Doctor of the Church. In 1093 he became archbishop of Canterbury, which meant he was Primate of the English Church. He is author of many works in which he reflects on the essence of God, the proof of God's existence, and divine truth among other issues. His main critics during the Middle Ages were William of Ockham and Thomas Aquinas. See Helmut Meinhardt, "Anselm v. Canterbury", in *Lexikon für Theologie und Kirche*, vol. 1, ed. Walter Kasper [and others] (Freiburg im Breisgau: 1993), 711–712.

51 Here the term "predestination" is not understood in the sense of the Calvinist doctrine.

52 The Venerable Bede (672–735) was a monk living in Northumbria. He was the author of biblical commentaries as well as of hagiographies, epigrams and writings concerning metrics. Most renowned, though, were his works on chronology. He became the most influential English historiographer and authority on English historical self-conception until the early Middle Ages. See Hanna Vollrath, "Beda Venerabilis", in *Lexikon für Theologie und Kirche*, vol. 2, ed. Walter Kasper [and others] (Freiburg im Breisgau: 1994), 116–117.

Chapter XI. About some false prophets who appeared in the past and about their deceits

28r[53]

Beside the principal error regarding matters of faith we have mentioned, our enemy[54] pretends to sow errors in what concerns the customs, because when those degenerate and with them the meaning and the ability to judge (from which God may relieve us by his infinite mercy), the rest will assist easily, and especially the sin of ambition is subjected to deceit by false prophecy, because the demon | promises them that they would achieve what they intend. And it is known of someone that not many years ago he promised the devil who appeared to be the Pope and then transfigured himself into Christ, and two others having been deceived in this vision, to the one he had promised that by lifting the host on a certain day he would show him his glory. And when the day came and he had made all the diligences that seemed appropriate to him, he said his late mass and the door being closed one of his companions helped him. And when lifting the host, he stopped und waited such a long time till he already got tired, and he lifted his voice and said: "Unclose, Lord, your glory", and as he did not reveal himself, he put the host into its place. And knocking with his hand on the altar, he said in a loud voice "I am betrayed", and by this way he became aware of his illusion, and he turned to the mercy of the Holy Church for his own and the others' remedy, and those who know the history which was public at his time, know that it was like this, and for the others it is not adequate to say who they were. And although it seems as if there are things in which the devil intends no more than mockery they always are obtrusive, | because between mockery and fooling a bad doctrine is washed ashore, and one bad though is sufficient for him to achieve a gain, and if it only was to have mockery with us, the most recent case would be the one of the dragon,[55] of whom is said that God created it in order to mock it, and it is commonly said, that when he had made the dragon wild, disdained and worthy of disregard, and this is what he provided us with, and when he cannot do more, he is satisfied with mocking us. And among other very bad mockeries has always been with much prejudice the one which pretended to have by medium of the ambassadors who with their diligence and modesty of those who listen to them, they make themselves prophets without being even of the false ones which the devil teaches, but there are people so much perverse that it seems as if they could

28v

29r

---

53   The pagination says "fol. 22r" here, but should read "fol. 28r" instead.
54   The devil is meant here.
55   Maybe a reference to the dragon described in Apocalypse 12 and 13.

teach the devils, and one of them was the false prophet Theudas,[56] of whom Josephus[57] writes who persuaded a major part of the Jews to follow him with their homesteads way down the River Jordan by promising them to part the water by his mere order, and he had deceived many, the Caesar's representative Cuspius Fadus[58] followed them and killed | many of them, also Theudas. The same author tells later on about an Egyptian who lived in Jerusalem and persuaded the Jews to climb the mountain of Olives, because from there they could see the city falling. This is what he understood from Felix[59], who sent soldiers who wakened them up by killing four hundred of them and captured two hundred, and not the deceiver, because he was diligent to escape.[60] About a Jew named Nathan who made himself a prophet and drew the people out of seclusion, writes the same author in "De Bello Iudayco" and who in the end was captured and in Rome they burnt him alive by the order of Vespasian,[61] and he also writes about others in the seventh book. Socrates Sozomeno[62] recounts

---

56   During the administration of the Roman procurator Cuspius Fadus (44–46), we have the account of a "false prophet" and "imposter" named Theudas living in Judea. The sources are the historian Flavius Josephus and the Acts of the Apostles (Acts 5:36). It is said that Theudas held very persuasive sermons and made the masses follow him to the River Jordan. There he could command the river to part so that they could easily cross it. The procurator Fadus, however, let him and many of his followers be captured. Theudas himself was decapitated. See Isaiah Gafni, "Theudas", in *Encyclopaedia Judaica*, vol. 19, ed. Fred Skolnik/Michael Berenbaum, 2nd ed. (Detroit: 2007), 703–704; Theudas was a released slave of his Master Trebianus. He was active in Rome in the summer of 46 A.D. F. Münster, "Theudas", in *Paulys Realencyclopädie der classischen Alterumswissenschaften*, series 2, vol. 6 (Neue Bearbeitung begonnen von Georg Wissow), ed. Wilhelm Kroll and Karl Mittelhaus (Stuttgart: 1936), 244.

57   Flavius Josephus, a Jewish historian and general (36/37–c.100 A.D.). He wrote a comprehensive history of the Jewish people. He is considered the most important reference for Jewish history during the two centuries before and after Christ. Roland Deines, "Josephus, Flavius", in *Calwer Bibellexikon*, vol. 1, ed. Otto Betz, Beate Ego and Werner Grimm, 2nd ed. (Stuttgart: 2006), 689.

58   See note 56.

59   This is probably Antonius Felix, the procurator of Judea from 52 to 60 A.D., a period which was characterised by constant unrest in the region. Lea Roth, "Felix, Antonius", in *Encyclopaedia Judaica*, vol. 6 (Jerusalem: 1996), 1218.

60   Ibid., with a reference to Acts 21:38.

61   The Roman Emperor Titus Flavius Vespasian (r.69–79 A.D.). After serving as proconsul in Africa, Nero entrusted him with the suppression of the rebellion in Judaea, a task which he accomplished until the middle of 68 (apart from Jerusalem). One of his characteristics was industriousness, and one of his most important achievements was to end the wars following Nero's death. Guy Edward Farquhar Chilver and Barbara Levick, "Vespasian (Titus Flavius Vespasian)", in *The Oxford Classical Dictionary*, ed. Simon Hornblower and Antony Spawforth, 4th ed. (Oxford: 2012) 1543–1544.

62   Probably Sozomen (Salamanes Hermeias Sozumenus), a church historian and advocate in

in his history the story of the false Moses in Creta who caused so much damage to the Jews by robbing them and throwing them alive [from the top of a mountain], and of this tell Adon and Sigeberto in their chronicles, that it was the devil in Moses' figure, and about the other who was called Dunaas, and also feigned to be Moses at the time of Justin[63] like Nicephorus[64] writes and says that in the end he came to kill Elesbass, captain of the Ethiopians.

Chapter XIII. About the feigned wonders and the way the devil is able to effect them 33ʳ

Saint Augustine[65] writes it in many places and the martyr Saint Justin[66] and other holy authors without the profane ones recount how the devil intended to authorise the famous enchanter Apollonius of Tyana[67] by performing mir- 33ᵛ

  Constantinople in the 5th century. He is the author of works on ecclesiastical history with a focus on monasticism, missions among the Armenians or Palestine local traditions. Jill Harries, "Sozomen (Salamanes Hermeias Sozomenus)", in *The Oxford Classical Dictionary*, 1387; Friedhelm Winkelmann, "Sozomenos", in *Lexikon für Theologie und Kirche*, vol. 9, ed. Walter Kasper [and others] (Freiburg im Breisgau: 2000), 801–802.

63 Justin Martyr was born in Samaria and died 165 A.D. in Rome. He was a teacher of Christian philosophy in Rome and maybe also earlier in Asia Minor. Justin Martyr is renowned as one of the most prolific Christian writers of the second century. Stefan Heid, "Justinos, Märtyrer", in *Lexikon für Theologie und Kirche*, vol. 5, ed. Walter Kasper [and others] (Freiburg im Breisgau: 1996), 1112–1113.

64 This is probably Nikephoros I, patriarch of Constantinople (c.750/758–828). Between 780 and 787, he wrote a historical work regarding the period from 602 until 769 (with interruptions). Otto Volk, "Nikephoros I. v. Konstantinopel", in *Lexikon für Theologie und Kirche*, vol. 7, ed. Walter Kasper [and others] (Freiburg im Breisgau: 1998), 839–840.

65 Augustine (354–430) was born in Numidia, a Roman province in North Africa, to his Christian mother Monica and his non-Christian father Patricius. After his studies in Milan, where he became professor of rhetoric in 385 and where he had listened to the preaching of the resident bishop, Ambrose, he converted to Christianity in 387. Ambrose was the one who baptised him. Driven by the wish to establish a monastic community in North Africa, he returned to the province where he was born. In 395 he became bishop of Hippo. Augustine was a writer of numerous works of very different genres, among them theological treatises, doctrinal writings, scriptural commentaries, homilies, but also lyrics and an autobiography. His influence on ecclesiastical institutions has been profound throughout history. Margaret R. Miles, "Augustine (354–430)", in *Encyclopedia of Early Christianity*, vol. 1, ed. Everett Ferguson, 2nd ed. (New York: 1997), 148–153.

66 Justin Martyr converted to Christianity and went to Rome, where he collided with the state over his refusal to sacrifice to the Roman gods because of his confession to the Christian faith, which led to his martyrdom by beheading. Justin was a teacher and prolific writer. He is mostly known for his apologetic works. Theodore Stylianopoulos, "Justin Martyr (d. c.165)", in *Encyclopedia of Early Christianity*, vol. 1, 647–650.

67 Apollonius of Tyana was a philosopher who lived in the first century. He was an itinerant

acles through him which were so extraordinary in apparition that the people dared to say that they were greater than those performed by Christ because the former were all deceits and illusions. Because the devil cannot do miracles which are clearly and explicitly for everybody, and those which he effects are like inventions of foolery with a subtlety of the hands, meaning that someone who understands them would laugh at those who become frightened because of not knowing what they are. And thus the devil is able to form figures in the air which are only apparent and not reality, as is practiced with the art of mirrors which can create a figure in the air which would be a representation of themselves. In this manner, in Rome on the day of the Sack[68] at the time of Pope Clement[69] the figure of a crucified Christ above a tower was spotted in the air and it was the artistry of the individual who was within it (i.e. the tower), also with a mirror and a painted figure and the figure | showed itself in the air in all its colours. With fire, things of great miracle can be performed which the devil could do, and these would appear like miracles not performed by any other individual which supposedly effects the rule that when natural bodies obey local movement, they are not affected by divine will. And in this way, one could hide a thing and bring another, although it may be from far away, and put it in its place so that it seems as if it would have converted into it. And thus, they display transformations which they pretend to effect like witches and in the manner used among some indigenous people when they allegedly transform themselves into foxes. And according to reports by Plinius,[70] they transform themselves into wolves and cause a lot of damage. Olaus Magnus[71] in his history also

teacher gathering traces of wisdom in different regions of the ancient world, from Ethiopia to India, and finally adopted a neo-Pythagorean lifestyle. Apollonius lived with the reputation of being a sage, but also a magician, and he had to face charges of magic upheld against him. Everett Ferguson, "Apollonius of Tyana (*d. c.*96–98 A.D.)", in *Encyclopedia of Early Christianity*, vol. 1, 81.

68 This refers to the Sack of Rome. See note 69.

69 Pope Clement VII (= prior to this: Giulio de' Medici) was born in 1478 in Florence. His pontificate, from November 1523 until September 1534, covered an extremely difficult period of time for the Roman Church. His attempts to stem the Imperial predominance of Charles V in Italy together with the French king Francis I led to the "Sacco di Roma" [Sack of Rome] in 1527, the complete devastation of the city by Charles' lansquenets. Georg Schwaiger, "Clemens VII. (19.11.1523–25.9.1534)", in *Lexikon für Theologie und Kirche*, vol. 2, ed. Walter Kasper [and others] (Freiburg im Breisgau: 1994), 1223.

70 Pliny the Younger (*d. c.*113) was a Roman writer, orator and governor. Among his most important writings are ten books of letters. Nine of these cover a great variety of topics, ranging from nature to administration. What is more, Pliny gave descriptions of Christian societies of the first two centuries. Michael P. McHugh, "Pliny the Younger (ca. A.D. 61–ca. 113)", in *Encyclopedia of Early Christianity*, vol. 1, 928.

71 Olaus Magnus (1490–1557), born in Linköping, was a Swedish geographer and historian.

relates similar transformations and remarkable cases among northern peoples. Without changing the humour with subtlety, this could produce figures which seem real; it is true what is stated later on, and the deceit consists primarily in the imagination which assents to those figures with such a power that it seems without doubt that they are real. And anyone who has himself suffered a serious illness like typhus fever will understand clearly when part of the imagination is weak and the spirits which rise in order to form the figures are so powerful that they create these figures; when the sick man imagines trees, he will see them and when he remembers persons which are dead, he will see them right before him. And it is not like the old (women) say who wish to die and call him due to the effects of their illness. And to sum up every kind of visual deceit, may it be representing figures in the air when the devils choose to manifest themselves in the air by densifying or rarefying it, and through light and dark which he unites like a great painter, although with things from the air, or deceiving the viewing by the alteration of the imagination, this is named with a particular prestigious name with which the famous enchanters have praised themselves like Apollonius, as we have mentioned, whose devilish life was described by Philostratus[72] with more elegance than truth. He does however tell the truth in a lot of matters because as George | Cedrenus[73] says, the devils intended to obscure Christ's miracles with deceits when they could. And in order to display evidence as to what the devil was able to do within this context with God's permission, there is no need for further proof, as recounted by the scripture of the wise men who resisted Moses while doing what he did. And in order to make it visible that this was with God's permission, he did not give them

34ᵛ

35ʳ

He was also appointed Roman Catholic archbishop of Uppsala, but could not carry out the office because of the implementation of the Lutheran Reformation in Sweden. Olaus Magnus is renowned for his map *Carta marina* which was published in 1539 in Venice and regarded as the most accurate picture of the Arctic region. In 1555 he published his *Historia de gentibus septentrionalibus* [History of the Northern people], an extensive description of Scandinavian political and social life. Trygve R. Skarsten, "Magnus, Olaus (1490–1557)", in *The Oxford Encyclopedia of the Reformation*, vol. 2, ed. Hans J. Hillerbrand (New York: 1996), 499–500.

72 Probably Philostratus (d. c.244–249), one of the leading Greek writers of the time with a very diverse variety of genres, among others biographies, dialogues and "love letters". He was highly esteemed in the Renaissance. Walter Manoel Edwards, Robert Browning, Graham Anderson and Ewen Bowie, "Philostrati", in *The Oxford Classical Dictionary*, ed. Simon Hornblower and Antony Spawforth, 4th ed. (Oxford: 2012), 1137.

73 Georgios Kedrenos was a Byzantine historian who lived in the first half of the 12th century. He wrote and compiled a historiographic work that comprised the time from the creation of the world until 1057. Johannes Koder, "Kedrenos, Georgios", in *Lexikon für Theologie und Kirche*, vol. 5, ed. Walter Kasper [and others] (Freiburg im Breisgau: 1996), 1383.

licence, so that they would be right in the easiest way, and then they started to see them, and the greatest power destroyed theirs in the way that Moses' serpent had engulfed the ones they had engulfed. And so they said "God's finger is here, which is God's power", according to the sentence in which there was another peculiarity regarding the fact that it is normal that God is able to achieve more than any other, meaning that he could demolish him with his finger. The devil has no power unless it is permitted (for him) and he never makes use of it for something good because of his malice, and although one might admit that some are worse than others and less prejudicial, there is no reason to admit that some of them would be provided with good conditions and be favourable to the people | as they could not stop this just by themselves. And those who in the tone of a landlord (this means goblin because they are goblins) want to show themselves friendly, in the end they deceive or at least mock, and sometimes even in a grave way. And to sum up, the miracle only derives from God who is able to newly create and return to nothing when what he has created is served, and this is what no creature can do. And through what someone sees which appears to him to be growing, one has to understand that it is not deceit in viewing because the seeds sowed by God will be visible in everything. And art can abbreviate or accelerate it, and this is what is said about the devil: that he is able to act swiftly, transferring the active things into passive ones.

And this is the quality of the miracles which are recounted of Apollonius and others; like those magicians who in Judea deceived the people whom they attracted, as written by Josephus, who afterwards became robbers and forgers and were punished by Felix, Judea's president. Amongst other acts of horror performed by the Gymnosophists in Ethiopia, who were their prophets | as recounted by Philostratus, was that the tree bent down to them and bowed to them with reverence and talked to them, and it is evident that this was as if they were doubling the devil and forming the voice in the air which is easy for them as we will tell later, when the crux of the matter is treated. And there would be a lot to say concerning the intention of these feigned miracles and what is important will be said when we will observe Magic and its deceits in which the principal divination is founded in those which the devil has introduced to the world, and what we have said will be sufficient. And actually, the greatest miracle which the devil can do for me is to say any truth and the more concerning the things to come, because he is the father of all lies and a friend of deceiving everybody, it is reasonable that we talk about the precise way in which he talks about some things.

Chapter XXII. About what to advise concerning revelations so that they will not cheat us.   56ʳ[74]

Anyone experiencing any type of revelation must examine his own conscience with great caution and start to see whether it is inclined to presumption and vain glory. If there is a trace of these attributes, it appears that the devil can find a large portal to enter and has a significant reason for entering. Should the individual find this the case, he can be sure that it is the work of his enemy, and to a greater degree in the air in which he deports himself, and from this time on, the devil will attempt to enter by implanting a contentment with himself and a certain arrogance that makes the individual think that he owes him these favours. This does not happen if the revelations come from God because they instead create a state of humiliation, planting peace in the soul and a new desire to serve and please God. And the devil with all his shrewdness is so stupid that from this time on he reveals the purpose for which he had come in order not to lose time. And more is not necessary when he blinds all comprehension at first glance and they believe him, as in the case recounted by Palladius in the history of the Holy Fathers, when there was a monk whom the devil deceived which appeared to him in the figure of Christ.

Firstly he sent him another devil in the figure of an angel who told him that   56ᵛ[75] he would see Jesus Christ, because he, Christ, loved his teaching, his liberty of life and the confidence he had in himself; the sinner could then begin to see that the trust could not be good because it was not completely in God, and the liberty of life also less good which should be subjected to holy obedience, and he did not pay attention to it before he expected it. And this damned individual (the Devil) appeared to him surrounded by a resplendence of fire and accompanied by many Angelicals who brought burning lamps; as he was lifted in the air, he (the Devil) told him: "Get out of your cell, and where you see me, adore me; and with this [order] you shall not do anything else". And after [the devil] had disappeared, the monk came out of his cell and saw the false Christ at [a distance of] one stadium, which is 125 steps, through the light of the lamps which accompanied him, and he adored him, so that from there on he was very satisfied. What is more, he was so deranged that it seemed to him no longer necessary to go to church or to communion. And when the others scolded him because of this, he said that | he did not feel any necessity for it. The compan-   55ʳ ions had pity because of his madness and when they had tied him and cured

---

74   This ought to be fol. 54ʳ following the pagination's order.
75   This ought to be fol. 54ᵛ following the pagination's order.

him, he convalesced like a sick person and he (the Devil) vanished. In this, we see an ordinary trick of the devil, and as soon as he has chosen someone to be under his hand, he tries to drive him to irrationality, so that he cannot return to himself and repent, especially concerning matters of idolatry. And the sin of weakness is characterised in its manner by something of this, in what we see being outside of oneself whilst feeling like having been put under certain spells like those which are utilised by the devil. But concerning the purpose which we mentioned when the devil deceives by apparitions which attempt to switch off the brain, there is an admirable example beyond what has already been mentioned which is described by the same Palladius, where he speaks about a holy monk who spent three years within a cave and did not eat for the whole week, until he received the Holy Communion on Sunday, the holy form which was brought to him by a priest. And one day Satan stepped forward in the figure of a priest wearing a form suitable for his hand, and because the Saint knew who he was, he told him: "O father of malice and of deceit, enemy | of every justice, will you not cease deceiving the soul? And so you dare to mock the sacraments?" And to this the devil answered: "Well, you do not seem to have been far from where you fell, and thus I have deceived one of your companions, and because of what I told him, he turned mad."

The second advice which every individual has to take heed of for himself is not to trust oneself in any way because there is more need for advice than in any other issue. And it is not sufficient to end with not believing in anything because the devil also knows to be tenacious and to enter by different ways; and no wise person will ever stop needing advice or at least he will understand it like this. And concerning another way to act when speaking of the truth, we could state what Saint John Climacus[76] said which was that he had no need for the devil to seduce him because he was the one who in similar matters was reluctant to accept any advice. And when the person to whom this happens would be God-fearing, and according to what he understands what seems to be the truth, what kind of trouble will he cause with another person to whom he communicates this | matter? Just because God is one within himself and in all that he does this should not be believed because it is not possible that he says something as one person and something else as another. And more would be saved if the necessary help and relief was never lacking in his church, enlightened by his ministers, and helping them so that they would fulfil their office properly. And they will all fulfil it accurately, especially when they treat it with

---

76   The abbot at Sinai, John Climacus (d.649), author of *The Ladder of Divine Ascent* (or *of Paradise*), which was widely received within the Eastern Church. Frederick W. Norris, "John Climacus (ca. 579–649)", in *Encyclopedia of Early Christianity*, vol. 1, 624.

humility and rectitude as God wishes because when they elevate themselves like scholars, even though they are such, they will not succeed. And above all it is necessary to entrust oneself to our Lord and to beg for his help, that he does not allow us to be deceived. And this is also well explained in what Saint Bonaventura teaches us concerning adoration in which he asks whether the one who will adore the devil has any excuse. By pointing to the figure of Christ, he says that he has none, because he had three remedies which are: to cancel one's own discernment, to beg for others' advice and to supplicate our Lord for his divine help who will grant it to those who live within him and will never lack him. And according to this in the remaining considerations, although some might be quite common, we will have to talk about those who advise these persons.

Chapter xxiiii: About some notorious cases which have succeeded by the deceit which the devil has ordered with feigned revelations 59ᵛ

For all this that has been mentioned and for what can be said concerning the cases which occur every day, it is reasonable in a meaningful way | to take notice 60ʳ of the examples of the things which have succeeded because they can teach us a lot, and beyond what we have already said, we have to mention a number of notable things.

In the year 847 a woman lived in Swabia who by the order of a cleric who intended to benefit from her deceits began to prophesy by feigning to have heavenly visions and to talk to the angels and the saints who revealed to her what she was to say. And many followed her and venerated her like a saint. And he [the cleric] wished to know her secrets until she came to understand his concern and she confessed this in the church of Saint Alban when Rabanus [Maurus][77] was bishop and present at that time. In addition to her public shame, she was whipped while being bound to a post. After this, she stopped her prophesying. And among other things she said was that the world would come to its end in that year; and it is common among the false prophets to treat this as the most secret issue which would frighten people to the highest degree.

---

77 (H)Rabanus Maurus (c.780–856), Benedictine monk and renowned teacher at the important abbey of Fulda, Germany, for twenty years (822–842), who attracted pupils from far away. He became Archbishop of Mainz in 847. Hrabanus was a prolific writer of biblical commentaries, sermons, pedagogic works, statements concerning ecclesiastical questions and others. Raymund Kottje, "Hrabanus Maurus, osb", in *Lexikon für Theologie und Kirche*, vol. 5, ed. Walter Kasper [and others] (Freiburg im Breisgau: 1996), 292–293.

And in parallel, Agathius[78] recounts of some in Constantinople at the time of Emperor Anastasius[79] who feigned having admirable vi|sions, declaring things to come, and that the world would end soon, with which they convinced some persons to the feigned penitence; but when they referred to, [Jean] Gerson[80] tells the history of a woman who lived in the land of Savoy who said that she was one of five women sent by God in order to redeem many souls from hell, because he was sorrowful of those who would be lost, and she had already deceived a lot of young women and other people with her illusions, especially by telling many of them their sins. According to Saint Augustine, the devil can understand this and reveal it to his followers, not by what is hidden in the secret of the heart but showing himself through exterior signals. She had ecstasies in which she said that he communicated her great secrets, and that in them she experienced things of great wonders; she lived in abstinence and apparently led a very good life, wearing two pieces of coal tied to her feet of which she claimed that they tortured her every time a soul went to hell. She said that she liberated three | souls every day, one and two without effort and the third with great difficulty. And by discovering this deceit, God was served, like many others who were similarly discovered. And she acknowledged that the devil put her into him and helped her and that the ecstasies were epilepsy which dissimulated from those fictions, and that the beginning had been the ambition to sustain herself because she was very poor. And this happened in the year 1424. And not less considerable is the case of Magdalena de la Cruz in Córdoba[81] which is notorious among us, and someone outside the kingdom describing her in great detail was not inaccurate. To sum up: when she was a little girl, the devil appeared before her as a black figure, and yet with flattery and caresses which did not

---

78 Probably Agathias (also called Scholastikos) (c.532–c.579/582), a Byzantine compiler and historian. Joseph David Frendo, "Agathias, gen. Scholastikos", in *Lexikon für Theologie und Kirche*, vol. 1, ed. Walter Kasper [and others] (Freiburg im Breisgau: 1993), 226–227.

79 The Byzantine Emperor Anastasios I (r.491–518). He was an important ruler who initiated reforms throughout the political system. Carmelo Capizzi, "Anastasio I., byz. Kaiser (491–518)", in *Lexikon für Theologie und Kirche*, vol. 1, 600–601.

80 The Frenchman Jean Charlier de Gerson (1363–1429) was one of the most influential medieval theologians. In 1393 he became chancellor of the University of Paris. He also acted as a legate at the papal court of Clement VII and attended the Council of Constance. Jean Gerson was the author of more than 400 theological works. Martin Bauer, "Johannes Charlier Gerson", in *Lexikon für Theologie und Kirche*, vol. 5, 909–910.

81 The Franciscan nun Magdalena de la Cruz (d.1560) spent most of her life in a monastery in Córdoba, where she was known and venerated as a "living saint" because of her visions of Christ, Mary, and various saints for almost forty years until she fell into disgrace. Ana Cristina Cuadro García, "Tejiendo una vida de reliquia. Estrategias de control de conciencias de la santa diabólica Magdalena de la Cruz", *Chronica Nova* 31 (2005), 307–326, *passim*.

scare her off; before they made friends, he talked to her every day. He threatened her not to reveal to anyone what had happened and taught her things which were unsuitable for her age; he began to place her in a manner of sanctity with everyone admiring her, and she began to feel vanity. Here the de|vil found the entrance he wanted and offered that when she married him, he would make her be viewed as a saint and that she would do miracles, and so she agreed to this bad marriage. And with this bigotry lasting for many years, God allowed her to be held as a saint because she feigned miracles and discovered secrets, saying that she had revelations sent by the good angels. In this manner, she predicted the capture of the king of France for the same day on which it took place, and also the entry into Rome in the times of [pope] Clement VII.[82] And because her fame of sanctity grew with similar deceits, the rulers recommended themselves in their prayers, until God was served when she discovered herself repenting and asking God and the ministers of his church for mercy in the year 1546. In these days there was another notorious case which due to the prelate's good memory to whom it happened, had to restrict himself to the mere statement that the devil was capable of doing so much that within many years he made this working girl, to whom he had appeared when she was nine years | old, to be considered as a saint, and he stipulated with her that he would make her be held for a saint while she would give herself to him. And from that time on, he showed great miracles through her and they grew in a way that the prelate saw himself obligated to honour her and gave orders for her to be imprisoned, and wherever she had gone with great caution, and with gifts and favours, it happened that people of religion and science talked about her as a saint. And it pleased God that among them was one who because of the differentiation of the spirits of which Saint Paul talks about, or because of considering the rules we have mentioned, he found the trace of deceit. And it pleased God that it all went wrong when she had begun feigning cicatrices and crowns of thorns on the head which the devil was able to make and he (the prelate) always tried to disavow the real miracles and the miracles made by God, when he did not have to abbreviate his hand, before they saw extraordinary cases, about which one could talk and write of in full at the time, but now no longer.

---

82   The "entry into Rome" here refers to the Sack of Rome.

2   María de la Concepción, beata
    Seville, in the Year 1645[83]

Cover sheet

Mairena   +   1645

Inq[uisiti]on[84] of Seville

Acts initiated by the Commission of the most illustrious Señor bishop of Plasencia Inq[uisid]or Gen[era]l y s[eñore]s de el q[...]o De la s[an]ta gen[era]l Inquissiçion dada
a
El s[eñ]or D[oct]or Don Agustin de villaueçençio apostolic (?) Inq[uisit]or de La Inq[uisiti]on of Seville.
Concerning the case of[85]
Maria de la Conçepción, a Beata
Resident of the town of Mairena =

---

83 AHN, Inq. 2061, Exp. 12. This file consists of a summary of 15 pages plus some notes and envelopes.
84 The literature concerning the Spanish Inquisition and its impact on religion, society and social control in early modern Spain is extensive. I would like to name some of the most important works on the topic here: José Martínez Millán, *La Inquisición española* (Madrid: 2009); Gustav Henningsen, *The Witches' Advocate. Basque Witchcraft and the Spanish Inquisition (1609–1614)* (Reno: 1980); James M. Anderson, *Daily life during the Spanish Inquisition* (Westport: 2002); Sara Tilghman Nalle, *God in La Mancha. Religious Reform and the People of Cuenca, 1500–1650* (Baltimore: 1992); Allyson M. Poska, *Regulating the People. The Catholic Reformation in Seventeenth-Century Spain* (Leiden: 1998); Jaime Contreras, *Historia de la Inquisición española (1478–1834)* (Madrid: 1997); Henry Kamen, *The Spanish Inquisition. A historical Revision* (London: 1997); Ricardo García Cárcel and Doris Moreno Martínez, *Inquisición. Historia crítica* (Madrid: 2000); Doris Moreno, *La invención de la Inquisición* (Madrid: 2004); Bartolomé Bennassar, *L'Inquisition espagnole. XVe–XIXe siècles* (Paris: 2001); Francisco Bethencourt, *L'inquisition à l'époque moderne: Espagne, Italie, Portugal XVe–XIX siécle* (Paris: 1995); still valid also: Henry Charles Lea, *A History of the Inquisition of Spain and the Inquisition of the Spanish Dependencies*, 5 vols (1906–1908; repr. London: 2011); and a bit more general: Julio Caro Baroja, *Vidas Mágicas e Inquisición*, 2nd ed., 2 vols (Madrid: 1992). Regarding especially women tried by the Spanish Inquisition, see Stacey Schlau, *Gendered Crime and Punishment. Women and/in the Hispanic Inquisitions* (Leiden: 2013); Lisa Vollendorf, *The Lives of Women. A New History of Inquisitorial Spain* (Nashville: 2005); Mary E. Giles (ed.), *Women and the Inquisition. Spain and the New World* (Baltimore: 1999); María Isabel Barbeito Carneiro (ed.), *Cárceles y mujeres en el siglo XVII. Razón y forma de la Galera. Proceso Inquisitorial de San Plácido* (Biblioteca de escritoras 21) (Madrid: 1991).
85 The underlined sections follow the original text.

[*Following some comments which seem to have been added later in a different handwriting; not reproduced here.*]

N[ota]ry De Gonçalo Flores

This petition has been brought before the council in whose copy is accompanied by this document against a *beata* from Mairena who has agitated and is still agitating this region with superstitions by answering to future contingents. And after having consulted [the case] with the most illustrious bishop of Plasençia the General Inquisitor has appeared [and said] Señor, you shall induce an inquiry of the content in which don Juan de la Vega, the notary of this Inquisition's Secreto[86] [= Secret], is undermined and to the others you shall answer that for them [...] of commission in form and when having finished the beginning of the lawsuit with the voice appearing [...] [...] the 22nd of June 1645, and the same inquiry you shall induce with the referred in the mentioned petition concerning the case of the commissary Pedro López de Cabra.

1r

[*following four signatures next to one another*]
D[oct]or Don Pedro
Pacheco Inquisitor

Licenciado Don Fran[cis]co Çapata
y Mendoça Inquisitor

D[oct]or Don Isidoro
De S[an] Vicente Inquisitor

Don [...]
Bishop

[*On the lower margin, the following is written:*]
Inquisitor D[oct]or Don Agustin de Villauiçencio
de off[ici]o Seville

[*five lines which seem to be the address = envelope; not reproduced here.*]

1v

---

86   Secreto [= Secret] means: "Bureau of the faith cases over which the ancient ecclesiastical tribunal of the Inquisition had the competence in a separated way" ["Despacho de las causas de fe, en las cuales entendía secretamente el antiguo tribunal eclesiástico de la Inquisición"]. *Diccionario de la lengua española de la Real Academia Española* (http://dle .rae.es/?id=XPKxnKN|XPMvDJ8|XPNR6xt, accessed on 6 January 2018).

2ʳ   +

Most illustrious P[...]a Señor Inquisitor

During the last months at the Inquisition's court of Seville a trial was initiated against a *Beata* from Mairena, [which is] at a distance of four miles from [Seville] who had scandalised and rioted[87] this land with her superstitions, especially, when she foretold future contingencies, because numerous persons, not only "the common", but from the most lucid and noble of Seville and its district[88] came to consult her, men as well as women. And when she was admonished by the tribunal not to foretell or to perturb in these issues it seems she remained silent for some days. And after a short time from this part the scandal has grown anew with more publicity because it was notorious that the Inquisitor Don Diego de la Fuente in company of a judge and of the bishop's notary Juan Lasso Cordero and with Atanassio de Torres de Avila, the notary of the Secreto had consulted her about different things. And especially they focused on the incident which the named Inquisitor and Athanasio, his great confidant and friend, have had in this visit, to whose responses it seems they gave credit to and which seem to have been not too favourable, because after the two returned from their visit to that woman, it was noticed that they were more frightened than ever before and that the Inquisitor did not speak about the journey to the mountain, which was undertaken with such commitment and with so much ostentation. And when the named Atanassio was in his office with considerable power which he had previously lacked

---

87   The risk of social riots caused by prophecies with extreme contents was indeed very real. The fear of uprising was not unjustified, bearing in mind the social disturbances and revolts occurring in Seville in 1652 because of bad harvests and extreme rises in prices. The local people were discontent to a high degree for a variety of reasons: a great number of soldiers from the Seville region had to serve the Spanish crown throughout the years of the Portuguese rebellion, as they already had done before in 1635 during the Spanish-French war; furthermore because of the ongoing economic crisis, resulting from, among other factors, the expulsion of 7500 *moriscos* from Seville in 1610. Antonio Domínguez Ortíz, *La Sevilla del siglo XVII* (Historia de Sevilla), 3rd ed. (Seville: 1986), 26, 71f., 110f., 113f. Bearing in mind the rebellions that had taken place in nearby Portugal just five years before, i.e. in 1640, the authorities in Seville remained careful to avoid social and political disturbances. These had indeed been a serious political matter because they led to Portugal's independence, which had been part of the Spanish empire since 1580. Mary Elizabeth Perry, *Gender and Disorder in Early Modern Seville* (Princeton: 1990), 43.
88   Domínguez Ortíz, *La Sevilla del siglo XVII*, 79. Seville was the most populous city in Spain at the time until the great plague epidemic of 1649 (Ibid., 73). Seville also had a highly heterodox social structure and a high percentage of members of the nobility, a fact that contributed to the city's reputation as a particular wealthy town. Ibid., 38f., 94, 96f.: "Sevilla el reino más rico de Castilla".

to stand before the public, he wished to ask in the Secreto that they would transfer him from this Inquisition's court to the one of the Indies. May it be scandals and presumptions, those give reason to minister similar ones with their actions so that they do not have | to be pressed by curiousness and if this together with the rest is the [...] of remedy only for Your Highness's consideration. 2ᵛ

[*The rest of the page appears in a different handwriting; not reproduced here.*]
[...]

In the royal castle of Triana[89] on the 6th of July 1645, being in his office the Señor Inquisitor Doctor Don Agustín de Villaviç[ençi]o. Saying that by the virtue that he owns by the commission he has from the Illustrious Señor General Inquisitor and the Señores of the Secreto of the Holy General Inquisition, he said that he accepted and accepts that under the date of 12th of June 1645 and for its compliance he used to name and named as writer before whom should pass the autos[90] which were sent by [the court] to me, Don Gonzalo Flores, notary of this Inquisition's Secreto and before everything. For this effect he received my oath in the form given by the law and I made and promised under the duty to keep inviolably the secret of anything that will pass to me and come to my conscience and the named Señor Inquisitor has signed it = 3ʳ

Inquisitor don Augustin   Before me
de Villauiçençio   Goncalo Flores, writer

1st witness
And then suddenly for the effect reported above the named Señor Inquisitor had ordered to appear before him

Don Juan de la Vega y Dauila, the Secreto's notary of this Inquisition court from whom | was received his oath in the form of the law and after having sworn he promised to tell the truth and to keep the secret and he said that he was older than 37 years. = 3ᵛ

He was asked whether he knew or presumed the reason why he had been called.

He said that he did not know nor presume why.

---

89   Triana is a neighbourhood of Seville situated on the other river bank, opposite the city of Seville. The river Guadalquivir separates Triana from the historic city centre of Seville. The castle of Triana is where the Inquisition's tribunal of Seville was located.
90   The term 'autos' signify documents resulting from a judicial decision.

He was asked whether he had any news of María de la conçepçion, a *beata* and resident of Mairena and of the trial which was initiated against her at this Holy Office and the form of its processing. =

He said that it must have been two or three years ago, little more or less, that he had heard a lot of news about the named *beata* María de la Conçepçion, resident of Mairena, because of the trial he had seen and he knew was initiated against her in this Holy Office because she was one of the women most mentioned in this kingdom[91] and he had also news about the processing of her trial which he wanted to remember: it was that they let her know that she should no longer respond to future contingencies like she had done before about what is referred to in the named case.

He was asked whether he knew what constant the referred and what by act of this Holy Office | was notified to the named that from that time on she should abstain from responding to future contingents: not only that she did not accomplish, contravening the named act since a good while from this part she had scandalised and disturbed this region with her prognostications and superstitions. By answering in this matter concerning future contingents, there are innumerable persons, not only commoners, but of the most illustrious of this town and district who used to consult her for this reason and certain persons in particular of great status and quality had consulted her. =

He said that about all he remembered was that before they had initiated a trial against the named *beata*, the notice arrived at the court that the commotion which her actions caused was to such a great extent and people from all states high and low[92] who came to consult and visit her, that when the tribunal realised having such a scandal the *comisario*[93] of Mairena did not justify it, nor did he give notice (about what he wanted | to remember), he wrote a letter to the named *comisario* (which without doubt must be among

---

[91] This seems to be a slight exaggeration, but it surely underlines the disturbances caused by her predictions.

[92] This gives an insight into the composition of the group of her clients. Both men and women wished to consult María. Cf. fol. 2ʳ.

[93] A "comisario" was a collaborator of the Inquisition who instead of a salary received some privileges as remuneration for his service. Comisarios normally were priests. Their function in the inquisitorial system was to represent the Inquisitor, publish edicts of faith, collect denouncements and send them to the tribunal. For the group of comisarios and their role, see Gonzalo Cerrillo Cruz, *Los familiares de la inquisición española* (Estudios de Historia) (Valladolid: 2000), especially 233–259; Sarah Tilghman Nalle, "Inquisitors, Priests, and the People during the Catholic Reformation in Spain", *The Sixteenth Century Journal* 18 (1987), 557–587, especially from 560 on; Moreno, *La invención de la Inquisición*, 49–50.

the files) in which he admonished his carelessness with repression and according to what the named *comisario* answered and little information which he referred to this witness it seemed that it could be something affecting the aforementioned *beata*, because although he examined some of the witnesses who testified concerning the aforementioned consults and about her <u>answers to future contingents</u> in the same complaints, one tried so hard to wipe this out with excuses (like the one we will see) that the tribunal was obliged to be content with little at that time during which they issued the named notification to him. And after that for a certain time this witness did not hear anything considerable concerning the aforementioned scandals of the aforementioned *beata* until a few days ago when he heard from different persons from this part that the aforementioned consultations and scandals have increased substantially more than | ever before, and this in particular after the letter of the Señores of the Secreto arrived in which they requested a report of the summary of the named case. Because on this occasion especially the Señor Inquisitor <u>Don Francisco Valero de Molina</u> said in the tribunal in the presence of almost all of his colleagues (if bad, he does not remember) and of this deponent who was most certain that the aforementioned *beata* today would bring more scandals than ever before with her answers and actions and when this witness was later interrogated in the Secreto, he heard that in the presence of the Secreto's ministers, one of <u>whom is Juan de Carmona</u>, that they came to Mairena from twenty leagues and more in order to consult the named *beata*. On the same occasion, <u>Don Carlos de Azme</u> answered that this would not mean a lot because he knew that two ministers from here inside and one Judge and Inquisitor had | gone to visit her or consult her and that this witness did not remember in particular the persons who before and after the named notification were said to have come to consult her, but that they had been numberless; he only remembers (in accordance to what had been referred to have said in the Secreto the named Don Carlos) that Señor Don Juan de Morales, prosecutor of this Holy Office, said to this witness that during the past months he had known for very certain that the Inquisitor Don Diego de la Fuente Peredo in the company of Athanasio Torres, the Secreto's notary, and of Juan Lasso Cordero, notary of imposed legal acts and of one judge whom he did not name, they had gone to see and consult the named *beata* about what this witness after perhaps a few days wrote to Señor Don Juan Escobar de el Corro, prosecutor of the Secreto, although the zeal of the named Don Juan de Morales is such that he did not stop reporting it to your Highness because this witness saw him being very scandalised. And this being by | similar ministers / although it was for mere curiousness / they would have been encouraged by their visit or consults (if it had been them), of a woman to whom they would have been

5ʳ

5ᵛ

6ʳ

obliged by their possessed offices to lend her a hand and castigate her should she contravene to the named notification which was given as an order to her by the court, and this would consist of the trial which was initiated against her. And around this point and after this visit, the scandal and the number of people who turned to the aforementioned *beata* had grown again: he referred this to what the named Señor Fiscal Don Juan de Morales = and those who he would cite = would say to him. It just seems to be condign to substitute what he had forced to receive new information in Mairena, not only did he not commit them to the Comissario of that town, but although the witnesses could be taken into account, they were not examined there but in Seville, because it is so near because they were persuaded that hereby nobody would dare to say anything substantial because they saw the named *beata* greatly assisted and favoured by

6ᵛ so many | persons of lustre[94] and of such authority,[95] particularly when they should investigate to ascertain the trip and visit of the named Señor Inquisitor Don <u>Diego de la Fuente Peredo and his great confidant</u> Athanasio Torres de Avila and Juan Lasso Cordero, being that certain and being such in which the named Señor Inquisitor had confidence in the named Athanasio and favoured him like he had proved in different particular commissions which the Señor Inquisitor Don Agustin de Villauiçençio has had in which the present notary of the Secreto has been witness. One could also prove during the visit and as it is now ultimately known in the pretension that it is notorious to have had the named Athanasio in the office of this Inquisition's rapporteur, for whose management it is necessary to be at ease with wealth, and despite costing many more ducats, for the deficit and lack of revenue paid to the treasury as well as for the punctuality that is precisely needed for the payment of the great number of consignments of the Secreto's salaries. And it seems he remains for

7ʳ all, because it is notorious that in the named pretension he has offered ten | thousand ducats as a bailment and [when] assigned he will give them in two merchants of silver, because they are a constant thing. Thus the named merchants would never trust only in such great nor in such very moderate quantity, but he has the power over the quantity in which they trust because in his office it is forbidden: and he redresses this witness so much more in order to see how much more than this which was offered to the named Athanasio who has such luminosity and such a rich salary which is public and shows in his person and his case because he had just as little time in which he exerts without earnings

---

94 Symptomatic of Seville in early modern times was the high percentage of members of the nobility. See note 88.

95 This shows that some of María's clients and supporters must have been influential members of Seville's society and public life.

or help concerning any court fee, the office of the Secreto's notary then had entered in it [exactly] at the time when he abandoned for this effect a poor apothecary which he had and with which he maintained in the Franconian street in this town. This was so public that there was nobody who did not know it and it is very notorious in this Holy Office and in particular to this witness who talked about it and gave him the title of 'botanist' in this Inquisition after the named having pretended it many days. It was also notorious that for the pre|tension of the named office of the Secreto's notary, he guarded the money or credit which allowed him to go to Madrid at the request of a business owned by a Portuguese, his brother-in-law, with whom he contributed for help concerning the dowry of a woman who was—as understood by this witness—the housemaid of a Lady of the Palace; and although this did not satisfy him completely, because this witness remembers most of all that before this, there was litigation which did not emerge in which he requested from the named Athanasio 500 ducats which he owed him from what he had and ceded or an amount similar to that as it seemed to him; he showed the document and this is what he answered = 7ᵛ

He was asked whether he knew that the persons who were mainly referred to in the previous question, the Señor Inquisitor Don Diego de la Fuente Peredo and the aforementioned Athanasio Torres de Avila and Juan Lasso Cordero had gone to the aforementioned town of Mairena in order to consult the aforementioned *beata* about a number of matters and in particular the aforementioned Señor Inquisitor Fuente and Athanasio Torres de Avila concerning the incident which they experienced in the past | visit, whose hearing and decision is pending today. After having returned from the town of Mairena, they had been more anxious about this than ever, and after the aforementioned Señor Inquisitor interrupted the trip to the mountain which he had specially prepared for, the aforementioned Athanasio announced publicly that he would endeavour to be transferred to a different Inquisition. It was conjectured that the answer which the named *beata* had given them would not have been favourable for them and that they believed her.— 8ʳ

He said that the haste is publicly known showed by the Señor Inquisitor Don Diego de la Fuente when he issued the cancellation of their trip to the mountain, mentioning in the tribunal the estimations which usually were the expenditure and illustriousness of his preparations concerning a unique and very grand travel bed which he was organising alongside other things, although this seemed superfluous for a Cardinal. Also notorious are the times which | the named Athanasio had simultaneously insinuated in the Secreto that he wished to move to a different Inquisition, from hearsay to the Indies; although he remembers that once in the tribunal, when some of the Secreto were present, 8ᵛ whom specifically he does not remember, the Señor Inquisitor Don P[edr]o de Sant Eliçes said that the aforementioned Athanasio indicated that he wanted to move to the Inquisition of Cuenca and he had asked him to endeavour that although he was the notary of the Secreto, he would exchange his office with him and hear this news shortly before having visited the named *beata* (according to the time which he heard). This indicated that the aforementioned Señor Inquisitor Fuente and Athanasio were also present at this Inquisition, and the aforementioned Señor Fuente made much preparation with such illustriousness out of fear of their trip about which he has said no more in so many days is the truth. That this witness and the aforementioned Señor prosecutor Don Juan Morales—he does not remember well that other persons who had resumed in the material—have inferred that the answers of the aforementioned *beata*

9ʳ must not have been favourable concerning the incident | which they could expect as a result from the visit of this Inquisition, because both became cautious and secretive and one had already tried to move away and the other did not talk about his mentioned trip. And he answered thus and that this is the truth under the declaration of the oath that he has sworn, and having it read out as aforementioned, he said that it is written well and signed it—the 22nd of the aforementioned notification—Vaesa—

Don Juan de la Vega y Dauila
Before me, Gonçalo Flores.

[witness]—[*written on the margin*]
In the royal Castle of Triana on the 7th July 1645, the aforementioned Señor Inquisitor Don Agustin de Villauiç[ençi]o for the investigation of the content he received in his commission on the oath in the legal form of
Witness No. 2—[*written on the margin*]
The Señor Licenciado Don Juan de Morales Fiscal of this Inquisition of Seville after having sworn he promised to say the truth and to keep the secret about all that would be given as information to him and he stated that he was older than 48 years.

9ᵛ Being asked whether he knew or presumed or suspected the reason why he had been called.
He said that he did not know nor presume why.
Being asked whether he was aware of María de la Concepción, a *beata* and resident of Mairena and about the trial which was initiated against her in this Holy Office and the form of its decision, he said that he had notice about the trial which was initiated against the named María de la Concepción, *beata*, that there is a process in the Secreto's chamber and that he refers to.

Being asked whether he knew that the referred would be on the records and what by this Holy Office's act was announced to the aforementioned that from this time on she should abstain from answering to future contingencies. Not only that she did not comply to this, but from some time on, she on her part contravened the named act and had scandalised and caused disturbances in this region with her prognostications and superstitions by answering to issues concerning future contingencies. There are countless persons, not only from the common people, but [also] from the most illustrious of this town and its district who came to consult her for the named reason and which persons in particular had been from this type and from which estate and quality.

He said that he did not know anything that con|cerns the matter, and if there was something in it, it may have been issued a few days after this report because if the content had come to his notice in the question or individual issues, he would have requested it in the tribunal and solicited the relief. All that he could say is that when this deponent came from San Lucar, he came to see her a bit from the part he has which is near Mairena whose name is Pedro Miguel Borreguero and he stated that he should declare that during these days there had been there a Señor Inquisitor and a secretary to see the *beata saludadora*[97] and this deponent presented who they were and said that he knew it, and when he had returned to the aforementioned town of Mairena he wrote the paper which he presents in which he states the identity of the aforementioned Inquisitor and secretary. = And then he exhibited a paper written on a half sheet folded as a quarto sheet or rather a quarto sheet folded in the middle which began with "Señor Inq[uisid]or" and ended on "La saludadora" and on the reverse there was a superscription saying "To the Señor Don Juan de Morales prosecutor of [this Inquisition]".

In all this, the witness referred to several ministers of this Holy Office, who were much scandalised because an Inquisitor searching for the aforementioned woman seems like giving her a tacit | licence for answering these questions and approving her and this is what he knows and no other things.

Being asked whether he knew that the aforementioned Señor Inquisitor Don Diego de la Fuente Peredo and Athanasio Torres having gone to the aforemen-

---

96 Before fol. 10ʳ, there are two leaves which look like they have been interspersed: one is blank, the other one is folded and looks like an envelope addressed "To Señor Juan de Morales, prosecutor of the Holy Inquisition and our Señor [in Triana]" from "Señor Inquisitor D[on] Diego de la Fuente Peredo, the secretary D[on] Athanassio de Torres y Avila, the secretary Juan Laso Cordero—Señor judge D[on] Diego Aredondo—these gentlemen are those who came to this town to visit the *saludadora*."

97 "Saludadora" refers to someone who pretends to cure or prevent harm and illnesses of cattle, but also of humans through a combination of certain performances, blessings and use of incantations.

tioned town of Mairena in order to consult the aforementioned *beata* about a number of matters, particularly concerning the incident they experienced in the past visit whose session and decision is pending today. After having returned from the named town they had been more anxious than ever and that about this and of having the aforementioned Señor Inquisitor suspended the trip to the mountain which he prevented with illustriousness and having published the aforementioned Athanasio that he had asked to be transferred to another Inquisition, they had inferred that the answer which the aforementioned *beata* had given them must not have been favourable for them and that they had believed her.

He replied that he did not know anything of the question's content although he presumed all, but to visit this woman could not be for anything other than to consult her [...]

11ʳ in affliction. He realised the sensitivities of the ministers of this tribunal acting in such a manner as in this suspension of the visit and that he did not know any other thing and that this, what he had said, is the truth under the declaration of the oath, his statement was read to him and he said that it was well written and signed it.

Licenciado Juan de Morales

Before me, Gonzalo Flores [writer].

Witness No. 3 [*written on the margin*]

In the aforementioned royal castle of Triana on the 10th of July of the same year, the aforementioned Señor Inquisitor Don Agustin de Villaviçençio was resident. He summoned before him a man of whom, when being present, was given the oath in the form used by law and having sworn, he promised to tell the truth and said that he was called Pedro Miguel Borreguero and that he was a worker and inhabitant of the town of Mairena which is four leagues away from this town of Seville and that he is around the age of 50.

Being asked whether he knew, presumed or suspected the reason why he

11ᵛ had been called, | he replied that he did not know nor presume why.

Being asked whether he had notice or knew a *beata* called María de la Concepción, resident of Mairena, who predicts the things to come and whether he knows that some people come to consult her and whether he knew any of those who had visited her.

He replied that he knew the aforementioned María de la Concepción, who is an inhabitant of the town of Mairena, where he knew her for many years and he knew that they called her *la saludadora* and that she predicted and answered contingents about future effects and that a lot of people from every part consulted her: in particular to this part he knows that they went to the aforementioned town in order to consult the aforementioned *beata* (he does not know what about) a certain Señor Inquisitor and a secretary or two of this Inquisition and a judge because this witness saw them in the aforementioned town and that they stopped in order to talk to the aforementioned *beata.* This witness related this version when in conversation with the Señor Don Juan de Morales, who is prosecutor of this Inquisition on the occasion of having come to see one of this witness's sons who assisted him, and this witness was not able to say the name or names of the aforementioned Señor Inquisitor and secretary and judge, he asked the aforementioned Señor Don Juan de Morales whether he would know who they had been and if he would be advised in whose ful|filment. The witness presented him to the licenciado Juan Garcia, inhabitant of the aforementioned town, he told him how the aforementioned Señor Inquisitor and secretaries and judge were called, who had gone to see the aforementioned *beata* in the aforementioned town and the aforementioned licenciado Juan Garcia replied to him that the aforementioned Señor Inquisitor was called Señor Don Diego de la Fuente Peredo and the secretaries Don Athanasio Torres de Avila and Juan Lasso Cordero and the judge Don Diego de Arredondo (what he remembered), and this witness, because he did not forget it and could advise the aforementioned Señor Don Juan de Morales regarding it and because he did not know the [...], he asked Balthasar Rodrigues de Fuente, resident of the aforementioned town, to write down the names mentioned for him as he did on a little piece of paper of half of a quarto sheet which he remitted with a superscription to the aforementioned Señor Don Juan de Morales. 12ʳ

Being asked whether he would recognise the aforementioned piece of paper which he remitted, he replied that yes, he would.

And then a piece of paper was shown to him which is exhibited and presented in these written acts on half of a quarto sheet which began with "Señor Inquisitor Don Diego de la Fuente Peredo" and ended with "La saludadora" with a superscription on the reverse which says "To the Señor Don Juan de Morales, prosecutor of | the Holy Inquisition s[...]de m[...]e s[ant]a in Triana", having it seen this witness and heard all of what the aforementioned piece of paper contained. 12ᵛ

He said that he recognised it as the one he remitted to the aforementioned Señor Don Juan de Morales and that to this witness wrote the aforementioned Balthasar Rodrigues de Fuentes for the effect of announcing the referred names, and that this what he has said is the truth and what he knows of what they have asked him under the obligation of the mentioned oath, the above mentioned was read out to him and he said that it is so well written, and because he did not know to affirm the aforementioned Señor Inquisitor affirmed it.

Por Don Agustin   Before me

de Villaviçençio   Gonçalo Flores, writer

Witness No. 4 [*written on the margin*]
In the royal castle of Triana on the 13th July of the aforementioned year, being in his bureau the aforementioned Señor Inquisitor, who ordered to appear before him, Don Carlos de Azme y Arrias, notary of the Secreto of this Inquisition, inhabitant of this City of Triana, who received the oath in the form owed by the law. After having sworn he promised to tell the truth and to keep the secret.

13ʳ He said that he was of the age of 23 years, | little more or less.

Being asked, whether he knew, presumed or suspected the reason why he had been called.

He said that he did not know nor presume the reason.

Being asked, whether he was aware of María de la Concepción, a *beata*, resident of Mairena and the trials which have been initiated against her in this Holy Office and the form of its processing, he said that he was aware of the aforementioned María de la Concepción, a *beata* and inhabitant of Mairena for many years from this part and in the same way he had notion of the trial sued against her before this Inquisition because he had heard it mentioned in the Secreto although he had not seen this case nor know the form of its processing.

Being asked whether he was aware that the aforementioned María de la Concepción answered and announced the things to come and that she had caused disturbances and scandalised this republic [sic!] with her prognostics and superstitions about which she is consulted by many persons, both commoners and higher ranked individuals. Could he tell whether he was aware of anyone of those who had come for a consultation.

He said that he knew because it was a public and notorious matter that a
13ᵛ lot of people came | from every part to consult the aforementioned *beata* who foretold the future. In particular he remembered having heard said on different occasions, although he does not remember which occasion, that the Señor Inquisitor Don Diego de la Fuente Peredo and Don Athanasio Torres de Avila and Juan Lasso Cordero, notary of the Secreto and a judge had gone to the aforementioned city of Mairena to see and consult the aforementioned *beata* for a short time. [...] Within this context, they had talked in the Secreto about the aforementioned *beata* that she had been notified by this tribunal that she should not respond to future contingencies and that nevertheless she continued to respond, said this witness. This was not much because he knew that two ministers from here and one Señor Judge and Señor Inquisitor had gone to visit her or consult her, who are the same individuals which he had already stated

and the case in question was having it heard like he had said and in the aforementioned occasion he heard the named secretary Don Athanasio <u>saying that this was nothing of importance, because the</u> aforementioned *beata* <u>only used to bless</u>[98] <u>and that up there she had blessed him two times;</u>

<u>here he confessed having gone to see her and he did not deny that it was the aforementioned Señor Inquisitor and the others to whom he has referred</u>, and that this, what he has said is what he knows of what he had been asked and the truth under the obligation of the mentioned oath was read to him and he said that it was written well and signed it. =

14ʳ

Don Carlos de Azme y Arrias
Before me
Gonçalo Flores, writer

Very mighty Señor

In conformity with the letter and commission of Your Highness of 12th of June of the previous year and of the memorial which I send together with it in reference of Your Highness, which forms the core of these acts. Therefore, I have arranged to procure an authorised copy for the examination of the second and last point which concerns doctor Garçilopez de Cabra Razionero of the Holy Church of Cádiz and the commissioner of absence in the aforementioned town, who had to adapt in a separate paper | and having concluded it, he brought it to Your Highness. I have received the declarations of Don Juan de la Vega, a notary of this Holy Office's Secreto and have examined three other attestors about the trip which the Inquisitor Doctor Don Diego de la Fuente Peredo and Athanasio Torres de Avila, notary of the Secreto, and Juan Lasso Cordero, notary of positive legal acts of this Inquisition made to the Town of Mairena in this district, where the *beata* María de la Concepción lives, whom they call *The saludadora*. And how Your Highness' intent (apparently) is not to ascertain now whether she responds to future contingencies, but Your Highness would have written this to order her to the tribunal (in case that your [Highness] would not have this notice) so that one could provide new information on this matter and following its summary administer justice. But rather for Your Highness being informed whether the aforementioned Inquisitor and officials went to the aforementioned town of Mairena, it seemed [right] to me to drop the examination of the Inquisitor Doctor Don Francisco Valero de Molina and of J[ua]n de Carmona, notary of the Secreto, because they are only cited

14ᵛ

---

98   "Bless" in the sense of "saludar" referring to *saludadora*, see note 97.

in relation with the scandal and notation which the aforementioned *beata* had caused with her actions and answers to future contingents.—

15ʳ   Concerning the trip to Mairena the Inquisitor Don Diego de la Fuente and the notary Señor Athanasio Torres de Avila and Juan Lasso Cordero. It says to all appearances Pedro Miguel Borreguero, witness no. 3, page 11, referring to the third question, and Don Carlos des Azme, notary of the Secreto and witness no. 4, page 14 in the 6th question, who reports that Athanasio himself had told him that it was the truth that he was in the town of Mairena and that the aforementioned *beata* had blessed[99] him and he did not deny the coming of the aforementioned Inquisitor Don Diego de la Fuente (from whom I heard it said). With the occasion of having Your Highness ordered to the tribunal, he would advise (as he had done) in the state of the case which they had continued against the aforementioned *beata*), that he had been in Mairena a few days ago; he did not dare to affirm whether he assented to having talked to her, with which it seemed not doubtable that the aforementioned Inquisitor had been in the aforementioned town, and although they could infer from the way that in that place there had been nothing of exhilaration which would have made the trip obligatory. And that he undertook the visit in order to see the aforementioned *beata*, as the third witness, page 11 in the 6th question, affirms that he talked to her. Therefore, in order to advance the inquiry

15ᵛ   in this point | (examining the licenciado Juan Garcia, resident of Mairena and cited by the third witness on page 12), would endanger the secret of this case with an unfavourable deficit: to me his declaration did not seem to be necessary.

Señor [*written on the margin*]

If the Inquisitor Don Diego had been to Mairena and talked to the *beata*, in my opinion he had to excuse it, because of the case that was initiated against her, because of the one they had to newly initiate against this woman (following the common voice from its marginal amendment). I would feel most relieved when being her judge, and even freer of the notification which could cause this action because of the reasons which had to be considered. I, Señor, am very sorry for this, and am equally anxious of the damage resulting from this if you would understand that Your Highness deserved the satisfaction of this and other commissions and the credit of more reports. For Your Highness's account is the basis of my calm and my honour. And may Your Highness provide in all that may convene. May our Lord guard Your Highness as we as his chaplains wish for. Seville, 18th July 1645.

---

99   "Bless" in the sense of "saludar" referring to *saludadora*, see note 97.

Don Agustin
de Villauiçençio

[*The next page is blank.*]

[*On the next page the only written text is placed right in the middle*]:

Señor Don Agustin de Villa
Viçençio |

[*The next page is blank*]
[*The next page is blank.*]

[*The document on the next page has no foliation: it seems to be a letter.*]

In M[adri]d 1st of August 1645   +   To the King
Very Mighty Señor

With this I remit to Your Highness on 15 pages (some of which are written on complete pages and some on parts of the pages) the summary that I have compiled in commission of Your Highness concerning the journey of the Inquisitor Doctor Don Diego de la Fuente Peredo to the Town of Mairena in this district, where the *beata saludadora* lives, with substantial relation of what it contains, and my consideration, which begins on page 14 of the documents.

With your insight, Your highness may provide what may mostly convene. May our Lord guard Your Highness as we as his chaplains wish for. Seville, 18th July 1645.

   Por
   Don Agustin
   De Villauiçençio

[*The next page is blank.*]

[*The next page is blank.*]

[*The next page looks like the envelope of a letter:*]
To the supreme council of
His Majesty of the Holy [and] General Inquisition
Inquisitor Doctor Don Augustin de Villaui[çençi]o
Madrid

In M[adri]d on the 6th September 1645

Your most illustrious Señores Salaçar = Aragon = S[eñ]or Videte

There is evidence that María de la Concepción, *beata* from Mairena has again incited responds to future contingents: this should be written to the Señores Inquisitors of Seville who will be undertaking the inquiry and when ongoing they shall initiate a trial against her.

[End of the page and of the document]

CHAPTER 8

The So-Called Italian Quietism: Siena in the 1680s

Adelisa Malena

Introduction

It is likely that the first mention of the "Quietists" was made by Innico Caracciolo, Archbishop of Naples, in a letter dated 30 January 1682 that he sent to Pope Innocent XI to request his intervention:

> For some time, Holy Father, here in Naples and, from what I understand, in other parts of this Kingdom, there has been widely disseminated among many people the frequent practice of the passive prayer which is called "of pure faith and of quiet." These people, who are acquiring the name of "Quietists", place themselves in a supplicant attitude of prayer, yes, but they do no recite vocal prayers, nor do they meditate; they remain in total quiet, mute and in silence, like the dead. And because they think they are making mental passive prayer, they try to cast out of their minds and even from their eyes every matter for meditation, exposing themselves, as they say, to the lights and to the divine influences they expect to receive from Heaven. Without observing rules or methods and without the preliminary preparation of points and spiritual lessons that spiritual masters usually assign to beginners for meditation, and without using the light of meditation to see their own defects, passions and imperfections in order to emend them, they presume to ascend by themselves to that sublime degree of passive prayer of contemplation that God by his free gift concedes to whom he wants, when he wants. [...][1]

---

1 Massimo Petrocchi, *Il Quietismo italiano del Seicento* (Rome: 1948), 147–177; I quote from the English translation provided by Brendan M. Dooley (ed.), *Italy in the Baroque: Selected Readings* (New York—London: 1995), 579–580. See Adelisa Malena, *L'eresia dei perfetti. Inquisizione romana ed esperienze mistiche nel Seicento italiano* (Rome: 2003); Eadem, *La costruzione di un'eresia. Note sul quietismo italiano del Seicento*, in *Ordini religiosi, santi e culti tra Europa, Mediterraneo e Nuovo Mondo (secoli XV–XVII)*, ed. R. Michetti, B. Pellegrino, G. Zarri, vol. 1 (Lecce: 2009), 165–184; Moshe Sluhovski, *Believe not Every Spirit. Possession, Mysticism & Discernment in Early Modern Catholicism* (Chicago—London: 2007), 115–136.

The alarmed cardinal informed the Pope that the Quietists took daily communion yet refused to practice most acts of external worship and denied the efficacy of confession. He invoked an intervention by the Pope, as a "great Father of a family", so that "by [his] most potent Apostolic Arm" he should cut off, or rather eradicate what he—"as a worker, however unworthy, assigned to labour in this vineyard"—thought to be the seedlings of a "pestiferous root".

At that time, the practices described in such detail by Caracciolo could be found, with minor variations, in various towns in Italy, some quite distant from each other. Although disturbing news about apparently deviant practices and behaviour was reaching Rome from all sides, the ecclesiastical hierarchy seemed far from ready to issue a condemnation. Moreover, the men considered to be the masters and promoters of the Prayer of Quiet could count on powerful protection within the Curia and from Innocent XI himself, at a time when the works of their adversaries, like the Jesuits Paolo Segneri and Gottardo Belluomo, were being placed on the Index of Forbidden Books.[2]

It was in this changeable context full of contradictions that a document playing a key role in the strategy adopted by the Catholic Church in subsequent years was drawn up, providing us with valuable insight into the process by which the Quietist heresy was constructed: Cardinal Albizzi's *Report on Quietism* (April 1682).[3] By then, the debate over "new mysticism" had been ongoing for some time, involving theologians from various religious orders and resulting in the supporters of Quietism prevailing. The aged Cardinal Albizzi did not base his analysis on theological arguments but on practical considerations and the need for discipline. He believed that it was necessary to ban the so-called

---

2   A Decree of the Congregation of the Holy Office (26 November 1681) suspended "donec corrigantur" the following books: *Il pregio e l'ordine dell'orazioni ordinarie e mistiche*, by Gottardo Belluomo S.J., printed in Modena by Bartolomeo Soliani's heirs in 1678 and *Concordia tra la fatica e la quiete nell'oratione* by Paolo Segneri S.J., printed in Florence by Ippolito della Nave in 1680. On 15 December 1682 the same Congregation forbade the works: *Clavis aurea, qua aperiuntur errores Michaelis de Molinos in eius libro cui titulus est La guida spirituale*, by Alessandro Regio, printed in Venice by Pontio Bernardon in 1681; *Lettera di risposta al sig. Ignatio Bartalini sopra le eccettioni che dà un direttore de moderni quietisti* [...], by Paolo Segneri (under the pseudonymus Francesco Buonavalle), printed in Venice by Andrea Poletti. See *Index des livres interdits*, ed. Jesús Martínez De Bujanda, vol. XI (Sherbrooke—Geneva: 2002), 118, 175, 749.

3   Dooley, *Italy*, 572–580. On Albizzi, see Lucien Ceyssens, *Le cardinal François Albizzi (1593–1684). Un cas important dans l'histoire du jansènisme* (Rome: 1977); Alberto Monticone, *Albizzi, Francesco* in *Dizionario Biografico degli Italiani*, vol. 2 (Rome: 1960), 23–27 (online: http://www.treccani.it/enciclopedia/francesco-albizzi_%28Dizionario-Biografico%29/, accessed 29 October 2018); Adelisa Malena, *Albizzi, Francesco*, in *Dizionario storico dell'Inquisizione*, ed. Adriano Prosperi, vol. 1 (Pisa: 2010), 29–31.

"prayer of quiet" and the contemplative methods diffused among spiritual groups throughout Italy because of the subversive potential of the uncontrollable phenomenon of mysticism. Using the approach typical of the Holy Office, where Albizzi had worked for over half a century, he drew upon a series of cases documented in the Inquisition archives. He cited the main decisions made by the Congregation with regard to this matter, referring to documents, provisions, letters from peripheral tribunals, and bishops.[4] He linked together facts, names, and episodes dug up from the distant past of the inquisitorial institution in a continuous sequence going from the Beghards to the Alumbrados, to the "Pelagians" in Valcamonica, to form a kind of genealogy of Quietism.[5] This long, uninterrupted series clearly revealed—from Albizzi's point of view—that the Catholic Church had condemned mystical prayer throughout its history, not in itself, but "because of the disorders that it causes". It was therefore a matter of urgency for inquisitors and bishops to act in concert to introduce repressive measures that would eradicate the poison darnel at the root where it obtained its nourishment, in the relationships between spiritual directors and devoted men and women. The confessors and "especially the [spiritual] directors of nuns" had to be advised not to admit "to this contemplation anyone except perfect souls, totally separated from the ways of the world, and those who, by special grace of the Blessed God, show that Our Lord has conceded to them the infused grace, which can only be acquired with difficulty". In Albizzi's opinion it was therefore necessary "to suspend permission for all the books that are printed in the vernacular languages—French, Spanish and Italian—on this matter", and are thus also accessible to laypersons and to all women.[6]

During the changing events and shifting balances of subsequent years, the anti-mystical approach outlined by Albizzi would become established and ultimately prevail. However, it would be a far from straightforward process given the many different positions and attitudes within the Roman hierarchies. The Roman Inquisition began by concentrating its forces on building up the theological paradigm of Quietism. The watershed moment took place in 1687 with the conclusion of the trial against the Spanish cleric Miguel de Molinos (1628–1696).[7]

---

4   Caracciolo's letter, which I quoted at the beginning of this essay, is one of the documents inserted by Albizzi in his *Report*.
5   On the so-called "Pelagians" (Pelagini) in Valcamonica, see Gianvittorio Signorotto, *Inquisitori e mistici nel Seicento italiano. L'eresia di Santa Pelagia* (Bologna: 1989).
6   Dooley, *Italy*, 579.
7   On Molinos, see Paul Dudon s.j., *Le Quiétiste Espagnol Michel Molinos (1628–1696)* (Paris: 1921); Ignacio Tellechea Idigoras, *Molinosiana. Investigaciones históricas sobre Miguel* Molinos

Only a few years after his arrival in Rome in 1663, Molinos had become a much-sought-after spiritual director among men and women from all social classes. Among those asking for his advice were Roman aristocrats and even Cardinals and members of the Curia. In 1675 he published the *Brief Treatise on Daily Communion* and some months later his most famous book: the *Spiritual Guide*.[8] Both books were published by the printer and bookseller Michele Ercole. In his texts of spiritual guidance—which circulated as published works and in numerous manuscript copies—he proposed an internal, passive way to contemplation and union with God that was to be pursued by annihilating the powers of the soul: memory, intellect, and will. Devotees were called upon to follow an itinerary of pure faith and passive abandonment to the will of God under the expert guidance of a wise director, obeying him unconditionally. Molinos' preferred form of prayer was a contemplative prayer known as the prayer of Quiet, a kind of inner prayer without meditation that did not use discursive thought or images. However, this approach could also be interpreted in terms of orthodox mysticism, making it very difficult for the theologians appointed by the Holy See to examine his writings to prove the error of those spiritual teachings that had so rapidly attained such an extraordinary success in a cross-section of society. The letters and reports drawn up by the Inquisition consultants and advisers reveal their constant sensation of fatigue due to the complexity of the trial and the intangible nature of the "poison" of Quietism. Ultimately, however, they would succeed in their difficult endeavour, as the sentence passed against Molinos reveals. The grounds for the conviction skilfully wove together the serious crimes of which he was accused—mainly sexual misconduct justified by the pretence of impeccability—and the dogmas that he put forward, permanently linking this heresy to sin. Although the immoral behaviour attributed to Molinos and to his followers undoubtedly cast a dark

---

(Madrid: 1987); Eulogio Pacho, *Molinos, Miguel de*, in *Dictionnaire de Spiritualité*, ed. Marcel Villier et al., 17 vols (Paris: 1937–1994), vol. 10 (1980), 1586–1514; Adelisa Malena, *Molinos, Miguel de*, in *Dizionario Storico dell'Inquisizione*, vol. 2, 1059–1060; Robert P. Baird, 'Introduction: Part One' and Bernard McGinn, 'Introduction: Part Two', in Miguel de Molinos, *The Spiritual Guide*, ed. and trans. Robert P. Baird (New York—Mahwah, NJ.: 2010), 1–20, 21–39.

8 Molinos' *Spiritual Guide* was first published in Spanish as *Guia espiritual que desembaraza al alma, y la conduce por el interior camino, para alcanzar la perfecta contemplacion, y el rico tesoro de la interior paz*, En Roma, por Miguel Hercules, 1675, and soon after in Italian: *Guida spirituale che disinvolge l'anima, e la conduce per l'interior camino all'acquisto della perfetta contemplatione, e del ricco tesoro della pace interiore [...]*. In Roma, per Michele Ercole, 1675. Critical spanish edition: Miguel de Molinos, *Guía Espiritual: Edición crítica, introducción y notas*, edited with an introduction by José Ignacio Tellechea Idígoras (Madrid: 1976). On the editions of this book, see Tellechea, 'Introducción'; Paola Zito, *Il veleno della quiete. Mistica ereticale e potere dell'ordine nella vicenda di Miguel Molinos* (Naples: 1997).

shadow over Quietism, ultimately the doctrine was condemned in its own right. This was the most effective or rather the only way of definitively solving the problem of the "new mystics". The sixty-eight heretical propositions attributed to Molinos and listed in the papal bull *Coelestis Pastor* issued by Innocent XI defined the new heresy of Quietism at doctrinal level. The definition of the dogma, of the paradigm of a Quietist heresy, provided a mirror that would subsequently be held up to suspected cases of mysticism in the present, future and even in the past. The reality of these actual cases would now be viewed through the new lens of doctrine according to an approach identifying Molinos as the master, heresiarch or spreader of the *pestifera quiete*, and many mystics, both old and new, as his disciples, victims, or even, as paradoxical as this may seem, his ancestors.[9]

Trials for Quietism in Siena

In the late 1680s, Siena, like other Italian cities, was inundated by a tidal wave of trials for Quietism. The investigations focused in particular upon a group of men and women, both lay believers and ecclesiastics from various social classes, devoted to the Prayer of Quiet.[10] The hub of Sienese Quietism was identified as the Ospedale di Santa Maria della Scala, a leading civic hospital, orphanage, hostel for pilgrims and the poor, and hospice for the sick where Antonio Mattei, a hermit considered to be the leader of the local movement, worked as a nurse. The trial began when Mattei spontaneously turned himself in on September 1687, but in fact the Holy Office had been investigating his case since the summer of that same year, following a report from Rome.[11] Thanks to his charisma, Mattei, who was considered a holy man, had become the spiritual guide of a large number of people including nuns, tertiaries, and clergymen—some of whom were spiritual directors in their own right—as well as lay persons. Mattei gave his many disciples a number of guidelines, but one text in particular aroused the suspicions of the inquisitors: the so-called *Protest of the Offering of the Will* (*Protesta dell'offerta della volontà*), which was widely

---

9   Malena, *L'eresia*, c.1 and 5; Eadem, *Wishful thinking: la santità come tentazione. Intorno ai quietismi del Seicento*, in *Tra Rinascimento e Controriforma. Continuità di una ricerca*, ed. Massimo Donattini (Verona: 2012), 247–268.
10 Malena, *L'eresia*, c.3 and 4.
11 On this point, see Hermann Schwedt, *Gli inquisitori generali di Siena, 1560–1782*, in *Le Lettere della Congregazione del Sant'Ufficio all'Inquisitore di Siena 1581–1721*, ed. Oscar di Simplicio (Rome: 2009), IX–LXXVI, LXIII.

circulated, especially in convents.[12] By discovering where this document had ended up, the inquisitors were able to reconstruct the network of relations between the members of the group. The Holy Office decided to turn Mattei's trial into an exemplary case. In the end he was condemned as a dogmatic heretic, forced to make a public abjuration, to wear yellow sackcloth and sentenced to life imprisonment: he was spared from excommunication because he had repented. Ten years later, Mattei died in the inquisitorial prison after a long, painful illness.

However, even after his conviction, the case of the Sienese Quietists was far from resolved. Mattei's trial was only the start of a lengthy investigation that would uncover many more names, writings and networks, thus leading to further trials and sentences. In the eyes of the inquisitors, the practices, ideas, and relationships that were emerging were all the more suspicious and dangerous the closer they were to the practice of spiritual direction; and all the more uncontrollable the closer they were to a terrain that is intrinsically unmanageable: that of mysticism. Many other spiritual directors were caught up in the Inquisitors' network of repression, including religious men and women. Among them there was suor Caterina Ottavia Carpia, a nun from the convent of St Jerome of the Abbandonate, the first person to receive Mattei's "protest" as well as a number of people who had died some years earlier, including the tertiary nuns Francesca Toccafondi (1638–1685) and Barbara Squarci (1626–1662), who had been the true charismatic mothers of the group for many years. These holy women were both already dead at the time of the trials, but their writings were thoroughly examined by the Inquisition. Toccafondi's writings were later prohibited by inquisitorial decree and the holy woman received a posthumous condemnation for the simulation of sanctity and for heretical propositions with Quietist leanings.[13]

The Inquisition also uncovered older stories of spiritual direction like those involving the Camaldolese monk Vitale Perini and the Augustinian friar Ottone Petrucci as well as discovering links between the Sienese group and Spirituals from other parts of Italy, like the Marchesan Capuchin friar Antonio Francesco Candelari, who had contacted other members of the group around 1670. The Siena Spirituals considered Candelari a spiritual life master, experienced in the ways of mysticism, collecting his letters, copying them and circulating them

---

12   On the *Protest*, see also Malena, *L'"offerta della volontà". Pratiche (sospette) di direzione spirituale nella Siena del Seicento*, in *Inquisizioni: percorsi di ricerca*, ed. Giovanna Paolin (Trieste: 2002), 181–202.

13   On 3 September 1691 (i.e. six years after Toccafondi's death). Malena, *L'eresia*, 203.

amongst themselves. And so in November 1688, Candelari, by now old and sick, was put on trial by the Inquisition of Ancona and then sentenced.

Primary Source Material

1. *The* Protest of the Offering of the Will

Mattei described the so-called "protest" of the offering of will as a "sentiment" that God inspired in his mind while he prayed. The hermit set down in writing his reflections and inspirations—or "lights" as he called them—then used those writings to guide other minds along the paths of the spirit. The "protest" was a vow, made in writing, that bequeathed the writers' will and freedom of choice to God in order to quieten their conscience, allowing them to free themselves from scruples and the fear of sinning. From that moment onwards, sin would only be possible after explicitly renouncing the protest "with the heart, tongue and pen". The state of serenity and spiritual quiet attained by means of this "vow" would allow the person concerned to give themselves up to contemplation and abandon themselves to the divine will. This text was a kind of *Leitmotiv* in the Sienese trials: it was the guiding document par excellence and its circulation—according to the Inquisitors—constituted a kind of map of the diffusion of the heretical contamination.

2. *Letter from the Hermit Antonio Mattei to Suor Caterina Ottavia delle Abbandonate, 14 January 1683*

When news first reached Siena about the *querelle* raging in Rome around Molinos and the new mysticism, Mattei became rather alarmed about the diffusion of his writings, the "protest" in particular: the letter published below shows that he was no longer able to control the circulation of this document and that he was clearly aware of the risks inherent to spiritual direction.

3. *Antonio Mattei's Depositions*

Various extracts from the depositions given by Mattei to the judges of the faith from September 1687 onwards are published below. Mattei, who had led a rather adventurous life until that point, went to Siena in the 1650s. Here he put on the habit of a hermit of St Antony and was ordained a priest. He served as a nurse at the hospital of Santa Maria della Scala for twenty-seven years as well as engaging in an intense activity of spiritual direction. Although he had only a modest educational formation and lacked a theological background, his services were highly requested for many years because he was considered a spiritual man, an "illuminated" director and good servant of God, expert in the direct practice of the mystical ways. However, the search of his house and his depositions to the inquisitors show that he was acquainted with important texts on contemplation: works by John of the Cross, Teresa of Avila, Catherine of Genoa, Hendrik Herp, Achille Gagliardi, Lorenzo Scupoli, Jean de Bernières Louvigny, Benedict of Canfield and the so called "new mystics" François Malaval, Miguel de Molinos, Pier Matteo Petrucci and others. His approach would have been one of active reading and these books would have nourished a direct experience of the ways of the spirit. During questioning Mattei provided a very apt description of his relationship with spiritual books "that impregnated my mind (*mi ingravidava la mente*) when I read them. It is possible therefore that when writing down my prayers I drew upon some features learnt from those books."[14]

The "impregnation" that took place through the spiritual experience therefore gave rise to other writings. In fact, we know that Antonio Mattei was the author of several texts concerning the "sentiments" and "enlightenment" received during his prayers, in other words, the words that God inspired in his mind. These texts were passed from hand to hand within the group, taking on an exemplary value and becoming texts of spiritual instruction and devotion in turn. During questioning he repeatedly mentioned that he had been taught to write down personal prayers and their effects and to draft a general confession by the Jesuit spiritual directors who had guided him for so many years. He seemed to be fully aware that the guidance of the Jesuits—sworn enemies of the Quietists—could in his case represent a patent of orthodoxy. He reiterated that the Jesuits had alway approved of the writings that he circulated among his spiritual sons and daughters.

During his audience with the inquisitors, Mattei stood up for his opinions, defending mysticism and showing that he was aware of the controversy then raging around these issues in the heart of the Catholic church. In his depositions he mentioned that, a few years earlier, during the polemic between the "meditative" Jesuit Paolo Segneri and masters of the new mysticism like Molinos and Pier Matteo Petrucci, he had assumed a role of advocacy among his disciples. He involved himself in this theological debate by sending to Rome his writings in defence of contemplation along with the writings of other Sienese spirituals such as the priests Virgilio Cenni and Silvestro Nelli; the noble Tomaso Bandinelli and the noblewoman Celia Piccolomini.

This episode represents an interesting example of how the ongoing theological debate was received in modest social circles, as well as revealing the

---

14   Malena, *L'eresia*, 127.

continuous intersecting of the different levels of the Quietist phenomenon, which should not, therefore, be investigated separately. These levels are the theological and doctrinal level concerned with the reception of texts and ideas and the level involving the practice of preaching and spiritual direction, and, therefore, of the orientation and tendencies of the single groups. The judges charged Mattei with writing propositions that were censored and condemned by the Church either for their association with Molinos's heresy or for "relaxing the Christian discipline" or being "close to heresy". Unresigned, Mattei, who never sought to deny his authorship of those writings and strove to the last to defend his beliefs, concluded, "I must add that if I were erudite or had a good memory, I would find these propositions in a number of mystical books and that it is not enough to pick out a truncated proposition without considering the entire context of the discourse".[15] This decontextualisation, which he considered unacceptable, was actually a distinguishing feature of the Inquisition procedure.

4. Mattei's Letters of Spiritual Direction
The texts of some of Antonio Mattei's spiritual letters appear below. They introduce the reader to the practice of spiritual direction. Mattei practised and taught contemplative prayer: the core of his spiritual practice was an "exercise" of the presence of God that was performed through an act of faith, without perceptible images, which involved the complete annihilation of the self and a "drowning" in the divinity.[16] A further instrument of the "expropriation of self" was blind obedience to a spiritual father, who acted as a protective guide on the path to perfection. Mattei was a mystic and was recognised within the group as a master and as a charismatic figure, yet he was not the only one. In circles like these, it was not uncommon for extraordinary mystical experiences to spring up in close proximity to a situation of exceptional spirituality with paths of "holiness" and perfection that reflected one another like a series of mirrors. In terms of spiritual direction, this complicated the relationship between guide and disciples, which were no longer univocal and tended to develop on multiple levels: in many cases spiritual fathers became spiritual sons; spiritual daughters could become spiritual mothers, and so on.[17] This was

---

15   Malena, *L'eresia*, 145.
16   On this kind of prayer, see Michel Dupuy, *Présence de Dieu*, in *Dictionnaire de Spiritualité*, XII/2 (Paris: 1986), 2107–2136.
17   Adelisa Malena, *Pratica della perfezione. Forme e linguaggi della direzione in una comunità di spirituali. (Siena, XVII sec.)*, in *Storia della direzione spirituale*, ed. Gabriella Zarri, vol. 3 (*L'età moderna*) (Brescia: 2008), 437–458. On the complex relationship of spiritual direc-

one of the reasons that prompted inquisitors to seize numerous letters, documents of spiritual direction and devotional images that were jealously guarded by the members of the group, and especially by the nuns. In fact, the invisible identity of the Sienese group had crystallised around these writings and around the memoranda of the spiritual masters and mistresses.

The letters that Mattei addressed to Sister Caterina Ottavia Carpia reveal the latter's leadership within the Sienese group. They also disclose some of the peculiar traits of Caterina's personality: she seems to be a very unquiet soul, deeply troubled by scruples. Mattei proposed to her an inner and contemplative spiritual path. He suggested that the only way to remove her scruples and spiritual doubts was the complete obedience to the spiritual director and a total and passive abandonment of the self to the will of God. Mattei invited Caterina to annihilate herself by renouncing her will. In Mattei's view, the first step in the path to perfection was the acknowledgment of the nullity of the self and of sin: it was necessary to create a vacuum in the soul to reach a state of detachment from the world. The state of indifference, pursued through a passive attitude, was the precondition for the so-called "freedom of spirit" or, in other words, for attaining spiritual perfection.

Conclusion

The many trials for Quietism that were held in Italy from the final decades of the seventeenth century onwards reveal an extremely varied constellation of groups, networks, texts, and spiritual practices that cannot be constrained in narrow inquisitorial categories. The Siena trials allow us to analyse some facets of this complex picture and to investigate the forms that spiritual guidance could assume in the groups gathering around charismatic leaders. One of the unique characteristics of the Sienese group seems to be the key role—identified by the Inquisitors—of the text of the "protest". I think it may be useful to apply to this case the category of "textual community" used by the theorist of literature Brian Stock to define "microsocieties organised around the common understanding of a script", where "concepts appear first as they are acted out by individuals or groups in everyday life".[18]

---

tion in the Early Modern Age, see Jodi Bilinkoff, *Related Lives. Confessors and Their Female Penitents, 1450–1750* (Ithaca, N.Y.: 2005), 77–85; Patricia Ranft, *A Woman's Way. The Forgotten History of Women Spiritual Directors* (New York: 2001), 108–128.

18   Brian Stock, *Listening for the Text. On the Uses of the Past* (Philadelphia: 1996), 13; 23.

Throughout Italy, and not only in Siena, these communities were not exclusively made up of scholars but also had members who were illiterate or semi-illiterate, placing it halfway between a written and non-written culture. Consequently, the ways in which the text was appropriated by the members of the Sienese community take on particular significance. The fundamental text of the "protest" was part of Antonio Mattei's writing, but the vow was to be made "with the heart, tongue and pen" meaning that the contracting parties were obliged to copy it in their own handwriting, read it out loud on the altar of the Holy Sacrament, and carry it around with them almost as if it were a relic. The rituality of the vow seems to have played a significant role in endowing this act with an aura of sacrality. And it was this pact or written "contract" that quietened the soul and allowed the vow-maker to set aside scruples and doubts.

The oblation or offering up of one's self, faculties and will was nothing new and can be found in monastic vows and in numerous other examples of self-sacrifice throughout Christian history.[19] However, I suggest that the model adopted by Mattei—and that he would therefore have been very familiar with—was the offering of self that takes place in the fourth week of the spiritual exercises of Ignatius of Loyola, when the "practitioner" praises the Lord with an extraordinarily powerful prayer expressing his or her devotion: "Take, Lord, and receive all my liberty, my memory, my intellect, and all my will, all that I have and possess. Thou gavest it to me: to Thee, Lord, I return it! All is Thine, dispose of it according to all Thy will. Give me Thy love and grace, for this is enough for me".[20] This was the lyrical peak of a strenuous process of constant inner perfectioning and of the continuous daily construction of a new self. The interpretation of oblation by the mystic Mattei is clearly rather different. In fact, it involves the annihilation of the person and the expropriation of their will, and is not a destination but the beginning and end of the journey, an alpha and omega. I maintain that this is one of the many possible examples of an original and active reception of a spiritual text within a specific context. Discussions of seventeenth-century Italian Quietism should also take into account examples such as these. These all form part of what we designate when referring to "Quietism".

---

19   See André de Bovis and Willibrord-Christian Van Dijk, *Offrande*, in *Dictionnaire de Spiritualité*, vol. 11 (Paris: 1982), 720–733.

20   Ignatius of Loyola, *The Spiritual Exercises and Selected Works*, ed. George E. Ganss S.J. (New York—Mahwah: 1991), 177.

The Siena Quietist Trials

1   The Protest of the Offering of the Will[21]

The Protest *is inserted in a letter by Antonio Mattei to Suor Caterina Ottavia delle Abbandonate of 4 March 1675. In the first lines of the letter Mattei affirms to send her a "protest made by God knows who". Mattei adds that he liked this "protest" very much and urges her to pass it on to the other nuns to read.*

[…] this evening, as I was praying […] more anguished and desperate than ever before, God soothed me in this way, speaking in my mind and asking, "Would you like me to teach you a way that will allow you to always be calm and at peace even in the midst of countless battles and enemies that will accompany you throughout your mortal life? Do therefore as I tell you: swear to me and promise to me on the altar of the Most Holy Sacrament, in the presence of my divinity and of all the celestial, terrestrial, and internal creatures, that you wish—helped by my divine Grace and with the fullness of your freedom and the will of your soul—that I be in eternity the God that I am, that you wish to love me in all eternity in the same way that I love myself; that in all eternity you wish to do my will, and that in all eternity you wish to hate sin as I do hate it.

You must then renew your oath,[22] giving me all your freedom, your soul, your body, and all your works in all eternity, and [promising] that you will never renounce this offer and oath, unless you renounce them expressly in the three distinct ways described above, doing so with your heart, your tongue, and your pen, saying and writing, 'I renounce God and all of the aforesaid', swearing against me, renouncing me, and taking back your freedom and your will that you gave to me. And you are free to do this whenever you so desire because, for as long as you shall live, I would never take back the freedom that I have given to you. And should you not carry out these three distinct acts—as I have

---

21   The letter is contained in a dossier titled *Lettere Speciali* (*Special Letters*) from the section *Inquisizione di Siena* (Inquisition of Siena = *Siena*) of the Archive of the Congregation for the Doctrine of the Faith (= ACDF) in Rome, that is to say the central archive of the Roman Inquisition. The dossier contains letters of spiritual direction. Other copies of this text are contained in the dossiers of the Sienese trials for Quietism (Vatican City, ACDF, *Siena, Processi* 57).
22   The Italian word in the text is "voto", i.e. "oath" but also "vow".

said, with the heart, the tongue, and the pen—never, in all eternity, in the case of any adversity, whether from without or within, that may afflict you, will I be offended by your actions. On the contrary, by virtue of the said acts, which will be extremely welcome to me, anything, whether internal or external, that you may do after having carried them out will be dear to me and accepted with pleasure, even if you should believe the contrary, due to the power and vehemence of the passions that will overwhelm you and even if you may feel that you have failed to maintain your promise to me.

And I promise that I will not take any account of this, unless—by means of those three separate acts—you renounce me, taking back your freedom: and in this way you will always live happily and calmly even in this vale of misery.

Should you ever feel that you have committed some sin, whether minor or grave, I desire that you go and confess it but [I do not wish] you ever to believe that you have offended me, at least not deliberately, if you did not carry out those three acts mentioned earlier. Because if you begin to believe that you have voluntarily offended me, you will immediately lapse from the aforementioned remedy, and anxieties, scruples, and doubts will once again afflict your every action. [Rather] you should firmly believe that you have not in any way offended me even though your fragility may have got the better of your inferior nature, causing some fault. But your superior nature, which is the nature that I hold in high regard, will never be damaged if you have not carried out those three acts above, with the heart, with the tongue, and with the pen.

I therefore tell you to be steadfast and firm in this belief and truth. You can laugh at the devil, at the world, and the flesh! They may fight you and crucify your inferior nature that comes to you from Adam but they will never overcome your superior nature unless you decide to take back those three acts that you once gave me—in other words, your freedom.

Now I have taught you how to behave in all your actions, which will be almost infinite as long as you live and which I wish to permit you [to have] and which I believe to be right and which will crown you with even greater worth if you should so desire. And do not tell me 'I cannot', 'I always fall', 'I become confused' or similar things, because I am the one who sends out light and darkness, comfort and unfeelingness. 'What I want' and 'What I do' should no longer matter because you no are longer yours but mine. You have given me yourself—your freedom—because that is the only thing that belongs to you.

And I will now conclude and leave you to begin putting into practice what I have taught you."

Suor Caterina,[23] consider these words carefully, pondering on them, because if you do not succeed in calming all your actions by means of this protest I have no better remedy to offer you.

Finally, I commend myself to your prayers.

From the Hospital[24] on this day 4 March 1675

Yours in the Lord,

Antonio Mattei Eremita.

---

23   The lines at the end of the letter as the lines at the beginning, addressed directely to suor Caterina Ottavia Carpia.
24   The Hospital of Santa Maria della Scala in Siena, where Antonio Mattei worked as a nurse.

2 Letter from the Hermit Antonio Mattei to Suor Caterina Ottavia delle Abbandonate, 14 January 1683[25]

Suor Caterina Ottavia,

Do you by chance remember that around four years ago[26] I wrote you a letter in the form of a protest to calm your mind, which was troubled by countless fears and scruples. And moved by zeal with regard to some other souls tormented by similar matters, you spoke to some persons about this, and they then spoke to others, as usually happens in such cases.[27]

Now word has reached our superiors via persons worthy of every respect who have come to the conclusion, together with our superior,[28] that [the protest] is not suited to every kind of person because some might make improper use of it. Just as there are different kinds of spiritual infirmity so must there be different remedies. Therefore, hearing the explanations of those representing God on earth, governed or ruled by the Holy Spirit, whom we should obey as we obey God himself, I say to you that we should trust them more than we trust our own feelings, as good as we may believe them to be, even though only God really knows our intentions.

We must therefore deny ourselves and believe in them because so doing we can never be mistaken.

Should you remember whom you sent it to, please show them the following declaration: that we both believe and firmly maintain all that is upheld and believed by our Holy Mother Church of Rome, as represented to us by her

---

25 A copy of the letter opens the dossier of the Sienese trials for Quietism. ACDF, Siena, Processi 57, fol. 1ʳ.

26 As far as we know, it was indeed eight years before: in 1675.

27 It was a common practice among these Sienese spirituals to circulate the text of spiritual direction among the members of the group: the letters were often read aloud in the female convents; a letter addressed to a single nun could contain also words of advice to other nuns; the recipients of the letters passed them to other spiritual men and women, lay or religious. In this case the same Mattei had invited Caterina Ottavia to circulate the "protest" (see 3.1).

28 In 1683 one of the nuns of the convent of St Jerome (San Girolamo) of the Abbandonate gave a copy of the "protest" to the Jesuit Annibale Marchetti, confessor of the nuns. Marchetti forwarded the text to the Archbishop Leonardo Marsili, praying him to behave "as a father, rather than as a judge" (ACFD, *Siena, Processi* 57, fol. 386ᵛ). The Archbishop Marsili summoned Mattei and compelled him to withdraw his writing and to assert that it was not suited to everybody. The Archbishop also urged Mattei to write to Caterina Ottavia and to collect all the copies of the "protest" circulating among the nuns.

members, for whom we are bound to pray to His Divine Majesty, and also by those pious persons who ceaselessly watch over our souls so that we may not be deceived by the snares of our infernal enemies.

Finally, I commend myself to your prayers.

Yours in the Lord,

Antonio Mattei Eremita

3   Antonio Mattei's Depositions

Although Mattei appeared before the inquisitor of Siena in September 1687, the Holy Office had been on his trail since the time of the arrest in Rome on 31 July of the Sienese canon Agostino Taia on suspicion of Quietism.[29] *The depositions made by the Sienese hermit contain a fascinating account of the reception in more peripheral contexts of the battle being fought in Rome against this "new mysticism". These documents also provide us with insight into the spiritual practices and doctrines diffused in the Sienese group, revealing their profusion, their complexity, and their originality.*

The account of the search of Mattei's house is invaluable in providing us with a reconstruction of the library of a "provincial Quietist", both its contents and materiality. Alongside mystical texts, we find minor devotional works, popular pamphlets, numerous manuscripts by Mattei himself (spiritual letters, reports written by order of his confessors, transcriptions of prayers and of the effects of mental prayer) as well as devotional images.

Mattei's depositions also provide an outline of the relations within the group. The dense network of relations within the city of Siena included secular clergy, regular clergy, nuns from various convents, tertiary nuns, laymen and laywomen. His statements also reveal the relationships existing between members of the group and persons outside the Sienese context.

∴

– 21 September 1687
Appearing in person before Reverend Father General Inquisitor of Siena, friar Modesto Paoletti from Vignanello O.F.M.,[30] is Fra Antonio Mattei from Altiani[31] in the Kingdom of Corsica, priest, hermit of St Antony, resident at Siena in the Society of San Giuseppe, declared age sixty-eight years, who asks to be heard in order to ease his conscience in the Holy Office, to whom this is conceded and who is required to swear an oath that he will tell the truth [...] testifies as follows:

"This morning, before coming to Your Most Reverend Fatherhood I paid a visit to the illustrious Monsignor Archbishop to explaine to him—although his illus-

---

29   Schwedt, *Gli inquisitori generali di Siena, 1560–1782*, LXIII.
30   Friar Modesto Paoletti of Vignanello was Inquisitor of Siena from 1677 to 1688. See Schwedt, *Gli inquisitori*, XXXI.
31   Altiani is a village in the north-eastern part of Corsica.

trious Lordship was already aware of the matter—that around twelve years ago, while I was under the spiritual direction of the Jesuit fathers of this city, I did a protest before God for the sake of my quietness, writing it down on a piece of paper to keep with me (although I later lost it).

Now, during the time in which I was in the Ospedale della Scala where I worked for twenty-seven years as a nurse, the hospital was visited by a certain priest called Don Virgilio Antonio Cenni who was confessor to the girls living there and who died three or four years ago. After finding out that I had made this protest, the said priest asked me to show it to him, and as he was my friend, I did so. Having read it and liked it, he asked whether he might make a copy to send to Suor Caterina Ottavia Carpia of the Congregation of the Abbandonate, which is not under the authority of the bishop but of the aforementioned hospital. This nun is still alive and I believe from what she told me that she received great relief from this protest and great benefit for her conscience, which was troubled by many scruples. And although I protested that I had not written this letter in person—as was in fact the case—for safety's sake and to ensure that Suor Caterina Ottavia believed it to be mine, I signed it.

Around five years ago,[32] a certain Father Marchetti,[33] a Jesuit, who was at that time rector to the College of this city, went to confess the nuns of the Congregation of the Abbandonate and the aforementioned letter ended up in his hands. He thought it contained some difficulties and so he took it to Monsignor Archbishop[34] who, after examining it, summoned me in order to hear my opinion on the contents of this letter. I stated to him—as I am now doing before Your Most Reverend Fatherhood—that, as God is my witness, I never had any intention to write or do anything that could go against the authority of our Holy Mother Church, whose every decree and pronouncement I will always believe and profess. And I said that I had been convinced to allow this letter to reach the hands of the aforementioned Suor [Caterina] Ottavia only to eliminate her scruples and for no other end. I also added that should any error—made out of ignorance and never deliberately—be discovered in the said letter or protest, I intended to submit myself to the judgement of our Holy Mother Church. After

---

32   In 1683.
33   Annibale Marchetti S.J., see note 29. Some months later, on 5 April 1688, Marchetti—at that time rector of the Jesuit college in Fermo—was questioned about the Sienese "Quietists" by the Inquisitor of Fermo on account of the Inquisitor of Siena.
34   Monsignor Leonardo Marsili (b.1641, bishop of Siena in 1682–1713).

expressing myself in these terms to the aforementioned Monsignore, I became calm and thought no more of it nor did anyone speak of it to me again.

Now, however, hearing the statements made by our Holy Mother Church with regard to Molinos,[35] I began to have my suspicions, and this morning—as I have already mentioned—I paid a visit to his Excellency, Monsignor Archbishop to remind him again of that letter and the Monsignore advised me to come and consign it to Your Most Reverend Fatherhood as I am now doing: and this is the letter that Monsignore has had in his possession for the past five years."

At this point he produced the sheet of paper now attached to the documents and marked "A" [letter of 4 March 1675].[36]

"[…] although the Monsignor Archbishop seemed satisfied with my statements, he advised me to write to the aforementioned Suor Caterina Ottavia Carpia, retracting my writing, as I, in fact, did, saying that our ecclesiastical superiors believed that the letter and protest in question were not suited to every type of person and that it therefore would be wise to obey and comply with the orders of those superiors representing God on earth. And this is what I wrote to Suor Caterina Ottavia in the letter that I am now handing over to you. […]"

In accordance with the archbishop's advice, Mattei gave the Inquisitor other letters of spiritual direction that had been returned to him at his request by numerous nuns in the city, adding:

"All of these letters were written in my own hand and sent to the aforementioned nuns, with the exception of the first, which is not in my handwriting but which I composed while I was being cruelly tormented by the devil, without having consulted any book or any manuscript by others, as I have been a hermit for forty-six years and have never, in all of this time, by the grace of God, ever neglected my mental prayer.

I have nothing more to say other than repeating that if there should be anything in these letters contrary to the Holy Catholic faith then I do now renounce it forever, professing my desire to always live and die in the Holy Catholic Apostolic Roman Church. […]"

---

35 Miguel de Molinos (1628–1696). On him and his trial, see the introduction to this essay.
36 See above, section 2.

In the following days, the Inquisitor gave orders to search Mattei's home:

In the first room, they found the following: a paper crucifix; St Anthony of Padua and other paper images of male and female saints; the image of Suor Francesca Toccafondi[37] on painted canvas. A closet contained five copies of the image of Suor Francesca Toccafondi. In the room where Padre Antonio slept, they found his bed with two mattresses, a straw pallet, sheets and blankets.

There was also a small table on top of which there was a large breviary and a booklet about the preparation of mass. In the drawer of the same table, a private letter *quae non facit ad rem*. On the door of the aforementioned room a copper portrait of suor Francesca Toccafondi and another image of her hanging on the wall, upon the table. Other images, precisely of the blessed Catherine of Genoa[38] and of the servant of God Armelle,[39] who died in 1671; two crucifixes and other sacred images.

---

37 The Franciscan tertiary Francesca Toccafondi (1638–1685) had been one of the charismatic mothers of the Sienese group. See above, section 2.

38 Caterina Fieschi Adorno (1477–1510), otherwise known as Catherine of Geona, was an Italian mystic and author of many mystical treatises (the so-called *Corpus Catharinianum*). During her life she was considered a spiritual mother and teacher by her many spiritual sons and daughters, both lay and religious. She spent most of her life and her means serving the sick (especially the incurable ones, notably during outbreaks of plague in 1497 and 1501), as well as the outcasts. She was beatified in 1675 and canonised in 1737. On her, see Sosio Pezzella, *Caterina Fieschi Adorno (Caterina da Genova), santa*, in: *Dizionario Biografico degli Italiani*, vol. 22 (Rome: 1979), 343; Giovanni Pozzi and Claudio Leonardi, *Scrittrici mistiche italiane* (Genoa: 1988), 346–362; Daniela Solfaroli Camillocci, "Il corpo, l'anima e l'amor proprio. Carità e vita devota nell'esperienza religiosa di Caterina da Genova e della sua cerchia, tra regola di vita spirituale e costruzione biografica", *Archivio italiano per la storia della pietà*, 18 (2005), 265–286; Eadem, *I devoti della carità. Le confraternite del Divino Amore nell'Italia del primo Cinquecento* (Naples: 2002).

39 Armelle Nicolas (1606–1671), otherwise known as "the good Armelle", was a French mystic of very humble origins: she came from a peasant family, was illiterate and worked as a servant. Her biography was published in [Jeanne de la Nativité], *Le Triomphe de l'amour divin dans la vie d'une grande servante de Dieu nommée Armelle Nicolas, décédée l'an de Nôtre-Seigneur 1671, fidèlement écrite par une religieuse du monastère de Sainte-Ursule de Vennes, de la Congrégation de Bordeaux* [...] (Vennes: 1676). The book had an Italian translation containing Armella's burin-graved portrait: *Il trionfo dell'amor diuino nella vita d'vna gran serua di Dio nominata Armella Nicolas passata a miglior vita l'anno del Signore 1671. Fedelmente descritta da vna religiosa del Monasterio di S. Orsola di Vennes della Congregatione di Bordeaux in lingua francese. E trasportata nell'italiana da vn sacerdote secolare distinta in due parti. All'illustriss. e reuerendiss. signore monsignor Petrucci vescovo di Iesi* (Jesi: 1686). It's very likely that Mattei's image came from this book.

On a stall a book *in quarto* titled Theologia Mistica Henrici Harfii [...];[40]
In the shelves two breviaries and a daily office;
The Spiritual Combat by Father Lorenzo Scupoli, printed in Bologna in 1663;[41]
Brief compendium on Christian perfection, where is shown an admirable practice to conduct the souls to the union with God, whose author is Father Achille Gagliardi, Jesuit, printed in Siena;[42]
Office of the Holy Week;
Compendium by Cardinal Toledo;[43]
another breviary;
Life of the blessed Sorore of Siena;[44]
A copper image of suor Francesca Toccafondi; the Franciscan Chronicles, two volumes in quarto; the Life of St Philip Neri;[45] Ascent of the Soul to God,

---

40   The *Theologia mystica* by Hendrik Herp (d.1477) contained many writings of the Flemish mystic, collected by his disciples after his death. The book, written in Latin, was often reprinted in the 16th and 17th centuries all over Europe: the first edition was published at Cologne in 1538 by M. Novesianus. Two Italian editions are known: Rome 1586 and Brescia 1601. The first editions of this book had been censored by the Catholic Church in 1585; nevertheless these editions, as well as other works by Herp, continued to circulate widely. In 1598 an *Index expurgatorius* was printed in Paris, with all the required changes and suppression. See *Herp (Henri de; Harpius)* in *Dictionnaire de Spiritualité*, vol. X, 346–366, 361. We do not know which edition Mattei had in his room.

41   The first edition of the Spiritual Combat (*Combattimento spirituale*) by the theatine Lorenzo Scupoli (c.1530–1610) was printed in Cremona in 1584. I was not able to find an edition printed in Bologna in 1663; it is possibly an error in the manuscript. There was a Bolognese edition in 1653: *Combattimento spirituale. Dal M.R.P.D. Lorenzo Scupoli chierico regol., per l'acquisto della Christiana Perfettione* [...] (Bologna: 1653). On the edition of this book, see Paola Barni, *Un secolo di fortuna editoriale: Il Combattimento Spirituale di Lorenzo Scupoli, 1589–1700*, in *La lettera e il torchio. Studi sulla produzione libraria tra XVI e XVIII secolo*, ed. Ugo Rozzo (Udine: 2001), 249–336.

42   A. Gagliardi, S.I., *Breve Compendio intorno alla Perfezione Cristiana. Dove si vede una pratica mirabile per unire l'anima con Dio. Del Padre Achille Gagliardi* [...]. *Aggiuntovi l'altra parte con le sue Meditazioni*. In Siena, per il Gori, s. a. [1644].

43   There are many 17th-century "compendia" of the *Summa casuum coscientiae* by the Spanish Jesuit Cardinal Francisco Toledo (1532–1596). We do not know which one Mattei owned.

44   The "blessed Sorore" was the legendary founder of the hospital of Santa Maria della Scala. In one of the wonderful scenes of the *Pellegrinaio* (pilgrim hall) frescoes in Santa Maria della Scala, the painter Vecchietta depicted a scene of Sorore's life: the vision that Sorore's mother was alleged to have experienced before his birth, announcing the founding of the hospital.

45   St Filippo Neri (1515–1595) was the founder of a society of secular clergy called the Congregation of the Oratory. He was canonised in 1622. His first printed biography by the Oratorian Antonio Gallonio was published in Rome in 1600 (Latin) and in 1601 (Italian):

by Father Giuseppe di Giesù, discalced carmelite, printed in Rome in 1664;[46] the Mystical day, or elucidations of prayer, by Father Peter of Poitiers, capuchin;[47] a volume titled Splendors, reflections of Heavenly Wisdom delivered by the glorious hierarchs Thomas Aquinas and Teresa of Jesus on the Interior Castle, the mystical garden and metaphors by the holy woman, by Father Baldassarre di S. Caterina da Siena, printed in Bologna 1671;[48] Exercises by Father Rodriguez, a volume *in quarto*;[49] Works of the blessed John of the Cross, a volume *in quarto*.[50]

Antonio Gallonio, *Vita beati p. Philippi Neri Florentini Congregatione Oratorio fondatoris in annos digesta* [...] (Rome: 1600); Id., *Vita del beato P. Filippo Neri fiorentino fondatore della Congregazione dell'Oratorio, scritta, e ordinata per anni da Antonio Gallonio romano sacerdote della medesima congregatione* (Rome: 1600).

46 *Salita dell'anima a' Dio. Che aspira alla diuina vnione. Opera del m. reu. p.f. Gioseffo di Giesù Maria* [...]. *Tradotta dalla spagnuola nella lingua italiana dal p.f. Baldassaro di Santa Caterina di Siena* (Rome: 1664). The author of this book was the Spanish carmelite José de Jesús María (Quiroga). The first Spanish edition was printed in Madrid in 1656: José de Jesús María, *Subida del alma a Dios que aspira a la divina unión* [...] (Madrid: 1656). See Malena, *L'eresia*, 300; Enrique del Sdo. Corazon O.C.D., "Notas del Proceso Inquisitorial contra la Subida del Alma a Dios del P. José de Jesús María (Quiroga), O.C.D.", *Revista de Espiridualidad*, vol. 14 (1955), 76–82.

47 Pierre de Poitiers (d.1684) was a French capuchin friar. There is an Italian edition of this book, printed in Rome in 1675: *Il giorno mistico overo Dilucidatione dell'oratione e teologia mistica composto in lingua francese dal M.R.P. Pietro da Poitiers predicatore,* [...] *tradotto nell'idioma italiano da fra Serafino da Borgogna,* [...] *dedicato all'eminentissimo, e reurendissimo signor cardinale Paluzzo Altieri* [...] (Rome: 1675). The only French 17th-century edition that we know is: Pierre de Poitiers, *Le jour mystique, ou l'éclaircissement de l'oraison ou théologie mystique* [...] (Paris: 1671).

48 Baldassarre di Santa Caterina da Siena, *Splendori riflessi di Sapienza celeste vibrati da' gloriosi gerarchi Tomaso D'Aquino e Teresa di Giesù sopra il castello interiore, e mistico giardino metafore della santa. Opera del P.F. Baldassarro di S. Catarina di Siena carmelitano scalzo* [...] (Bologna: 1671).

49 *Esercitio di perfettione e di virtu christiane. Composto dal Reu. Padre Alfonso Rodriguez ... della Compagnia di Giesù. Diuiso in tre parti. Diretto a' Religiosi della medesima Compagnia, e ad ognuno, che desideri* [...] (Venice: 1686). We don't know which edition Mattei had. The first Spanish edition of this book was printed in Sevilla in 1609: Alonso Rodríguez, S.J., *Exercitio de perfeccion y virtudes cristianas* [...] (Sevilla: 1609). On Rodriguez and his work, see John Patrick Donnelly s.J., "Alonso Rodriguez 'Ejercicio': a neglected classic", *Sixteenth Century Journal* 11:2, (Summer 1980), 16–24.

50 Juan de la Cruz (1542–1591) was a Spanish carmelite friar, priest, mystical, author of many spiritual treatises and poems. He was beatified in 1675 and canonised in 1726. His works had numerous editions in different European languages. We don't know which edition of his works Mattei had. An Italian edition *in quarto* is the following: *Opere spirituali che conducono l'anima alla perfetta vnione con Dio, composte dal ven. P.F. Giouanni della Croce primo Scalzo della riforma del Carmine,* [...] *con vn breue sommario della vita*

In the kneeling bench, four handwritten volumes *in quarto*, titled "Lights and spiritual affections, sent by God to a soul", bound in parchment with leather laces.[51] Another manuscript without cover and title [...]. A manuscript booklet titled "Prophecy to be read in the life of St Angiolo". [...] In a box behind the bed the following books were found: The Interior Christian by Alessandro Cenami, in octavo;[52] The Help for the Dyings by Father Giovan Francesco Pomi;[53] Declaration of the Psalms by Panigarola;[54] Instruction for Confessors by Medina;[55] Extasy of the Contemplating Soul;[56] Adoration in Spirit and Truth by Father Nieremberg, Jesuit;[57] Exercises of the Interior Christian by Father Argentan, capuchin;[58] Life of the Blessed Catherine of Genoa;[59] [...] a box with glasses; [...].

Mattei signed the list after recognising the objects as his and his signature is followed by the signatures of the witnesses.

---

      dell'autore, [...] Tradotte dalla spagnuola in questa nostra lingua italiana dal P. Fr. Alessandro di S. Francesco definitore generale della congregazione d'Italia de' medesimi Scalzi (Rome: 1627).

51   One of these volumes contained the "protest".

52   *Il Christiano Interiore, o vero la Conformità Interiore che devono havere li Christiani con Giesù Christo. Opera tradotta dalla lingua francese nell'italiana dal Signor Alessandro Cenami, Priore di S. Alessandro di Lucca* (Venetia: 1666).

53   *L' aiuto de' moribondi opera utile, e necessaria per consolare i poveri infermi, & aiutarli nel tempo della morte.* [...] *Dal padre d. Gio. Francesco Pomi canon. Reg. del Salvatore* (Siena: 1656).

54   *Dichiaratione de i salmi di David, fatta dal R. P. F. Francesco Panigarola, minore osservante* [...] (Venice: 1586). We don't know which edition Mattei owned.

55   [Bartolomè de Medina, 1526?–1580?], *Breve istruttione de' confessori, come si debba amministrare il sacramento della penitenza, del molto r.p.f. Bartolomeo de Medina,* [...] *Nella qual si contiene tutto quello che deve sapere, & fare il savio confessore* [...] *Tradotta dalla lingua spagnuola nella italiana* (Bergamo: 1584). We do not know which edition Mattei owned.

56   *Estasi dell'anima contemplante, che s'incamina al cielo, col mezo delle meditazioni de' tre santi padri, lumi della Chiesa; S. Agostino vescouo. S. Bonauentura card. S. Bernardo abbate. Raccolte tutte in questo volume, a beneficio delle persone diuote* (Venice: 1639).

57   *Dell'adoratione in ispirito, e verità cioè dello spirito vero con cui nella legge di gratia si deve seruire à Dio. Opera del padre Gio: Eusebio Nierembergh* [...] (Venice: 1671). We do not know which edition Mattei owned. Juan Eusebio Nieremberg (1595–1658) was a Spanish Jesuit, author of many religious, historical and philosophical works.

58   *Esercizi del Cristiano Interiore, nel quale s'insegnano le pratiche per conformare il nostro interiore a quello di Gesù Cristo, e per vivere nella sua vita, composti dal P. Luigi Francesco d'Argentano cappuccino* (Venice: 1671). We do not know which edition was in Mattei's room.

59   Cattaneo Marabotto, *Vita della beata Caterina Adorni da Genova. Con un dialogo diviso in dua capitoli, tra l'Anima, il Corpo, l'humanità, l'Amor proprio, & il Signore, composto dalla medesima* [...] (Venice: 1590). We do not know which edition was in Mattei's room.

– 29 September 1687

Friar Francesco Leoni, lay OFM Conv.[60] prison custodian and *socius* of the Inquisitor, informed the inquisitor and the registrar that the imprisoned Mattei had requested another hearing.

The inquisitor went to receive his deposition, asking Mattei what he wished to add [to his previous statement]:

"In addition to the letters[61] that I spontaneously submitted to this Holy Tribunal, I wish to profess that I never intended to do or write anything sinful or contrary to the dogma of our Holy Mother Church and that I retract and utterly abominate any errors that she [our Holy Mother Church] might note in my letters or discourses with others. Moreover, if this Holy Tribunal should have any other evidence against me that will keep me imprisoned in this place, I declare and confess before God, who will be my judge after death, that I have never in my life freely done, said or written anything either against the Holy Faith or against the rites of our Holy Mother Church.

In order to ease my conscience in the best possible way and to enlighten this Tribunal about the persons with whom I have practised and spoken about things relating to God, I declare that if there were errors, I am going about amending them, [...] and that I have always practised with people who were religious, God-fearing and eager to serve and love God, to avoid sin and to acquire virtues. And if they had not been such people, I would not have associated with them, and I confess that I am the greatest sinner in the world. If Your Most Reverend Fatherhood wishes to know the single names of the people with whom I associated, they are as follows: firstly, a certain priest called Cenni,[62] confessor to the girls at the hospital, who died a number of years ago although I cannot recall exactly when; Signor Silvestro Nelli[63] who is the sacristan at the aforementioned hospital; Don Andrea Castellucci; Signor Giuseppe Bizzarri, and Don Pietro Draghi. We spoke on various occasions about God or about virtues and vices. I only occasionally associated with other priests.

---

60   Order of Friars Minor Conventual.
61   On 21 September 1687 Mattei had delivered all his letters of spiritual direction to the inquisitor.
62   Virgilio Antonio Cenni (see above).
63   The priest Silvestro Nelli was taken to trial and condemned as a quietist to the abjuration *de vehementi* and to prison. See Malena, *L'eresia*, 161–180.

The nuns with whom I have had dealings, either by writing, speaking, or sending messages, are as follows: Suor Catarina Ottavia Carpia[64] and Suor Catarina Girolama Buoninsegni, as I testified during my spontaneous presentation. In addition to these two nuns, I have practised with two converse nuns at the Refugio, albeit rarely, one called Suor Angiola Cecilia, the other Suor Giulia.[65] In the convent of Santa Petronilla[66] I had dealings with another nun nicknamed "La Turca" (or "the Turk") because she was really Turkish, writing her occasional letter at the request of the Hospital Rector because she had been among the girls at the hospital for some months. Because of her constant infirmities and struggles, I sometimes sought to comfort her by paying her visits or by sending her letters. I am connected to the convent of Paradiso through ties of friendship and practice with the aforementioned Suor Caterina Girolama Buoninsegni, who is currently the sub-prioress.[67] I began to visit this convent at the request of Signor Niccolò Gori, deputy,[68] because at that time there was a certain nun called Rosa Maria—deemed a great servant of God at her death—and on that occasion I entered into the confidence of the other nuns too and would speak with them at the parlour grille.

I am on friendly terms with Suor Rubera Melari at the convent of S. Abbondio[69] and usually visit her once or twice a year.

I also pay occasional visits to the convent of the Capuchin nuns[70] and during the thirty years that I have worked at the Hospital and have been a member of the Society of Saint Joseph I may well have written letters, depending on their needs, but I have never kept any of their replies—the struggles expe-

---

64 Suor Caterina Ottavia Carpia was also put on trial for Quietism and condemned. Her abjuration took place in private in the convent's sacristy, before the Inquisitor Serafino Gottarelli, the Archbishop's vicar Orazio Piccolomini and two witnesses, on 29 July 1691. See Malena, *L'eresia*, 149–161.
65 On the Conservatorio del Refugio, see Alfredo Liberati, "Chiese, monasteri, oratori e spedali senesi. Chiesa e conservatorio di San Raimondo detto del Refugio", *Bullettino senese di storia patria*, 56 (1949), 152–153.
66 St Petronilla was a Franciscan convent.
67 The nuns of St Catherine called del Paradiso were Dominican tertiaries.
68 In Tuscany the deputies (Deputati sopra i monasteri) were secular gentlemen, relatives of the nuns, who had to supervise the administration and the discipline of the convent. See Arnaldo D'Addario, *Aspetti della Controriforma a Firenze* (Rome: 1972), 480–482.
69 The nuns of St Abbondio were "gesuate".
70 The convent of St Egidio.

rienced by the enclosed nuns are known to us all. And I universally profess that I have never practiced, written or spoken to the aforementioned nuns as their director but merely motivated by truth and because of the recognition and friendship that they showed me.[71] Nor am I aware of having ever taught them anything that was not concerned with acquiring virtues and eradicating sin.

But wishing to describe the course of my life I should tell you that for seventeen years I was under obedience to five Jesuit rectors who told me to write down my prayer as is customary for their novices. Thus I would often show these rectors what I had written and I believe that most of my earliest originals [manuscripts] are at the college of these fathers because after I had copied them, they would keep them. I do not remember them ever suggesting that there were any mistakes in my prayers. On the contrary, they were always urging me to write, something that I could not always do because of my duties caring for the sick in the hospital, and I believe that they were very charitable to listen to all of the mistakes I believe that I made. The names of the father rectors are as follows: the first was Father Lorenzo Sozzifanti from Pistoia; the second Father Sebastiano Bellucci; the third Father Domenico Bernardini from Lucca; Father Conti[72] from Pistoia. Father Bernardini, who was the rector of the Roman seminary for a number of years (I do not know exactly how many) ordered me on a number of occasions to send the aforementioned writings with my prayers to Rome;[73] I did so and he informed me when returning them that they contained no errors.

I also showed these books containing my prayers to the Vicar and to Father Inquisitor Massafra,[74] your predecessor, who told me that he wished to take them to Rome to have them printed without my name because he was very impressed by them. I also took a fifth volume to Monsignor Archbishop on

---

71 Here Mattei seems to suggest a distinction between the role of the institutional "director" and his role. The nuns asked him for spiritual counseling because of his own experience of the mystical path and because of his charisma, but he wasn't their "official" or institutional spiritual director.

72 Sebastiano Conti (before 1637–1694).

73 On the Jesuits in Siena, see Raffaele Argenziano, *La beata nobiltà*, in *I Libri dei Leoni. La nobiltà di Siena in età medicea (1557–1737)*, ed. Mario Ascheri (Siena: 1996), 285–328.

74 Friar Giuseppe Amati da Massafra, Inquisitor of Siena from 1664 to 1677. See Schwedt, *Gli inquisitori*, XXXI.

the same morning that he sent me to take the aforementioned letters to Your Most Reverend Fatherhood. And, if I am not mistaken, paper 17 of this book contains the same protest that the aforementioned Signor Cenni copied and took to the aforementioned Suor Caterina Ottavia, and that I spontaneously presented to Your Most Reverend Fatherhood (he also said something similar to me or else I would have burnt them).[75] Should the Holy Church recognise something contrary in these writings, I would like them to be given to the flames because I wrote them not to print them but only in obedience and it is for this reason that I asked to be heard; in order to further ease my conscience."

Mattei's deposition ends in this manner, without interruption, and with a signature by his hand.[76]

– 2 October 1687
The prison custodian Francesco Leoni again informs the Inquisitor[77] that Mattei has something to say:

"I have requested another hearing with Your Most Reverend Fatherhood in order to inform you that I have always believed that anything I may have written or said would have been something that one could teach to anyone aspiring to perfection, according to the capacity of the person whom I was writing to or with whom I was talking. And in fact whenever I have had the chance and hope of being successful, I have taught these propositions expressed in my letters, either through the spoken or written word.

I believed that I was doing something that would have met with God's approval and that I was promoting perfection, which is found more often on the inner path than on the common road, according to the teachings of all the saints.[78] Nonetheless, if all that I have said, written, and held to be true should be considered a mistake by our Holy Mother Church, then I desire and yearn to be corrected for the benefit and wellbeing of my soul, and for the greater glory of God. And I declare that in this Holy Tribunal I do not intend to argue either with reasons or other means or defend myself in any regard; I would like to

---

75 See above, sections 1 and 2.
76 "Io Antonio Mattei Eremita ho deposto quanto sopra *manu propria*".
77 Friar Modesto Paoletti of Vignanello.
78 Once again Mattei was trying to defend the mystical path and contemplative prayer.

emphasise that I have never at any time had any bad intentions with regard to any evidence that the Holy Office may have against me because my purpose—may God be my witness—was not only holy but very holy, and by the grace of God, I have never carried out any evil deed nor am I capable of so doing, and the entire city of Siena, which has been my home for forty years, can testify to this.

And should Your Most Reverend Fatherhood wish to know something of the diversity of the people with whom I have practiced and conversed I can tell him that I have practiced with Monsignor Ugolini, Bishop of Grosseto, who has been known to me for at least forty years and that I have spoken to his Illustrious Lordship about matters of the soul and about his household affairs.

I have also practised with Mr. Don Bernardino Venturini, who is blind, and he was one of the first people whom I saw regularly. I always discussed spiritual matters with him because it is my habit to abhor worldly matters, preferring to speak always of God, to shun vice and to acquire virtues.

I have also practised with Signor Niccolò Gori, who was very close to Suor Francesca Toccafondi, and who came to me for the purpose of talking about her.

I have also spoken on many occasions with Father Angioloni, a Dominican, discussing spiritual things with him and speaking of my occasional difficulties. He has never told me that I erred on my spiritual path.

I have also talked with Father Carlo from Pitigliano, a Capuchin and expert in mystical matters. In fact, I gave him my manuscripts to read and not only did he not find any mistakes in it, he told me that these were very sound principles. And the reason that I showed my writings to erudite people is because I did not trust myself. With this Carlo, as with other guardians pro tempore, I have always spoken of God, of virtue, and of prayer. I became acquainted with this father, and with all of the Capuchins, because they often came to the hospital for medicaments, and I would joke merrily with them, saying 'I want to become more holy than you' and other similar things. I would raise my eyes to the heavens and say 'Love, love, when will I come?' or I may have said: We do God a huge injustice to fear him so when he reveals himself to be a loving Father in so many ways. Because there should be no limits in this life in believing, in hoping, and in loving, and this is why so few people attain freedom of the spirit. […]

I also practised with a certain Father Antonio Francesco,[79] a Capuchin from Ancona, who came to this Capuchin convent fifteen or sixteen years ago to purge himself and to take the waters of San Casciano. The Father Guardian of that time, who was called Fra Bernardino da Uzzano, sent for me and put me in contact with the aforementioned Father Antonio Francesco, and speaking with him I realised that he was very experienced in the mystical ways so I had him speak to Suor Francesca. The aforementioned father recognised her great spirit, and became fond of her, writing to her often and consoling her during her serious illnesses. And on those occasions I revealed my inner self to him, sometimes writing to him on spiritual matters. And when Suor Francesca died, this Monsignor Archbishop gave orders for an inquiry to be carried out and for her life story to be drawn up and placed in the archbishop's chancery together with her writings.[80] And the Chamberlain of the Hospital, Signor Ottavio Marsilii, had a copy made at his expense, and given that the Suor Francesca's many supporters were in favour of having it printed, [...] Monsignor Archbishop gave the copy to three theologians to examine—to the Deacon Piccolomini, to Father Angeloni and to the aforementioned Father Carlo, who mutually agreed that it contained no mistakes but as it was written by a woman they thought it advisable to have it examined by a mystical theologian before having it printed.[81] Given that there was no such person in the city capable of carrying out this task, I informed the Capuchin father Antonio Francesco who was in Jesi at that time and he replied telling me that if I sent him the text he would give it to Monsignor Petrucci[82] to check as well as reading it himself; he told me [...] to

---

79   Antonio Francesco Candelari (1639/40–1714). See Mario Scaduto s.J., "Il P. Antonio Francesco (Candelari) da Ancona e il Quietismo marchigiano", *Miscellanea Melchor de Pobladura*, 2, (1964), 327–345; Callisto Urbanelli, *Il cappuccino Antonio Candelari e il movimento quietista della seconda metà del secolo XVII*, in *Ascetica Cristiana e ascetica giansenista e quietista nelle regioni d'influenza avellanita*, [Atti del I convegno del Centro di studi avellaniti] (Fonte Avellana: 1977), 245–276; Malena, *L'eresia*, 219–237.
80   This was the common praxis for men and women who died in odour of sanctity.
81   See above, note 13.
82   Pier Matteo Petrucci (1636–1701) Bishop of Jesi, created Cardinal by Innocent XI, was author of many mystical books and is considered one the leaders of Italian Quietism. He was put on trial and condemned to retract in private fifty-four propositions (concerning the "active annihilation", the "passive mortification", the alleged impeccability in the contemplative state). His writings were put on the Index. See Malena, *Petrucci, Pier Matteo*, in *Dizionario Storico dell'Inquisizione*, 3 (Pisa: 2010), 1206–1207; Sabrina Stroppa, *Petrucci, Pier Matteo*, in *Dizionario Biografico degli Italiani*, 82 (Rome: 2015), (http://www.treccani.it/enciclopedia/pier-matteo-petrucci_(Dizionario-Biografico)/, accessed 24 November 2018); *Mistica e poesia. Il cardinale Pier Matteo Petrucci (Jesi 1616-Montefalco 1701)* ed. Curzio Cavicchioli and Sabrina Stroppa (Milan-Genoa: 2006).

send it to the secretary of the said Monsignor Petrucci and so I did so. And after having kept these writings for a number of months, the secretary had them returned to me in August by Signor Federico Galli, chaplain to the Most Serene Cardinal Carlo de' Medici, informing me that the writings appeared most holy to him, but that in these times it was not wise to touch or have dealings with such materials. [...] Signor Tommaso Bandinelli,[83] a highly spiritual man, was rector of the hospital at that time and I spoke with him on many occasions about spiritual matters and prayer, given that he was a man devoted to prayer, also doing so with Signor Ottavio Marsili, the treasurer of the Hospital.

I must also say that around six or seven years ago, if I remember correctly, a certain Capuchin father called Fra Clemente of Monte Latrone, an old friend of mine, turned up in Siena, telling me that he was going to Loreto and that it would have been no trouble to him to travel from there to Jesi to speak to Monsignor Petrucci. He therefore persuaded me to write a letter [to Monsignor Petrucci], commending myself to his prayers, and although I was reluctant, not wishing to be in his debt, I nonetheless wrote to him because I had heard that he was a good servant of God but I never received a reply. When I expressed my regret to this Capuchin friar, he told me that he pitied [the Monsignore] because he was always so busy.

Finally, I would like to say that for forty-six years I have always sought to engage in mental prayer, which I considered my guide and my vocation [and without which] I would have found it impossible to resist my free youth, without religious vows, even though—after all—I have always been obedient to a father who was my spiritual director. And therefore when I hear people criticise mental prayer, I answer them fervently, saying that the contemplation taught by Christ in the Gospel of the Magdalen—who *optimam partem elegit*,[84] etc.— could not possibly be anything but good. And this is what happened when the disputes flared up between Petrucci and Segneri leading me to conclude that whenever I either approved or taught the prayer of pure faith—or of quiet, contemplation, meditation, or whatever other name you wish to use, of a mystical, interior nature—either in writing or using my voice according to the disposition of the person I encountered, whether religious or lay, or a member of one sex or the other—I have always, always, with the grace of God, intended

---

83 Tommaso Bandinelli was a Sienese nobleman who had been rector of the Hospital of Santa Maria della Scala. He was put on trial for quietism in Perugia. See Malena, *L'eresia*, 184–187.

84 Luke 10:42.

to make a sacrifice to Holy God in order to help his creatures get to know him and to love him more, and to teach them that good, perfect contemplation that Christ taught the Magdalen. Never [have I intended] anything else as you will see from my writings. And I therefore submit those writings and every other thing belonging to me for correction and judgement by our Holy Mother Church and I am ready to obey her every gesture because I may have erred but if I have done so it was never out of malice. And it is for this reason that I asked to be heard again by V. P. R.ma in order to tell you all my inner thoughts. I have nothing else to add."

The deposition ends with his signature.

– 9 October 1687
The inquisitor of Siena intended to continue with the proceedings against Mattei and gave orders to attach to the trial evidence of the propositions taken from the letters and above all from the "protest" submitted by Mattei himself. He had the documents validated by presenting them to Mattei for recognition.

Mattei was accompanied out of the prison on that same day for this very purpose. The propositions were read out loud to him—along with other marked passages from "the protest" and from other letters—for him to recognise, which he did. His letters were also submitted to him and he recognised those written in his hand and by others. In response to the inquisitor's question, he recognised the propositions as his and referred to the depositions that he had already made. He signed them and the propositions were then attached to the trial documents.

Following the completion of Mattei's depositions in the autumn of 1687, numerous other witnesses were examined and other trials for suspected Quietism began: for instances against the nun Caterina Ottavia Carpia, of the convent of the Abbandonate; against the priest Silvestro Nelli; against the noble Tommaso Bandinelli.[85]

Mattei made further depositions from June 1688 onwards.[86] *The first examination (9 June 1688) began with the usual questions about his name, country of origin, age and profession. In his self presentation Mattei described his adventurous youth*

---

85   See above, section 2.
86   In 1688 there was a new Inquisitor of Siena: friar Serafino Gottarelli of Castelbolognese a kind of "Quietist-hunter", who brought the Sienese trials for Quietism to a conclusion. See Schwedt, *Gli inquisitori*, XXI; Malena, *L'eresia*, 129–137.

and the unconventional religious path that he had followed before becoming one of the charismatic leaders of the group.

Before replying to the question, the hermit knelt, folding his hands, and asked to make a statement for the record. After making the sign of the cross, he began to speak:

"I protest and confess in this Holy Tribunal, which represents the place of God on earth, that I believe and profess everything believed, hoped, and loved by the Holy Catholic Church, militant as well as triumphant, and that, by the grace of God, I was born in the bosom of the Holy Mother Church where I wish to live and die, and that if I have ever said or written anything not in keeping with Catholic doctrine, I declare that I have never done so out of malice or with bad intentions but through my ignorance—not being a man of learning—even though I do not know where exactly I have erred, with the exclusion of anything that I may have stated during my spontaneous appearance and during subsequent depositions to which I refer.

[...]: my name is Antonio and I was baptised Antonio Giovanni. My father was called Christofano from the Mattei family and my mother Veronica came from the Felici. I was born in 1619 on All Hallows' Eve in the Bonicardo lands in the parish of Altiani, in the diocese of Aleria on the island of Corsica, I was baptised in the church of the Santissima Annunziata di Felie, and I became a priest in 1658.

[...] A.: Until the age of seventeen I remained in my home country and I studied a little grammar, which was taught to me by my brother Antonio Bello who was a priest and who died in around 1659 in the hospital where the priests live in Rome—I think it is in the Via Giulia. After reaching my seventeenth birthday, I went to Genoa, living there for three years and associating with some of my fellow countrymen who were serving the Republic of Genoa as officers. From there I went to Verona where I remained for seven months, also associating with my fellow countrymen who were soldiers and officers. However, I did not study because I was only there to see the world. In Verona I received divine inspiration telling me to become a priest and so I went to Rome where I met Colonel Paolo Girolamo Pozzo di Borgo who wanted me to stay with him because he was my countryman and he received a stipend from the Apostolic Chamber as a colonel of the Corsican Nation. But I did not wish to stay there so I went to Viterbo because I had found out that there was a congregation of hermits living in great austerity there. And I begged the head [of their community] who was called Friar Francesco Pacini [to let me stay with them]. After admitting me as a lay member for a many days, he gave me the habit worn by those hermits, which was a simple sackcloth garment that I wore for six or seven years, living together with them in great hardship. When I was no longer able to continue, I left the community and came here to Siena where I went to Monsignor Piccolomini,[87] who was archbishop at that time, begging him for permission to wear the habit of St Anthony. He granted me permission in writing and I believe that piece of paper was found among my things. By virtue of this permission, I had a habit made and put it on myself, and soon after I was taken up by the fathers of St Francis of this convent and allowed to stay in accomodation near the tree of St Francis in order to look after the tree and the church, and I remained there for four years without interruption. During those four years there was a famine and the city of Siena gave shelter to 700 paupers in a place near Canto de' servi, and I was among the men appointed to care for these paupers, doing so for seven months. Next I went to Sinalunga, remaining there for four years. I then went to Rome and back. In the end, Signor Volumnio Bandinelli,[88] who later became a cardinal and is held in loving memory, convinced me to become a priest by virtue of the services I had rendered to the aforementioned poor. And so I went to Rome where, thanks to the Monsignor's intercession, I received a brief from His Holiness Alexander VII of Holy Memory allowing me to be ordained. [...] I took the brief back to my hometown where I was ordained by Monsignor Giovan Battista Imperiale, Bishop of Alesia, in the year 1657 or 1658 or thereabouts [...]. After becoming a priest I came here to Siena with my licences proving that I had been ordained and showed them to the aforementioned Monsignor Archbishop. With his blessing I celebrated my first mass in the Hospital of Santa Maria della Scalta where I became a nurse. I held this position for over twenty-seven years. I only studied up to the age of seventeen and in the four years that I lived by the tree of St Francis, Canon Ugolini who is now bishop of Grosseto came almost every day to revise grammar with me. I am well acquainted with this prelate and ever since we first met, thirty-eight or so years ago, we have had the habit of discussing spiritual matters. I have not carried out any other studies.[89]

Q.: Are you aware of any enemies, either now or in the past? If so, name them, give the reasons and dates and inform us whether you have since been reconciled.

---

87   Ascanio Piccolomini (1628–1671).
88   Volumnio Bandinelli (1598–1667).
89   Mattei had only a modest educational formation, did not follow a regular course of study and lacked a solid theological background.

A.: In my homeland there was enmity with a certain Simone in my village, Bonicardo, who [believed] that I had insulted his wife. A brawl later broke out between us and I shot him with an arquebus in defence. He subsequently died of his injuries forcing me to leave my homeland at the age of seventeen. I should add that I received a dispensation for this wrongdoing in the period that I obtained the brief to be ordained a priest. Before taking orders, I made my peace with the relatives of the victim. Here in Siena I have no enemies that I know of."

From that point on, the interrogation concentrated on Mattei's network, on the doctrines circulating in the Sienese group, and, above all, on spiritual direction. Many questions concerned the books owned by Mattei and now seized by the inquisitors: in particular, the mystical books.

On 27 September 1688 he was asked to provide more information about the books concerning contemplative prayer. Mattei answered as follows:

"Actually, I read many books concerning contemplation and prayer: all the books I could lay my hands on. For instance, the Blessed [John] of the Cross, Father Joseph of Gesù Maria, the Malaval, the Interior Christian, the Molinos—which I brought to the Inquisition—Petrucci, Saint Theresa's works, [the book by] a blind Carmelite Friar and other books on the same subject that impregnated my mind when I read them. It is possible therefore that when writing down my prayers I drew upon some features learnt from those books. But it is true that I usually wrote what came into my mind while doing mental prayer. I did not take anything from other authors, with the exception of some beautiful sentences that I could have heard at any time, from anybody."

On the following day Mattei again acknowledged his authorship of the propositions taken from his writings, which the inquisitors had labelled as "suspect", "sounding bad" or even "openly heretical", and concluded:

"I must add that if I were erudite or if I had a good memory, I would find these propositions in a number of mystical books and that it is not enough to pick out a truncated proposition without considering the entire context of the discourse. And, furthermore, I would add, as I have done on other occasions, that if an Angel sent by the Lord should come and tell me "You have to die right now, this very moment", I would have no regrets regarding this matter, other than the fact of the Church's disapproval."

4   Mattei's Letters of Spiritual Direction

4.1   Antonio Mattei to Suor Caterina Ottavia Carpia[90]

A.M.D.G.,[91]

In my mind's eye, I seem to see Suor Catarina Ottavia on the top of the Torre del Mangia like a paper weathervane that turns in whatever the direction the wind blows and not like the merlons of that tower, which have held firm for centuries.[92] O for the love of God, remain as firm and steady as a rock in God: obey, be silent and endure it as best you can! And when you can no longer do so, annihilate[93] even these activities, saying, "O my heart, I am clearly a nobody and can do nothing; but what matters that even if I could, I would not want power because we owe all our power entirely to God and not to a human creature." Having established this fundamental principle that is so essential for perfection, is there anything else that can worry us? Have you ever heard anyone say that is possible that nothing can do something? And if you ever heard someone making a similar claim, would you not say "He's insane!"? Therefore how much more insane must we be, when we believe and claim to be able to do something other than committing sins: and that is nothing.

We must reduce ourselves to that nothing[94] or, like it or not, we will end up racking our brains with a thousand worries. We must reduce ourselves to this, despite ourselves: and only then will we attain the freedom of spirit that will make suffering the same as experiencing pleasure, acting the same as not acting.[95] And then we will reduce ourselves to observing God with a simple remembrance[96] in faith and it will be like watching a calm sky, not like looking into the sun.

---

90   ACDF, *Siena*, Lettere speciali 216, dossier titled "Lettere trovate al Cenni" (s.d., s.p., n.p.).
91   Ad Maiorem Dei Gloriam = for the greater glory of God.
92   The Torre del Mangia is a medieval tower located in the Piazza del Campo, Siena's main square. It is the emblem of the city of Siena and the symbol of Sienese urban identity.
93   "Annihilation" and "nothing" are among the keywords of the 17th-century mystic.
94   See note 93.
95   "Freedom of spirit" is here equivalent to "Indifference". See on this subject: Stroppa, *Sic arescit*, 100; Mino Bergamo, *La scienza dei santi. Studi sul misticismo del Seicento* (Florence: 1984), 33; Georges Bottereau and Andrè Rayez *Indifférence*, in *Dictionnaire de spiritualité*, 5 (Paris: 1971), 1696–1708.
96   There is a correspondence between this "simple remembrance" and the "simple sight" that Mattei recalls 5 lines below. On the "oraison de simple vue" in the works of the French mystic François Malaval, see Sabrina Stroppa, *Sic arescit. Letteratura mistica del Seicento italiano* (Florence: 1998), 109–112. It is very likely that Malaval was Mattei's source. Nevertheless it is worth pointing out that Malaval does not use the image of the sky, but that of *"glace nette et polie"*.

Have you ever noticed, in the name of charity, the difference between observing the sky and the sun? It makes us unstable in our desires: by this I mean that when it is hot, we would like it to hide and when it is cold, we would prefer it to come out. When it is dark and cloudy, we would like it to rise and reveal itself. As a result we are never calm during its innocent doings—due to our flaw, not because of its fault. But when we look at the sky, things are different because we merely use simple sight. Why should this be? Because the sky is always the same. It is not like the sun whose eclipses are always causing confusion throughout the world.

Now let us come to morality and to how we must look at God in this mortal life. In his divine works he is that beautiful sky among skies that is always clear and serene. Although the clouds may bring a thousand storms with hail, thunder, lightning, rain, and other perturbations, he laughs in their face. Given that our souls are the living image of the beautiful sky of our God, why do we not always wish to remain the same, in the light as in darkness, in action as in inanction? Does God perhaps need my fasting, my discipline, my mortification or other similar actions? Of course not: what he really wants is my peace, my quiet, my humility, my annihilation, and other similar things.

Let us take care not to mistake the means for the end. When we can use them, it is as well to do so but with quiet and resignation, in one way as much as in another, because only by so doing will we be able to begin in this life what we will continue to do for all eternity in the next.

After all, my dearly beloved in Christ, I do not know what else I can tell you to help you. And should you wish to talk, send me a message and I will come. But remember to consult and obey your Spiritual Father first.

Remain quiet and in peace, and do as he says because it will be God commanding you through him.
   Goodbye.
   A.M.E.[97]

---

[97] Antonio Mattei Eremita.

4.2   *Antonio Mattei to Suor Caterina Ottavia Carpia*[98]
A. M. D. G.,

How long will the lamentations of the prophet Jeremiah endure? I think Holy Week must be over by now. O, my dear Suor Caterina, you shut yourself up in the prison of your own passions just as the silkworms do. But I console myself because these silkworms would never fly up to the heavens if they were not first imprisoned. In the same way I hope that after its many imprisonments, your soul too, enslaved and not free, will finally take flight and be lost from the sight of its enemies. I believe that with the grace of God you could bring about this union [with God] more swiftly if you slept in peace, following the example of St Peter[99] who slumbered so peacefully and quietly in prison beneath the shadow of desire. And such was his peace and trust that God immediately sent forth an angel to free him. And he would do the same for us if we were not so burdened by our thoughts and cares: [because] we wish to gnaw through the chains of our slavery, breaking them, but this is not our duty but that of the son of the Virgin, who came to free us all with the power of his divinity. And there is no need for us to blame ourselves or those who guide us because this liberation is not the task of the creatures but of their creator.

All that we must do is make ourselves passive and resigned, and endure, and become dead to all our plans and worries, and only then, in no time at all we will see the wonders and splendours of God. Read this letter then seal it and give it to Suor Vittoria; and tell Suor Girolama that I have the impression that she is abandoning herself to the way of the Lord and that the prize[100] is not won [just] by he who begins the race but by he who perseveres to the very end: only he will be rewarded.[101]

I thank you for your charity and God will pay tribute to you for this. Remember, Suor Caterina, that until you sacrifice yourself to living with faith, and not with the sentiment of everything that you feel within you, whether good or bad, you will always exist in hell: because our passions, both good and evil, form the

---

98   ACDF, *Siena*, Lettere speciali 216, dossier titled "Lettere trovate al Cenni". S.d; s.p.
99   Acts 12:6.
100   Mattei uses the word "palio", which refers to the local context and Siena's famous horse race. See Aurora Savelli, *Palio, contrade, istituzioni: costruire un modello di festa civica (Siena, 1945–1955)*, in *Toscana rituale. Feste civiche e politica dal secondo dopoguerra*, ed. Aurora Savelli (Pisa: 2010), 19–48.
101   In this letter to suor Caterina Ottavia, Mattei also wrote advices to other nuns of the Abbandonate. See note 28.

inferno[102] of a soul that believes in them, and this is why we must banish them and refuse to believe in them, going in with our eyes closed, with faith in that all: and let Him do with us in time and eternity as He wills.

Goodbye,

Forever yours in the Lord.

A.M.E.

4.3   Antonio Mattei to Unknown[103]

Ad Maiorem Dei Gloriam,

I would like to make a particular comparison. Which of the two lives, that is, the active or the contemplative life, does God most appreciate? I believe that this is the most certain and perfect comparison because we have it from the mouth of truth of the son of God when he replied to those two beloved sisters, Martha and Mary Magdalen, saying "optimam partem elegit sibi Maria".

But I believe, in as far as God has seen fit to enlighten me, that we can compare one—the active life—to the light of the moon at night and the other—the contemplative life—to the light of sun during the day. And maintaining the order of my simile—in as far as my ignorance permits—I will begin by looking at the active life, comparing it to the imperfect light of the night because when you walk at night, you always encounter many dangers. The first is [the danger] of falling or of stumbling due to the lack of light. Secondly, [if you walk at night, you] are more likely to be beset by thieves, by wild animals, a variety of weather conditions, by sinister clouds dimming the little light available and leaving you in the pitch dark, making it very hard to find your way if you are not familiar with the road. Moreover, there is also the disadvantage of seeing things imperfectly, especially small things, and then there is the fact that it is always colder at night than during the day and that all kinds of inconvenience and suchlike can occur to those walking at night.

Now the same things happen to those who have chosen the active life because they are more likely to lapse into grave sin or to come up against imperfections, to encounter infernal thieves who may steal their good works or in wild beasts who symbolise the evil people in the world who always seek to trap consciences with their tricks and guile. They are exposed to bad weather, that is, to our bad bodily humours, which often cloud the mind, preventing it from using reason

---

102   Hell.

103   ACDF, *Siena*, Lettere speciali 216, dossier titled "Lettere trovate al Cenni". S.d; s.p. (copy).

to distinguish good from evil. In the same way, attachment to things created dims the intellect, sometimes leaving us in total darkness, unable to distinguish imperfections and venial sins. Our fragility and carelessness cause us to make mistakes. But we must lose no time in getting back on the path, redressing matters humbly and lovingly, recognising that we are nothing and that God is all, knowing that only He can do every thing. Given that even during the day there may be storms and clouds may cover the sun, hail or rain may fall and there may be other adversities like excessive heat or cold or other such things—although they will never be like these nocturnal events—the same thing may also happen to contemplatives who may experience spiritual or temporal incidents allowed by God, like losing their health, their honour, their property, their inheritance or other similar things. However, they will never experience these trials and shadows in the same way as those leading an active life. This is because they will always be supported by secret consolation in the depths of their heart given that by God's grace they have acquired extensive experience in dying to their nature and to their own interests while they are intent upon those belonging to God. And God rewards them and never leaves them without His divine presence and His consolation because of their faith, filling them, in the depth of their souls with the [awareness] that everything that He allows is for His greater glory and for the merit of their faith. And the soul, recognising this truth, consoles herself in every adverse circumstance, rejoicing with glee just like the three boys in the Babylonian furnace[104] because she knows that this is the will of God whom she loves infinitely more than itself, realising that this is God teasing with her with loving jests. But then, in the same way that calm weather returns after the storm after every tribulation of the beloved soul, the Beloved returns lovingly to see his betrothed, the soul. Because when two lovers truly love each other, they cannot bear to spend much time angry at each other and apart.

Now, this is a brief description of the difference between one life and the other: may it please his divine Majesty to truly introduce us for once [...] through experience to this luminous, fertile contemplation, which once tasted will cause the soul to sell all that she holds good to buy this single pearl like the merchant described in the holy gospel [...].

---

104   Daniel 3.

4.4   Antonio Mattei to Massimilla[105]

A.M.D.G.,

Thanks be to God—my beloved sister in Christ—who undergoes no change but remains stable throughout eternity, and who, immobile in himself, gives movement and life to all creatures without ever moving one *iota* from his stability. And in truth we can see that in the same way that he is alone in himself, he is alone in this stability because we wretches [on the other hand] believe in one thing one moment, and in another the next. First we want, then we do not. First we are right up up in the heavens, then we are down on the ground. We are never firm and constant in a single proposition but like dust or leaves fluttering in every wind and those propositions that we thought were so solid just go up in smoke.

Therefore, my dear sister, let us recognise ourselves and seeing that we were made by God in his image and likeness, let us also resemble him in being strong in our faith and in the resolutions that we have so often made, that is, let us become his through and through, and dead to ourselves.

Do not answer, "I wish to love him but I do not really love him; I wish to die but in the meantime I continue to live."[106] Because if we believe our senses there will be no end to it and [our senses] will always make us restless while faith, which surpasses the senses, reassures us that we will receive all that we ask for, believe in, and hope for from God.

Once you have resolved to love God and to die to yourself, be strong and believe that you are dead and love God, paying no mind to any feelings that you might have to the contrary.[107] In fact, the more you feel the contrary, the more you will believe and have confirmation that you love God and that you have died to yourself with your will. While your senses will become more upset and agitated when they see that your soul is moving away from them in order to join God. And just as I explained to you, that union will take place in this faith: that is in firmly believing that you are dead to yourself and that you love God and desire none but him.

It is certainly true that this nature rebels and when it realises that it must die to make way for God, it would prefer to die a gentle death at least, dying little

---

105   ACDF, *Siena*, Lettere speciali 216, dossier titled "Lettere trovate al Cenni". S.d; s.p. (copy) Mattei told the Inquisitor that Massimilla was one of Don Cenni's spiritual daughters.
106   Massimilla, like Caterina Ottavia, seems to be a very scrupulous person.
107   This assertion seems to be in line with the content of the "Protest".

by little. But in this we must seek to resemble the God Incarnate, who died a violent, sudden, and shameful death, and resolve to put to death a disorderly nature, our *amour-propre*, and ourselves, and to do so soon, violently, agreeing to die on the cross if necessary. I mean [we should do this] even though nature opposes itself, our disorderly passions seethe, and we lack every kind of devoted sentiment and are filled, on the contrary, with tedium and aridity, feeling ourselves to be enemies rather than lovers of God. If in the midst of all these tribulations we can stand strong and believe that we love God, that we are in Him, alive to him and dead to ourselves, we will die on the cross and resemble our Lord Christ, to whom I commend you, beseeching him to make up for what you lack and I will tell him what you have written in our [letter].

Be constant in believing that you love God and do not doubt your love for him. May God make you a saint as I leave you in the holy wounds of Christ [...].

4.5   Antonio Mattei to Suor Caterina Ottavia Carpia [*"Copy of a Spiritual Letter"*][108]

How long, o my God, will we resist Your divine graces, I and that other soul who shall remain nameless? First we offended You through the extent of our treachery and infinite sins and now, like stubborn pharaohs, we constantly resist Your divine graces. And You, the highest communicable good, have never let Yourself be overcome by our faults, in exchange giving us so many joys and graces and heavenly rewards to make us resemble Your only-begotten Son, Jesus Christ our Lord, depriving us of all those consolations received from sentiment and sight.

And what is more, You wish to make us see and touch with our hands, something brighter than a thousand suns: the fact that hell holds no demons more abominable and evil than we are. All this serves to humiliate us and show us what we really are. This vision represents one of the greatest graces You can offer faithful souls in our mortal life [...]—whereby I mean You are mirroring them in Your divinity, allowing them to clearly see what they once were and what they could become on their own. You, the highest good, believe that you can use this continuous vision of ourselves to construct the machine of perfection upon our awareness while at the same time allowing us to know what You are: because we must first know ourselves in order to know you well.

---

108   ACDF, *Siena*, Lettere speciali 216, dossier titled "Lettere Caterina Ottavia Carpia". S.d; s.p. The letter is titled "Copia di una lettera spirituale". During the trial Mattei asserted that he sent this letter to Caterina Ottavia Carpia fourteen or fifteen years before, i.e. in 1673 or 1674. See ACDF, *Siena*, Processi 57, fol. 483^r.

But the demon, your mortal enemy and ours, uses all his powers and trickery to prevent us from knowing ourselves as he did who never wished to reflect on his state, which was [that] of a pure creature, or [on that of] God, the highest creator of all, and who was caused by his lack of this knowledge to fall into the infernal abyss of arrogance and eternal torments. Now he wishes us to become wretches [like him] by preventing us from knowing our being but disguising us with beautiful colours and appearances gilded with virtues and the zeal of the honour of God, he causes us to falter on our road to perfection, [tormenting us] with a thousand forms of despair, aridity, and shadows. He makes us say: "How can I always be so unfaithful and wicked to a God who deserves so much love? Is this the correspondence of good works with God? Is it possible therefore that I have never succeeded in truly serving Him and loving Him? I was certainly unable to explain myself to my confessors or they just did not understand me." And so I will have to rack my brains thinking back over my past life and brooding again in this bog of my conscience that seems to me like a cesspit overflowing with all the rubbish, sins and the ingratitude of this world.[109] And in addition to this, every four days I will have to carry out these duties because I will either go to another confessor or more shadows or thoughts will be blown in by the north wind. In other words, with a thousand fine objections, the devil, or our corrupt natures (which I hold to be no less evil than the devil and possibly even more so), demand to leave the orders of God who never demands anything but His greater glory and our sanctification, by the path of light as much as by that of darkness; either through knowledge of Him or of ourselves; or by suffering or through joy and other similar things. Yet we immediately lose heart and begin to judge first one thing then another: but who are we with our meagre intelligences to have the presumption to understand divine dispositions or the purposes and judgements of the most High? When the most fiery and wise seraphim and cherubim, the holiest men and the enlightened of the holy church have lowered the wings of their knowledge and [of their] curiosity, and with every humility and fear have always adored the divine ways and dispositions, saying, "These are the things and works of a God, and that suffices to calm us and prevent us from wishing to go any further". And we miserable little worms of the earth or ignorant, weak little women who are worse than worms, wish to fly in the face of heaven and understand divine secrets: whether we are on the right road or not, whether we are graced or in disgrace, regardless of whether we will continue to be ungrateful and sinners, and so on. And not

---

109   This statement seems to refer to the Jesuit practice of the general confession. See Moshe Sluhovski, *Becoming a New Self. Practice of Belief in Early Modern Catholicism* (Chicago: 2017), 96–120.

even all the wisdom of saints Paul, Augustine, and Solomon will appease them. There they are all day long tormenting the poor Spiritual Fathers with their many scruples and suspicions to the point that they have to rack their brains all day to find ways and means to quieten those melancholy,[110] twisted little brains. I believe that even if all the cherubim were to descend from the heavens with all the wisdom God gave to them, it would not suffice to quieten them.

But what I am saying? Even God himself can barely content them and appease them! They would make even Him lose his mind if He were capable of doing so. So He, the highest good and eternal wisdom, seeing that these creatures never trust either faith or even He himself, although He has assured them by so many means, He places these lovely brains in gloomy darkness or in solitudes that seem eternal and desperate, without all the light, tastes, and sentiments that one could desire, putting them inside a kind of portable hell, as a punishment because they wish neither to quieten themselves nor trust God despite having received so much proof of his protection and care.

And yet in the end we do not wish to trust either the proof of [what we have witnessed] so many times or the faith that tells us so many great things about this God who almost went mad out of love for this ungrateful, disloyal man who was never satisfied. And this loving God could tell us so many truths: "What could I possibly do for man that I have not already done? Whenever I sent him the slightest little difficulty to put his love and his faith to the test and have more opportunity to reward him justly, he would immediately languish and falter and despair, thinking I had completely abandoned him whenever things did not go his way. O man, how can it be possible that you always seek to pit your will against me and always impose it [your will] in everything! The more enlightenment and advantages I give you, the more you oppose me, refusing my divine dispositions. When I show that I love you and caress you, you convince yourself that you do not deserve it. If I show you that you are always ungrateful and sinful towards me, you despair. If I give you light and tenderness, you suspect you have been deceived. If I surround you with darkness, you scream in despair; if I caress you like a son or a bride, you reject my caresses feigning humility. If I

---

110 On religious melancholy, see the monographic issue: MELANCHOLIA/Æ. The religious experience of the "disease of the soul" and its definitions / *MELANCHOLIA/Æ. L'expérience religieuse de la « maladie de l'âme » et ses définitions*, of *Etudes Epistémè. Revue de littérature et de civilisation (XVIe–XVIIIe siècles)*, 28 (2015), ed. Sophie Houdard, Adelisa Malena, Lisa Roscioni, Xenia von Tippelskirch (https://journals.openedition.org/episteme/742, accessed 26 November 2018).

behave severely with you, you forget your humility and use every means at your disposal to escape from me, whatever state I place you in. Ultimately, if I were not God I would struggle to find the means to satisfy the most worthless old woman in the world who would still claim to know more than me or than all the men in the world, saying "They do not understand me or I have not made myself understood." And it seems that in order to make this old woman understand and to quieten her down it would be necessary for the divine word to descend on earth again with all the wisdom of God, three in one."

For the love of God, let us for once allow ourselves to be guided by this loving God, who knows and wishes to guide us to that end that he has ordered *ab eterno*, as the cause of our salvation is more his than ours. Let us not dwell so much on our delusions and passions. Indeed, how is it possible that we do not wish to trust a God who is our Father in so many respects—for creation, redemption, and conservation—and [we do not wish] to let him act as he chooses in our regard.

As for me, I do not know what else to say, because in as far as I can, I wish to leave the responsibility for caring for my soul to Him, and remain there like a child in his mother's arms, leaving it up to him in time and in all eternity [...].

4.6 Antonio Mattei to Suor Caterina Ottavia Carpia[111]

A.M.D.G.,

Suor Caterina, I thank you most heartily. I apologise for not being able to visit you this Lent because for almost a month now I have been caring for a soul, to whom one might say what the Holy Prophet said about himself: "*Veni in altitudinem maris et tempestas demersit me*".[112] And given that I have a duty to her, as I do to myself, I cannot abandon her until the end of such a fierce tempest and desperation is nigh. Therefore, for the grace of God, I ask you and your companions to pray to God to keep her strong in the fulfilment of his divine orders, which are truly so terrible and incomprehensible for a mortal creature.[113] This soul finds herself in this state because she is all at sea, as the saying goes, in lov-

---

111   ACDF, *Siena*, Lettere speciali 216, dossier titled "Lettere Caterina Ottavia Carpia". S.d; s.p.
112   Psalm 69:14–15: "deliver me [...] from the deep waters, do not let the floodwaters engulf me".
113   The men and women in the group were linked by multiple and complex relations of spiritual guidance that took place on various levels. For example, there were relationships between confessors and penitents (both men and women) and between fathers and their spiritual sons and daughters in accordance with the dictates of the Church of the Counter-Reformation. There were more equal relationships of a kind of spiritual friendship between people sharing devotional practices, methods of praying and ways to

ing too much and in blindly following her love. And with divine invention, and as if [he himself were] blind, God has led this soul to the high seas, or towards great solitude, leaving her there, completely abandoned. And so, poor mad fool, she finds herself on the edge of a precipice, and in desperation, seeing herself in a new world, surrounded by more perils and fears than there are stars in the sky, with so many sights and the cognition of herself, that is, of her nothingness, of her wickedness, her powerlessness, that would move a rock to compassion and pity. All she does is weep and turn to the side where she saw her Love depart, calling him cruel and worse than cruel an infinity of times, saying to him, "So you lead souls into an infinity of evils, battles and dangers, and then abandon them completely?". And he seems to laugh deep down in his heart and to taunt her, saying "You ended up there once and now you can remain there as you wish: how many times have you deceived me with your many pretences and with your obstinacy. It was for your sake that I consumed myself day and night. You are worse than cruel, ungrateful and faithless soul who followed my enemies: world, demon, and flesh! Now we will take turns in mocking each other and calling each other cruel. Go on and torment yourself as much as you like because in the end it is there that you must stay, like it or not."

Now you know in what a wretched state that creature finds herself so pity me as charity demands. And you, hide yourselves, flood yourselves, and transform yourselves into the Holy Side of Sweet Jesus[114] but take care that He does not do as Love does because they are part of the same being and share the same condition and understand each other. Take care, therefore, to be on your guard, and should you receive any kind of insult turn to your Father Confessor although it is possible that he might disagree [with my advice] and in that case I do not know to whom we should turn. Ultimately, if that is what they want, we will have to surrender and do things their way.
Goodbye.
Always Yours in the Lord,
A.M.E.

Texts translated by Oona Smyth

---

spiritual perfection. In this Letter Mattei informs Caterina Ottavia and the nuns in the Abbandonate about another of his spiritual daughters. He shares with the nuns his reflections on that case and asks them to pray for that soul.

[114] On this image and on Christ's humanity as "female", see Caroline Walker Bynum, *Jesus as Mother. Studies in the Spirituality of the High Middle Ages* (Berkeley—Los Angeles—London: 1984); eadem, *Holy Feast and Holy Fast. The Religious Significance of Food to Medieval Women* (Berkeley—Los Angeles—London: 1988).

CHAPTER 9

Saints in Revolt: The Anti-Ottoman "Vision of Kyr Daniel"

Marios Hatzopoulos

Introduction

The *Vision of kyr Daniel,* [*a story*] *very beneficial* [*Optasia tou kyr Daniel, pany ōphelimos*] is a Greek prophetic tract probably written around the mid-1760s. In manuscripts it can be found conjoined to the hagiographical account of Anastasius, the new martyr[1] whose martyrdom and sainthood are venerated by the Greek Orthodox Church on 17 November. An edited and annotated version of the *Vision of kyr Daniel* (hereafter *kyr Daniel*) was published by Pantelis Paschos in 1995 on the basis of two manuscripts: the Kozani Municipal Library 34, an 18th century manuscript kept at the municipal library of Kozani, Greece (referred to in my translation as "Kozani MS"), and the Athos Saint Anne 85.4, a 19th century manuscript kept at the monastic library of the skete of Agia Anna on Mount Athos (referred to in my translation as "St Anne MS"). Paschos has published the two manuscripts side by side.[2] My translation follows his edition. In particular it follows the text of the older Kozani MS while drawing in part on the later St Anne MS, as well as on Paschos's critical commentary when the meaning in the Kozani MS text is vague or unclear. *Kyr Daniel*'s manuscripts are found as well in several Athonite monasteries such as the Zographou, Panteleimon and Grigoriou monasteries, in the Romanian Academy in Bucharest and at least in one monastic library (Myrtidiotissa monastery) on the island of Corfu.[3]

---

1   The title of "new martyr" or "neomartyr" of the Greek Orthodox Church was given to persons who had opted for the Christian faith, and then put to death, instead of being converted to, or remaining in, Islam.
2   Pantelis Paschos, "Islam kai neomartyres. O ek Paramythias neomartis Anastasios kai o ismailitis [Mousa] Daniel o omologitis" [Islam and New Martyrs. The New Martyr Anastasius from Paramythià and the Ishmaelite [Mousa] Daniel the Confessor], *Epistimoniki Epetiris tis Theologikis Scholis Panepistimiou Athinon*, 30 (1995), 413–474.
3   See respectively Spyridon Lambros, *Catalogue of the Greek manuscripts on Mount Athos*, vol. 2 (Cambridge: 1900), 503; Andrei Timotin, "La Vision de kyr Daniel. Liturgie, prophétie et politique au XVIIIe siècle", in *The Greek world between the Age of Enlightenment and the 20th century*, vol. 1, ed. Konstantinos Dimadis (Athens: 2007), 127, note 1; Spyros Karydis "O neo-

Dating and Authorship

The dating of the work is debatable in spite of the chronological evidence appearing on the title of at least three Athonite manuscripts. The evidence might be useful in determining a timeframe for the work's production. According to the *Catalogue of the Greek Manuscripts on Mount Athos* compiled by Spyridon Lambros, the title of the Athos, Zografou 9.13 manuscript (Lambros 335) is: "The vision of kyr Daniel that was seen in the year 1764, November 18".[4] The same year is referred to in the Athos, Panteleimon 204.124 manuscript (Lambros 5711) kept at the Panteleimon monastery, whose title is somewhat more elaborate: "The splendid vision of the most venerable kyr Daniel, which he saw on the Queen of Cities in the year 1764, November 13".[5] Despite the different date contained in each one's title, both manuscripts agree on the year of the work's composition—that is 1764. The manuscripts, however, are not of the same period. The Zografou 9.13 was written in the 18th century while the Panteleimon 204.124 dates from the 19th century, and it is not unlikely that the latter has followed the former in matters of dating. The problem arises from a third manuscript, the Athos, Grigoriou 34.4 (Lambros 581) which is also from the 18th century and whose title dates the work some sixty years earlier. In addition to dating evidence, the title of this manuscript contains historical evidence and reads: "Vision of kyr Daniel the monk that occurred in the year 1704 during the reign of Sultan Mustafa".[6]

Indeed, the start of the 18th century did witness a Sultan named Mustafa on the throne of the Ottoman Empire, Mustafa II (1664–1703), who died in December 1703. It is noteworthy, however, that a Sultan of the same name sat on the throne in 1764 too, namely Mustafa III (r.1757–1774). Grigoriou 34.4 and the aforementioned Zografou 9.13 both originate from the 18th century, even though each manuscript sets a different date for the composition of the work. Was *kyr Daniel* written at the start of the century, according to Grigoriou 34.4, or in the middle of the century according to Zografou 9.13? The text itself provides a number of historical references or allusions in favour of the mid-18th century and, if we take into account the dating provided by Zografou 9.13 and Panteleimon 204.124, it could indeed be product of the mid-1760s. Given that in

---

martyras Anastasios 'o ek Paramythias' kai o monachos Daniel. Ta prosopa kai i geografia tou martyriou" [The New Martyr Anastasius from Paramythià and the monk Daniel. The Persons and the Geography of Martyrdom], in *Triakosto Tetarto Panellinio Istoriko Synedrio 31 Maiou–2 Iouniou 2013. Praktika*, ed. Vassilis Gounaris (Thessaloniki: 2016), 21–23.

4 Spyridon Lambros, *Catalogue of the Greek manuscripts on Mount Athos*, vol. 1 (Cambridge: 1895), 32.
5 Lambros, *Catalogue*, vol. 2, 328.
6 Lambros, *Catalogue*, vol. 1, 49. Meaning probably Mustafa II (r.1695–1703).

some codices *kyr Daniel* comes right after the hagiographical account of Anastasius the new martyr,[7] the year of Anastasius's martyrdom, which is known to have taken place in 1750, might provide a *terminus post* for the work's writing. The second hint in favour of the mid-18th century comes from a person twice referred to in *kyr Daniel* (§11 and §14), one Sophronius, metropolitan bishop of Ptolemaïs in Syria. Without much difficulty, Sophronius could be identified with the man who served as Patriarch of Jerusalem from 1771 to 1775 and then ecumenical Patriarch of Constantinople as Sophronius II from 1775 until his death in 1780. Born in Aleppo, Syria, Sophronius had been serving as metropolitan bishop of Ptolemaïs, Syria during the 1760s.[8] Moreover, it is known that he became involved in the great controversy of Kollyvades as Patriarch of Constantinople, which by the 1770s had begun to divide the monastic communities of Mount Athos.[9] Interestingly, Zografou 9.13 refers to "turbulence" occurring on Mount Athos (§11), while Panteleimon 281.39 identifies the "turbulence" with the Kollyvades controversy.[10] Another hint given in favour of a mid-18th century dating is the explicit reference of the text to Ottoman clothing laws taking effect at the time (§9). It is known that laws requiring Ottoman subjects to wear distinctive clothes according to one's religion were issued by Sultan Mustafa III (r.1757–1774).[11] *Kyr Daniel* does not name the then reigning Sultan, but if Mustafa III is taken into account, the text's allusion to a "most impious Mahmud" (§9) makes full sense as Mahmud I (r.1730–1754) had been a close predecessor of Mustafa III on the throne. Furthermore, if the text was drafted by the mid-18th century, the vague reference to "a teacher called Chrysanthus" (§4) could also be identified with Chrysanthus of Aetolia, the cleric-educator who was brother of the renowned preacher and new martyr, Kosmas of Aetolia (1714–1779).[12] Last but not least, though *kyr Daniel* allegedly foresees the Christian reconquest of Constantinople, no reference is made to the Russo-

---

7   Take for example Athos, Saint Anne 85.4; or Athos, Panteleimon 281.37–39 (Lambros 5788).
8   Paschos, "Islam kai neomartyres", 470–471.
9   The "Kollyvades" movement arose in 1754 out of a dispute within the Skete of Saint Anne at Mount Athos on whether memorial services should be held on Sundays. The Kollyvades monks insisted that it was improper to commemorate the dead on Sundays as it is the day of the Lord's resurrection. They also advocated the reception of communion by the faithful on a daily basis. In 1776 the movement was condemned and its leaders were excommunicated by a synod organised by, and convened under, Sophronius himself, then ecumenical Patriarch of Constantinople. The Kollyvades leaders, however, were later vindicated and their ideas turned out to be influential within the Orthodox Church.
10 Lambros, *Catalogue*, vol. 2, 349.
11 Donald Quataert, "Clothing Laws, State, and Society in the Ottoman Empire, 1720–1829", *International Journal of Middle East Studies* 29/3 (1997), 410.
12 Paschos, "Islam kai neomartyres", 471–472.

Ottoman war which was to break out in 1768. For these reasons therefore, *kyr Daniel* seems to be a product of the mid-18th century and possibly of 1764 or of the years around 1764, to the extent Zografou 9.13 and Panteleimon 204.124 are right.[13] In this case, the dating evidence contained in Grigoriou 34.4, that is 1704, must be regarded as anachronistic.

The work's author is also unknown. What is known is that the noun *"kyr"* which appears only once, merely in the title of the work, was used in Byzantine times to refer to the distinguished members of the court, the church and the laity. The term is an abbreviated form of the Greek noun *"kyrios"* meaning one exercising power over somebody or something, namely the master or the lord. *"Kyr"* preceded one's first name, all the more so after the 12th century, to denote the high respect that a man enjoyed in society. In case one was a priest or a monk, the usage of *"kyr"* underlined the man's spiritual and religious prominence.[14] Purportedly, *kyr Daniel* was authored by its very protagonist, the monk *Daniēl ex Hagarinōn* [Daniel from the Hagarenes] who lived in the mid 18th century. Daniel allegedly had a prophetic dream which he wrote down himself. According to recent research, Daniel was probably a real person and not a fic-

---

13   It has to be noted that the dating is provisional as it does not take into account all surviving manuscripts, whose exact number and location remains unknown, but merely the available manuscripts to date. Referring to hagiographical accounts of Saint Anastasius the new martyr, Karydis speaks of 23 manuscripts in total without clarifying which of them include *kyr Daniel*'s text; see Karydis "O neomartyras Anastasios", 26–27. On the other hand, Lambros's catalogue of Athonite manuscripts does not include Saint Anne 85.4, which was used and published by Pantelis Pashos ("Islam kai neomartyres") and thus does not seem to be exhaustive. Based mainly on Paschos who dated vaguely Kozani 34 and Saint Anne 85.4 in the 18th and 19th century respectively, Timotin dated *kyr Daniel* from 1763–1765; see Andrei Timotin, "Eschatologie post-byzantine et courants idéologiques dans les Balkans. La traduction roumaine de la *Vision de kyr Daniel*", in *Peuples, États et nations dans le Sud-Est de l'Europe, IXe Congrès international des études du Sud-Est européen, Tirana, 30 août–4 septembre 2004* (Bucarest: 2004), 123. Other experts, however, opt for a different dating. For example, Kariotoglou accepts the dating of Grigoriou 34.4 which he has mistakenly rendered as 1740 instead of 1704; see Alexandros Kariotoglou, *Islam kai christianiki chrismologia. Apo ton mytho stin pragmatikotita* [Islam and Christian Oracular Literature. From Myth to Reality] (Athens: 2000), 118; see also 291. Whereas Ziaka writes that the work was written during the reign of Sultan Mahmud I (*r.* 1730–1745); see Aggeliki Ziaka, *Metaxy polemikis kai dialogou. To Islam sti byzantini, metabyzantini kai neoteri elliniki grammateia* [Between Polemic and Dialogue. Islam in Byzantine, Post-Byzantine and Modern Greek Literature] (Thessaloniki: 2010), 416–417. None of the above has explained how they arrived at these dates. We will be able to establish a definite date for the work when all surviving manuscripts become available for research.

14   Anastasia Kontogiannopoulou, "I prosigoria kyr sti byzantini koinonia" [The Qualifier 'kyr' in Byzantine Society], *Byzantina* 32 (2012), 209–226.

tional character.[15] This, however, does not imply that Daniel the Hagarene, even if he really existed, would have also authored the piece, as prophetic works often assume authorship by an existing saint, sage or hero in order to gain credence for the predictions contained therein.[16] The second character of *kyr Daniel* is Anastasius the new martyr, a Christian from Epirus who was executed by the local Ottoman governor in 1750 for refusing to convert to Islam. He was thus given the title of "new martyr" by the Orthodox Church and was canonised as saint in the same manner as the martyrs of the ancient Church. What *kyr Daniel* offers to the reader is the sequel to this story.

The Rise of the Army of Saints

The preface of *kyr Daniel* gives an outline of the protagonist's identity and background. Before becoming Christian, Daniel the Hagarene was a Muslim named Musa. He was the young son of the Ottoman governor who had put Anastasius to death. Feeling remorse for the killing of an innocent and seemingly holy man, Musa started to lean towards Christianity. He escaped to the nearby island of Corfu, was baptised and became a monk under the name Daniel. After this introductory paragraph, the prophetic narrative starts unfolding in the main body of the text. Daniel arrived in the Queen of Cities (Constantinople) from Corfu. He had decided to confess publicly his faith in Jesus and face the consequences. He found the city tainted by what he described as impiety and godlessness, seeing Christians mistreated at the hands of Muslims. These experiences cemented his resolve for martyrdom. He started praying day and night seeking God's answer for the way ahead. Indeed, in the course of the night of 17 November, Anastasius the new martyr came to Daniel's dream and pledged to guide him in divine mysteries (§1). The pair started to wander about the streets of Constantinople / Istanbul. They visited former Christian sacred spaces, namely Byzantine churches that had ceased to exist or had been turned into mosques which, however, are found to be in use as if the glory days of Byzantium were back. One example is the Church of All the Saints (*Hagioi Pantes*) built by the Byzantine emperor Leo VI (r.886–912), which had ceased to be used by the 14th century; another example is the nearby Church of the Holy Apostles (*Hagioi Apostoloi*), the burial place of Byzantine emperors and

---

15 Spyros Karydis argued this quite convincingly on the basis of evidence from the archive of the Greek community of Venice; see Karydis, "O neomartyras Anastasios", 26–27.
16 Marios Hatzopoulos, *Ancient Prophecies, Modern Predictions: Myths and Symbols of Greek Nationalism*, unpublished PhD thesis (London: 2005), 25 and 96.

arguably one of Constantinople's most sacred sites, which had been demolished by the Ottomans in the 15th century. The sacred sites were found to be miraculously populated with saints whose presence, in turn, re-consecrated *de facto* each edifice (§ 3).

The story begins from the Church of All the Saints, where Daniel and Anastasius witnessed what could be described as the formation of a sacred army by All the Saints, namely the sum of the saints of the Christian Church. Then the army took out to the streets. Roaming the city and exercising their powers, the saintly army took back Christian sacred space or outright claimed Muslim sacred space as Christian. The Muslims began to flee in despair realizing that Constantinople is returning to Christian hands. Crescent symbols atop mosque domes cracked and fell apart in the face of the True Cross that All the Saints were holding upright. In case a mosque had been a church in the past, the saints did not resort to exercising supernatural power but also took physical action against the current occupiers throwing the theme of Muslim expansion into relief. Saint George, for example, appeared to be chasing the Muslims out of his church wielding a club (§ 4–5). The plot culminates in the former Byzantine cathedral of *Hagia Sophia* (Church of the Holy Wisdom) which Sultan Mehmed II the Conqueror (r.1444–1446 and 1451–1481) had turned into a mosque right after the conquest of Constantinople. Upon entering the cathedral's premises, the saints along with Daniel and Anastasius spotted a closed door. Inside there was a secret chapel fully ornamented as if it had never stopped functioning since the old days of the Byzantine Empire. Whereupon commenced an Orthodox divine liturgy, which is recounted in great detail in the text. The liturgy was carried out by All the Saints in the presence of the Virgin Mary, whereas Jesus Christ in full glory acted as archpriest. As the scene concludes, the first prophetic announcement is made: in response to his mother's plea, Jesus promised to liberate the Orthodox Christians "in a little while" (§ 9). Soon the prophecy becomes more specific. The Virgin headed to the Ottoman palace in the company of saints and publicly humiliated the then reigning Sultan whose name remained undisclosed. Next, she went on to address the Orthodox prelates and primates stressing that she had always been the liberator of Constantinople and so she would be forever. Finally, in what is undoubtedly the climax of the plot, the Mother of God prophesied that she would lead the Orthodox elites to rise up and annihilate the Ottoman kingship and people.

The Unseen Realm and Its Enemies

Kyr Daniel casts the world in terms of a struggle between light and darkness, good and evil. Within the confines of this Manichaean worldview, the Muslim Ottomans are portrayed as persecutors of the church and chastisers of Christians. Time and again, *kyr Daniel* contrasts Muslims with the followers of the true God, the eastern Christians, and their drama: like the Jews of ancient Israel, God has decided to chastise the Orthodox for their committed sins through bondage and captivity at the hands of an alien nation. Yet the Muslim Ottomans are more than this according to the work: they are irreverent (§8), impious (§9, 12) and godless (§12), sacrilegious and wicked (§14). To say the least, the way Muslims are presented is bleak. What must be borne in mind, however, is that *kyr Daniel* is not an account of history but an account of prophecy. *Kyr Daniel* is not interested in impartiality when it comes to inter-confessional relations, nor does it aspire to scrutinise the imperial policy towards non-Muslim communities in the Ottoman Empire. The work is a passionate polemic against the Ottoman power, rule and religion and, by the same token, a narrative of hope for those Christians who found it hard to feel accommodated within the political and social status quo of the Ottoman conquests.

Kyr Daniel aimed mainly at providing hope and encouragement to the community of the conquered Christians by offering "divine" affirmations that their political status was to be reversed at a foreseeable point in the future. Besides the loose ends allowing variant readings in the narrative—inherent features of all prophetic works—*kyr Daniel* had a double mission: first, to prevent the world view of the conquered community from collapse, which in the case of the eastern Christians would be tantamount to Islamisation; and second, to guide the defeated community in future actions. In so doing, however, the work had first and foremost to deal with a question posed if not by the fact of the Ottoman military success and expansion in South-eastern Europe, then by a bitter moral and spiritual dilemma implied thereby: if God protected his elect by bestowing victory over foes, could ever the one, true God be that of the victorious Muslims? *Kyr Daniel* comes to terms with this potentially explosive dilemma for the belief system of the defeated community by making a chain of allegations about the victors and their religion. Impiety, impurity, profanity and godlessness are not merely rhetorical vehicles. They are potent argumentative weapons meant to erase any sense of suspicion that the God of the conquered community has failed to protect His people and, ultimately, might be false and untrue.

It is in this light that the Ottoman rule is justified on grounds of human transgression and sin: Christians are chastised because they have sinned. On this point *kyr Daniel* is clear. When the Saints beg the enthroned Jesus for Christian freedom the reply is that Christians are deemed unworthy of heavenly protection for having been ungrateful to God (§ 8). When the Virgin goes on to intercede for them it is reiterated that God is inclined to set the Christians free, yet they remain in bondage for not regretting their sins (§ 9). When God allows three Orthodox prelates to be killed by the Sultan, it is stated that the prelates got what they deserved because they had been insincere in their faith. The argument comes full circle towards the end of the text, as the Mother of God proclaims that she has always been saving Christians and Constantinople from every harm, and whoever doubts it commits the heavy sin of thanklessness to God (§ 13).

The second aim of *kyr Daniel*, as stated before, was to guide the members of the conquered community in future actions. Here is when prophecy is called on duty. The work underlined that the Muslim "captivity" was a provisional measure so that penitent Christians be welcomed again—a pattern that was born and found its greatest elaboration in the Jewish tradition and scripture.[17] The political status of subjection, therefore, was going to be reversed soon. "I shall set them free in a little while" declared an all-glorious Jesus about the future of the Muslim-subjugated Orthodox (§ 9). The prophetic declaration of Christian freedom was spelled out in many ways: explicitly as in § 14 where it was stated again that "Christians [shall] come to power"; or more subtly as in § 11 where it was recounted that the oil-lamps of the secret chapel remained allegedly lit since the time of Byzantium will continue to be so "only for a short while more". That is to say, the rulers' might is running out of time so much as the oil lamps are running out of oil. What was generally proclaimed was that the Christian accession to power had been decreed by Heaven and the Mother of God would interfere in history with the aim to "liberate all the humbled Christians" (§ 13).

It is not by chance that Virgin Mary is mostly referred to throughout the text under the name of "Theotokos" (Birth Giver of God). This is a title of Mary used especially by eastern Christendom. The title had started to be used in the mid-3rd century but it became widespread only after the Council of Ephesus (431 AD). It was there that Cyril of Alexandria argued that Mary must be called *Theotokos* (Birth Giver of God), against the teaching of Nestorius that Mary must only be called *Christotokos* (Birth Giver of Christ). In Byzantium, Mary the Theotokos was perceived as guarantor of military success and defender of the empire. She was also regarded as the chief protector of the empire's cap-

---

17   See, for example, Jer. 25:8–14; Deut. 28.

ital. The dedication of cities to godly protection against man-made or natural disasters was inherited from antiquity, yet in Christian times it was patron or matron saints who were expected to entreat God on behalf of the city's citizens by virtue of their proximity to Him. All the more so, was the woman who bore God in herself, according to Christian doctrine, Mary the Theotokos.[18] The Theotokos had been addressed as intercessor by the 5th century but it was not until the late 6th century that she started to be regarded as the protectress of the Christian Roman empire as a whole. When in 626 the Avars besieged Constantinople and, according to tradition her miracle-working icon being carried around the walls saved the city, the Theotokos was turned into something of a fighter and a weapon for Roman Christians.[19] Ever since the Avar siege of 626 the Byzantine capital would be dedicated personally to her as a *Theotokoupolis* (city of the Theotokos).[20] Mary's intercessory role for the Roman Empire and capital would be celebrated in every Orthodox divine liturgy and the events of 626 would be re-enacted on the streets of Constantinople through custom and rite.[21] Prayers would extend to her in order to "[…] hurry and protect the faithful and to slay their foes as soon as possible".[22] Her icons would be treated as parts of the army's defensive arsenal: they would be carried along the walls during sieges and emperors would take them along when in campaign.[23]

---

18   Mario Baghos, "Theotokoupoleis: the Mother of God as Protectress of the Two Romes", in *Mariology at the Beginning of the Third Millennium*, ed. Kevin Wagner et al. (Eugene, Oregon: 2017), 51–54; as the author interestingly notes: "It was in this capacity that the Theotokos was considered the chief intercessor on behalf of not just Constantinople and Rome, but of Paris and Aachen"; ibid. 54.

19   This is quite evident in Orthodox hymnography. Take for example the renowned *prooimio* (preamble) of the Akathist Hymn which, echoing the events of 626, addresses the Theotokos as *Ypermachos Stratigos* [Defender General]: "Unto the Defender General / the dues of victory,/ and for the deliverance from woes, the thanksgiving / I, Thy city, ascribe Thee, / O Theotokos./ And having your might unassailable, / deliver me from all danger / so that I may cry unto Thee:/ Rejoice, O Bride unwedded".

20   Baghos "Theotokoupoleis", 57–65.

21   Alexei Lidov "Spatial Icons. The Miraculous Performance with the Hodegetria of Constantinople", in *Hierotopy. Creation of Sacred Spaces in Byzantium and Medieval Russia*, ed. Alexei Lidov (Moscow: 2006), 350–353.

22   Philip Slavin, "From Constantinople to Moscow: The Fourteenth Century Liturgical Response to the Muslim Incursions in Byzantium and Russia", in *Church and Society in Late Byzantium*, ed. Dimiter Angelov (Kalamazoo, Mich.: 2009), 213, cited in Anthony Kaldellis, "'A Union of Opposites': The Moral Logic and Corporeal Presence of the Theotokos on the Field of Battle", in *Pour l'amour de Byzance: Hommage à Paolo Odorico*, ed. Christian Gastgeber et al. (Frankfurt am Main: 2013), 143.

23   Kaldellis, "A Union of Opposites", 137–143; see also Anthony Kaldellis, "The Military Use

The militarisation of Theotokos, an otherwise utterly un-martial figure by any standard, stepped up considerably from the 7th until the 15th century. However, when Constantinople was conquered by the Ottomans in 1453, it was difficult for the faithful to reconcile the bitter reality with the age-old belief that the Theotokos protected the empire and the city. Distress and anguish gave way to legend and myth. One Greek legend held that as the Turks were breaking into the city walls, the last Byzantine emperor, Constantinos Palaeologos, noticed a woman looking like a Byzantine Queen enter a nearby church along with her entourage. The church was dedicated to the Mother of God and the emperor followed her inside only to find the Queen was Theotokos and her entourage a host of angels. Soberly, the Theotokos said to the emperor that she had been delivering the city from harm but this time she was unable to do so because "[...] the sins of your people have inflamed the anger of God". Therefore, she predicted that the city would fall to the Muslims and asked the emperor to leave his crown with her to keep "[...] until such time as God will permit another [one] to come and get it".[24]

Text and Contexts

To date, *kyr Daniel* has attracted less scholarly attention than it deserves. One reason for this may be the visionary character and the dreamy atmosphere of the work that make it alien to modern eyes. The religious fanaticism and fervour that characterise *kyr Daniel* have not increased the chance of its appreciation either. The work's stern religious element could be misleading, for experts have treated *kyr Daniel* as a work similar to religious tracts suggesting, for instance, that the author was interested in heavenly affairs, paying scant respect to the mundane ones.[25] This approach shifts the focus away from external "flesh and blood" enemies to internal ones—something far from the intentions of *kyr Daniel*'s author—thereby occluding the political dimension that is evident throughout the work. Not infrequently, moreover, *kyr Daniel*

---

of the Icon of the Theotokos and its Moral Logic in the Historians of the Ninth-Twelfth Centuries", *Estudios bizantinos: Revista de la Sociedad Española de Bizantinística* 1 (2013), 57–59.

24   *Anonymi Monodia de capta Constantinopoli*, ed. Spyridon Lambros, *Neos Ellinomnimon* 5 (1908), 248–250 cited in Donald Nicol, *The Immortal Emperor: The Life and Legend of Constantine Palaiologos, Last Emperor of the Romans* (Cambridge: 1992), 89–90.

25   Kariotoglou, *Islam kai christianiki chrismologia*, 102; see also 118, 291. See also Karydis, "O neomartyras Anastasios", 21.

figures out in bibliography as "apocalyptic"[26] or "eschatological".[27] In philological terms the work is indeed close to the literary genre of the Byzantine "apocalypses" or "visions"—a group of apocalyptic texts of varied dating and origin allegedly composed by renowned religious figures of Christianity (the Virgin, the Apostles Peter, John and Paul etc) or even anonymous monks.[28] As has been observed, however, two characteristics are always standard in Byzantine "apocalypses" in spite of the variety that characterises the genre: first, the elevation of the protagonist, and alleged author, to the heavens and, second, his or her contemplation about the damnation of sinners in hell and the reward of the righteous in paradise.[29] In the 10th century "Vision of Cosmas the monk", for example, the monk Cosmas leaves his body only to see the damned being hurled down in fiery hell. Afterwards, he is guided to Abraham's bosom whence he becomes witness to the riches and glory of the heavenly Jerusalem.[30] Another work of the genre that possibly triggers closer associations with certain parts of *kyr Daniel* (the scene of Divine Liturgy in particular) is the so-called "Vision of Saint Niphon"; or to be more precise, Saint Niphon's vision of Judgement which is contained in his *Vita*.[31] The vision describes, among other things, a liturgy being carried out in Heaven by the angels, the apostles and the entirety of saints. After the sinners are taken for punishment, Christ dispenses rewards to his saints starting from the apostles, who receive a throne and a crown each, and going through the prophets, the martyrs, the clergymen and finally the laypeople. The Mother of God escorted by virgins breaks into the scene and the angelic powers sing a hymn of praise which evolves into an

---

26   Nikolas Pissis, "Apokalyptikos logos kai syllogikes tautotites (170s–180s ai.)" [Apocalyptic Discourse and Collective Identities (17th–18th c.)], in *Identities in the Greek World (from 1204 to the Present Day)*, 4th European Congress of Modern Greek Studies, Granada 9–12 September 2010. Proceedings, vol. 3, ed. Konstantinos Dimadis (Athens: 2011), 692.

27   Asterios Argyriou, *Les exégèses grecques de l'apocalypse à l'époque turque (1453–1821). Esquisse d'une histoire des courants idéologiques au sein du peuple grec asservi* (Thessaloniki: 1982), 103, note 2; Andrei Timotin "La littérature eschatologique byzantine et post-byzantine dans les manuscrits roumains", *Revue des études sud-est européennes* 40 (2002), 161.

28   Timotin "La littérature eschatologique", 151–158, especially 155–158. The genre enjoyed some continuity after the 15th century with the "Vision of Sophiani" which was written in the 17th century; see Andrei Timotin, "Circulation des manuscrits en contexte historique. La traduction roumaine de la Vision de Sophiani", *Revue des études sud-est européennes* 42 (2004), 107–116.

29   Timotin, "La littérature eschatologique", 155.

30   Christina Angelidi, "La version longue de la vision du moine Cosmas", *Analecta Bollandiana* 101 (1983), 73–99.

31   Vasileios Marinis, "The Vision of the Last Judgment in the *Vita* of Saint Niphon (BHG 1371z)", *Dumbarton Oaks Papers* 71 (2017), 193–227.

unending song spreading everywhere.[32] All these might trigger some associations with *kyr Daniel*'s plot, yet in comparison the latter is different.

Kyr Daniel abstains from the overt apocalypticism of the medieval and early modern Greek eschatological literature gravitating towards mundane historical and political realities. It adopts and adapts an end-of-times imagery, with Jesus rewarding the believers and condemning the impious. It also contains a subtle apocalyptic reference to thrones being prepared [*hetoimasia*] for a synod that is about to unite the Church for the ages of ages (§ 6). But otherwise the work exhibits little interest in matters relating to the afterlife or end time. *Kyr Daniel* lacks an explicit apocalyptic or eschatological scenario: there are no "throes", no Antichrist, no Judgement, no end-of-the-world-as-we-know-it. The work does not dwell on the torments of eternal damnation nor is it concerned with rejoicing life in the heavens. Its central concern is political: the coming to power of eastern Christians (§ 14). The reward of the believers that is proclaimed in the text does not take place in Heaven but on earth: it takes place either in the streets or inside the built structures of Constantinople / Istanbul, like the Hagia Sophia, other churches turned-into-mosques of lesser importance, or the palace. The impious are not condemned for their sins in general as happens in the Byzantine and post-Byzantine *Visions* but, in particular, for the "injustice and harm" they have been inflicting on the true believers. It is indicative perhaps that when the Theotokos brings heavenly wrath down on the very embodiment of the Ottoman power, the Sultan, she first calls him "godless man", then "unlawful" [ruler] and finally "tyrant"—the latter two appellations being part of the vocabulary of the Enlightenment. The prophecy of liberation from the Ottoman rule is articulated within a context of politicised metaphysics spelled out on the threshold of modernity. If the work aims at something, it is at propagating rebellion through the medium of prophecy.

Historiography from and about the Balkans is inclined to treat a great deal of the early modern Greek prophetic literature, especially that of the 18th century, as manifestations of propaganda of the then-expanding Russian influence within the Ottoman-ruled Orthodox milieu.[33] In this way the importance of this literature as a source of shared beliefs and collective aspirations of the subjugated Christians of the East is undermined. Indeed, during the 18th century, and because of the recurrent wars against the Porte, the Russian Empire

---

32   Marinis, "The Vision of the Last Judgment", 195.
33   Recent research has challenged this tendency; see for example, Nikolas Pissis "Chrismologia kai 'rossiki prosdokia'" [Oracular Literature and the 'Russian Expectation'], in *Slavoi kai ellinikos kosmos. Praktika protis epistimonikis imeridas tmimatos slavikon spoudon* (Athens: 2015), 153, 166.

tried to take advantage of the fellow Orthodox living in the underbelly of the Ottoman Empire and stir them in its favour through all means available, one of whom were prophetic writings.[34] By the last quarter of the century, the visible decline of the Ottoman Empire and the weakness of Venice in the eastern Mediterranean had left ample space for the Russian expansion southwards. Tsarina Catherine II (r.1762–1796) took her chances with the Russo-Ottoman war of 1768–1774 which resulted in a landslide victory for Russia. During the course of the war, the Russians sailed for first time in the Mediterranean occupying briefly several Aegean islands. In 1770 they went as far as instigating a major revolt in the Greek and Albanian lands, known in the historiography as the Orlov revolt. But eventually the movement failed spectacularly and proved quite costly in terms of human loss and damage, especially for the Christians of Peloponnese. Gradually, Catherine II conceived what historiography refers to as the "Greek project", namely the plan of replacing the Ottoman Empire with a new "Greek empire" centred on Constantinople, which relied to a considerable degree on the support of the fellow Balkan Orthodox. To the extent *kyr Daniel* was drafted in the mid 1760s, it could be argued that it might be nothing but a piece of Russian propaganda clad in prophetic dress.[35] If *kyr Daniel* was actually a product of the years around 1764 it is not unlikely that its author would be aware of Catherine's first attempts to stir up the Greek Orthodox. This can be taken into account if one wishes to argue that the work was born out of, and fed by, a pre-war climate between Russia and the Porte. Spirits were exalted at the time and many were looking for God's signal acts in sky apparitions and natural phenomena. Richard Chandler, the British traveller and antiquarian who travelled extensively on both sides of the Aegean from June 1764 to July 1766 gave a thorough picture of the Christian beliefs and expectations at the time:

> In the first year of our residence in the Levant [1764], a rumour was current, that a cross of shining light had been seen at Constantinople pendant in the air over the Grand Mosque once a Church dedicated to St Sophia; and that the Turks were in consternation at the prodigy, and had endeavoured in vain to dissipate the vapour. The sign was interpreted to portend the exaltation of the Christians above the Mahometans; and this many surmised was speedily to be effected; disgust and jealousy then subsisting between the Russians and the Porte, and the Georgians con-

---

34 Timotin, "La Vision de kyr Daniel", 133–134.
35 This what Timotin suggests; see ibid. 134.

tending with success against the Turkish armies. By such arts as these are the wretched Greeks preserved from despondency, roused to expectation, and consoled beneath the yoke of bondage.[36]

However, even if this was the political, ideological and broadly cultural context that possibly inspired the author, it does not follow that the work was of Russian provenance. By 1764 Catherine's enterprise in the Greek lands had barely commenced, while her "Greek project" had not come to the fore until the 1780s.[37] Another sound argument running counter to the scenario of *kyr Daniel*'s Russian provenance is the way the work deals with the Russian factor. Generally, during the 18th century, a large part of Greek prophetic writings contained allusions in favour of Russians.[38] In this respect, it would be illuminating to see how the two published versions of the *kyr Daniel* (1995) deal with the issue. Right before the prediction about the Christian liberation (§ 12), the Theotokos discovers that the Sultan has gathered Christian prelates and primates in order to have them executed. As five of them lie down dead already she goes on to ask about the reason. The Sultan replies that he would wish to have all prelates and primates killed, not just the five, because they had dispatched letters moving the Sultan's enemies against him. In her reply the Theotokos first insists on their innocence and then predicts the liberation of Christians. In the earlier Kozani MS (18th century) her reply reads: "The case is not they [the Christian prelates and primates] wrote [letters] to your enemy, you most impious man. In fact, I shall lead them [i.e. the Christian prelates and primates] against you so they will annihilate you along with your people". Whereas in the later MS Athos the same sentence reads: "The case is not they wrote [letters] to your enemy, you most impious man. In fact, I shall lead your enemy against you so he [i.e. the enemy] will annihilate you along with your people". What separates the two versions is a slight change in words. While in both manuscripts the

---

36   Richard Chandler, *Travels in Greece: Or an Account of a Tour made at the Expense of the Society of Dilettanti* (Oxford: 1776), 137–138.
37   Gregory Bruess, *Religion, Identity and Empire: A Greek Archbishop in the Russia of Catherine the Great* (New York: 1997), 117.
38   For the first half of the 18th century, see Nikolas Pissis, "Tropes tis 'rossikis prosdokias' sta chronia tou Megalou Petrou" [The Course of the "Russian Expectation" in the Years of Peter the Great], *Mnimon* 30 (2009), 37–60. For the second half of the 18th century, see Argyriou, *Les exégèses grecques*, 357–689; Paschalis Kitromilides, *Enlightenment and Revolution: the Making of Modern Greece* (Cambridge, Mass.: 2013), 120–133; Nikos Rotzokos, *Ethnaphypnisi kai ethnogenesi. Orlofika kai elliniki istoriographia* [National Awakening and Ethnogenesis. Greek Historiography and the Orlov Revolt] (Athens: 2007), 254–257; Pissis "Chrismologia", 163–167.

unnamed "enemy" with whom the Christian elites allegedly had communication might be identified with the Russians, in the earlier 18th century Kozani MS, the Theotokos promises to lead the Orthodox prelates and primates against the Sultan and through them the subjugated community as a whole. Whereas in the later 19th century St Anne MS the Theotokos promises to lead the Russians against the Sultan. If *kyr Daniel* had been of Russian provenance, the earlier rendering of the sentence would have favoured the Russians instead of the local elites.

In Dreams Begins Responsibility

It has been suggested that *kyr Daniel* is one-of-the-kind a literary work.[39] What I would like to suggest, on the contrary, is that it does belong to a greater literary family which, in turn, is part of early modern Greek prophetic literature. As I have argued elsewhere,[40] the latter was a literature aimed at restoring hope and dignity to the community of Orthodox Christians by offering "divine" assurances that a communal state of decline and failure would not last. Political decline and military failure became apparent in Byzantine society from the 13th century onwards, hence the period witnessed the gradual development of a key myth that was about to play a considerable role in shaping shared beliefs and collective aspirations for the Orthodox after the fall of Constantinople. The term "myth" here is used in the sense of Anthony Smith's definition as a widely believed tale about the past reflecting current needs and legitimating future purposes within a given community.[41] In Smith's sense, myths structure communal thought and feeling by providing shared formulations of how to understand the present and how to proceed with the future. The myth under consideration suggested that God would restore Christians to their former glory, thus bringing the Ottoman Empire to an end, at a more or less foreseeable, and sometimes calculable, point of human history. The myth of Byzantine restoration (or "resurrection" in the language of this tradition) was articulated through a stream of medieval and early modern Greek prophetic writings known by the generic term "oracular literature".

---

39 Timotin, "La Vision de kyr Daniel", 130.
40 For an overview of early modern Greek prophetic literature and its distinctive streams see my chapter "Eighteenth-Century Greek Prophetic Literature", in David Thomas & John Chesworth (eds), *Christian-Muslim Relations. A Bibliographical History, Volume 14 Central and Eastern Europe (1700–1800)*, (Leiden: 2020), 382–402.
41 Anthony D. Smith, *The Antiquity of Nations* (London: 2004), 34.

For this stream of belief and thought, apocalypticism was not a necessary element.[42] Oracular prophecy was as much geared towards the future as it was towards the past. Because what it prophesied was the revival of a past phase, indeed a golden age, of the faithful's history. The Byzantine Empire was not a heavenly kingdom where no one would want for anything. It was a lived and shared historical experience of the Orthodox community, which ever since its demise has been transformed into a *lieux de mémoire* commemorated and celebrated through the written, oral, and visual culture of the Orthodox Church. Oracular prophecy strove to activate the past into the present. Building on the collective memories of Byzantine glory and, at the same time, on the historical experience of Ottoman conquest and subjection, oracular literature offered "divine" assurances that the political status of the Ottoman-ruled Orthodox is to be reversed inside the confines of human time and history.

Kyr Daniel is a piece of oracular literature. The work elaborated on the myth of "resurrection" of the Eastern Roman Empire with a view to guiding collective action among members of the Ottoman-ruled Orthodox community in the years before the Russo-Ottoman war of 1768–1774. *Kyr Daniel* was produced from within this community with the aim of legitimating rebellion against the Ottomans. Legitimation was sought, on the one hand, through the appeal to a previous state of religious-cum-imperial glory and on the other through the invocation of God's promise to restore the faithful to their former state. The promise of restoration was articulated through the means of God-sent dreaming. Dreaming has always been a principal mode for producing prophetic narratives and the so-called "vision" of the monk Daniel, literally taken, is nothing but a dream. It is through dreaming that the separation of past and present was overcome throughout the work's narrative and a sense of temporal simultaneity, or multi-temporality, was offered to the reader. The ecstatic journey of the monk Daniel into the world of saints produced a mythical narrative of liberation from the Ottoman rule that energised the self-assertion of Christians and delivered moral meaning onto the historical experience of Muslim subjugation. Ultimately, this mythical narrative was a source of agency: through imaginings of the future, the prophecy urged the faithful to plan action in the present.[43]

---

42   "[The] Oracles are not concerned with the end of the world, but with the fate of the Byzantine empire and especially of its capital". Mango remarks on the oracles of Leo the Wise in particular but a great deal of his insights can be generalised for the oracular literature as a whole; see Cyril Mango, "The Legend of Leo the Wise", in *Byzantium and its Image*, ed. Cyril Mango (London: 1984), 61; see also 62.

43   Charles Stewart, "Dreaming and Historical Consciousness", *Historically Speaking* 14/1 (2013), 28–30; Charles Stewart, *Dreaming and Historical Consciousness in Island Greece* (Cambridge Mass.: 2012), 3–5.

Assumed sacredness was a standard feature of oracular literature and this applies also to *kyr Daniel*.[44] Oracular works often claimed authorship by various saintly figures in order to be seen and treated as holy labour. As Alexandros Kariotoglou, an authority on Greek oracular literature, suggests, *kyr Daniel* could be using on purpose the name of a prophetic authority like the Biblical Daniel so as to raise the stakes of credibility on the basis of the name semblance.[45] Manuscripts testify to the fact that *Kyr Daniel* was perceived as and classified among religious literature. In Saint Anne 85.4, one of the two manuscripts published by Pantelis Paschos, the work comes right after the hagiographical account of Saint Anastasius the new martyr "as if it were a part thereof" and precedes the liturgical text in the Saint's honour (*akolouthia*).[46] *Kyr Daniel*, in this way, bridges Saint Anastasius's *vita* and *akolouthia* appearing as an integral part of a literary ensemble about the martyr's life, martyrdom and veneration. Similarly, in Panteleimon 281 (Lambros 5788) *kyr Daniel* follows once more the text on Saint Anastasius's life and martyrdom (281.36), yet in this case Daniel's visionary experience (281.38) is complemented with an account of Daniel's baptism (281.37) and another account "on the reasons that deterred Daniel from visiting Mount Athos", implying the monastic controversy of Kollyvades (281.39). Thus, in Panteleimon 281 the monk Daniel is elevated to become something of a saint himself for his life and action extends in three accounts compared to one dedicated to the fully canonised Saint Anastasius the new martyr. Indeed, one understands the great influence Daniel has exerted on the martyr's hagiography if one realises that Anastasius is venerated by the Orthodox Church on 18 November; that is the day Daniel had his dream-vision, instead of 22 July, which is actually the day of the Saint's martyrdom according to the manuscript tradition.[47] Eventually, Grigoriou 34 (Lambros 581) sets the picture straight by putting *kyr Daniel* in context: three out of the four manuscripts comprising the codex are oracular works (34.2, 34.3, 34.4) with *kyr Daniel* being the last of them (34.4).

Kyr Daniel does not frame its arguments in eschatological or apocalyptic contexts. Hence it cannot be regarded as a work of post-Byzantine eschatology.[48] Compared to other works of early modern Greek eschatology, *kyr Daniel* lacks the most important rhetorical *topoi* of the genre: it does not quote or

---

44   Marios Hatzopoulos, "Oracular Prophecy and the Politics of Toppling Ottoman Rule in South-East Europe", *The Historical Review/La Revue Historique* 8 (2011), 114.
45   Kariotoglou, *Islam kai christianiki chrismologia*, 118.
46   Paschos "Islam kai neomartyres", 417.
47   Karydis, "O neomartyras Anastasios", 32.
48   Cf. Argyriou, *Les exégèses grecques*, 103, note 2.

comment on Biblical prophecy, notably the Revelation of John; it does not associate the Muslim Ottomans with the devil and the supernatural evil in general;[49] it does not contain anti-Catholic polemic—as much important a *topos* for Greek eschatological literature as anti-Islamism.[50] Most importantly, however, the work lacks the basic premise of post-Byzantine eschatology that only faith and repentance would bring about Christ's Second Coming and only this, in turn, would terminate the Muslim "captivity". *Kyr Daniel* does not deal with the end of the Islamic religion. It deals with the end of Ottoman political power. The work puts forth and propagates an activist stance. Its foremost concern lies with Christians coming to power again. On a par with their supernatural power, the saintly figures exercise violence like humans do: they seize clubs and chase foes away (§ 4 and § 14), they damage property (§ 4) and cut heads with sword (§ 12). The message of rebellion conveyed is straightforward.

God Guides, Man Fights

Kyr Daniel draws on extra-Biblical prophecy and, in particular, on the lore and literature of post-Byzantine messianism. Out of the lore, *Kyr Daniel* utilises extensively the oral legend of the "unfinished liturgy" in Hagia Sophia. Nikolaos G. Politis, the pioneer of folklore studies in Greece who published this account in 1904, observed the great vogue it enjoyed throughout the 19th century and before.[51] The legend holds that there was a liturgy going on in Hagia Sophia when the Turks broke into the fallen Constantinople. The liturgy was stopped when one priest, with the communion cup in hand, miraculously disappeared into a crypt behind a heavy church wall. The conquerors put all their efforts into breaking down the wall and found that impossible. When the city will be retaken, the legend concludes, God will allow the wall to open again so that the priest will emerge and consummate the liturgy that has been

---

49 The Muslim Ottomans may be described as oppressors and persecutors of the Church which could be a hint for the Antichrist but they are literally defenceless vis-à-vis the army of Christian saints. Notably, the Sultan, whom Greek eschatological literature considers to be the Antichrist's embodiment, is clearly sketched (§ 12) as an all too human figure.

50 On the contrary, it could be argued that *kyr Daniel* might be alluding to a form of cooperation with western Christians: the text recounts for instance the Christian re-appropriation of *Yeni* Mosque (§ 5) in the area of Galata, formerly the Latin Church of Saint Francois. Apparently, the prophesied process of "liberation" includes every Christian sacred space of Constantinople, irrespective of denomination.

51 Nikolaos G. Politis, *Meletai peri tou viou kai tis glossis tou ellinikou laou. Paradoseis* [Studies on the Life and Language of the Greek People. Traditions], vol. 2 (Athens: 1904), 678.

left unfinished.[52] In his detailed commentary, Politis relates this oral tradition with another one current among Istanbul's Christians according to which there exists a gate made of gold inside Hagia Sophia remaining closed since the day of the conquest because the Turks are not capable of opening it. Nor are they willing to do so fearing that a great catastrophe would befall their empire.[53] *Kyr Daniel* comes to draw and elaborate on both oral traditions. Closed gates are first referred to in § 6 where a closed gate hides a fully working secret chapel inside Hagia Sophia. In this place the "unfinished liturgy" of the oral tradition would be consummated by no other archpriest than Jesus Christ in full glory. At the same place, the prophecy of Christian liberation would be uttered. Another reference to a closed gate is made in § 13 when a wandering Theotokos through the rooms of the Sultan's palace finds a closed gate hiding another secret chapel with vested priests living in secret. In essence, *Kyr Daniel* comes to build on the belief that, despite Muslim appropriation, Christian worship miraculously continues within Constantinople's sacred spaces. By the same token, it is implied that any act of Christian worship that was stopped at the very moment and because of the Muslim conquest would be resumed by the will of God. What the prophecy proclaims here is a total return to the past through mending the historical timeline which the Ottoman conquest had broken.

Out of the post-Byzantine messianic literature *Kyr Daniel* utilises in part the messianic figure of the sleeping king-redeemer who was expected to crush the Ottoman military might, wrest political power from Muslims and restore empire and glory to Christians. Prophetic compositions like *Oracles of Leo the Wise* and its accompanying texts elaborate on the man's features and redemptive function. He is called the True Emperor, the Chosen King, the Hoped-for or the Anointed; he has high moral and mental qualities; he lies dead or asleep in the western part of Constantinople; he is to be revealed in the end of the Muslim domination as an angel will instruct him to rise up, take revenge and banish impiety.[54] In *Kyr Daniel* the king-redeemer makes his appearance inside Hagia Sophia's secret chapel in the guise of a crowned and enthroned old man who sleeps on the lower left side of the Theotokos holding a gospel in hand (§ 6). Hagia Sophia's "unfinished liturgy" virtually finishes with him receiving Holy Communion from the hands of the archpriest Jesus.

---

52   See tradition no. 35 in Politis, *Meletai*, vol. 1, 23.
53   The tradition was published by Carnoy and Nicolaides in 1894. See Politis, *Meletai*, vol. 2, 678–679.
54   *Imperatoris Leonis cognomine sapientis: Oracula cum figuris et antiqua Graeca paraphrase*, in *Patrologia Graeca*, ed. J.-P. Migne, vol. 107 (Paris: 1857–1891), 1122–1168. See especially oracles XII–XVI as well as the text of the "anonymous paraphrase".

Kyr Daniel might be sketching the king-deliverer as God's instrument ready for action, yet it introduces a striking innovation in Greek prophetic literature as a whole. The work breaks away from earlier tradition that kept seeing the messianic figure of the king-deliverer as the main agent of Byzantine "resurrection". *Kyr Daniel*'s emperor stays surprisingly inactive because the focus shifted from one man's action to collective action. The restoration of the lost space and sovereignty to Christian hands becomes a matter of collective action. *Kyr Daniel* makes this point by portraying the saints acting collectively as they claim back Constantinople. To this end the saints collectively exercise violence either through physical or supernatural means. Could their actions ever be imitated by humans? The answer to this question comes straight from the lips of the Theotokos: "I shall lead them against you", she sternly warns a terrified and trembling Sultan implying the ecclesiastical and political leaders of the subjugated Orthodox, "so they will annihilate you along with your people" (§ 12). In this light, the prophetic message of *kyr Daniel* could be summarised in two sentences: toppling the Ottoman power on earth materialises the will of heaven. This undertaking requires divine guidance and human action on the communal level. The first sentence epitomises the beliefs and expectations of the oracular genre. The second sentence, however, constitutes a striking departure from earlier tradition—a tradition that proclaimed the coming of a king-redeemer expected to crush the Muslim military might, wrest sovereignty and space from Ottomans and restore it to Christians.[55] For *kyr Daniel* the vessel of divine election, the executor of God's will and, ultimately, the agent of the prophesied insurrection is none but the subjugated community with its religious and lay leaders. The prophecy, as it seems, did not take long to be fulfilled. Merely a few years later, in 1770, the Christian elites and masses of the Peloponnese, the west of Greece and the south of Albania rose in revolt against the Sultan.

---

55   Marios Hatzopoulos, "From Resurrection to Insurrection: 'Sacred' Myths, Motifs, and Symbols in the Greek War of Independence", in *The Making of Modern Greece: Nationalism, Romanticism and the Uses of the Past (1797–1896)*, ed. Roderick Beaton and David Ricks (London: 2009), 81–93; also Marios Hatzopoulos, "Prophetic Structures of the Ottoman-ruled Orthodox Community in Comparative Perspective: Some Preliminary Observations", in *Greek-Serbian Relations in the Age of Nation-Building*, ed. Paschalis Kitromilides and Sophia Matthaiou (Athens: 2016), 121–147.

1   The Vision of kyr Daniel

[Preface] *The Plot of the Present Account*

One Christian called Anastasius had been of service to a rich Hagarene[56] who tried to convert him to his own religion; and since there was no way Anastasius would renounce piety, the Hagarene had him decapitated. Finding hard to bear the injustice that had been committed, the Hagarene's son fled his father's domain; he went to Corfu where he received the holy baptism and then became a monk. This is the one called Daniel herein. Anastasius was his father's slave.[57]

The Vision of kyr Daniel, [a story] very beneficial

1. I, Daniel, the least among the monks, had been living on the island of Corfu for the sake of the miracle-working Saint Spyridon. After eight years spent in one monastic community, I longed for becoming worthy of martyrdom. Burning inside day and night, I looked for a sure way to become a martyr—for taking risks is alien to divine decrees. Keeping this craving secret, I left Corfu and with God's help I arrived at Constantinople, the Queen of Cities, when time was ripe for getting there. And seeing this city replete with impiety, and the men descending from Hagar being mad at Christians, my soul started again to burn with the desire to daringly confess faith in Jesus Christ the Lord.[58] I sought advice from spiritual fathers thereon but, as soon as I disclosed my aim, they wouldn't let me go on with what I was longing for. I then found one father[59] who, on learning

---

56   The term was used in Byzantine Greek to signify initially the Arabs and later any adherent of the Muslim faith. According to Genesis 16:1–16, an Egyptian slave named Hagar bore Abraham's first-born son Ishmael who, in turn, became progenitor of the Ishmaelites, i.e. the Muslims. The latter therefore were referred to by the Byzantines either as Ishmaelites or Hagarenes. In time, however, "Hagarene" acquired a rather pejorative meaning in Greek and it is in this sense that the term is used in *kyr Daniel*.

57   The paragraph occupies the whole of the Kozani MS, fol. 1091 serving as an introduction to the work, which literally begins in the next page (fol. 1092) with the title "The Vision of kyr Daniel [a story] very beneficial". The paragraph gives a very brief outline of the developments that preceded the story recounted in *kyr Daniel*. Another work entitled *Martyrdom of the new martyr Anastasius*, recounts these developments in detail. The *Martyrdom* together with kyr Daniel's *Vision* and a third work, the *Akolouthia of the new martyr Anastasius* consist of a literary triptych, which is contained as a whole in the St Anne MS (fols 693–722). The Kozani MS (fols 1091–1102), on the other hand, contains only the middle part of the set, namely the *Vision of kyr Daniel*.

58   Sentence translated according to the St Anne MS, fol. 703.

59   The Kozani MS, fol. 1092 does not reveal the man's identity but the St Anne MS fol. 703 states that he was Sophronius, metropolitan bishop of Ptolemaïs, Syria (?–1780), hence

my thoughts, urged me to beg for an answer by praying all the more fervently. And the answer would be revealed to me through signs whether God sanctions my plans or not. He urged me, therefore, to perform prayer upon prayer, and fasting upon fasting in order to become worthy of the revelation.

2. Seventeen days of November had passed and, towards the eighteenth,[60] I made my way to a grocery to buy two candles. When I returned to my little house I took to prayer as usual, yet that night it took me even longer to pray with tears, and so I did until the ninth hour of the night. And then exhausted as I had been, I fell asleep. Then the Lord remembered me; and I saw one young man of shining appearance asking me: "Why are you sad Daniel? You should be happy instead". And I said: "Who is saying I must be happy?" And the young man said: "Don't you know, my friend, who is speaking to you?" "No, I said, I don't know". "Am I not Anastasius, who was sent to the kingdom of heaven through martyrdom by your own father?" Then I said to the martyr: "Man of God, how did you deign to come to me, the sinner and the wretched one?" "Believe me", he said, "I have not neglected praying for you since you fled your father's house. Be glad and rejoice for today you will become worthy of seeing into great mysteries". Laying hold of my right hand, the martyr said: "Come with me".

3. We both took to the streets for long and when we arrived at an altar of the Hagarenes he said: "Do you see this altar? This was once the Church of All the Saints."[61] As we were getting closer we saw a man coming out from an open door saying: "Do come in quickly; for they are expecting you." We thought it right to do so. And inside we saw a multitude of people, young along with old ones, so I turned to Anastasius and asked: "Who are they?" "They are known as All the Saints", he replied. One of them said: "Daniel, here you are at last." "Yes, I am here the sinner" I replied. Then they began going out in pairs and we followed them arriving at another altar. They

---

explaining why Sophronius himself breaks into the story by the end of §11; another reference to him is made in §14. For the man and his illustrious career see the introduction.

60   18 November is the day the Greek Orthodox Church venerates Saint Anastasius the new martyr. Daniel's vision takes place on the eve of the saint's feast day.

61   The Church of All the Saints (*Hagioi Pantes*) was built by the Byzantine emperor Leo VI (886–912), initially as a memorial to his first wife Theophano. Probably it stood alongside and to the east of the church of the Holy Apostles. In 1390 it was demolished together with other buildings by the Byzantines themselves to provide stone for strengthening Constantinople's Golden Gate (*Porta Aurea*); see on this Glanville Downey, "The Church of All Saints (Church of St. Theophano) near the Church of the Holy Apostles at Constantinople", *Dumbarton Oaks Papers* 9/10 (1956), 301–305.

said to me "That was once the Church of the Holy Twelve Apostles."[62] And the doors opened as we came closer. Two young men came out, each holding one church pillar candle; another two deacons with incense burners in hand were standing by the door incensing the saints who were entering the church. In the end we were let in. And inside we saw the Twelve Apostles and Saint Constantine together with Saint Helena holding up the True Cross which shone brighter than the sun. Behold, Saint Marcianos[63] comes out [sic] dispensing candles; Saint Constantine comes out [sic] along with his mother holding the Cross in hand; so did the holy Apostles and all Saints following them. And when the True Cross finally came out, the crescent moon symbols sunk in the sea.[64]

4. Then we reached the district of Phanar[65] after a long walk. Passing by a house, the dwelling of a teacher called Chrysanthus,[66] I turned to the martyr and said: "Servant of the Lord, one friend of mine who has entertained and helped me many times stays here; would you want to see

---

62 Being second in size and sacredness only to Hagia Sophia, the church of the Holy Apostles served as the burial place of emperors and patriarchs from the 4th to the 11th century. Right after the Ottoman conquest the building was re-assigned to Christians to house the ecumenical patriarchate but it was soon abandoned. Being in poor condition, the building was finally demolished in 1462 by Mehmed II to provide space for the construction of his own *Fatih Mosque* on the same site.

63 Saint Marcianos (c.450–474) was the treasurer [in Byzantine: *Oikonomos*] of Hagia Sophia. By virtue of this title, he was second only to the patriarch. Marcianos spent his fortune in restoring Constantinopolitan churches. He is also believed to have been a miracle worker; see Manouil Gedeon, *Byzantinon eortologion. Mnimai ton apo tou 4ou mechri meson tou 15ou aionos eortazomenon agion en Konstantinoupolei* [Byzantine Calendar of Saints. Feast Days of Saints in Constantinople from the 4th to the 15th century] (Constantinople: 1897), 271–277.

64 Destruction through sinking in the sea is a well-established motif in the Byzantine apocalyptic literature. Originally, however, the motif referred to the eschatological destruction of Constantinople itself; see Petre Guran, "Historical Prophecies From Late Antique Apocalypticism To Secular Eschatology", *Revue des études sud-est européennes* 52 (2014), 53, 59; see also ibid. 53 note 24. The motif surfaced in the oracular tradition through the Oracles of Leo the Wise; see Jeannine Vereecken and Lydie Hadermann-Misguich, *Les oracles de Léon le Sage illustrés par Georges Klontzas. La version Barozzi dans le codex Bute* (Venice: 2000), 127, 150, 193–194, 247, 308. The "crescent moon symbols" of the text are those found atop the mosque domes and minarets.

65 The *Phanar* [Turkish: *Fener*] district is the area where the ecumenical patriarchate of Constantinople has been located since 1586. The district has also been home to many of the city's Greek-speaking Orthodox.

66 As Pantelis Paschos suggests, this "Chrysanthus" might well be the brother of the new martyr Kosmas of Aetolia (1714–1779) who served high posts at Constantinople's Patriarchal Academy and elsewhere; see Pantelis Paschos, "Islam kai neomartyres", 471–472.

him?" He replied: "I am aware of the one you are talking about; be silent and follow me." After he said so, we walked a long way. Behold, we see Saint George the trophy-bearer who says to the saints: "Come also by my church,[67] now turned into an altar, so that the [crescent] moon establishments will sink in the sea." Before we make it to the spot the Great George was already there and, seeing Hagarenes therein, he seized a club and chased them out. Then he threw away the furniture and the carpets with which they had covered the floor and indignantly said: "I just cannot stand your abomination any longer, you most unholy people." Then the True Cross arrived and the execrable crescent moon symbol sunk in the sea.

5. As we walked ahead, we started listening to a most sweet and pleasing melody. It was the hymn "Rejoice O Queen".[68] As we headed straight, we saw Hagarenes shouting: "woe, woe to us, we must be going because the Romans have arrived!" We reached what the Hagarenes call *Yeni* Mosque, got into the courtyard, set the Cross up and praised the Lord with hymns.[69] As the doxology was drawing to a close, an *Imam*[70] climbed up to yell. Constantine the Great rose up his gaze at him and angrily said: "Damned man, you see the Cross elevated and yet you keep yelling and blaspheming?" And they elevated the Cross and the mosque domes collapsed taking down the *Imam*.[71]

---

67   It is not clear which church that could be. Andrei Timotin suggests it could either be the monastery Church of Saint George of the Mangana or the Church of Saint George in the city's quarter known as *Deuteron*. Saint George of the Mangana occupied a prominent position close to the cape in the east of the city. After 1453, the church had been briefly occupied by dervishes before it was demolished by the Ottoman authorities to make space for the *Topkapi* palace. Saint George of Deuteron, on the other hand, was a church of lesser importance but it was actually situated much closer to the site of the Church of All the Saints and the nearby Church of Holy Apostles; see Andrei Timotin, "La Vision de kyr Daniel", 130.

68   Irmos of the 9th ode of the Pentecost (excerpt): "Rejoice O Queen, glory of mothers and virgins. No tongue, however sweet or fluent, is eloquent enough to praise you worthily [...]".

69   It is worth noting that the verbs of the sentence suddenly shift from first person plural to third person plural in both Kozani MS, fol. 1094 and St Anne MS, fol. 705. I have opted for retaining the first person plural throughout the sentence for reason of clarity.

70   Kozani MS, fol. 1094 uses the term "*ontassimanis*" while St Anne MS, fol. 705 uses a variant term, "*tassimanis*"; both are used respectively once more in §14. The words are apparently Greek transliterations of Turkish terms. Paschos ("Islam kai neomartyres", 472) suggests that the term "*ontassimanis / tassimanis*" is a transliteration of the Persian-Turkish term "dānishmand" meaning the leader of Islamic worship services, the *Imam*.

71   Ibid.

6. Then we headed to the *Hagia Sophia* [Church of the Holy Wisdom].[72] On our arriving, a gate opened and two deacons appeared wearing priestly robes and holding two incense burners ornamented and gilded in gold. I asked the martyr "who are they?" and he said "the one on the right is Stephen the Protomartyr[73] and the one on the left is Lawrence the archdeacon."[74] They offered incense to the venerable Cross and to the multitude of Saints; in the end we got in. On the right, by the *bema*,[75] there was a closed gate which had now been opened and the Cross and the Saints went in. We too entered and saw a frightening miracle. In there was a temple worth seeing and beautifully decorated. It was fully equipped with icons, suspended oil-lamps, candelabra, and other sacred vessels all made of gold. At the place where the icon of the Mother of God is usually to be found, there was a throne where the ever-Virgin Queen was seated encircled by a legion of angels. Lower to the throne, on the left, there was another one where an old man was seated—I am not sure whether he was sleeping or awake—who bore a crown on the head and a nicely decorated and closed Gospel book in hand. Other thrones stood all around the church. Then I asked the Saint, "whom are those thrones for?" and he replied that "those thrones are for the prelates who once sat thereupon and carried out the ecumenical councils; now they are prepared anew so that the prelates shall again seat to unite the Church and anathematise the schisms, thereby leaving the former undisturbed to the ages of ages". In this way, the venerable Cross was placed in the middle.
7. Marcianos in turn, taking the candles from our hands, placed them onto the venerable Cross. Then the door of the *bema* opened and young men appeared dressed in white carrying an all-glorious and shining out throne. As they placed the throne at the spot where the archpriests normally sit, we saw Christ the Lord coming out accompanied by angels, vested in splendour and crowned with unwaning light. He sat on the throne that had been prepared for Him. Then James the brother of the Lord com-

---

72   Built in 537 by the Byzantine emperor Justinian I, *Hagia Sophia* [Turkish: *Ayasofya*] was the Roman Empire's first Christian cathedral and arguably the most sacred space of Byzantine Constantinople. It was converted into a mosque as soon as the city was conquered by Sultan Mehmed II in 1453.
73   Venerated as the Protomartyr or first martyr of Christianity, Stephen was killed by stoning in 34 AD.
74   Lawrence or Laurence was one of the seven deacons of the city of Rome who were martyred in the persecution by the Roman Emperor Valerian in 258 AD.
75   Originally meaning orator's podium, *bema* is a raised area within a Christian church composing the sanctuary and is usually approached by steps.

menced the Divine Liturgy. Jesus Christ the great archpriest made the First Entrance[76] into the holy *bema* together with all who were present. When the time arrived for reading the Acts of the Apostles, Saint Lawrence read this; and the reading went like "Brothers, All the Saints by faith conquered kingdoms" and the rest.[77] Protomartyr Stephen read the holy Gospel from the *ambo*[78] and the reading went like "I am the vine, you are the branches" and the rest. When the time arrived for the Great Entrance,[79] Christ the Lord stood up and blessed everyone. The same He did to the holy offerings when the latter were placed on the altar. Then the communion hymn was sung and Stephen came out [of the sanctuary] saying "With fear of God, faith and love draw near". Christ the Lord stood by the Royal Doors[80] holding the chalice. Then John the Chrysostom[81] and Saint Metrophanes of Constantinople[82] awakened from sleep the old man who was seated on the throne. The old man's crown was taken off by Saint Metrophanes of Constantinople and his Gospel book by [John the] Chrysostom. Then they rose him up and together they approached the Mother of God kissing the edge of her sacred robe. Then they moved before the Royal Doors where the Lord was standing. The old man kneeled before Christ and received Holy Communion from the chalice. Taking the crown from St Metrophanes's hands, the Lord placed it on the old man's head. Taking the Gospel book from Chrysostom's hands, the Lord placed it on the old man's hands.

---

76 The "Entrance" is a liturgical act occurring during the Divine Liturgy of the Orthodox Church. It is a procession during which the clergy enter into the sanctuary through the Royal Doors; for the Entrance and the Royal Doors see also notes 79 and 80 respectively.

77 Heb. 11:32–33, excerpt somewhat distorted. In the original the sentence reads "Gideon, Barak, Samson, Jephthah, David, Samuel, and the prophets, who by faith conquered kingdoms [...]".

78 An elevated desk or pulpit reserved for reading out the gospels and the epistles. In an Orthodox church the *ambo* is normally found at the left (north) side of the building.

79 The "Great Entrance" is a liturgical act of high importance during the Orthodox Divine Liturgy (see also note 76), when the Gifts (bread and wine) to be offered are solemnly carried before the faithful to be eventually placed on the church altar.

80 Royal Doors, or Beautiful Gate, is the appellation for the central door of iconostasis [i.e. the wooden screen separating the sanctuary from the nave in an Orthodox church].

81 John Chrysostom (349–407 AD) was Archbishop of Constantinople and a major figure among the Fathers of the early church.

82 Metrophanes I was bishop of the city of Byzantium [see note 87] from 306 to 314 AD. Tradition has it that the emperor Constantine made him the first Patriarch of Constantinople. On Metrophanes see Gedeon, *Byzantinon eortologion*, 111.

8. When the Divine Liturgy ended, Christ the Lord headed to the throne where he had been previously seated. And immediately all the Saints bowed before Him saying with one voice: "Oh Lord we, Thy servants, are begging for Thy mercy and for the power of Thy kingdom. Please wrest the Christians and the city from the hands of the irreverent ones." And the Lord replied saying: "I wouldn't free them but I would be eager to keep them in bondage for longer. For they have proved unworthy". So the Saints spoke no more. Then Saint John the Theologian and Saint John Chrysostom bowed before the Lady Theotokos and said: "Our Lady Mother of the Lord we, Thy servants, are begging you to intercede for us to Thy son and our God in order to set the Christians free from the Hagarenes."

9. Rising up from her throne, the Theotokos, and along with her the Cross and all the Saints, bowed before Him saying: "My son, you see your faithful servants, standing in fear and shame before you, begging for the freedom of Christians who are too Thy faithful servants. I am joining them in begging Thy goodness to show mercy and set them free from bondage". Then the Lord said to the Theotokos: "My Mother, please be aware that I wanted to set them free since the time of the most impious Mehmed. However, it is them who have not regretted their sins and remained ungrateful. Therefore, I have allowed the king to issue an order that they have to be dressed only in black[83] as the black [colour] might make them change their mind and repent. However, they remain senseless fuelling my anger every single day." Then again, the Queen of All said: "My son, give them a hard time if you wish. But please don't leave the Hagarenes to disturb them [any longer]." And He replied: "Oh Mother, because of your intercession for the unthankful ones, and thanks to your love and the prayers of my saints, I shall set them free in a little while."

---

83   In the 18th century, both Sultan Osman III (1754–1757) and his successor Mustafa III (1757–1774) issued laws requiring that Ottoman subjects had to wear distinctive clothes or badges according to their respective religion. Generally, clothing laws are regarded as disciplinary actions taken in times of economic and political crisis; see Donald Quataert, "Clothing Laws, State, and Society in the Ottoman Empire, 1720–1829", *International Journal of Middle East Studies* 29/3 (1997), 403–425. See, for example, the imperial edict of 29 May 1761 (No. 2727) from the *Kadi* court archives of Heraklion, Crete. The edict, however, speaks of the obligation of Christians "to put on black fez and headscarf along with the attire that is pertinent to their religion", in contrast to *kyr Daniel*'s all-out dressing in black; see Nikolaos Stavrinidis, *Metafraseis tourkikon istorikon eggrafon aforonton eis tin istorian tis Kritis* [Translations of Turkish Historical Documents Regarding the History of Crete], vol. 5 (Heraklion: 1985), 160–161. See also the somewhat similar edict of 25 August 1762 (No. 2771); Stavrinidis, *Metafraseis*, 195.

10. Then the Lord's Mother and all the Saints prostrated to Him. The Theotokos went to sit on her throne. And the saints made pairs and kneeled before Christ the Lord kissing his kneecap. Last of all, myself and the martyr Anastasius appeared before Him. I, the unworthy, approached Him and said: "Lord, help me." He said to me: "Daniel, you would rather not come out now as you may put yourself in great danger." I said to Him: "Oh Lord, Thy will be done." Then some young men encircled in light came out of the *bema*; the church's roof broke in two and they lifted Christ the Lord up and in this way He ascended to Heaven.

11. Due to the prospect of the liberation of Christians, [the Saints and] those who stood by the Mother of God [i.e. angels?] went very happy. We were let to know that she was expecting us. When we appeared before her I expressed how grateful and, at the same time, how sorry I was. I was grateful for becoming worthy of witnessing the visitation of Our Lady and her Son but, at the same time, I was sorry for not achieving what I was longing for [i.e. martyrdom]. Then she said: "Don't be sorry; should you come out, you would bring about terrors on the Church and on every Christian. Moreover, you wouldn't be spared from their evil-doings.[84] Because these cunning people [i.e. the Muslims] intended to have you locked up in a house with girls so as to defile you. Last year your father was here and wondered what the place of your baptism was; for it had been revealed to him through divination that you had converted to Christianity and become a monk and that you would come to the City [i.e. Constantinople]. He thought you had received baptism in Hungrowallachia[85] hence he expected you to arrive from there. Therefore he sent there a man, who was pretending to be a Christian, to look up for you and, for the same reason, he also left some people here in Constantinople. However, what would be the need for [your] martyrdom? If you observe my Son's commandments you will rejoice over the Kingdom come." Then I said: "My Lady, please know that I also yearned for converting my own parents to the true faith." And she said: "You would rather stop caring about them, for your mother died last year and, thanks to your prayers, she was delivered [from her sins]. As for your father who has done much harm to Christians,

---

84   Sentence translated according to St Anne MS, fol. 709. The meaning of the sentence in Kozani MS, fol. 1098 is unclear.

85   "Hungrowallachia" was the early modern Greek name for the Danubian Principality of Wallachia which, in the latter half of the 19th century, was united with the Principality of Moldavia (referred to respectively in the Greek sources as "Moldowallachia") thus forming modern Romania.

and still does, do not beg for him for he would not have been convinced [to abandon his own religion] even if he had seen the dead coming back to life." Then I said again: "My Lady Theotokos, there is one more favour I will ask from you: please leave me here to light up the oil-lamps and be at your temple's service." She said to me: "Be aware that these oil-lamps have been lit for three hundred years and so will be for a short while more; no man is allowed to stay here so get out immediately. Do not go to Mount Athos as the place is undergoing much turbulence and there is more to come. Go and tell what you have seen to the metropolitan bishop of Ptolemaïs[86] who is my true servant."

12. Then I saw a man entering the church and saying: "Let the Queen know that the king is going to have the prelates and primates executed." Immediately the Theotokos got up from the throne and so did everyone. As we were heading there, the crescent moon symbols were sinking in the sea at her nod. We arrived somewhere within the city of Byzas[87] and we found the prelates and primates with hands tied at the back. Three of the former and two of the latter had already been decapitated. Then the Mother of God nodded at Saint Christopher and he, wresting the sword out of the executioner's hands, cut his head off.[88] Then the ever-Virgin Lady went inside the palace, found the tyrant seated on a throne and said to him: "You most impious and unlawful man, how did you dare to capture and kill the prelates and primates?" He audaciously replied: "Who are you that you come over here and speak so daringly?" And the entourage of Theotokos said: "Godless man, don't you see the Queen of heaven and earth standing before you?" Then Saint Christopher pulled him down from the throne. And the Mother of the Lord sat thereupon and said angrily to him: "What is the reason for which, you unlawful [ruler], have had prelates and primates killed in this bitter way?" And the king said: "I would also be eager to kill the rest of them." And the Theotokos said: "What have they done to you, tyrant?" And the tyrant[89] said to her: "They

---

86 For the metropolitan bishop of Ptolemaïs Sophronius (?–1780) see introduction; see also here note 9.
87 The "city of Byzas" means Constantinople but the exact place of arrival is unspecified. Byzas was the mythological founder of Byzantium, the city built at the very site where Constantinople came later to be founded by Constantine I.
88 According to Christian tradition, Saint Christopher was tall and robust, as his duties in *kyr Daniel*'s recount.
89 The usage of "tyrant" here likely reflects the ideas of the Enlightenment. The Sultan is not only impious and godless because of his religion; he is also tyrannical and unlawful because of his politics. Notably, the text reserves for him the title "king" too, albeit with small "k".

have written [letters] to my enemy to move against me." The Theotokos replied to him: "The case is not they wrote to your enemy, you most impious man. In fact, I shall lead them against you so they will annihilate you along with your people. For I cannot bear any more the utmost injustice and harm you inflict on Christians."

13. Then the Mother of God left and wandered in every room of the palace in the company of Saints. The great Christopher was with them too carrying the throne. Then they met a closed gate which was opened with merely a nod. Therein existed a temple with oil-lamps lit, and three prelates clad in vestments. No sooner had they seen the Theotokos, they bowed before her saying: "We thank you, our Lady Theotokos, Queen of heaven and earth, because you are going to liberate all the humbled Christians." The Saints placed the throne inside the temple, the prelates stayed there, and we all went to the place where the bound-in-chains prelates and primates were kept. By order of the Theotokos, St Christopher unbound everyone. They prostrated themselves before her saying: "We thank you, all-glorious Queen, because you turned us away from the gates of Hades and set us free from the great calamity." And she said to them: "You have become forgetful, hence ungrateful. Am I not the one who has been rescuing this city from great calamities so many times and for so long? Now go in peace and do not be ungrateful to your benefactor any more." Then [Saint John] the Theologian said to the Mother of God: "My Lady Theotokos why have you permitted the unlawful one [the Sultan] to kill these three prelates?" And the Theotokos said to him: "Do you see the prelates lying dead? They have never been true servants of God, neither have they been mine. Therefore, they have not only lost their earthly lives, but they also went away into eternal punishment."

14. Upon leaving the palace, we headed to Hagia Sophia [Church of the Holy Wisdom]. But the Mother of God took the martyr Anastasius by the arm and said: "My child, take Daniel to King Constantine's Church so that he offers veneration to the icons." So the Theotokos and all the Saints went into Hagia Sophia while I and the martyr, after a long walk, reached the church now turned into a mosque.[90] And the gate opened when the

---

90 Both Kozani MS, fol. 1101 and St Anne MS, fol. 710bis use the Greek transliteration of the Turkish term *"metzition"* [Turkish: *mecidiye* or *mecit*] which makes no sense as it means a gold coin minted by Sultan Abdulmejid I (1839–1861). Paschos ("Islam kai neomartyres", 473–474) has therefore corrected the term to *"mestitzion"* [cf. *masjid* in Arabic = mosque] so that it does makes sense in the context. It is uncertain which structure that might actually have been.

martyr made the sign of the venerable Cross. And inside we saw the sacrilegious and wicked priests of the Hagarenes.[91] The martyr seized a club and chased them out. When we entered,[92] we saw an icon of the most holy Theotokos radiant and blazing with light. We venerated the icon and the martyr said: "Do you see this icon? When Christians come to power it is going to perform great miracles, even resurrections of the dead. It is for this reason that a great church shall be erected here." We covered the icon in cloth, then made it out and headed back to my house. The martyr said to me: "now go to church because you will miss the *Orthros*."[93] I insisted, however, that both of us should go and visit the Metropolitan bishop of Ptolemaïs, as Theotokos had ordered. The martyr said to me: "Go there alone and tell him what you have seen; as for me, I am off to my duties." Just as I was pressing him to stay for a while, he said: "The candle is burnt out". Then I opened my eyes and saw the candle nearly burnt to the end of the wick. Praising the name of the Lord, and that of his servant too, I went off to the church and took to reading the psalter.

⁂

[91] Kozani MS, fol. 1102 reads "*ontassimanous kai miareis tōn Hagarinon*" whereas the St Anne MS, fol. 710*bis* reads "*etoimasmenous miareis tōn tes Hagar*". For the term "*ontassimanous*" see note 70 here.

[92] Kozani MS, fol. 1102 merely reads "entered in", yet Anastasius and Daniel were already inside the church turned-into-mosque. Whereas St Anne MS, fol. 710*bis* reads "entered in the holy *bema*" despite the fact the edifice was currently a mosque.

[93] *Orthros* (= daybreak) is the service of the Eastern Orthodox church which is held early in the morning just before the beginning of the Divine Liturgy on Sunday and feast day mornings.

Bibliography

Manuscripts

Istanbul, İstanbul Süleymaniye Kütüphanesi, Ms. Hacı Mahmud Efendi 1657, Yazıcıoğlu Aḥmed Bīcān. el-Münteha.

Istanbul, İstanbul Üniversitesi Nadir Eserler Kütüphanesi, Ms. T. 3263, Mevlānā ʿĪsā, Cāmiʿüʾl-meknūnāt.

Kozani, Kozani Municipal Library, Ms. 34, fols 1091–1102, *Optasia tou kyr Daniel, pany ophelimos* [*The Vision of kyr Daniel, (a story) very beneficial*].

Lisbon, Biblioteca Nacional de Portugal, Codex 4371, Castro, D. João de, *Da Quinta e última Monarquia futura, com muitas outras coisas admiráveis dos nossos tempos* (Paris: 1597).

Lisbon, Biblioteca Nacional de Portugal, Codex 4388, Fundo Geral, Castro, João de, Tratado dos Portugueses de Veneza ou ternário, scenario ou Novenário que em Veneza solicitaram a liberdade d'El Rey Dom Sebastião, 1621–1622.

Lisbon, Biblioteca Nacional de Portugal, Códice 4388, Fundo Geral, Obras de D. João de Castro, "Dos nove Portugueses que procuraram em Veneza pella liberdade d'El Rey Dom Sebastião nosso Senhor'", livro 5, *c*.3.

Lisbon, National Archives "Torre do Tombo", Cód. 774, manuscritos da Livraria.

Lisbon, National Archives "Torre do Tombo", Tribunal do Santo Ofício, Inquisição de Lisboa, Proc. 1664, "Processo de Padre Antônio Vieira" (http://digitarq.arquivos.pt/details?id=2301562).

Madrid, Archivo Histórico Nacional (AHN), Inquisition 2061, Expediente 12, records of the inquisitorial trial against María de la Concepción.

Madrid, Biblioteca Nacional de España (BNE), Ms 5305, ff. 61^r–67^v, Moriscos adaptation of John of Rupescissa's *Vade mecum in tribulation*.

Mount Athos, Skete of Agia Anna Library, Ms 85.4, fols 703–711*bis*, *I thavmasia Optasia in eiden o ex Ismailiton Daniel monachos, en Konstantinoupolei, en etei 1764, Noemvrio 14, o kai ieromonachos isteron genomenos* [*The Splendid Vision seen by Daniel from the Ishmaelites, in Constantinople, in the year 1764, November 14, who subsequently became a monk*].

Paris, Bibliothèque Nationale de France (BnF), Ms 774, ff. 294^r–301^r, Aljamiado rendering of Isidore's *Plaint of Spain*.

Valladolid, Archivo General de Simancas (AGS), Estado, Leg. 1214, doc. 143, Greek prophecies about King Philip II of Spain.

Valladolid, Archivo General de Simancas (AGS), Estado, Leg. 1498, doc. 256, sixteenth century rendition of a prophecy attributed to the Crusader king of Jerusalem Guy de Lusignan (*d*.1194)

Vatican City, Archive of the Congregation for the Doctrine of the Faith (ACDF), Inquisizione di Siena, Processi 57.

Vatican City, Archive of the Congregation for the Doctrine of the Faith (ACDF), Inquisizione di Siena, Lettere speciali 216.

Printed Primary Sources

Anon., "Ad serenissimum principem et invictissumum regem Alfonsum Nicolai Sagundini opratio", in *La caduta di Constantinopoli. L'eco nel mondo*, ed. Agostino Pertusi (Verona: 1976), 129–135.

Anon., *Il trionfo dell'amor diuino nella vita d'vna gran serua di Dio nominata Armella Nicolas passata a miglior vita l'anno del Signore 1671. Fedelmente descritta da vna religiosa del Monasterio di S. Orsola di Vennes della Congregatione di Bordeaux in lingua francese. E trasportata nell'italiana da vn sacerdote secolare distinta in due parti. All'illustriss. e reuerendiss. signore monsignor Petrucci vescovo di Iesi* (Jesi: 1686).

Bandarra, Gonçalo Annes, *Trovas do Bandarra Apuradas e impressas, por ordem de hum grande Senhor de Portugal. Offereçidas aos verdadeiros Portugueses, devotos do Encuberto* (Nantes: 1644).

Besselaar, José van den (ed.), *Antônio Vieira. Profecia e polêmica* (Rio de Janeiro: 2002).

Bocarro Francês, Manuel, *Tratado dos cometas que apareceram em Novembro passado de 1618* (1619; facsimile ed. Lisbon: 2009).

Castro, D. João de, *Discurso da vida do sempre bem vindo, e aparecido Rey Dom Sebastião nosso senhor o Encoberto desde seu nascimento até o presente: feito e dirigido por Dom João de Castro aos três Estados do Reino de Portugal: convém a saber ao da Nobreza, ao da Clerezia e ao do povo* (Paris, 1602). Facsimile edition by Aníbal Pinto de Castro (Lisbon: 1994).

Castro, D. João de, *Paraphrase e Concordância de algumas profecias de Bandarra, sapateiro de Trancoso, por Dom João de Castro* (Paris: 1603). Facsimile edition by José Pereira Sampaio (Bruno) (Porto: 1901).

Castro, João de, *Paraphrase et concordancia de alguas propheçias de Bandarra: çapateiro de Trancoso* (1603; repr. Porto: 1942).

Chuchiak, John F., (ed.), *The Inquisition in New Spain, 1536–1820. A Documentary History* (Baltimore: 2011), 111 [Edict of faith of 8 March 1616].

Ciruelo, Pedro, *Tratado de reprobación de supersticiones y hechizerías* (Alcalá de Henares: 1530).

Ciruelo, Pedro, *Tratado en el qual se repruevan todas las supersticiones y hechizerías* (Barcelona: 1628).

Colleção das leys, decretos y alvarás, que comprehende o feliz reinado Del. Rey Fidelissimo D. Jozé o I, t. II (Lisbon: 1770).

Dryer, Abigail and Kagan, Richard. *Inquisitorial Inquiries. Brief Lives of Secret Jews and Other Heretics* (Baltimore: 2011).

Floristán Imízcoz, José Manuel, *Fuentes para la política oriental de los Austrias: la documentación griega del Archivo de Simancas (1571–1621)* (León: 1988).

Gagliardi, Achille s.j., *Breve Compendio intorno alla Perfezione Cristiana. Dove si vede una pratica mirabile per unire l'anima con Dio. Del Padre Achille Gagliardi [...]. Aggiuntovi l'altra parte con le sue Meditazioni* (Siena: 1644).

Gallonio, Antonio, *Vita beati p. Philippi Neri Florentini Congregatione Oratorio fondatoris in annos digesta* [...] (Rome: 1600).

Gallonio, Antonio, *Vita del beato P. Filippo Neri fiorentino fondatore della Congregazione dell'Oratorio, scritta, e ordinata per anni da Antonio Gallonio romano sacerdote della medesima congregatione* (Rome: 1600).

Horozco y Covarrubias, Juan, *Tratado de la verdadera y falsa prophecia* (Segovia: 1588).

Ignatius of Loyola, *The Spiritual Exercises and Selected Works*, ed. George E. Ganss, s.j. (New York-Mahwah: 1991).

[Jeanne de la Nativité], *Le Triomphe de l'amour divin dans la vie d'une grande servante de Dieu nommée Armelle Nicolas, décédée l'an de Nôtre-Seigneur 1671, fidèlement écrite par une religieuse du monastère de Sainte-Ursule de Vennes, de la Congrégation de Bordeaux* [...] (Vennes: 1676).

Juan de la Cruz, *Opere spirituali che conducono l'anima alla perfetta vnione con Dio, composte dal ven. P.F. Giouanni della Croce primo Scalzo della riforma del Carmine,* [...] *con vn breue sommario della vita dell'autore,* [...] *Tradotte dalla spagnuola in questa nostra lingua italiana dal P. Fr. Alessandro di S. Francesco definitore generale della congregazione d'Italia de' medesimi Scalzi* (Rome: 1627).

Lambros, Spyridon (ed.), *Anonymi Monodia de capta Constantinopoli*, Neos Ellinomnimon 5 (1908), 242–247.

Lambros, Spyridon, *Catalogue of the Greek manuscripts on Mount Athos*, 2 vols. (Cambridge: 1900).

Liberati, Alfredo, "Chiese, monasteri, oratori e spedali senesi. Chiesa e conservatorio di San Raimondo detto del Refugio", *Bullettino senese di storia patria* 56 (1949), 152–153.

Lucena, João de, *História da Vida do Padre Francisco de Xavier*, 2 vols. (1600; facsimile ed. Lisbon: 1952).

Marabotto, Cattaneo, *Vita della beata Caterina Adorni da Genova. Con un dialogo diviso in dua capitoli, tra l'Anima, il Corpo, l'humanità, l'Amor proprio, & il Signore, composto dalla medesima* [...] (Venice: 1590)

Mármol Carvajal, Luis del., *Historia del rebelión y castigo de los moriscos del reino de Granada*, ed. Javier Castillo Fernández (Granada: 2015).

Mello, Homem de, *Resorreiçam de Portugal e Morte fatal de Castella* (Nantes: 1650).

Menezes, Luiz de (Conde da Ericeira), *História de Portugal Restaurado*, vol. 2 (Lisbon: 1751).

Migne, Jacques Paul (ed.), *Imperatoris Leonis cognomine sapientis: Oracula cum figuris et antiqua Graeca paraphrase*, in *Patrologia Graeca*, vol. 107 (Paris: 1857–1891), 1122–1167.

Molinos, Miguel de, *Guia espiritual que desembaraza al alma, y la conduce por el interior camino, para alcanzar la perfecta contemplacion, y el rico tesoro de la interior paz* (Rome: 1675)

Molinos, Miguel de, *Guía Espiritual: Edición critica, introducción y notas*, ed. José Ignacio Tellechea Idígoras (Madrid: 1976).

Molinos, Miguel de, *Guida spirituale che disinvolge l'anima, e la conduce per l'interior camino all'acquisto della perfetta contemplatione, e del ricco tesoro della pace interiore* [...] (Rome: 1675).

Molinos, Miguel de, *The Spiritual Guide*, ed. and trans. Robert P. Baird (New York—Mahwah, NJ: 2010).

Monfasani, John (ed.), *Collectanea Trapezuntiana: Texts, Documents, and Bibliographies of George of Trebizond* (Binghamton, N.Y.: 1984).

Monzón, Francisco, *Avisos Spirituales que enseñan cómo el sueño corporal sea provechoso al espíritu* (Lisbon: 1563).

Muhana, Adma Fadul (ed.), *Os Autos do processo de Vieira na Inquisição: 1660–1668* (São Paulo: 2008).

Nieremberg, Juan Eusebio S.J., *Dell'adoratione in ispirito, e verità cioè dello spirito vero con cui nella legge di gratia si deve seruire à Dio. Opera del padre Gio: Eusebio Nierembergh* [...] (Venice: 1671).

Panigarola, Francesco, *Dichiaratione de i salmi di David, fatta dal R. P. F. Francesco Panigarola, minore osservante* [...] (Venice: 1586).

Paschos, Pantelis, "Islam kai neomartyres. O ek Paramythias neomartis Anastasios kai o ismailitis [Mousa] Daniel o omologitis" [Islam and New Martyrs. The New Martyr Anastasius from Paramythià and the Ishmaelite [Mousa] Daniel the Confessor], *Epistimoniki Epetiris tis Theologikis Scholis Panepistimiou Athinon* 30 (1995), 413–474.

Pierre de Poitiers, *Il giorno mistico overo Dilucidatione dell'oratione e teologia mistica composto in lingua francese dal M.R.P. Pietro da Poitiers predicatore,* [...] *tradotto nell'idioma italiano da fra Serafino da Borgogna,* [...] *dedicato all'eminentissimo, e reurendissimo signor cardinale Paluzzo Altieri* [...] (Rome: 1675).

Pierre de Poitiers, *Le jour mystique, ou l'éclaircissement de l'oraison ou théologie mystique* [...] (Paris: 1671)

Pomi, Giovan Francesco, *L' aiuto de' moribondi opera utile, e necessaria per consolare i poveri infermi, & aiutarli nel tempo della morte.* [...] *Dal padre d. Gio. Francesco Pomi canon. Reg. del Salvatore* (Siena: 1656).

Quiroga, José de Jesús María O.C.D., *Salita dell'anima a' Dio. Che aspira alla diuina vnione. Opera del m. reu. p.f. Gioseffo di Giesù Maria* [...]. *Tradotta dalla spagnuola nella lingua italiana dal p.f. Baldassaro di Santa Catarina di Siena* (Rome: 1664).

Regio, Alessandro, *Clavis aurea, qua aperiuntur errores Michaelis de Molinos in eius libro cui titulus est La guida spirituale* (Venice: 1681).

Río, Martín del, *La magia demoníaca* (libro II de las *Disquisiciones mágicas*) (Leuven: 1599).

Rodrigues Lobo, Francisco, *Corte na Aldeia*, ed. José Adriano da Fonseca (Lisbon: 1991).

Rodríguez, Alonso, *Esercitio di perfettione e di virtu christiane. Composto dal Reu. Padre Alfonso Rodriguez ... della Compagnia di Giesù. Diuiso in tre parti. Diretto a' Religiosi della medesima Compagnia, e ad ognuno, che desideri* [...] (Venice: 1686).

Rodríguez, Alonso, *Exercitio de perfeccion y virtudes cristianas* [...] (Sevilla: 1609).

Sánchez Álvarez, Mercedes, *El manuscrito misceláneo 774 de la Biblioteca Nacional de París: Leyendas, itinerarios de viajes, profecías sobre la destrucción de España y otros relatos moriscos* (Madrid: 1982).

Scupoli, Lorenzo, *Combattimento spirituale. Dal M.R.P.D. Lorenzo Scupoli chierico regolare per l'acquisto della Christiana Perfettione* [...] (Bologna: 1653).

Segneri, Paolo (pseud. Francesco Buonavalle), *Lettera di risposta al sig. Ignatio Bartalini sopra le eccettioni che dà un direttore de moderni quietisti* (Venice: 1681).

Segneri, Paolo, *Concordia tra la fatica e la quiete nell'oratione* (Florence: 1680).

Silva, José Seabra da, *Deducção Chronologica e Analytica*, 4 vols (Lisbon: 1768).

Stavrinidis, Nikolaos, *Metafraseis tourkikon istorikon eggrafon aforonton eis tin istorian tis Kritis* [Translations of Turkish Historical Documents Regarding the History of Crete], vol. 5 (Heraklion: 1985).

Teixeira, José, *The Strangest Adventvre That Ever Happened: Either in the ages passed or present. Containing a discourse concerning the successe of the King of Portugall Dom Sebastian* (London: 1601).

Teixeira, José, *The True Historie of the Late and Lamentable Adventures of Don Sebastian King of Portugall* (London: 1602).

Vasconcelos, João de, *Restauração de Portugal prodigiosa*, 2 vols. (Lisbon: 1643–1644)

Vereecken, Jeannine and Hadermann-Misguich, Lydie (eds), *Les Oracles de Léon le Sage illustrés par Georges Klontzas. La version Barozzi dans le codex Bute* (Venice: 2000).

Vieira, António, *António Vieira: Six Sermons*, ed. and trans. Mónica Leal da Silva and Liam Brockey (Oxford: 2018).

Vieira, Antônio, *Defesa perante o tribunal do Santo Ofício*, 2 vols (Salvador, Brazil: 1957).

Vieira, António, *Livro anteprimeiro da História do Futuro*, ed. José van den Besselaar (Lisbon: 1983)

Vieira, António, *Obra completa*, 30 vols (Lisbon: 2013).

Vieira, António, *The Sermon of Saint Anthony to the Fish and Other Texts*, trans. Gregory Rabassa (Dartmouth: 2009), 77–106.

Vieira, Antonio. *Sermoens do P. Antonio Vieira da Companhia de Jesu*, 15 vols (Lisbon: 1679–1748).

West, Delno C. (ed. and trans.), *The Libro de las profecías of Christopher Columbus* (Gainesville: 1991).

Secondary Sources

Art. "legua", in *Diccionario de la lengua española de la Real Academia Española* (http://dle.rae.es/?id=N5P0XDE, accessed on 2 September, 2018).

Art. "secreto", in *Diccionario de la lengua española de la Real Academia Española* (http://dle.rae.es/?id=XPKxnKN|XPMvDJ8|XPNR6xt, accessed on 6 January 2018).

Ahlgren, Gillian T.W., *The Inquisition of Francisca: A Sixteenth-Century Visionary on Trial* (Chicago: 2005).

Albuquerque, Martim de, O valor politológico do sebastianismo, *Estudos de Cultura Portuguesa*, vol. 2 (Lisbon: 2000).

Alden, Dauril, "Some Reflections on Antonio Vieira: Seventeenth-Century Troubleshooter and Troublemaker", *Luso-Brazilian Review* 40/1 (Summer 2003), 7–16.

Alden, Dauril, *The Making of an Enterprise. The Society of Jesus in Portugal, its Empire, and Beyond, 1540–1750* (Stanford: 1996).

Alencastro, Luiz Felipe de, *O Trato dos Viventes* (São Paulo: 2000).

Amir-Moezzi, Mohammad Ali, *The Divine Guide in Early Shi'ism: The Sources of Esotericism in Islam*, trans. David Streight (Albany, N.Y.: 1994).

Amirav, Hagit, "John Chrysostom", in *Encyclopedia of the Bible and its Reception (EBR) online*, vol. 5, ed. Dale C. Allison Jr. [and others], 263–267 (accessed on 2 January 2018).

Anderson, James M., *Daily Life During the Spanish Inquisition* (Westport: 2002).

Angelidi, Christina, "La version longue de la vision du moine Cosmas", *Analecta Bollandiana* 101 (1983), 73–99.

Aram, Bethany, "La reina Juana entre Trastámara y Austrias", in *Gobernar en tiempos de crisis: las quiebras dinásticas en el ámbito hispánico (1250–1808)*, ed. José Manuel Nieto Soria and María Victoria López-Cordón (Madrid: 2008), 31–44.

Argenziano, Raffaele, La beata nobiltà, in *I Libri dei Leoni. La nobiltà di Siena in età medicea (1557–1737)*, ed. Mario Ascheri (Siena: 1996), 285–328.

Argyriou, Asterios, *Les Exégèses grecques de l'apocalypse à l'époque turque (1453–1821). Esquisse d'une histoire des courants idéologiques au sein du peuple grec asservi* (Thessaloniki: 1982).

Atienza López, Ángela, "De beaterios a conventos. Nuevas perspectivas sobre el mundo de las beatas en la España moderna", *Historia social* 57 (2007), 145–168.

Azevedo, João Lúcio de, *A Evolução do Sebastianismo* (1918; repr. Lisbon: 1984).

Azevedo, João Lúcio de, *História de António Vieira*, 2 vols (1918; repr. Lisbon: 1992).

Baer, Marc David, *The Dönme: Jewish Converts, Muslim Revolutionaries, and Secular Turks* (Stanford: 2010).

Baghos, Mario, "Theotokoupoleis: The Mother of God as Protectress of the Two Romes", in *Mariology at the Beginning of the Third Millennium*, ed. Kevin Wagner et al. (Eugene, Ore.: 2017), 55–77.

Bähr, Andreas, "Furcht, divinatorischer Traum und autobiographisches Schreiben in der Frühen Neuzeit", *Zeitschrift für Historische Forschung* 34/1 (2007), 1–32.

Barbeito Carneiro, María Isabel (ed.), *Cárceles y mujeres en el siglo XVII. Razón y forma de la Galera. Proceso Inquisitorial de San Plácido* (Biblioteca de escritoras 21) (Madrid: 1991).

Barni, Paola, *Un secolo di fortuna editoriale: Il Combattimento Spirituale di Lorenzo Scupoli, 1589–1700*, in *La lettera e il torchio. Studi sulla produzione libraria tra XVI e XVIII secolo*, ed. Ugo Rozzo (Udine: 2001), 249–336.

Bauer, Martin, "Johannes Charlier Gerson", in *Lexikon für Theologie und Kirche*, vol. 5, 909–910.

Bennassar, Bartolomé, *L'Inquisition espagnole. XVe–XIXe siècles* (Paris: 2001).

Bercé, Yves-Marie, *Le roi caché. Sauveurs et imposteurs. Mythes politiques populaires dans l'Europe moderne* (Paris: 1990).

Bergamo, Mino, *La scienza dei santi. Studi sul misticismo del Seicento* (Florence: 1984).

Besselaar, José van den, "A Profecia Apocalíptica de Pseudo-Metódio", *Luso-Brazilian Review*, 28/1 (Summer 1991), 5–22

Besselaar, José van den, *Sebastianismo—uma história sumária* (Lisbon: 1987).

Bethencourt, Francisco, *L'inquisition à l'époque moderne: Espagne, Italie, Portugal XVe–XIX siécle* (Paris: 1995).

Bilinkoff, Jodi, *Related Lives. Confessors and Their Female Penitents, 1450–1750* (Ithaca, N.Y.: 2005).

Binbaş, Evrim, "The Jalayirid Hidden King and the Unbelief of Shāh Mohammad Qaraqoyunlu", *Journal of Persianate Studies* (forthcoming, Winter 2020).

Bisaha, Nancy, "Pius II's *letter to Mehmed II*. A reexamination", *Crusades* 1 (2002), 183–200.

Bom Meihy, José Carlos Sebe, "A ética colonial e a questão jesuítica dos cativeiros índio e negro", *Afro-Asia* 23 (2000), 9–27.

Boone, Rebecca Ard., *Mercurino di Gattinara and the Creation of the Spanish Empire* (London: 2014).

Bottereau, Georges and Rayez, Andrè, *Indifférence*, in *Dictionnaire de spiritualité*, vol. 5 (Paris: 1971), 1696–1708.

Bovis, André de and Van Dijk, Willibrord-Christian, *Offrande*, in *Dictionnaire de Spiritualité*, vol. 11 (Paris: 1982), 720–733.

Boxer, Charles R., *A Great Luso-Brazilian Figure: Padre Antonio Vieira, S. J., 1608–1697* (London: 1957).

Brandão, Mário, *Coimbra e D. Antônio Rei de Portugal. Documentos de 1582 a 1598* (Coimbra: 1947).

Brown, William P., "Ecclesiastes, Book of, I. Hebrew Bible/Old Testament", in *Encyclopedia of the Bible and its Reception (EBR) online*, vol. 7, ed. Hans-Josef Klauck (and others), 274–278 [accessed on 2 January 2018].

Bruess, Gregory, *Religion, Identity and Empire: A Greek Archbishop in the Russia of Catherine the Great* (New York: 1997).

Buescu, Ana Isabel, "Vínculos da Memória: Ourique e a fundação do reino", in *Portugal: Mitos revisitados*, ed. Yvette Kace Centeno (Lisbon: 1993), 11–50.

Bynum, Caroline Walker, *Holy Feast and Holy Fast. The Religious Significance of Food to Medieval Women* (Berkeley—Los Angeles—London: 1988)

Bynum, Caroline Walker, *Jesus as Mother. Studies in the Spirituality of the High Middle Ages* (Berkeley—Los Angeles—London: 1984).

Caetano, Antonio Filipe Pereira, "'Para aumentar e conservar aquelas partes …': Conflitos dos projetos luso-americanos para uma conquista colonial (Estado do Maranhão e Grão-Pará, séculos XVII–XVIII)", *Revista Estudos Amazônicos* VI/1 (2011), 1–20.

Camenietzki, Carlos Ziller, "O Cometa, o Pregador e o Cientista: Antônio Vieira e Valentim Stansel observam o céu da Bahia no século XVII", *Revista da Sociedade Brasileira de História da Ciência* 14 (1995), 37–52.

Campagne, Fabián Alejandro, "Witchcraft and the Sense-of-the-Impossible in Early Modern Spain: Some reflections based on the literature of superstition (ca. 1500–1800)", *The Harvard Theological Review* 96/1 (2003), 25–62.

Capizzi, Carmelo, "Anastasio I., byz. Kaiser (491–518)", in *Lexikon für Theologie und Kirche*, vol. 1, 600–601.

Caro Baroja, Julio, *Vidas Mágicas e Inquisición*, 2nd ed., 2 vols (Madrid: 1992).

Carolino, Luís Miguel, *Ciência, Astrologia e Sociedade. A teoria da Influência Celeste em Portugal (1593–1755)* (Lisbon: 2003).

Castro, José de, *O Prior do Crato* (Lisbon: 1942).

Cavicchioli, Curzio and Stroppa, Sabrina (eds), *Mistica e poesia. Il cardinale Pier Matteo Petrucci (Jesi 1616-Montefalco 1701)* (Milan-Genoa: 2006).

Cerrillo Cruz, Gonzalo, *Los familiares de la inquisición española* (Estudios de Historia) (Valladolid: 2000).

Ceyssens, Lucien, *Le Cardinal François Albizzi (1593–1684). Un cas important dans l'histoire du jansènisme* (Rome: 1977).

Chambouleyron, Rafael, "'Ásperas proposições': Jesuítas; moradores e a Inquisição na Amazônia seiscentista no tempo de Vieira, missionário", *Revista Lusófona de Ciência das Religiões* 13–14 (2013), 94–96.

Chambouleyron, Rafael, "Indian Freedom and Indian Slavery in the Portuguese Amazon (1640–1755)", in *Building the Atlantic Empires: Unfree Labor and Imperial States in the Political Economy of Capitalism, ca. 1500–1914*, ed. John Donoghue and Evelyn P. Jennings (Leiden: 2016), 54–71.

Chambouleyron, Rafael, "Uma missão 'tão encontrada dos interesses humanos'. Jesuítas e portugueses na Amazônia seiscentista", in *Vieira. Vida e Palavra*, ed. Silvia Azevedo and Vanessa Ribeiro (São Paulo: 2008), 29–53.

Chandler, Richard, *Travels in Greece: Or an Account of a Tour made at the Expense of the Society of Dilettanti* (Oxford: 1776).
Christian, William A. *Apparitions in Late Medieval and Renaissance Spain* (Princeton: 1989).
Coelho, Geraldo Mártires, "A pátria do Anticristo: A expulsão dos jesuítas do Maranhão e Grão-Pará e o messianismo milenarista de Vieira", *Luso-Brazilian Review* 37/1 (2000), 17–32.
Cohen, Thomas, "Millenarian Themes in the Writings of Antonio Vieira", *Luso-Brazilian Review* 28/1 (Summer 1991), 23–46.
Cohen, Thomas, *The Fire of Tongues. António Vieira and the Missionary Church in Brazil and Portugal* (Stanford: 1998).
Contreras, Jaime, *Historia de la Inquisición española (1478–1834)* (Madrid: 1997).
Corey, Stephen, *Reviving the Islamic Caliphate in Early Modern Morocco* (Farnham: 2013).
Costigan, Lúcia Helena, "Judeus e Cristãos-Novos nos escritos de letrados do Barroco espanhol e de Antônio Vieira e Menasseh Ben Israel", in *Diálogos da Conversão*, (Campinas: 2005), 123–154.
Crome, Andrew (ed.), *Prophecy and Eschatology in the Transatlantic World, 1550–1800* (London: 2016).
Cruz, Maria do Rosário de S.T.B. de Azevedo, *As regências na menoridade de D. Sebastião. Elementos para uma história estrutural*, 2 vols (Lisbon: 1992).
Cuadro García, Ana Cristina, "Tejiendo una vida de reliquia. Estrategias de control de conciencias de la santa diabólica Magdalena de la Cruz", *Chronica Nova* 31 (2005), 307–326.
Cunha, Mafalda Soares da, A questão jurídica na crise dinástica in José Mattoso (ed.), *História de Portugal*, vol. 3: No alvorecer da modernidade (1480–1620) (Lisbon: 1993–1994).
D'Addario, Arnaldo, *Aspetti della Controriforma a Firenze* (Rome: 1972).
D'Antas, Miguel, *Os falsos D.Sebastião*, 2nd ed. (Odivelas: 1988).
Deines, Roland, "Josephus, Flavius", in *Calwer Bibellexikon*, vol. 1, ed. Otto Betz, Beate Ego and Werner Grimm, 2nd ed. (Stuttgart: 2006), 689.
DeVun, Leah. *Prophecy, Alchemy, and the End of Time: John of Rupescissa in the late Middle Ages* (New York: 2009).
Di Simplicio, Oscar (ed.), *Le Lettere della Congregazione del Sant'Ufficio all'Inquisitore di Siena 1581–1721* (Rome: 2009).
Domínguez Ortíz, Antonio, *La Sevilla del siglo XVII* (Historia de Sevilla), 3rd ed. (Seville: 1986).
Donnelly, John Patrick s.J., "Alonso Rodriguez 'Ejercicio': a neglected classic", *Sixteenth Century Journal* 11/2, (Summer 1980), 16–24.
Dooley, Brendan M. (ed.), *Italy in the Baroque: Selected Readings* (New York—London: 1995).

Downey, Glanville, "The Church of All Saints (Church of St. Theophano) near the Church of the Holy Apostles at Constantinople", *Dumbarton Oaks Papers* 9/10 (1956), 301–305.

Dudon, Paul S.J., *Le Quiétiste Espagnol Michel Molinos (1628–1696)* (Paris: 1921).

Dupuy, Michel, *Présence de Dieu*, in *Dictionnaire de Spiritualité*, XII/2 (Paris: 1986), 2107–2136.

Edwards, Walter Manoel, Robert Browning, Graham Anderson and Ewen Bowie, "Philostrati", in *The Oxford Classical Dictionary*, ed. Simon Hornblower and Antony Spawforth, 4th ed. (Oxford: 2012), 1137.

Eisenberg, José, "António Vieira and the Justification of Indian Slavery", *Luso-Brazilian Review* 40/1 (2003), 91–92.

El Alaoui, Youssef, "Carlos V y el mito de la cruzada contra el islam", in *Autour de Charles Quint et son empire*, ed. Augustin Redondo (Paris: 2005), 113–130.

Elliott, John Huxtable, *Imperial Spain 1469–1716* (London: 1969).

Emmerson, Richard K., "Apocalyptic Themes and Imagery in Medieval and Renaissance Literature", in *The Encyclopedia of Apocalypticism, vol. 2: Apocalypticism in Western History and Culture*, ed. Bernard McGinn (New York/London: 2000), 402–441.

Enrique del Sdo. Corazon O.C.D., "Notas del Proceso Inquisitorial contra la Subida del Alma a Dios del P. José de Jesús María (Quiroga), O.C.D.", *Revista de Espiridualidad*, vol. 14 (1955), 76–82.

Falbel, Nachman, "Menasseh Ben Israel e o Brasil", in *Judeus no Brasil* (São Paulo: 2008), 121–133.

Farquhar Chilver, Guy Edward and Barbara Levick, "Vespasian (Titus Flavius Vespasian)", in *The Oxford Classical Dictionary*, ed. Simon Hornblower and Antony Spawforth, 4th ed. (Oxford: 2012), 1543–1544.

Ferguson, Everett, "Apollonius of Tyana (d. ca. 96–98 A.D.)", in *Encyclopedia of Early Christianity*, vol. 1, 81.

Fernández Luzón, Antonio, "Profecía y transgresión social. El caso de Lucrecia de León", *Historia Social* 38 (2000), 3–15.

Figueiredo, Luciano Raposo de Almeida, "Brazilian Machiavellians: dissimulation, political ideas, and colonial rebellions (Portugal, 17th–18th century)", *Tempo* 20 (2014), 1–24.

Fleischer, Cornell H., "A Mediterranean Apocalypse: Prophecies of Empire in the Fifteenth and Sixteenth Centuries", in "Speaking the End Times: Prophecy and Messianism in Early Modern Eurasia", ed. Mayte Green-Mercado, *JESHO—Journal of the Economic and Social History of the Orient* 61 (2018), 18–90.

Fleischer, Cornell H., "The Lawgiver as Messiah: The Making of the Imperial Image in the Reign of Süleymân", in *Soliman le Magnifique et son temps*, ed. Gilles Veinstein (Paris: 1992), 159–177.

Fleischer, Cornell H., "The Lawgiver as Messiah: The Making of the Imperial Image in the Reign of Süleymân", in *Soliman le Magnifique et son temps*, ed. Gilles Veinstein (Paris: 1992), 159–177.

Flemming, Barbara, "Public Opinion under Sultan Süleymān", in *Süleymān the Second [i.e. the First] and His Time*, ed. Halil İnalcık and Cemal Kafadar (Istanbul: 1993), 49–57.

Flemming, Barbara, "The Cāmi'ül-meknūnāt: A Source of 'Ālī from the Time of Sultan Süleymān", in *Essays on Turkish Literature and History*, trans. John O'Kane (Leiden: 2018), 169–182.

Flores, Luiz Felipe Baêta Neves (ed.), *Padre Antônio Vieira. Catálogo da Biblioteca Nacional* (Rio de Janeiro: 1999).

Floristán Imízcoz, José Manuel, "Felipe II y la empresa de Grecia tras Lepanto (1571–78)" *Erytheia: Revista de estudios bizantinos y neogriegos* 15 (1994), 155–190.

França, Eduardo D'Oliveira, *Portugal na Época da Restauração* (1951; repr. São Paulo: 1997).

Franco, José Eduardo, and Reis, Bruno Cardoso, *Vieira na Literatura Anti-Jesuítica* (Lisboa: 1997).

Frendo, Joseph David, "Agathias, gen. Scholastikos", in *Lexikon für Theologie und Kirche*, vol. 1, ed. Walter Kasper [and others] (Freiburg im Breisgau: 1993), 226–227.

Frohnapfel-Leis, Monika, "An enchantress, a saint and a prophetess. How religious deviance is described in Spanish Inquisition trials", in *Recounting Deviance. Forms and Practices of Presenting Divergent Behaviour in the Late Middle Ages and Early Modern Period*, ed. Jörg Rogge (Mainz Historical Cultural Sciences 34), (Bielefeld: 2016), 77–95.

Gafni, Isaiah, "Theudas", in *Encyclopaedia Judaica*, vol. 19, ed. Fred Skolnik and Michael Berenbaum, 2nd ed. (Detroit: 2007), 703–704.

Gantet, Claire, "Zwischen Wunder, Aberglaube und Fiktion. Der Traum als politisches Medium in Frankreich, 1560–1620", in *Traum und res publica. Traumkulturen und Deutungen sozialer Wirklichkeiten im Europa von Renaissance und Barock*, ed. Peer Schmidt and Gregor Weber (Berlin: 2008), 307–326.

García Cárcel, Ricardo and Doris Moreno Martínez, *Inquisición. Historia crítica* (Madrid: 2000).

García-Arenal, Mercedes, *Ahmad al-Mansur: The Beginnings of Modern Morocco* (Oxford: 2009).

Gedeon, Manouil, *Byzantinon eortologion. Mnimai ton apo tou 4ou mechri meson tou 15ou aionos eortazomenon agion en Konstantinoupolei* [Byzantine Calendar of Saints. Feast Days of Saints in Constantinople from the 4th to the 15th century] (Constantinople: 1897).

Giles, Mary E. (ed.), *Women and the Inquisition. Spain and the New World* (Baltimore: 1999).

Goldish, Matt, *The Sabbatean Prophets* (Cambridge, MA.: 2004).
Gomes, Plinio Freire, *Um herege vai ao Paraíso. Cosmologia de um ex-colono condenado pela Inquisição (1680–1744)* (São Paulo: 1997).
Green-Mercado, Mayte, "Morisco Prophecies at the French Court (1602–1607)", *Journal of the Economic and Social History of the Orient (JESHO)* 61 (2018), 91–123.
Green-Mercado, Mayte, "The Mahdi in Valencia: Messianism, Apocalypticism, and Morisco Rebellions in Late Sixteenth-Century Spain", *Medieval Encounters* 19 (2013), 193–220.
Green-Mercado, Mayte, *Visions of Deliverance. Moriscos and the Politics of Prophecy in the Early Modern Mediterranean* (Ithaca, N.Y.: forthcoming).
Greene, Molly, "The Early Modern Mediterranean", in *A Companion to Mediterranean History*, ed. Peregrine Horden and Sharon Kinoshita (Hoboken, N.J.: 2014), 91–106.
Gril, Denis, "L'Enigme de la Šağara al-Nuʿmāniyya fī l'Dawla al-ʿUthmāniyya, atribuee a Ibn ʿArabī", in *Les traditions apocalyptiques au tournant de la chute de Constantinople*, ed. Benjamin Lellouch and Stéphane Yerasimos (Paris: 2000), 51–71.
Grimm, Werner, "Jona", in *Calwer Bibellexikon*, ed. Otto Betz, Beate Ego and Werner Grimm, 2nd ed., vol. 1 (Stuttgart: 2006), 682.
Guadalajara Medina, José, *Las profecías del anticristo en la edad media* (Madrid: 1996).
Guran, Petre, "Historical Prophecies From Late Antique Apocalypticism To Secular Eschatology", *Revue des études sud-est européennes* 52 (2014), 47–62.
Gutierrez Cuadrado, Juan, "Covarrubias y Horozco, Sebastián", in *Diccionario de Literatura Española e Hispanoamericana*, ed. Ricardo Gullón, vol. 1 (Madrid: 1993), 389.
Hansen, João Adolfo, "Educando Príncipes no Espelho", *Floema* II:2 (2006), 133–169.
Hansen, João Adolfo, "Prefácio. A Chave dos Profetas: Deus, Analogia, Tempo", in António Vieira, *Obra completa*, t. V, vol. 1 (Lisboa: 2013), 11–56.
Hansen, João Adolfo, "Razão de Estado" (1996), *Artepensamento: ensaios filosóficos e políticos* (https://artepensamento.com.br/item/razao-de-estado/, accessed on 12 December 2018).
Hansen, João Adolfo, *A Sátira e o Engenho: Gregório de Matos e a Bahia do século XVII* (São Paulo: 2004).
Harries, Jill, "Sozomen (Salamanes Hermeias Sozomenus)", in *The Oxford Classical Dictionary*, 1387.
Hatzopoulos, Marios, "Eighteenth-Century Greek Prophetic Literature", in David Thomas & John Chesworth (eds), Christian-Muslim Relations. *A Bibliographical History, Volume 14 Central and Eastern Europe (1700–1800)*, (Leiden: 2020), 382–402.
Hatzopoulos, Marios, "From Resurrection to Insurrection: 'Sacred' Myths, Motifs, and Symbols in the Greek War of Independence", in *The Making of Modern Greece: Nationalism, Romanticism and the Uses of the Past (1797–1896)*, ed. Roderick Beaton and David Ricks (London: 2009), 81–93.

Hatzopoulos, Marios, "Oracular Prophecy and the Politics of Toppling Ottoman Rule in South-East Europe", *The Historical Review/La Revue Historique* 8 (2011), 95–116.

Hatzopoulos, Marios, "Prophetic Structures of the Ottoman-ruled Orthodox Community in Comparative Perspective: Some Preliminary Observations", in *Greek-Serbian Relations in the Age of Nation-Building*, ed. Paschalis Kitromilides and Sophia Matthaiou (Athens: 2016), 121–147.

Hatzopoulos, Marios, *Ancient Prophecies, Modern Predictions: Myths and Symbols of Greek Nationalism*, unpublished PhD thesis (London: 2005).

Haven, Alexander van der, *From Lowly Metaphor to Divine Flesh: Sarah the Ashkenazi, Sabbatai Tsevi's Messianic Queen and the Sabbatian Movement*, Menasseh ben Israel Instituut Studies 7 (Amsterdam: 2012).

Heid, Stefan, "Justinos, Martyrer", in *Lexikon für Theologie und Kirche*, vol. 5, ed. Walter Kasper [and others] (Freiburg im Breisgau: 1996), 1112–1113.

Henningsen, Gustav, *The Witches' Advocate. Basque Witchcraft and the Spanish Inquisition (1609–1614)* (Reno: 1980).

Hermann, Jacqueline, "An Undesired King: Notes on the Political Career of D. Antônio, Prior do Crato", *Revista Brasileira de História* 30/59 (São Paulo, 2010).

Hermann, Jacqueline, "Politics and Diplomacy in the Portuguese Succession Crisis: The Candidacy of D. Antônio, Prior of Crato (1578–1580)", *Giornale di Storia* 2014 (www.giornaledistoria.net).

Hermann, Jacqueline, "Um papa entre dois casamentos: Gregório XIII e a sucessão portuguesa (1578–1580)", *Portuguese Studies Review* 2015.

Hermann, Jacqueline, *No reino do Desejado*. A construção do sebastianismo em Portugal, séculos XVI e XVII (São Paulo: 1998).

Houdard, Sophie; Malena, Adelisa; Roscioni, Lisa; von Tippelskirch, Xenia (eds), MELANCHOLIA/Æ. The religious experience of the "disease of the soul" and its definitions / *MELANCHOLIA/Æ. L'expérience religieuse de la « maladie de l'âme » et ses définitions*, of *Etudes Epistémè. Revue de littérature et de civilisation (XVIe–XVIIIe siècles)* 28 (2015), online (https://journals.openedition.org/episteme/742).

Jordán Arroyo, María, "Francisco Monzón y 'el buen dormir': La interpretación teológica de los sueños en la España del siglo XVI", *Cuadernos de Historia Moderna* 26 (2001), 169–184.

Jordán, María V., *Soñar la Historia. Riesgo, creatividad y religión en las profecías de Lucrecia de León* (Madrid: 2007).

Kadir, Djelal, *Columbus and the Ends of the Earth. Europe's Prophetic Rhetoric as Conquering Ideology* (Berkley: 1992).

Kagan, Richard, *Lucrecia's Dreams Politics and Prophecy in Sixteenth-Century Spain* (Baltimore: 1990).

Kaldellis, Anthony, "'A Union of Opposites': The Moral Logic and Corporeal Presence of the Theotokos on the Field of Battle", in *Pour l'amour de Byzance: Hom-*

mage à Paolo Odorico, ed. Christian Gastgeber et al. (Frankfurt am Main: 2013), 131–144.

Kaldellis, Anthony, "The Military Use of the Icon of the Theotokos and its Moral Logic in the Historians of the Ninth-Twelfth Centuries", *Estudios bizantinos: Revista de la Sociedad Española de Bizantinística* 1 (2013), 56–75.

Kamen, Henry, *The Spanish Inquisition. A historical Revision* (London: 1997).

Kariotoglou, Alexandros, *Islam kai christianiki chrismologia. Apo ton mytho stin pragmatikotita* [Islam and Christian Oracular Literature. From Myth to Reality] (Athens: 2000).

Karydis, Spyros, "O neomartyras Anastasios 'o ek Paramythias' kai o monachos Daniel. Ta prosopa kai i geografia tou martyriou" [The New Martyr Anastasius from Paramythià and the monk Daniel. The Persons and the Geography of Martyrdom], in *Triakosto Tetarto Panellinio Istoriko Synedrio 31 Maiou–2 Iouniou 2013. Praktika*, ed. Vassilis Gounaris (Thessaloniki: 2016), 21–34.

Kitromilides, Paschalis, *Enlightenment and Revolution: The Making of Modern Greece* (Cambridge, Mass.: 2013).

Knauf, Ernst Axel, "Joshua (Book and Person), I. Hebrew Bible/Old Testament", in *Encyclopedia of the Bible and its Reception (EBR) online*, vol. 14, ed. Christine Helmer [and others], 757–762 [accessed on 2 January 2018].

Koder, Johannes, "Kedrenos, Georgios", in *Lexikon für Theologie und Kirche*, vol. 5, ed. Walter Kasper [and others] (Freiburg im Breisgau: 1996), 1383.

Kontogiannopoulou, Anastasia, "I prosigoria kyr sti byzantini koinonia" [The Qualifier 'kyr' in Byzantine Society], *Byzantina* 32 (2012), 209–226.

Kottje, Raymund, "Hrabanus Maurus, OSB", in *Lexikon für Theologie und Kirche*, vol. 5, ed. Walter Kasper [and others] (Freiburg im Breisgau: 1996), 292–293.

Lea, Henry Charles, *A History of the Inquisition of Spain and the Inquisition of the Spanish Dependencies*, 5 vols (1906–1908; repr. London: 2011).

Lévy, Florence, "La prophétie et le pouvoir politico-religieux au XVIIe siècle au Portugal et en Hollande: Vieira et Menasseh Ben Israel", in *La prophétie comme arme de guerre et des pouvoirs*, ed. Augustin Redondo (Paris: 2000).

Lidov Alexei, "Spatial Icons. The Miraculous Performance with the Hodegetria of Constantinople", in *Hierotopy. Creation of Sacred Spaces in Byzantium and Medieval Russia*, ed. Alexei Lidov (Moscow: 2006), 349–372.

Lima, Luís Filipe Silvério and Megiani, Ana Paula (eds), *Visions, Prophecies, and Divinations. Early Modern Messianism and Millenarianism in Iberian America, Spain, and Portugal* (Boston: 2016).

Lima, Luís Filipe Silvério, "O percurso das *Trovas* de Bandarra: circulação letrada de um profeta iletrado", in *O Império por Escrito. Formas de transmissão da cultura letrada no mundo ibérico (séc. XVI–XIX)*, ed. Leila Algranti, Ana Paula Megiani (São Paulo: 2009), 441–452.

Lima, Luís Filipe Silvério, "Prophetical hopes, New World experiences and imperial expectations: Menasseh Ben Israel, Antônio Vieira, Fifth-Monarchy Men, and the millenarian connections in the seventeenth-century Atlantic", *AHAM* XVII (2016), 359–408.

Lima, Luís Filipe Silvério, "Um 'apócrifo' de Vieira: discursos sebastianistas, leitura de impressos e circulação de manuscritos (séc. XVII–XVIII)", in *Poderes do Sagrado. Europa Católica, América Ibérica, África e Oriente portugueses (séculos XVI–XVIII)*, ed. Jacqueline Hermann and William Martins (Rio de Janeiro: 2016), 53–83.

Malena, Adelisa, *Albizzi, Francesco*, in *Dizionario storico dell'Inquisizione*, ed. Adriano Prosperi, vol. 1 (Pisa: 2010), 29–31.

Malena, Adelisa, *L'"offerta della volontà". Pratiche (sospette) di direzione spirituale nella Siena del Seicento*, in *Inquisizioni: percorsi di ricerca*, ed. Giovanna Paolin (Trieste: 2002), 181–202.

Malena, Adelisa, *L'eresia dei perfetti. Inquisizione romana ed esperienze mistiche nel Seicento italiano* (Rome: 2003).

Malena, Adelisa, *La costruzione di un'eresia. Note sul quietismo italiano del Seicento*, in *Ordini religiosi, santi e culti tra Europa, Mediterraneo e Nuovo Mondo (secoli XV–XVII)*, ed. R. Michetti, B. Pellegrino, G. Zarri, vol. 1 (Lecce: 2009), 165–184.

Malena, Adelisa, *Molinos, Miguel de*, in *Dizionario Storico dell'Inquisizione*, ed. Adriano Prosperi, vol. 2 (Pisa: 2010), 1059–1060.

Malena, Adelisa, *Petrucci, Pier Matteo*, in *Dizionario Storico dell'Inquisizione*, ed. Adriano Prosperi, vol. 3 (Pisa: 2010), 1206–1207.

Malena, Adelisa, *Pratica della perfezione. Forme e linguaggi della direzione in una comunità di spirituali. (Siena, XVII sec.)*, in *Storia della direzione spirituale*, ed. Gabriella Zarri, vol. 3 (*L'età moderna*) (Brescia: 2008).

Malena, Adelisa, *Wishful Thinking: la santità come tentazione. Intorno ai quietismi del Seicento*, in *Tra Rinascimento e Controriforma. Continuità di una ricerca*, ed. Massimo Donattini (Verona: 2012), 247–268.

Mandalà, Giuseppe, "Tra mito e realtà: L'immagine di Roma nella letteratura araba e turca d'età ottomana (secoli XV–XVI)", in *Italien und das Osmanische Reich*, ed. Franziska Meier (Herne: 2010), 29–56.

Mango, Cyril, "The Legend of Leo the Wise", in *Byzantium and its Image*, ed. Cyril Mango (London: 1984), 59–93.

Marinis, Vasileios, "The Vision of the Last Judgment in the *Vita* of Saint Niphon (BHG 1371z)", *Dumbarton Oaks Papers* 71 (2017), 193–227.

Martínez de Bujanda, Jesús (ed.), *Index des livres interdits*, 11 vols. (Sherbrooke-Geneva: 1984–2002).

Marques, Guida, "'Por ser cabeça do Estado do Brasil'. As representações da cidade da Bahia no século XVII", in *Salvador da Bahia: retratos de uma cidade atlântica*, ed. Evergton Sales Souza, Guida Marques and Hugo R. Silva (Salvador: 2016), 17–46.

Marriott, Brandon, *Transnational Networks and Cross-religious Exchange in the Seventeenth-century Mediterranean and Atlantic Worlds* (Farnham: 2015).
Martínez Millán, José, *La Inquisición española* (Madrid: 2009).
Maurício, Carlos Coelho, "Entre o silêncio e o ouro—sondando o milagre de Ourique na cultura portuguesa", *Ler: História* 20 (1990), 3–28.
McGinn, Bernard. *The Calabrian Abbot: Joachim of Fiore in the History of Western Thought* (New York: 1985).
McHugh, Michael P., "Pliny the Younger (ca. A.D. 61–ca. 113)", in *Encyclopedia of Early Christianity*, vol. 1, 928.
McKay, Ruth, *The Baker who Pretended to be King of Portugal* (Chicago: 2012).
Meinhardt, Helmut, "Anselm v. Canterbury", in *Lexikon für Theologie und Kirche*, vol. 1, ed. Walter Kasper [and others] (Freiburg im Breisgau: 1993), 711–712.
Meserve, Margaret, *Empires of Islam in Renaissance historical thought* (Cambridge, MA.: 2008).
Miles, Margaret R., "Augustine (354–430)", in *Encyclopedia of Early Christianity*, vol. 1, ed. Everett Ferguson, 2nd ed. (New York: 1997), 148–153.
Milhou, Alain, *Colón y su mentalidad mesiánica en el ambiente franciscanista español* (Valladolid: 1983).
Moin, A. Azfar, *The Millennial Sovereign. Sacred Kingship and Sainthood in Islam* (New York: 2012).
Monteiro, Rodrigo Bentes, and Dantas, Vinícius, "Machiavellianisms and governments in Portuguese America: two analyses of ideas and political practices", *Tempo* 20 (2014), 1–26.
Monticone, Alberto, *Albizzi, Francesco* in *Dizionario Biografico degli Italiani*, vol. 2 (Rome: 1960), 23–27 (online: http://www.treccani.it/enciclopedia/francesco-albizzi _(Dizionario-Biografico)).
Moreno, Doris, *La invención de la Inquisición* (Madrid: 2004).
Muhana, Adma Fadul, "O processo inquisitorial de Vieira: aspectos profético-argumentativos", *Semear* 2 (1998), 9–19.
Münster, F., "Theudas", in *Paulys Realencyclopädie der classischen Alterumswissenschaften*, series 2, vol. 6 (Neue Bearbeitung begonnen von Georg Wissow), ed. Wilhelm Kroll and Karl Mittelhaus (Stuttgart: 1936), 244.
Muraro, Valmir, *Padre Antônio Vieira. Retória e Utopia* (Florianópolis: 2003).
Nalle, Sarah Tilghman, "Inquisitors, Priests, and the People during the Catholic Reformation in Spain", *The Sixteenth Century Journal* 18 (1987), 557–587.
Nalle, Sarah Tilghman, *God in La Mancha. Religious Reform and the People of Cuenca, 1500–1650* (Baltimore: 1992).
Nalle, Sarah, "*El Encubierto* revisited: Navigating between visions of Heaven and Hell on earth", in *Werewolves, witches, and wandering spirits*, ed. Kathryn A. Edwards (Kirksville, MO.: 2002), 77–92.

Nicol, Donald, *The Immortal Emperor: The Life and Legend of Constantine Palaiologos, Last Emperor of the Romans* (Cambridge: 1992).

Norris, Frederick W., "John Climacus (ca. 579–649)", in *Encyclopedia of Early Christianity*, vol. 1, 624.

Novinsky, Anita, "Sebastianismo, Vieira e o messianismo judaico", in *Sobre as naus da iniciação*, ed. C.A. Iannone (São Paulo: 1998), 65–79.

Olivari, Michele, "Milenarismo y política a fines del quinientos: notas sobre algunos complots y conjuras en la monarquía hispánica", in *En pos del tercer milenio*, ed. Adeline Rucquoi et. al. (Salamanca, 1999), 137–160.

Olsen, Eric, *The Calabrian Charlatan, 1598–1603: Messianic Nationalism in Early Modern Europe* (Basingstoke: 2003).

Osborne, Roger, *The Dreamer of the Calle de San Salvador. Visions of Sedition and Sacrilege in Sixteenth-Century Spain* (London: 2002).

Pacho, Eulogio, *Molinos, Miguel de*, in *Dictionnaire de Spiritualité*, ed. Marcel Villier et al., vol. 10 (1980), 1586–1514.

Paiva, José Pedro (ed.), *Padre António Vieira. 1608–1697. Bibliografia* (Lisbon: 1999).

Paiva, José Pedro, "Revisitar o processo inquisitorial do padre António Vieira", *Lusitania Sacra* 23 (2011), 151–168.

Parker, Geoffrey, "Some Recent Work on the Inquisition in Spain and Italy", *The Journal of Modern History* 54 (1982), 519–532.

Parker, Geoffrey. "Messianic Visions in the Spanish Monarchy, 1516–1598", *Calíope: Journal of the Society for Renaissance and Baroque Hispanic Poetry* 8/2 (2002), 5–24.

Pascoe, Louis, *Church and Reform. Bishops, Theologians, and Canon Lawyers in the Thought of Pierre D'Ailly (1351–1420)* (Leiden: 2005).

Pécora, Alcir, "O processo inquisitorial de Antônio Vieira", in *Sobre as naus da iniciação*, ed. C.A. Iannone (São Paulo: 1998), 49–64.

Pécora, Alcir, "Vieira e a condução do Índio ao Corpo Místico do Império Português (Maranhão, 1652–1661)", *Sibila* (24 March 2009), online (http://sibila.com.br/mapa-da-lingua/o-padre-vieira/2703, accessed 18 July 2018).

Peloso, Silvano, *Antônio Vieira e o Império Universal. A Clavis Prophetarum e os documentos inquisitoriais* (Rio de Janeiro: 2007).

Pérez García, Pablo and Catalá Sanz, Jorge Antonio, *Epígonos del encubertismo. Proceso contra los agermanados de 1541* (Valencia: 2000).

Perry, Mary Elizabeth, *Gender and Disorder in Early Modern Seville* (Princeton: 1990).

Petrocchi, Massimo, *Il Quietismo italiano del Seicento* (Rome: 1948).

Pezzella, Sosio *Caterina Fieschi Adorno (Caterina da Genova), santa*, in *Dizionario Biografico degli Italiani*, vol. 22 (Rome: 1979), 343.

Pietsch, Karl, "The Madrid Manuscript of the Spanish Grail Fragments. I", *Modern Philology*, 18/3 (1920), 147–156.

Pietsch, Karl, "The Madrid Manuscript of the Spanish Grail Fragments. II", *Modern Philology*, 18/11 (1921), 591–596.

Pissis Nikolas, "Chrismologia kai 'rossiki prosdokia'" [Oracular Literature and the 'Russian Expectation'], in *Slavoi kai ellinikos kosmos. Praktika protis epistimonikis imeridas tmimatos slavikon spoudon* (Athens: 2015), 149–168.

Pissis, Nikolas, "Apokalyptikos logos kai syllogikes tautotites (170s–180s ai.)" [Apocalyptic Discourse and Collective Identities (17th–18th c.)], in *Identities in the Greek World (from 1204 to the Present Day), 4th European Congress of Modern Greek Studies, Granada 9–12 September 2010. Proceedings*, vol. 3, ed. Konstantinos Dimadis (Athens: 2011), 687–695.

Pissis, Nikolas, "Tropes tis 'rossikis prosdokias' sta chronia tou Megalou Petrou" [The Course of the "Russian Expectation" in the Years of Peter the Great], *Mnimon* 30 (2009), 37–60.

Politis, Nikolaos G., *Meletai peri tou viou kai tis glossis tou ellinikou laou. Paradoseis* [Studies on the Life and Language of the Greek People. Traditions], 2 vols (Athens: 1904).

Poska, Allyson M., *Regulating the People. The Catholic Reformation in Seventeenth-Century Spain* (Leiden: 1998).

Potestà, Gian Luca, *Il tempo dell'Apocalisse: vita di Gioacchino da Fiore* (Rome: 2004).

Pozzi, Giovanni and Leonardi, Claudio, *Scrittrici mistiche italiane* (Genoa: 1988).

Prosperi, Adriano, *America e apocalisse e altri saggi* (Pisa: 1999).

Puntoni, Pedro, *O Estado do Brasil* (São Paulo: 2013).

Quataert, Donald, "Clothing Laws, State, and Society in the Ottoman Empire, 1720–1829", *International Journal of Middle East Studies* 29/3 (1997), 403–425.

Ranft, Patricia, *A Woman's Way. The Forgotten History of Women Spiritual Directors* (New York: 2001)

Reeves, Marjorie, *Joachim of Fiore and the Prophetic Future* (New York: 1977).

Reeves, Marjorie, *The Influence of Prophecy in the Later Middle Ages. A Study in Joachimism* (Notre Dame, IN.: 1993).

Riedl, Matthias, "Einleitung: Prophetie als interzivilisatorisches Phänomen", in *Propheten und Prophezeiungen—Prophets and Prophecies*, ed. Matthias Riedl and Tilo Schabert (Würzburg: 2005), 9–16.

Romeiro, Adriana, *Um visionário na corte de D. João V* (Belo Horizonte: 2001).

Roth, Lea, "Felix, Antonius", in *Encyclopaedia Judaica*, vol. 6 (Jerusalem: 1996), 1218.

Rotzokos, Nikos, *Ethnaphypnisi kai ethnogenesi. Orlofika kai elliniki istoriographia* [National Awakening and Ethnogenesis. Greek Historiography and the Orlov Revolt] (Athens: 2007).

Saraiva, António José, "António Vieira, Menasseh ben Israel e o Quinto Império", in *História e utopia* (Lisbon: 1992), 75–107

Savelli, Aurora, *Palio, contrade, istituzioni: costruire un modello di festa civica (Siena,*

1945–1955), in *Toscana rituale. Feste civiche e politica dal secondo dopoguerra*, ed. Auroro Savelli (Pisa: 2010), 19–48.

Scaduto, Mario s.j., "Il P. Antonio Francesco (Candelari) da Ancona e il Quietismo marchigiano", *Miscellanea Melchor de Pobladura*, vol. 2 (1964), 327–345.

Schlau, Stacey, *Gendered Crime and Punishment. Women and/in the Spanish Inquisition* (The Medieval and Early Modern Iberian World 49), (Leiden: 2013).

Schwaiger, Georg, "Clemens VII. (19.11.1523–25.9.1534)", in *Lexikon für Theologie und Kirche*, vol. 2, ed. Walter Kasper [and others] (Freiburg im Breisgau: 1994), 1223.

Serafim, João Carlos Gonçalves, D. João de Castro (?1550–?1628), Um resistente que se tornou profeta, *Via Spiritus* 6 (1999).

Serafim, João Carlos Gonçalvez, *D. João de Castro, "O Sebastianista". Meandros de vida e razões da obra*, 3 vols (Porto: 2004).

Serrão, Joaquim Veríssimo, *O reinado de D.Antônio, Prior do Crato*, vol. I (1580–1582) (Coimbra: 1956).

Signorotto, Gianvittorio, *Inquisitori e mistici nel Seicento italiano. L'eresia di Santa Pelagia* (Bologna: 1989).

Silva, Jacqueson Luiz da, "Arquitetura do Quinto Império em Vieira", PhD dissertation (Campinas: 2007).

Şişman, Cengiz, *The Burden of Silence: Sabbatai Sevi and the Evolution of the Ottoman-Turkish Dönmes* (New York: 2015).

Skarsten, Trygve R., "Magnus, Olaus (1490–1557)", in *The Oxford Encyclopedia of the Reformation*, vol. 2, ed. Hans J. Hillerbrand (New York: 1996), 499–500.

Slavin, Philip, "From Constantinople to Moscow: The Fourteenth Century Liturgical Response to the Muslim Incursions in Byzantium and Russia", in *Church and Society in Late Byzantium*, ed. Dimiter Angelov (Kalamazoo, Mich.: 2009), 201–229.

Sluhovski, Moshe, *Becoming a New Self. Practice of Belief in Early Modern Catholicism* (Chicago: 2017)

Sluhovski, Moshe, *Believe not Every Spirit. Possession, Mysticism & Discernment in Early Modern Catholicism* (Chicago—London: 2007)

Smith, Anthony D., *The Antiquity of Nations* (London: 2004).

Smoller, Laura Ackermann, *History, Prophecy, and the Stars: The Christian Astrology of Pierre D'Ailly, 1350–1420* (Princeton: 1994).

Solfaroli Camillocci, Daniela, "Il corpo, l'anima e l'amor proprio. Carità e vita devota nell'esperienza religiosa di Caterina da Genova e della sua cerchia, tra regola di vita spirituale e costruzione biografica", *Archivio italiano per la storia della pietà* 18 (2005), 265–286.

Solfaroli Camillocci, Daniela, *I devoti della carità. Le confraternite del Divino Amore nell'Italia del primo Cinquecento* (Naples: 2002).

Stewart, Charles, "Dreaming and Historical Consciousness", *Historically Speaking* 14/1 (2013), 28–30.

Stewart, Charles, *Dreaming and Historical Consciousness in Island Greece* (Cambridge, MA.: 2012).

Stock, Brian, *Listening for the Text. On the Uses of the Past* (Philadelphia: 1996).

Stroppa, Sabrina, "Petrucci, Pier Matteo", in *Dizionario Biografico degli Italiani* 82 (Rome: 2015), online (http://www.treccani.it/enciclopedia/pier-matteo-petrucci_(Dizionario-Biografico)/)

Stroppa, Sabrina, *Sic arescit. Letteratura mistica del Seicento italiano* (Florence: 1998).

Stylianopoulos, Theodore, "Justin Martyr (d. ca. 165)", in *Encyclopedia of Early Christianity*, vol. 1, 647–650.

Subrahmanyam, Sanjay, "Sixteenth-Century Millenarianism from the Tagus to the Ganges", in *Explorations in Connected History: from the Tagus to the Ganges* (Oxford: 2005), 102–137.

Tähtinen, Lauri, "The Intellectual Construction of the Fifth Empire: Legitimating the Braganza Restoration", *History of European Ideas* 38/3 (2012), 415–416.

Tavares, Pedro, *Pedro Henequim. Proto-mártir da separação (1744)* (Lisbon: 2011).

Tavim, José Alberto, "Revisitando uma carta em português sobre Sabbatai Zvi", *Sefarad* 67/1 (2007), 155–190.

Tellechea Idigoras, Ignacio, *Molinosiana. Investigaciones históricas sobre Miguel Molinos* (Madrid: 1987).

Timotin Andrei, "La littérature eschatologique byzantine et post-byzantine dans les manuscrits roumains", *Revue des études sud-est européennes* 40 (2002), 151–166.

Timotin, Andrei, "Circulation des manuscrits en contexte historique. La traduction roumaine de la Vision de Sophiani", *Revue des études sud-est européennes* 42 (2004), 107–116.

Timotin, Andrei, "Eschatologie post-byzantine et courants idéologiques dans les Balkans. La traduction roumaine de la *Vision de kyr Daniel*", in *Peuples, États et nations dans le Sud-Est de l'Europe, IXe Congrès international des études du Sud-Est européen, Tirana, 30 août–4 septembre 2004* (Bucarest: 2004), 123–132.

Timotin, Andrei, "La Vision de kyr Daniel. Liturgie, prophétie et politique au XVIIIe siècle", in *The Greek world between the Age of Enlightenment and the 20th century*, vol. 1, ed. Konstantinos Dimadis (Athens: 2007), 127–134.

Torgal, Luis Reis, *Ideologia Política e Teoria de Estado na Restauração*, 2 vols (Coimbra: 1981).

Toro Pascua, María Isabel, "Milenarismo y profecía en el siglo XV: La tradición del libro de Unay en la Península Ibérica", *Península. Revista de Estudios Ibéricos* n. 0 (2003), 29–38.

Turri, Serena, "Il Tratado de la verdadera y falsa prophecía di Juan de Horozco: Una nota su Lucrecia de León", in *I racconti delle streghe. Storia e finzione tra Cinque e Seicento*, ed. Giulia Poggi (Pisa: 2002), 217–224.

Urbanelli, Callisto, *Il cappuccino Antonio Candelari e il movimento quietista della seconda metà del secolo XVII*, in *Ascetica Cristiana e ascetica giansenista e quietista nelle regioni d'influenza avellanita*, [Atti del I convegno del Centro di studi avellaniti] (Fonte Avellana: 1977), 245–276.

Vainfas, Ronaldo, *Antônio Vieira* (São Paulo, 2011).

Valdez, Ana, "Making of a Revolution: Daniel, Revelation and the Portuguese Restoration of 1640", *Oracula* 9/14 (2013), 5–20.

Valdez, Ana, *Historical Interpretations of the "Fifth Empire": The Dynamics of Periodization from Daniel to António Vieira, s.J.* (Leiden: 2011).

Valérian, Dominique, "The Medieval Mediterranean", in *A Companion to Mediterranean History*, ed. Peregrine Horden and Sharon Kinoshita (Hoboken, N.J.: 2014), 77–90.

Vaz, João Pedro, *Campanhas do Prior do Crato. 1580–1589, Entre Reis e Corsários pelo trono de Portugal* (Lisbon: 2004).

Vázquez de Parga, Luis, "Algunas notas sobre el Pseudo Metodio y España", *Habis* 2 (1971), 143–164.

Velloso, J.M. Queiroz, *D. Sebastião (1554–1578)*, 3rd ed. (Lisbon: 1945).

Velloso, J.M. Queiroz, *O interregno dos governadores e o breve reinado de D. Antônio* (Lisbon: 1953).

Velloso, J.M. Queiroz, *O reinado do Cardeal D. Henrique*, A perda da independência (Lisbon: 1946).

Verd Conradi, Gabriel María, "Las poesís del manuscrito de fray Miguel de Guevara y el soneto *No me mueve, mi Dios, para quererte*", *Nueva Revista de Filología Hispanica* LXV (2017), 471–500.

Villier, Marcel et al. (eds), *Dictionnaire de Spiritualité*, 17 vols (Paris: 1937–1994).

Volk, Otto, "Nikephoros I. v. Konstantinopel", in *Lexikon für Theologie und Kirche*, vol. 7, ed. Walter Kasper [and others] (Freiburg im Breisgau: 1998), 839–840.

Vollendorf, Lisa, *The Lives of Women. A New History of Inquisitorial Spain* (Nashville: 2005).

Vollrath, Hanna, "Beda Venerabilis", in *Lexikon für Theologie und Kirche*, vol. 2, ed. Walter Kasper [and others] (Freiburg im Breisgau: 1994), 116–117.

Wachtel, Nachtan, "Theologies Marranes. Une configuration millénariste", in *Des Archives aux Terrains* (Paris: 2014), 465–505.

Weiner, Jack, "El indispensable factótum Sebastián Covarrubias Horozco (1539–1613), pedagogo, cortesano y administrador", *Artifara* 2 (2003), sezione Addenda (http://www.artifara.com/rivista2/testi/covar.asp, accessed on December 26, 2017).

Whalen, Brett Edward, *Dominion of God: Christendom and Apocalypse in the Middle Ages* (Cambridge, MA: 2009).

White, Lorrain, "Dom Jorge Mascarenhas, Marquês de Montalvão (1579?–1652), and Changing Traditions of Service in Portugal and the Portuguese Empire", *Portuguese Studies Review* 12/2 (2004–2005), 63–83.

Wiegers, Gerard, "Jean de Roquetaillade prophecies among the Muslim minorities of medieval and early-modern Christian Spain: An Islamic version of the *Vademecum in Tribulatione*", in *The transmission and dynamics of the textual sources of Islam*, ed. Nicolet Boekhoff-van der Voort (Leiden: 2011), 229–247.

Winkelmann, Friedhelm, "Sozomenos", in *Lexikon für Theologie und Kirche*, vol. 9, ed. Walter Kasper [and others] (Freiburg im Breisgau: 2000), 801–802.

Wulz, Gabriele, "Jeremia", in *Calwer Bibellexikon*, ed. Otto Betz, Beate Ego and Werner Grimm, 2nd ed., vol. 1 (Stuttgart: 2006), 639–641.

Yates, Frances A., *Astraea. The Imperial Theme in the Sixteenth Century*, 2nd ed. (London: 1993).

Zafra Molina, Rafael, "Nuevos datos sobre la obra de Juan de Horozco y Covarrubias", *Imago* 3 (2011), 107–126.

Ziaka, Aggeliki, *Metaxy polemikis kai dialogou. To Islam sti byzantini, metabyzantini kai neoteri elliniki grammateia* [Between Polemic and Dialogue. Islam in Byzantine, Post-Byzantine and Modern Greek Literature] (Thessaloniki: 2010).

Zito, Paola, *Il veleno della quiete. Mistica ereticale e potere dell'ordine nella vicenda di Miguel Molinos* (Naples: 1997).

Index

1666 (year of) 93n53
Aaron (Moses's brother) 170
Abbandonate, Congregation of the 206, 207, 212, 215, 218, 231, 237n101, 245n113
Abraham 94–95, 151n286, 170, 172, 256, 266n56
Afonso I, King of Portugal 48n56, 127n188& 189, 132, 133n206
Afonso VI, King of Portugal 82, 84, 93n53, 106n104, 137n227, 149n276
Africa 8, 18, 20, 32, 34n33, 40, 42–46, 48, 51–54, 68, 77, 79, 115, 150, 156, 169, 174n61, 175n65
Agathias / Agathius 182n78
Aḥmad al- Manṣūr, Sultan of Morocco 5–6
Albizzi, Francesco (Cardinal) 202–203
Alcazarquivir / Alcacer Quibir, Battle of (1578) 20, 21–26, 34n33, 43n46, 44n47, 46, 79, 150n278
Alcantara, Battle of (1580) 23, 62
Alemany, Juan 14
Aleria, Corsica 232
Alexander VII, Pope 233
Alexander XVII, Pope 105
Alfonso the Magnanimous, King of Aragon 3
'Alī b. Abī Ṭālib 15
Alpujarras Revolt 7, 16, 17, 169
Altiani (Corsica) 217, 232
Alumbrados 203
Amati, Giuseppe of Massafra, Franciscan friar and inquisitor 226n74
Americas 6, 73, 76–77, 90, 91n51, 153n296, *see also* Portuguese America
Amerindians 74, 75, 76, 90, 126n183, 176
Anastasios I (Anastasius), Byzantine Emperor 182
Anastasius, the new martyr (Saint of the Greek Orthodox Church) 246, 248, 249, 262, 267n60
Andalusia 162, 163
annihilation (spiritual) 209, 211, 229n82, 235n93, 236
annihilation 251, 259, 265, 275
Anselm / Anselmo, Saint 172

Antonio, Prior of Crato 21, 22, 23, 25, 26, 49n59, 51, 57n73, 62n82, 69
Anthony, Saint 118, 220, 233
Antichrist 11, 18, 126, 257, 263n49
apocalypticism 1–19, 80, 87, 93n54, 112n133, 145n258, 256, 257, 261
Augustine of Hippo, Saint 139, 175, 182, 243
Avars 254

Babylon, Kingdom of 36
Bahia 74, 78, 84, 100n76, 101, 153, *see also* Brazil
Balkans 257
Bandarra, Gonçalo Annes 24, 25, 32–34, 36, 38, 61–62, 65–66, 79, 83–84, 92n52, 94–95, 110, 149, 156, *see also* Trovas (of Bandarra)
Bandinelli, Tomaso 208, 230, 231, 233
beata 165n26, 167, 168, 184–200
Bede, The Venerable (Beda Venerabilis) 162, 172
Beghards 203
Bellucci, Sebastiano 226
Belluomo, Gottardo 202
Ben Israel, Menasseh 80, 86–87, 121n168
Bento, Friar ("Frade Bento") 147
Berber kingdoms 44
Bernardini, Domenico S.J. 226
Bernardino da Uzzano, Capuchin friar 229
Bernières Louvigny, Jean de 208
Bizzarri, Giuseppe 224
Bocarro, Manuel Francês (*aka* Jacob Rosales) 118n158, 153n296
Bonaventura, Saint 181
Bonicardo, Corsica 232, 234
Bouray, Nicolas 88–89
Brazil 73–75, 78, 80, 90–91, 99–102, 106n105, 126n184, 147n265, *see also* Portuguese America
Buoninsegni, Caterina Girolama, nun 225
Byzantine apocalypses 256

Camões, Luís de 133n207
Candelari, Antonio Francesco, Capuchin friar 206, 207, 229n79
Canfield, Benedict of 208

Caracciolo, Innico, Archbishop of Naples 201, 202
Carlo of Pitigliano, Capuchin friar 228, 229
Carpia, Caterina Ottavia, nun 206, 207, 210, 212, 214n23, 215, 218, 219, 225n64, 227, 231, 235, 237, 241, 244–245
Castellucci, Andrea, priest 224
Castile, kingdom of 14, 31, 41, 44, 45, 58, 60, 69, 98, 109, 136, 142, 150, 155, 156
Castro, Dom Alvaro de 22, 26
Castro, Dom João de 20–27, 32, 40, 41, 43, 49–51, 57, 61, 81, 118n158, 130n198
Catherine II, Tsarina of Russia 258–259
Catherine of Genoa, Saint (Caterina Fieschi Adorno) 208, 220, 223
Catherine of Habsburg, Queen of Portugal 21, 22, 32, 41, 150n276
Catholic Church 27, 34, 63, 95, 134, 143, 162, 176n69, 202, 208, 219, 221n40, 232
Catizone, Marco Tulio 25, 40n42, 58n76
Caussin, Nicolas 153, 154
Cenni, Virgilio Antonio, priest 208, 218, 224, 227, 240n105
Chandler, Richard (British traveller) 258–259
Charles V, Holy Roman Emperor 4, 5, 41, 150, 176n69
Christopher, Saint 274–275
Christotokos, *see* Mary, the Virgin
Chrysanthus of Aetolia (teacher, brother of Kosmas) 248, 268
Church of All the Saints [*Hagioi Pantes*] (Constantinople) 250, 267
Church of the Holy Apostles [*Hagioi Apostoloi*] (Constantinople) 250, 267–269
Church of the Holy Wisdom [*Hagia Sophia*] (Constantinople) 251, 263–264, 268, 270, 275
Ciruelo, Pedro 164, 168
Clavis Prophetarum 83–84, 90
Clement VII, Pope (= Giulio de' Medici) 176, 183
Clemente of Monte Latrone, Capuchin friar 230
Climacus, Saint John 180
Coelestis Pastor 205
Columbus, Christopher 11

Concepción, María de la 162, 165, 168, 184–200
Constantine I (Constantine the Great / Saint Constantine), Roman emperor 3, 268–269, 271, 274–275
Constantinople 14, 18, 182, 250, 251, 253–255, 257–258, 260, 263–268, 270–271, 273, 274
  Ottoman conquest of (1453) 1, 4, 12, 251, 255
  prophecies of the Christian reconquest of 116, 117, 119, 129, 156, 248
Constantinos XI Palaeologos (last Byzantine Emperor) 255
Contemplation 201, 203–204, 207–209, 230, 234, 239
Conti, Sebastiano 226
Corfu 246, 250, 266
Cruz, Magdalena de la 182
Cuspius Fadus 174

D'Ailly, Pierre 11
Daniel, biblical prophet 24, 35, 126, 151n285, 262
deceit 159, 162, 164, 168, 173, 176–178, 180–183
Devil 53, 54, 63, 133n206, 160, 161, 163, 168, 173, 175–183, 213, 219, 242, 263
divination 159, 160, 163, 166, 178, 273
Dönme 8
Draghi, Pietro 224
dreams, prophetic 35, 62, 65, 97, 98, 100, 104, 110–114, 116, 119, 121–123, 126, 128, 132–134, 141, 151, 152, 159–161, 164n17, 165, 169, 249–250, 260–262

early modern Greek prophetic literature 257, 260, 262
Ecclesiastes, Book of 170
edict of faith 161–163, 165, 188n93
Elizabeth I, Queen of England and Ireland 50n63
Encoberto / Encobierto / Encubierto (Hidden king, Hidden one) 6, 14, 15, 16, 18, 20, 24–26, 51–52, 60, 79, 97n68, 108n120, 116, 118, 137–138, 148n268
Enlightenment 89, 257, 274n89
  spiritual 109, 208, 242, 243
Ezekiel, Book of 123, 126–127, 151

INDEX 301

Ezra, Book of (IV Ezra or 2 Esdras)   121n167, 126

Faṭimī / Fatimí   18
Felici, Veronica   232
Felix (Antonius Felix)   174, 178
Ferdinand I, Grand Duke of Tuscany   58
Ferdinand II, King of Aragon   5, 11, 111, 120, 135, 150
Fernandes, André, Bishop of Japan   72–73, 84–85, 88, 92, 93n54, 153
Fifth Empire   37, 72, 78–84, 86–91, 126n184
Fifth Monarchy   15, 24, 35, 36, 81
figure / figural Interpretation   117n155, 127n188, 138n233
five wounds of Christ   127–128, 132–133
France   49, 51, 57, 79, 120, 183

Gagliardi, Achille   208, 221
Galli, Federico   230
Gama, Vasco Luís da, Marquis of Niza   79
Genoa   232
George, Saint   251, 269
Georgians   258
Gerson, Jean Charlier de   182
Gori, Niccolò   225, 228
Gottarelli, Serafino of Castelbolognese, Franciscan friar and inquisitor   225n64, 231n86
Greek project (planned by Tsarina Catherine II)   258–259
Grigoriou monastery (Mount Athos)   246

Habsburg dynasty   4, 41n43, 56n70, 76, 99n73, 130
ḥadīth   3
Helena (Saint Constantine's mother)   268
Henequim, Pedro de Rates   90–91
Henrique (Cardinal)   21–23, 26, 34, 41, 42, 150n276, 155
heresy / heretics   83–84, 90, 161, 205–207, 234
Herp, Hendrik   208, 221n40
Hezekiah, King of Judah   171
Holy Office, see Inquisition
Holy Roman Emperor   4, 12, 60
Hope of Israel   87
Hopes of Portugal ("Esperanças de Portugal")   72–73, 82–90, 92–158

Horozco y Covarrubias, Juan   162–164, 170
Horozco y Covarrubias, Sebastián   163

Ibn 'Arabī   13, 16
Ignatius of Loyola, Saint   211
Imperiale, Giovan Battista, Bishop of Alesia   233
Innocent X, Pope   105n100&101
Innocent XI, Pope   201, 202, 205, 229n82
Inquisition
  Portuguese Inquisition   24n19, 25n22, 32, 79–80, 82–90, 92n52, 98n69, 126n183&184
  Roman Inquisition   202n2, 203–209, 212n21, 217, 228, 231, 234
  Spanish Inquisition   9, 16, 159, 161, 162, 165–169, 184, 185, 188–200
Isaiah, biblical prophet   124, 126, 170, 171
Isidore of Seville [*pseud.*]   97n68, 118n158, 147n265, 148n266, 148n268
Isidore, Saint, Archbishop of Seville   14, 15, 16, 17, 31
Islam   3, 4, 5, 8, 9, 12–17, 28, 36, 43, 48, 68, 246, 250–253, 263, 269, 273
Istanbul, *see* Constantinople
Italy   3, 9, 103, 112–116, 119, 145, 156, 202, 203, 206, 210, 211

James, Saint (brother of Jesus)   270
Jeremiah (Hieremias), biblical prophet   36, 70, 151n284, 171, 237
Jerusalem   11, 13–15, 17, 49, 111, 113, 118, 121n166, 122, 124, 129, 132, 151n284, 248, 256
Jesuits   72–76, 78, 82, 89, 158n316, 202, 208, 226
Jesus Christ   4, 12, 15, 48n56, 78, 80, 127, 128, 133, 140, 144, 147, 156, 179, 230–231, 241, 245, 251, 264, 266, 271–273
Joachim of Fiore   10–11, 13, 30, 36
Joachimism   11, 13, 30, 148n266
John I, King of Portugal   133n206
John III, King of Portugal   21, 22, 32, 41, 109, 150n277
John IV, King of Portugal   72, 76n14, 78–80, 83, 86, 88, 90, 92–95, 99n72&74, 105, 106n104, 110–111, 129–131, 134–139, 145, 147, 155

Jean de Roquetaillade (John of Rupescissa)
  11, 18, 148n266
Jofores   7, 16–18
John of the Cross, Saint   208, 222, 234
John the Chrysostom   171, 271–272
John, Saint (the Theologian)   272, 275
Jonah, prophet   171
Josephus, Flavius   174, 178
Joshua, biblical prophet   170
Judea   174n59, 178
Justin Martyr, Saint   175

Kariotoglou, Alexandros   249, 255, 262
Kedrenos, Georgios (= George Cedrenus)   177
Kollyvades controversy (Mount Athos)   248, 262
Kosmas of Aetolia (Saint of the Greek Orthodox Church)   248, 268
Kozani Municipal Library, Greece   246
Ksar El-Kibir, Battle of, see Alcazarquivir / Alcacer Quibir, Battle of (1578)

Lambros, Spyridon   246–249, 255, 262
Lawrence the archdeacon   270–271
León, Lucrecia de   164, 165, 169
Levant   119, 129, 131, 136
Lisbon   23, 26, 32, 45, 47, 57, 64, 73, 74, 78, 84–85, 88, 90, 93, 99n74, 106n106, 118n157, 140, 155, 157
lost tribes of Israel / ten tribes of Israel   121, 123, 126–127, 129, 156
Luis, Prince of Portugal   21
Luisa de Guzmán, Queen of Portugal   72, 82, 85, 106n104, 149
Lusignan, Guy de   11–12, 13

Madrid   8, 9, 165, 169, 191, 199, 200
Magnus, Olaus   176, 177
Mahdī   3, 4, 5, 6, 14, 15, 18
Mahmud I, Sultan of the Ottoman Empire   248, 249n13
Mahometans, see Islam
Mairena   166, 167, 184–186, 188–194, 196–200
Malaval, François   208, 234, 235n96
Maranhão and Grão-Pará, State of   72–76, 82, 84, 93, 95n60, 105, 107, 157, see also Portuguese America
Marchetti, Annibale   215n28, 218

Marcianos, Saint   268, 270
Marguerite de Valois   22
Marsili, Leonardo, Archbishop of Siena   215n28, 218n34
Marsili, Ottavio   229, 230
martyrdom   246, 248, 250, 262, 266–267, 273
Mary, the Virgin   251, 253–256, 270–275
Mascarenhas, Jorge de, Marquis of Montalvão   78, 99–101
Mattei, Antonio Giovanni, hermit   205–212, 214–224, 226n, 227, 231–238, 240, 241, 244, 245n
Mattei, Cristofano   232
Maurus, (H)Rabanus   181
Medici, Carlo de', Cardinal   230
Mehmed II the Conqueror, Sultan of the Ottoman Empire   3, 12–13, 251, 268n62, 270n72
Melari, Rubera, nun   225
messiah   80, 121n168
messianism   1, 4–10, 14, 16, 20, 24, 73, 81n26, 83–84, 92n52, 263
Methodius [*pseud.*]   15, 145–147
Metrophanes, Saint (of Constantinople)   271
Minas Gerais   90–91, see also Brazil
Miriam (Moses's sister)   170–171n45
Mission   9, 74, 76, 82, 90, 139n237, 158n317
Molinos, Miguel de   203–205, 207–209, 219, 234
Monzón, Francisco   164, 165, 168
Moors   43, 44, 46, 48, 68, 120, 129n195, 169
Moriscos   6, 7, 15–18, 186n87
Morocco   5, 8, 21, 25, 40, 43, 44, 99n73
Mount Athos, Greece   246, 248, 262, 274
Mullah Mahamet   44
Mullah Maluco   44–46
Mustafa II, Sultan of the Ottoman Empire   247
Mustafa III, Sultan of the Ottoman Empire   247–248, 272
mysticism   7, 9, 202–204, 206–208, 217

Naples   8, 25, 58, 131, 136, 201
Nelli, Silvestro, priest   208, 224, 231
new Christians   80, 129n195
New World   73, 77, 90–91, see also Americas
Nicephorus (Nikephoros I), patriarch of Constantinople   175

Nicolas, Armelle   220n39
Nineveh   171
nobility   5, 20, 21, 26, 40, 99n71, 169, 186, 190n94

oracles / oracular literature   12, 13, 260–262, 265, 268
Orlov revolt (1770)   258, 265
Ottoman Empire   7, 8, 12, 13, 14, 16, 114, 156, 247, 252, 258, 260
Ourique, Battle and miracle of   48, 78, 127n188, 133n206

Pacini, Francesco   232
Panteleimon monastery (Mount Athos)   246, 247
Paoletti, Modesto of Vignanello, Franciscan friar and inquisitor   217, 227n77
Paschos, Pantelis   246, 248–249, 262, 268, 269, 275
Paul IV, Pope   150
Paul, Saint   94, 170, 183
Pelagians   203
Perini, Vitale, Camaldolese monk   206
Petrucci, Ottone, Augustinian friar   206
Petrucci, Pier Matteo, Bishop of Jesi, Cardinal   208, 220n39, 229, 230, 234
Phanar (Istanbul district)   268
Philip I, King of Portugal   23
Philip II, King of Spain   5, 6, 7, 8, 21, 23, 26, 34, 41, 44, 45, 48–50, 57, 109, 169
Philip IV, King of Spain   101
Philostratus   177, 178
Piccolomini, Ascanio   233
Piccolomini, Celia   208
Piccolomini, Orazio   225n64, 229
Piedrola, Miguel de   8–9
Pius IV, Pope   150
Pius V, Pope   150
Pliny the Younger   176n70
Politis, Nikolaos G.   263–264
Portugal, Kingdom of   6, 14, 20, 24, 26, 34, 38, 40, 48, 49, 61, 73, 75–76, 78–79, 81–82, 89, 90–91, 92, 97–98, 103, 105, 109, 122, 125, 127, 132–134, 149, 155
Portuguese America   72–74, 76–77, 90, see also Brazil and Maranhão
Portuguese Coat of Arms   127–128, 132, see also Ourique; Five Wounds of Christ

Portuguese Empire   72–74, 76–77, 79, 82, 89–90, 93n54, 101n84
Portuguese Jews in the Netherlands   80
Pozzo di Borgo, Paolo Girolamo   232
Prayer of Quiet   202–205
Prester John   52
prognostications   3, 4, 5, 6, 7, 16, 17, 159, 162, 165, 169, 188, 193
Protest of the Offering of the Will   205–207, 210–212, 214, 215, 218, 219, 227, 231, 240n107

Quietists / Quietism   9, 201–205, 210, 211, 212n21, 215n25, 217, 225n64, 229n79, 230n83, 231

Restoration of Portugal   76, 78–82, 84, 88, 99n74, 104n98, 106n105, 130n198, 132n206
revelations   9, 30, 32, 48, 49, 59, 159, 169, 170, 172, 179, 181, 183
Revelation, Book of   121n167, 125n180, 152, 263
Río, Martín del   164, 168
riots   96n63, 186
Roman Inquisition, see Inquisition
Roman Empire   2, 3, 36, 254
Romanian Academy, Bucharest   246
Rome   3, 4, 5, 12, 13, 14, 16, 17, 18, 53, 84, 104–105, 114, 122, 140, 143, 145, 155, 254, 270
Russians / Russian empire   257–260
Russo-Ottoman war (1768–1774)   248–249, 258, 261

Sack of Rome   176, 183n82
saludadora   193–197, 198n99, 199
Salutio, Bartolomeo (Bartolomeo Cambi)   112, 140, 142
Salvador of Bahia   74, 78, 84, 99–100, see also Bahia
San Lucar of Barrameda   25, 58n76, 193
Santa Maria della Scala, hospital   205, 207, 214n24, 218, 221n44, 230n83
São Luís do Maranhão   74, 85, 93, 107n115, see also Maranhão and Grão-Pará
Satan   28, 180, see also Devil
Savoy   182
scandal   159–162, 165–167, 169, 186–190, 193, 196, 198

Scupoli, Lorenzo 208, 221
Sebastian I, King of Portugal 5, 6, 14, 20–26, 32, 34, 39, 40–61, 65–69, 79, 89, 93, 98n72, 108n120, 111n125, 118n158, 133n206, 134, 149–151
Sebastianism 6, 20, 23, 24, 26, 30, 33, 79–82, 84, 86, 88–89, 92–93, 98n72, 141n246, 145, 150–151
Segneri, Paolo 202, 208, 230
Segovia 162–164, 170
Seville 184–186, 187n89, 190, 192, 194, 198
Siena 201, 205–207, 210, 211, 212n21, 214n24, 215n28, 217, 218n33&34, 221, 222, 226n73&74, 228, 230, 231, 233, 234, 235n92, 237n100
simulation of sanctity (Pretence of Holiness) 206
Sinalunga 233
Skete of Agia Anna (Mount Athos) 246, 248n9
Sky, apparitions in the 258
sleeping king-redeemer (Byzantine prophetic figure) 14, 264–265
Smith, Anthony David 260
Sophronius II, Patriarch of Constantinople 248, 266–267, 274
Sozomeno, Socrates 174, 175n62
Sozzifanti, Lorenzo 226
Spain 14–15, 17–18, 24, 74, 78, 82, 104n98, 154–155, 156, 159–200
Spanish Empire 186
Spanish Inquisition, see Inquisition
spiritual direction / guidance 204, 206, 207, 209, 210, 212n21, 215n27, 218, 219, 224n61, 234, 235, 244n113
spiritual exercises 211
spiritual mothers 209, 220n38
Spyridon, Saint 266
Squarci, Barbara, tertiary nun 206
Stephen of Sampaio, Friar 51
Stephen, Saint (the Protomartyr) 270–271
street prophets 162, 164
Süleymān the Magnificent, Sultan of the Ottoman Empire 4, 5, 14
Swabia 181

Teixeira, José 145n258, 147n264
Temudo, Diogo Marchão 141–142

Theodosius / Teodósio of Braganza, Prince of Portugal 105–106, 136n218
Teresa of Avila, Saint 164, 208
tertiary nun 165, 206, 217, 220n37, see also beata
Theotokos, see Mary, the Virgin
Theotokoupolis (city of the Theotokos) 254
Theudas (false prophet) 174
time (concept of) 10–11, 76–77
Toccafondi, Francesca, tertiary nun 206, 220, 221, 228, 229
Trent, council of 164
trial (before an Inquisition's court) 83, 84, 86, 162, 165–167, 169, 186, 188, 190, 192, 196, 200, 203–207, 225n64, 229n82, 230n83, 231, 241n108
trovas (of Bandarra) 24, 25, 32, 34, 79, 84–88, 90, 93n54, 94–98, 100–102, 104–106, 107n115, 108–117, 118n158, 119–141, 142n247, 143–145, 147–158
True Cross 251, 268–270, 272
Tyana, Apollonius of 175, 176

Ugolini, Cesare, Bishop of Grosseto 228, 233
unfinished liturgy (Greek folklore legend) 253, 264
uprisings 7, 14, 17, 96n63, 169, 186n87, 258
Urban VIII, Pope 105

Valcamonica 203
Vasconcelos, Joane Mendes de 106–108
Vasconcelos, João de 98n69, 130n198
Venice 12, 13, 25, 39, 40, 49, 50, 51, 53, 54, 57, 58, 59, 81, 113, 258
Venturini, Bernardino 228
Vespasian, Titus Flavius 174
Vieira, Antônio 72–93, 95n60, 97n67, 98–99, 102n90, 103n92, 105n102, 107n114, 108n120, 111n127, 126n183, 130n197, 138n233, 146n260, 147n265, 153n296&297, 158n314
Vision of Cosmas the monk (Byzantine apocalypse) 256
Vision of Saint Niphon (Byzantine apocalypse) 256
Viterbo 232
Volumnio Bandinelli, Cardinal 233

INDEX

Wādī al-Makhāzin 5, *see also* Alcazarquivir

Xavier, Saint Francis 139

Yeni mosque 263, 269

Zevi, Sabbatai 7–8, 9
Zographou monastery (Mount Athos) 246